WORKIN

MAN BLUES

COUNTRY MUSIC IN CALIFORNIA

GERALD W. HASLAM

with *Alexandra Haslam Russell and Richard Chon*

VERSITY OF CALIFORNIA PRESS   BERKELEY   LOS ANGELES   LONDON

University of California Press
Berkeley and Los Angeles, California

University of California Press, Ltd.
London, England

© 1999 by the Regents of the University of California

Library of Congress Cataloging-in-Publication Data

Haslam, Gerald W.
    Workin' man blues : country music in California /
       Gerald W. Haslam ; with Alexandra Haslam Russell
       and Richard Chon.
          p.   cm.
    Includes bibliographical references (p.   ) and index.
    ISBN 0-520-21800-0 (alk. paper)
       1. Country music—California—History and criticism.
I. Haslam, Alexandra R., 1963–   . II. Chon, Richard.
III. Title.
ML3524.H28   1999
781.642'09794—dc21   98-43061
                                CIP
                                MN
Manufactured in the United States of America

10   9   8   7   6   5   4   3   2   1

The paper used in this publication meets the minimum
requirements of ANSI/NISOZ39.48-1992 (R 1997)
(Permanence of Paper). ♾

For my wife, Jan,

who has taken for better

or for worse seriously,

with all my love.

◄ ► ◄ ► ◄ ► ◄ ► ◄ ►

The publisher gratefully acknowledges the generous
contribution to this book provided by
CALIFORNIA STATE LIBRARY FOUNDATION
GREAT VALLEY CENTER

CONTENTS

Country music pervaded Oildale, my hometown. The fiddles and guitars of what was called Okie music were as common on local jukeboxes and at local dances as tumbleweeds on a vacant lot. Like the biscuits and gravy offered at neighborhood cafes, like the stock car races every Saturday night, like the tent meetings held on a lot near our house, they were simply part of when and where I grew up.

One street north of the house where I was reared, a railroad spur led to the Golden Bear oil refinery. Black cylindrical tank cars moved up and down that track daily. Two of my sixth-grade classmates in the 1940s, Billy Thorp and Merle Haggard, deep in the thrall of songs about lonesome whistles and clacking rails, became ramblers when they jumped aboard one of those cars and ended up stranded a hundred miles north in Fresno. The Thorps, both Texans, and Mrs. Haggard, from Oklahoma, retrieved their adventurous sons and likely blistered their butts. Yet to J. D., Peanut, Joe Ed, and me, to Sarajane, Joline, Ilene, and Tootsie, to our entire class, in fact, they were heroes and more than heroes: they were men.

The next year I became distinctly aware that Oildale wasn't all of California when my parents sent me to school in nearby Bakersfield. There, Okie music was disdained and I put it away, praising the records of Johnny Ray, Joni James, or Nat "King" Cole. When I returned home each day, though, I'd watch the shows hosted by Jimmy and Louise Thomason or Cousin Herb Henson on a neighbor's television (my folks didn't own one). This bifurcation was prompted by the area's undisguised class consciousness: "Okie music" at school tagged you as a hick, and like many insecure adolescents, I wanted to fit in. Besides, I liked the other music, too.

Then one day, for reasons I no longer remember, a slight, disheveled boy named Norman Zumwalt stood before our class at Garces Junior

High School and, poker-faced, launched into a nasal rendition of Hank Snow's great hit "I'm Movin' On." My classmates, used to uncomfortable clowning when other students performed, at first sat stunned—this guy was *serious* about his singing. The class fidgeted, giggled, and laughed. I cringed because part of me stood there with Norman, but I lacked his courage.

A few years later when Carl Perkins, Jerry Lee Lewis, and Elvis Presley introduced a new, irresistible version of country music in the mid-1950s, I came out of the closet, and so did several of my classmates. Forty years later, having completed this manuscript with the help of coconceptualizer and editor Alexandra Haslam Russell as well as interviewer *par excellence* Richard Chon, I think again of gutsy Norman, wherever he is.

Special thanks are owed to Jonny Whiteside, Bill Woods, Louise Thomason, Sharon Mize, Steve Fjeldsted, Jim Shaw, Steve Emanuels, Archie Green, Norm Cohen, Heather Eisenman, and Jim Clark.

Penngrove, California

BAKERSFIELD, 1994

Nodding in rhythm to the music, the big man wears boots, Wranglers, a pearl-snapped shirt, and a battered five-gallon hat. His face appears to have been gouged out of metal; his shoulders are wide; his belly ample; his hips nonexistent. Noticing him, Jimbo whispers to me, "That guy was flew over by the butt fairy and landed on by the gut fairy." I stifle a laugh.

One of the large man's boots is planted on the floor, while the other touches the wall behind his flexed knee. At the end of an arm ruddy as terra-cotta, his right hand holds a long-necked bottle of Bud. He crooks his left thumb into a pocket of his jeans, the next two fingers clamp a cigarette: the classic stance. Then he says to me out of one corner of his mouth, "This sure is a great deal they're a-throwin' for ol' Billy, idn't it?"

I've never seen him before, but he is as familiar as sweat. "Damn right," I agree. Our mutual presence in that smoky room tells us all we need to know about one another. We're here to listen to fiddles and guitars and voices that sometimes crack—to real folks—not to banks of violins or backup choruses or echo chambers.

The "Tribute to Billy Mize" my older daughter Alexandra and I are attending is held at a venue called the Casa Royale. The Casa no longer seems very Royale—but then, neither do many of us middle-aged fans who are gathering today. Handsome Billy Mize had been a prominent member of the cadre of young entertainers from Bakersfield who four decades ago extended the popularity of country music, while at the same time staying close to its roots.

Mize had gone on to enjoy a career as sideman, singer, bandleader, and songwriter in the Los Angeles area, where his television program—and Billy himself—won multiple awards. While riding high, he was always willing to appear at benefits. Now two severe strokes have cut his career short, costing him his ability to sing or even to speak, so he has moved back to Bakersfield to rehabilitate close to family and friends.

We old fans have not forgotten him, and the Casa Royale's ballroom is filled far beyond capacity, standing-room only, with folks crowding out to the lobby. Cowboy boots and jeans dominate male attire, and they are worn mostly by guys with faces seared by outdoor work

1

and hands hard as Corn-Nuts. A much smaller percentage are younger, with curls hanging behind their dip-brim straw Stetsons. Many women who used to pour themselves into jeans and frilly blouses are now layered in skirts and jackets. Everyone appears happy and familiar: "My gosh, what're those kids of yours up to now?" asks a pert, gray-haired lady. Near her a middle-aged man says to another, "You're a grandpa! I always knew you was old, but…"; laughter and shoulder punches follow. Some of us recognize faces from shindigs past: "Aren't you ol' Bud's sister?"

On the floor, one eightyish couple dances to every tune—no rest. Near them, a young man sways and slowly turns with a legless woman, her arms tightly around his neck, his arms encircling her waist and bottom. A few affluent-looking younger couples practice choreographed line dancing never seen in a Kern County honky-tonk in the halcyon days; they seem as out of place as ballerinas.

The city of Bakersfield, the county of Kern, and the state of California have declared this "Billy Mize Day." The guest of honor, still movie-star handsome, accepts the accolades, but he does not speak. He can, but it is a torturous process, so he merely smiles and waves.

On the bandstand, Billy's songwriter brother, Buddy, reads a telegram from Merle Haggard, congratulating the recuperating entertainer and expressing sorrow that he can't be present, and heads in the crowd nod: you know ol' Merle'd be here if he could. Hell, he's a local boy.

The list of performers who are in attendance, though, and who have signed up to entertain reads like a Bakersfield Who's Who. Tommy Hays of the Country Music Museum serves as M.C., while Jimmy Sanders and the Stage Riders play; Jimmy's dad, the legendary fiddler Jelly Sanders, joins them. Many fans cluster near the bandstand to greet the man acknowledged to be the most important pioneer of Bakersfield music and Billy's one-time employer, Bill Woods. "'Member this buckle, Bill?" asks an angular, hard-looking man. He shows Woods a silver inlaid guitar the size of a large hand.

"Hell, yeah," Bill smiles, and they launch into talk of old friends and old adventures.

There are fine musical moments: Glen Duncan's baritone version of "Deep Water"; fiddler Richard Chon's electric "Take Me Back to Tulsa"; Oscar and Richard Whittington's bluesy, fiddle-and-sax rendition of "Night Train"; the Johnny Mosby band's bilingual numbers and his humor: "Don't ever get an Arkie up here on the bandstand," he calls as his set extends beyond the time limit; "you won't never get him off."

Bonnie Owens, who had come here as the teenage wife of Buck in 1951 and who remains a treasure to local folks, contributes a rollicking batch of songs, topped by yodeling runs in "I Want to Be a Cowboy's Sweetheart." Her banter is replete with first-name greetings and song dedications to old chums in the audience.

Billy Mize had been a prominent entertainer in Bakersfield in the 1950s who
contributed to the popularity of country music but stayed closed its roots.
Gerald Haslam Collection.

At midafternoon, a murmur surges through the room: Buck's here. He's brought the
Buckaroos. Buck's here.

*Buck Owens is, with Haggard, one of two superstars with roots in this town. Rumor has
it, though, that he and Billy had had a falling out some years back, so folks this afternoon
have openly wondered what would transpire if he appeared. They needn't have worried.
Buck Owens is part of this community, and he, too, has recently endured ill health, so he
understands well the ephemerality of life and the importance of friendship.*

Buck and the Buckaroos enter through a side door and mount a bandstand so low that

3

the musicians are actually among the audience without guards or barriers, tuning their instruments and greeting old chums. Bonnie approaches her former husband and says, "You're behind in your child support."

"Oh my God," Owens replies, then laughs. Their children have long since grown into adulthood.

A few moments later, Buck and the Buckaroos launch into "Act Naturally," and a bright spotlight immediately highlights the fit-looking star. When the number ends, Owens calls, "Not havin' a mic' here reminds me of the old Blackboard! I lived there for ten years." The crowd—made up of many former patrons of that fabled nightspot—applauds and cheers.

"Listen," the star calls, "why don't you turn that light off," and the beam on him is extinguished. This is Billy's day, and Buck literally refuses the spotlight. When he begins another of his hits—"Together Again"—the dance floor is dangerously crowded, couples having to sway in place.

"Love's Gonna Live Here Again," another number-one hit, follows, and that big man leaning against the wall next to me murmurs, as though in benediction, "Ol' Buck. . . ."

The star works his way through hit after hit, his voice in fine form. During instrumental interludes, he recognizes old friends in the crowd: "I thought you was in jail!" he calls, pointing at a Stetsoned man. "Boy, I see a lot of people tonight. Looky here," he smiles in recognition at an older couple. The Buckaroos are playing "Crying Time" behind him. "Hi Don! Hi Wanda!" A moment later, in mock anger, he growls toward a dancer, "Hey, you got my five dollars!" and the crowd roars.

"Ol' Buck . . ." that big guy on the wall mutters again, smoke exploding from his nostrils.

Buck Owens, like Merle Haggard, is the peak of a pyramid, we fans its base. But the pyramid's material is exactly the same for all of us, and everyone acknowledges that. There is scant distance between star and crowd, physically or emotionally. Buck is the community's laureate, and the community embodies his songs.

After performing a Billy Mize hit—"Who'll Buy the Wine?"—the band begins another tune, but the leader silences them: Billy has risen from his chair and mounted the bandstand next to Buck. The old pals embrace, then Mize struggles to speak.

"Listen up a minute folks!" calls Buck, trying to quiet the excited crowd, but Billy's faint words can't be heard. "Billy Mize, ladies and gentlemen!" calls Buck, louder, and finally the room stills.

The guest of honor again struggles with words, and this time we hear him rasp, "Thank you . . . Buck . . . so much."

The craggy man next to me, the one who looks like he not only could wrestle badgers but has, brushes his eyes. I, too, am blinking hard.

With his arm around Billy's shoulders, Buck says, "Let me tell you a story, folks. When I first came to town in 1951, things got kinda tough and I hocked my guitar. I got a chance to work for a few days, and I didn't have a guitar. Billy heard about it, and he said, 'I got a guitar over at the house he can borrow,' and he'd never even met me." *The deeper message is not missed: In this business, in this community, in this culture,* we don't forget.

Billy returns to his seat, and Buck launches into his most recent number-one song, "The Streets of Bakersfield." *I tell my Bakersfield-born daughter that with the town's prominence in country music waning we may be in the midst of its final great moment and that this also may be the most poignant one—beyond commercialism, beyond flash—a gathering sacred in its communion: we are one community and that pyramid embodies us all.*

Yet even this moment is bittersweet. Country music as a distinct regional and working-class phenomenon may be dying, while a variation of pop music called "contemporary country" becomes more popular nationwide. What has happened to the promise of country music in Bakersfield is the same that has happened to nearly all of California's country music and to the nation's, too.

It has been diluted by the commercial homogenization of the nation; folks eat at McDonald's instead of Bunky's Drive-In, they sleep at Motel 6 instead of Bud's Motel, they shop at Wal-Mart not Curnow's Dry Goods—the former establishments not significantly different in Tulsa or Tampa or Taft.

At 6:14 A.M. the next day, Alex and I enter McDonald's in nearby Oildale, my hometown. A fortyish waitress is talking to the only other customer, an older man who sits at a nearby table smoking a cigarette and nursing a cup of coffee. "Me and Georgie left about four, four-thirty," she says, "and it was still full. I'll tell you, Jack, he sure deserved it. He deserved every bit of it."

At first, we don't catch what she's talking about.

"Ol' Buck showed up and sang. And Bonnie, too," she adds.

"Is that a fact?" comments Jack, shaking his head. "Ol' Buck hisself."

The woman turns toward my daughter and me and asks, "Did you want cream with that coffee?"

"Please," I smile.

After serving us, she turns toward Jack again and says, "You know, Billy he recognized Georgie right away, and Buddy did, too." *Her voice reveals that Billy and Buddy are as much neighbors as celebrities.*

Although I say nothing, I am moved by what I hear because I am implicated. This is my hometown; I am and always will be part of it. The overheard conversation reminds me how much Buck and Billy, Bonnie and Buddy mean to all of us. They are our voices, for they, too, have been disdained, but they have triumphed and they have refused to abandon their roots.

They are country.

Exactly what that means, however, is open to considerable debate.

COUNTRY MUSIC–ROOTS AND STEMS

In June of 1922 country music's roots and stems were powerfully, if unintentionally, reflected in the outfits worn by two southwestern fiddlers, Henry C. Gilliland and Alexander C. "Eck" Robertson. Fresh from entertaining at a Confederate Army reunion in Virginia, they trooped uninvited into the New York City offices of the Victor Talking Machine Company, Gilliland decked out in a reb uniform, Robertson clad in a cowboy costume. The folks at Victor wondered what in the world they were dealing with. The company's catalog later recounted, "They told us they could play the fiddle, and asked for a hearing. As we knew several thousand persons who could play the fiddle, more or less, we were not especially impressed, but we asked them to begin."

On June 30 and July 1 Gilliland, an Oklahoman, and Robertson, a Texan, were allowed to cut six sides for Victor, country music's first recording session. The rest, as they say, is history, and those costumes— as well as the business suits worn by Victor's executives—symbolize the diverse musical reality that developed: southern, western, and definitely entrepreneurial.

But notions about *country*, the word itself, have tended to be more romantic, perhaps more mystical, than southern, western, or even commercial. A college-educated aficionado from Canada told researcher Melissa Ladenheim that "country" meant

> the simplicity, you know, not having to worry about schedules or organizations: a sort of natural rhythm and flow of things, things that are intrinsically interesting and fulfilling to do. . . . I think of country people as being honest, . . . talking only when necessary. . . . There's a kind of attitude about making things work and fixing things or using things, a knowledge

of tools—physical and mental—that comes with rural living. . . . That is, you know, resourceful in the way that you use something that is available to get done what has to get done and you do so, you know, with a kind of easy and slow-moving wisdom rather than a frenetic desire to get it done as fast as possible.

This is of course a statement of faith, harking to nostalgia for an agrarian past, real or imagined.

What, then, really *is* country music? This is not necessarily a simple question. The current, fashionable "top-40" version is actually a southern style of pop music so middle-of-the-road that a white line should be painted on it. In fact, it is probably more southern now than ever, thanks to Nashville's command of the business. Still, contemporary themes—featuring soft-focused ruralism—are increasingly cosmopolitan, thus less limited by class, region, or race, despite a continuing revision of the music's history that seeks to make it appear more folk, more southern, and even more "mountain" than it actually has been.

This music's legion of newer fans seems increasingly diverse, better educated, and significantly more affluent than earlier buffs. Perhaps as a result, sales of country albums have doubled since 1990 and are now twenty times higher than they were in 1970: country has become America's most popular music. Still, many old-time fans agree with music journalist Tony Scherman, who asserts that "the price of acceptance has been the music's pungency—more, its very identity."

Country was originally recorded in 1922 and '23, energized in part by technology—especially the availability of radios—and by the move of rural folks to cities—particularly the southern diaspora—as well as by the fact that many of its early tunes were largely familiar throughout rural and small-town America. Its surge of popularity in the 1980s and '90s may be linked to the suburban flight, to the blandness of competing pop music, and to America's continuing rural romanticism. Of course that has led traditionalists to ask if this electronically perfected contemporary stuff presented by Garth Brooks and the rest is *really* country music a-tall.

What writer Scherman has called the "oatmeal" now produced by major labels sure isn't what folks raised on Hank Williams and Lefty Frizzell would call country, but that's exactly why the audience has grown so large. Former *Playboy* model and sometime vocalist Barbi Benton explained what had led her to country: "The beat has changed. It's on a cusp between country and rock." Then she added, "I don't know if I would have liked 'Your Cheatin' Heart' in the old days." Probably not. This new stuff is increasingly homogeneous music for an increasingly homogeneous America—southern soft rock—yet it is also country's latest legitimate variation. Like everything else, this music changes.

What has historically evolved in country is assorted forms of music assembled under a single name. Any examination of acts on television's enduring "Austin City Limits" will reveal not only obvious versions such as western swing, bluegrass, honky-tonk, and rockabilly, but also zydeco, gospel, "old-timey," cowpunk, spirituals, blues, folk ballads, boogie-woogie, Tex-Mex, Cajun, cowboy ballads, story songs, undisguised pop, and some styles for which no title yet exists. Even the musically conservative "Grand Ole Opry" might present any of those elements—albeit, later and more reluctantly.

Variety has become country music's defining characteristic. When people say, "I don't like country, but I love rockabilly," they're really saying that rockabilly is a kind of country they love. Jo Walker, longtime executive director of the Country Music Association, admitted in 1970, "We used to spend a lot of time trying to define what a country song was. A committee was even appointed to work up a definition. We finally gave up."

The name, itself, hasn't always been clear-cut. William Ivey, former executive director of the Country Music Association Foundation, credits the 1968 publication of Bill C. Malone's landmark book *Country Music U.S.A.* with having finally established the term *country* as the accepted catchall for what might fairly be termed "nonpop" popular music—everything from Patsy Montana's yodeling to Lester "Smiley" Burnette's croaking, with a few dangerously high notes from Bill Monroe tossed in. For years, no one knew what to call such an assortment: "folk," "old-time," "hillbilly," "hill country music," "songs of mountains and plains," "old familiar tunes," "country-western," and, in California 50 years ago, "Okie music" (as with "hillbilly music," the term was often used pejoratively). In the Southeast this state's music has been labeled "West Coast country" or sometimes simply "coast country."

Despite (or because of) country's variety, many admirers remain quick to assert what the gen-u-ine deal is, usually something old and southern, but such assertions are just variations of an enduring "countrier-than-thou" phenomenon. An unidentified man at a 1996 old-time fiddling

A rural dance hall, the Pumpkin Center Barn, in the 1950s. Courtesy of Kern County Museum. Used by permission.

competition in Oroville said, "This is what country really is, mountain music." Sorry, pardner, it really is *everything* it is.

Country music arose in the 1920s as industrialization, urbanization, mechanization—as modernism itself—threatened old ways, and many country lyrics have revealed resistance to such changes. In the 1980s, for example, Merle Haggard's hit "Are the Good Times Really Over" celebrated this enduring topic. As a result, a series of generally popular themes have distilled as listeners from Carolina to California to Canada responded to its simple tunes and often frank verse. Country lyrics have tended to face reality, or some version of it anyway, head on. In what

10

other popular music, for example, have songs celebrated birth control ("The Pill"), reliable farm equipment ("The John Deere Tractor Song"), interracial romance ("Irma Jackson"), or dashing around naked in public ("The Streak")?

Despite its dynamism and recent catering to mass-market tastes, this domain retains a conservative core, celebrating traditional values—family, church, nation, and work—during periods when other forms of popular music seem to be without orthodoxy. As a consequence it has not infrequently offered anthems to those unhappy with or threatened by contemporary existence. Says songwriter/singer Tom T. Hall,

> You know, since day one of the Declaration of Independence, the American working man . . . [has] been jerked around from one calamity to another. And so that's where the songs come from. It's not easy out there if you wonder where the next refrigerator payment is coming from, or if the kids are going to eat, or if they're going to close down the plant where you work.

Scholars exploring country's choice of topics agree that love of one kind or another still dominates and that a romanticized rural motif remains pervasive. John Buckley's list of subjects in country songs, for example, includes (1) satisfying and fulfilling love relationships, (2) unsatisfactory love relationships, (3) home and family, (4) country (the agrarian ideal), (5) work, (6) individual worth, (7) rugged individualism, and (8) patriotism.

◄ ►   ◄ ►

All of Buckley's subjects are present among songs that have been created in California:

1. Satisfying and fulfilling love relationships. This subject/theme has run the gamut from Stuart Hamblen's 1950 classic "(Remember Me) I'm the One Who Loves You," to John Hartford's countrypolitan hit "Gentle on My Mind," with several fine examples by Harlan Howard, Buck Owens, and Merle Haggard.

Asked what inspired his song, Hamblen remembered that one day his wife, Suzy, asked, "Why not write a song about me? Remember me, I'm the one who loves you." Bingo.

2. Unsatisfactory love relationships. The list is long here, too, with Dallas Frazier's Country Music Association's 1967 song of the year, "There Goes My Everything," Haggard's "Holding Things Together," and (with Red Simpson) "You Don't Have Very Far to Go" especially strong. During Howard's stay in California, he produced several remarkable examples, among them "Heartaches by the Number," "Pick Me Up on Your Way Down," and (with Owens) "Excuse Me (I Think I've Got a Heartache)."

Of the last number, Howard explained that he and Wynn Stewart inadvertently found themselves in the midst of a friend's collapsing marriage, and the friend said, "Well, you guys'll have to excuse me. I think I've got a heartache."

3. Home and family. This is another popular subject/theme in California, a state of so many transplants. Most "home songs," such as Woody and Jack Guthrie's "Oklahoma Hills" refer to places left behind. The hankering for the home that couldn't support you is linked of course with a more genuine yearning for family and friends. Perhaps that's why Lefty Frizzell had a great hit in the Golden State with "Mom and Dad's Waltz," for it proclaimed a sentiment with which literally thousands of transplants could identify.

4. Country (the agrarian ideal). Closely related to home and family, some variation of this positive agrarian image—or illusion—seems to exist in most country songs. In this state it can be linked to disillusionment because the old rural ways so seldom lead to a decent living, as is exemplified by Dallas Frazier's "California Cottonfields" or Haggard's "Hungry Eyes." It can also show country resourcefulness, as seen in Tommy Collins's "Shade Tree (Fix-It Man)." The best example of all may be Haggard's "Big City."

5. Work. Closely tied to number 4 above, this subject/theme is owned by Haggard, with everything from "Tulare Dust" to "Workin' Man Blues" and plenty in between.

6. Individual worth. Haggard leads again with "I Take a Lot of Pride in What I Am" and "My Own Kind of Hat," and lots of others.

7. Rugged individualism. Haggard reigns once more with such songs as "I've Done It All" and "Mama Tried," among others.

8. Patriotism. This term is generously defined here, so numbers as varied as Haggard's "The Fightin' Side of Me," Kris Kristofferson's "The Vietnam Blues," and Country Joe McDonald's "I-Feel-Like-I'm-Fixin'-to-Die Rag" all count.

◄ ►　　　◄ ►　　　◄

Any deep understanding of the themes—indeed, of the metaphysics—of country music demands some examination of the larger issue of national culture or perhaps of what it has meant to be an American. In her stimulating 1931 volume, *American Humor: A Study of the National Character,* Constance Rourke argued that culture—ever dynamic—moved from the masses to the elite not vice versa, and she denied the existence of a "high" culture separate from "popular" culture; to her, they were parts of the same whole, with considerable shared middle ground.

Country music—in its forms, in its themes, in its very existence—seems to validate Rourke's thesis. Its heterogeneous nature embraces the elements of her prototypical American "comic trio": the Yankee, the Backwoodsman, the Negro. Recognizing the blended essence of this nation's traditions, she wrote: "The mythic trio's comedy, their irreverent wisdom, their sudden changes and adroit adaptations, provide emblems for a pioneer people who required resilience as a prime trait." Unaltered, the scholar's words might describe country music, especially in its earliest forms.

This music's traditional independent and improvisational tone has reinforced many characteristics central to the development of our national personality. Illusions of its British or European origins notwithstanding, country music—like its even more distinct cousin, jazz—has been essentially American, especially in its feisty nature. But that nature has become less feisty, less independent, and certainly less innovative since big business in the guise of top-40 stations, cookie-cutter producers, electronically smoothed performances, and so on, began clamping a hammerlock on artists and songwriters four decades ago. That country retains much of its original power at all represents a triumph of popular taste over commercialism and is largely the product of this music's contemporary margins—especially in California and Texas—not its mainstream.

In 1972 sociologists John D. McCarthy, Richard A. Peterson, and William L. Yancey flatly stated that country's fans were "predominately southern and white." Even today, when observers suggest that country music has remained close to its origins, they usually mean its *southern* origins. This branch of the music business certainly did originate in the South, where various American commercial styles combined with British and African traditions—themselves much Americanized—to produce some unique works. Those in turn resonated with the experiences and the nostalgic tastes of rurally identified folks nationwide. The music is more complex and varied now because it has borrowed widely, mostly for commercial reasons, and it seems more southern than it is because Nashville has become its commercial home and because the music's major image-shaper, the Country Music Association, is located there.

In fact, two questionable "givens" regarding the southernness of this music have come to be widely accepted: One is that Nashville has always been the center of country music; the other is that country music started with British songs retained in the mountain South. Neither is true. The former myth is simple to refute. According to the editors of *Country Music* magazine, Atlanta dominated the 1920s, Chicago the 1930s, and Hollywood the 1940s, then Nashville attained prominence, and it has steadily built preeminence.

The latter myth, however, is more persistent because so many folks want it to be true. A few of country's oldest songs can indeed be traced to music from Britain, but they are just the oldest, not the most or the most important. Country music was commercial from the start. During the first two years of recording country music, performers were indeed primarily rural and southern, and they were allowed to choose their own songs. Scholars Anne and Norman Cohen identified about 70 percent of those selections and found that only 2 percent were of pre-1800 British origin; 6 percent were from post-1900 Tin Pan Alley; 7 percent were from post-1900 American folk sources; 26 percent were from 1860–1900 Tin Pan Alley; 59 percent were from pre-1900 American folk or early minstrel sources.

J. K. Johnson, a musician reared in rural California recalled, "Well, when those new records from the South came out in the twenties, we mostly recognized the songs. They sang some dandy ones." He pointed out one difference, though: "Here we played most of the same ones they did, but Spanish stuff too—'El Rancho Grande' or 'La Golondrina.' And we really liked that Haywire Mac [McClintock] and his hobo songs. I sure bought his records."

"Spanish stuff" was common in the Southwest, of which the southern half of California was a cultural extension; Texas music, too, was much influenced by Latino styles. That's revealing because most popular definitions of the musical South seem to focus on the Southeast, due in no small measure to Nashville's present prominence and perhaps some skillful revisionism by the Country Music Association. But the Southwest has

Hollywood helped spread country music. Merle Travis and Carolina Cotton harmonize in a 1940s film short. Playing steel at the far left is songwriter Bonnie Dodd. From the Gid Tanner Artist File #NF1996, The Southern Folklife Collection, Wilson Library, The University of North Carolina at Chapel Hill.

certainly held its own in this music in terms of styles, of performers, and of audiences, and it has most influenced California's country music.

"Southwest" in this context does not refer to the mesas of New Mexico or Arizona but to a variation of what historians refer to as the "Old Southwest," in this case Arkansas, Missouri, Louisiana, Oklahoma, Texas—a tier of states that has contributed so much to settlement on the West Coast. Moreover, those states, with their more heterogeneous histories and populations than the Deep South's, have had at least as much in common with the Golden State—including varied ethnic music—as with Tennessee or Georgia.

In a memorable article published in the spring 1975 issue of the *Journal of Country Music*, "The Fertile Crescent of Country Music," sociologists Richard A. Peterson and Russell Davis, Jr., made two central points: One, "notable country musicians have been, and continue to be, primarily country born"; two, "the South has been, and still is, the cradle of country music." They define the fertile crescent as an "arc of states beginning with West Virginia in the Northeast continuing south and west encompassing most of the Southeast, as well as including Texas and Oklahoma."

That interesting designation, however, isn't necessarily as significant as it seems. The inclusion of Texas and Oklahoma moves the fertile crescent well beyond the Deep South. John Shelton Reed and Dale Volberg Reed point out in 1001 *Things Everyone Should Know About the South* that in their southernness "Texas and Oklahoma are marginal but show an east-to-west gradient"; the eastern sections of those states were much more influenced by Dixie, while their central and western sections (the particular areas that most contributed population and culture to California) escaped reb homogeneity in their populations and music. In fact, as Peterson and Davis also pointed out, Texas has produced more country-music notables than any other state—many of whom, from Stuart Hamblen to Bob Wills to Buck Owens, have chosen to reside in California—which indicates that they have avoided domination by the Southeast. Oklahoma and Missouri have sent nearly as many important musicians to the Golden State.

California has provided few native-born stars. At the time Peterson and Davis were writing, only Cliffie Stone, Sammi Smith, and Merle Haggard were California-born luminaries; for each of them, there have been dozens of outstanding transplants—the Rose Maddoxes, the Gene Autrys, the Merle Travises, and the Dwight Yoakams. It's important to note of course that this state's general population (and especially its population of entertainers) has been characterized by a large number of folks born elsewhere, and that some areas of it have served as virtual enclaves of this culture or that one. In the entertainment industry today, it seems difficult *not* to have a California connection, no matter when or where you were born.

More to the point, the eclecticism and independence of many musicians in the Southwest and California have linked them as outsiders (or, trendily, "outlaws") since Nashville gained control of this business on the cusp of the 1940s and '50s. A decade after that a fan named Frank Chase said, "They used to call it country and western, but now they ought to call it country and southern." He was of course commenting on a subtle musical change that dated from Nashville's rise to dominance. By the 1980s John Denver would identify himself as a "western singer not a country singer" because by then Tennessee's version of the music had come to be so thoroughly identified with southern styles. Ironically, following Denver's death in 1997, fully six of his albums were listed in the country-music top 10.

Today, with pop techniques in vogue nationally, the gap that has grown between "country" and "western" remains clear: they are different threads of a cloth. Suggests singer U. "Utah" Phillips, "in Nashville, you have to wear a new hat; in the West, you have to run over your hat with a truck before you wear it." Sonoma County favorite Ace Atkins summarizes the difference this way: "Western singers sing about their horses and they never kiss women. Country singers sing about drinking and chasing women. And they do both."

Ironically, the openness to new ideas that emanated mainly from the Southwest—including Southern California—has arguably proved at least as predictive of what country music has now become as have narrower early southeastern definitions. Perhaps the most important single lesson Californians learned from their southwestern neighbors, for example, was that country music should be danceable, as were western swing, honkytonk, and rockabilly.

Peterson and Davis's use of "production of notables" as a criterion, while interesting, is by no means a definitive revelation of the music's hub. Nashville now dominates country, and many stars from elsewhere cluster there, just as they historically have in the Golden State, America's favorite destination since 1848. In fact, enthusiastic audiences, varied venues, movie opportunities, radio and television programming, and regional recording labels along with the West Coast impulse to reinvent not only self but music, too, seem to have established California as second to Tennessee in country music's history; only Texas challenges. Such an assertion may run counter to this state's and this music's images, but history (even as regards a domain as public as the entertainment industry) contains many surprises.

The production of fans and the intensity of their identification have

Bob Wills (third from left) in the 1950s with a group that includes (left to right) Cliff Crofford, Will Ray (?), Billy Mize, Jean Shepard, Johnny Cuviello (partly obscured), Bill Woods. Two people on the right are unidentified. Courtesy of Kern County Museum. Used by permission.

been a revealing gauge. A national community has been created by country, and its concerns have of course been national (perhaps universal) not regional; the music's blue-collar and countercultural connotations, for example, have endeared it to people who have been shadowed or luminated by their own experiences in the class-conscious Golden State. When fans see Buck Owens on stage, they don't see Bakersfield, California, or Sherman, Texas; they see themselves and their dreams.

Historically, most of America, including the rural South, was much influenced by various commercial music well before the dawn of recording.

Sears Roebuck, for example, was sending millions of copies of catalogs (featuring everything from fiddles to songbooks) to rural folks by 1920. Traveling minstrels and vaudeville revues (both still common in the early 1920s), medicine shows, sacred "singing schools," and sheet music (published of course in cities) were other early shapers of this commercial genre. Dixie indeed remained a unique realm when in 1916 the British musicologist Cecil Sharp observed of the region, "I found myself for the first time in my life in a community in which singing was as common and almost as universal a practice as speaking."

Sharp collected 1,600 versions of 500 traditional songs in the southern mountains between 1916 and 1918, yet logged almost no instrumental music. Conversely, Roy Acuff, perhaps the greatest of singers in the southern hill-country tradition, reported that when he was young, he and his friends didn't often sing a song outside of church; mainly, they played instrumental music for their neighbors at parties and dances. Early hillbilly recordings, even those with vocals, were dominated by instrumentals.

The prototypes of country music, whatever their sources, enjoyed a national reach from the start; as scholar D. K. Wilgus explains, while its "manifestation was of the South; its essence was of rural America."

> That hillbilly music is a phenomenon solely of the South in general and of the Southern Appalachians in particular is a myth in the best sense of the word. . . . Early hillbilly performers came not only from the lowland and upland South, but from the Great Plains and the Midwest—and eventually New England, Nova Scotia, and Alberta.

Folklorist Roderick J. Roberts agrees, saying that "tradition-oriented people outside the South bought commercially recorded Southern music because it was the closest available . . . to their musical aesthetic."

Scholar Robert Cantwell adds a telling point: "Hillbilly music has never been anything but entrepreneurial and commercial, prospering in the one commodity which in America is ever in short supply—the past." The title of a recent book by sociologist Richard A. Peterson is also informative: *Creating Country Music: Fabricating Authenticity.*

At its inception, this music's underlying sentiment certainly jibed with a prevailing national mood; its primary theme, as sociologist Alex Freedman summarizes, was that "the country is good and the city is bad—

there is no in-between position," an almost perfect expression for rural people caught in the process of urbanization.

"Poor-but-proud" is another enduring motif; this has not been the music of big shots. If country's first powerful connotation was rural and its second was southern, its third has been white people in blue collars. That identification is no coincidence, since folks near the bottom of America's class-conscious society have been acutely aware of their position; scorning country music's fans has, until recently at least, been common. When country became increasingly popular in the Golden State during the 1940s, it was often called "Okie music." Said Spec Haslam, "They called it 'Okie,' but that didn't mean Oklahoman or southern, it meant poor mostly. Someone it's okay to look down your nose at."

This music can, in fact, be viewed as a survivor of a forgotten nineteenth-century battle between promoters debating what American music—and by implication, American society—should be. Musicologist Charles Seeger points out that aristocrats and urbanites then "were at loggerheads with respect to what was good, but in agreement upon one that was bad, the folk art favored by rural people." Then as now, class tensions were persistent. While gentry supporting European "classics" competed with urban dwellers who endorsed newly emerging commercial American sounds (such as Tin Pan Alley's), the traditional songs that endured in every village and on every farm were viewed as unfit for high culture or perhaps for any culture at all.

Of course this hasn't been an entirely one-sided struggle. Many hard-working pioneer Americans have considered classical music to be a foreign affectation of the idle rich. Disparaging art, and anti-intellectualism in general, have been popular practices among those who identify with what historian James Gregory calls "plain-folks Americanism." Long before there was country music, there was social awareness; it's still an important aspect of country music's world, well summarized by Lester Flatt and Earl Scrugg's song title, "Don't Get above Your Raising." A Stetsoned habitué of Penngrove's Twin Oaks Saloon in 1996 winked as he said, "Hell no, I sure wouldn't wanta miss an opera or one of those ballet deals"; in the background his pals laughed.

The roots of country music actually penetrated California with the Gold Rush. Fiddle music was common in the camps on holidays, and miners danced with one another if ladies (professional or otherwise)

Honky-tonkin' at the Blackboard in Bakersfield during the 1950s. On the bandstand are Bill Woods and his Orange Blossom Playboys, featuring young Buck
Owens on guitar. Courtesy of Kern County Museum. Used by permission.

weren't available. Often such music was one of the few touches of home
lonely men retained. By the time the Civil War raged in the East, young
William Henry Brewer, a leader of the California Geological Survey party,
traveled about the state, and he found a decidedly heterogeneous society,
including many southerners, referred to scornfully as "Secessionists."

Fiddle music was often heard in rural California, and it would eventually prove central to the development of commercial country music.
Scholar Douglas B. Green explains that because the instruments were
portable as well as versatile, "fiddles came over with the earliest settlers
and became a part of the American folk tradition." Certainly, fiddlers
were the favorite musicians in rural nineteenth-century America, whether
on a farm or in a mine, in a village or at a cattle camp. Generation after
generation of some families passed fiddle playing down, and few communities were without someone who could "pull that bow."

Competitions among fiddlers became a tradition, and those contests
eventually provided a training ground for many of country music's first
performers, as the sobriquets of Fiddlin' John Carson, Fiddlin' Sid

Harkreader, and Fiddlin' Bob Hayes, among others, illustrate. In *San Antonio Rose*, his biography of Bob Wills, Charles R. Townsend describes a West Texas contest that involved Bob's father:

> Eck Robertson and John Wills were selected for the finals. . . . Eck went to the platform first and probably played "Beaumont Rag" . . . whatever he played was good, and when he left the platform everyone knew he would be difficult to beat. John Wills, in his turn, probably played "Gone Indian," for that was one of his best. When John reached a certain place in the tune, he began hollering and held an elongated cry about an octave above his fiddle music so that his voice harmonized with the fiddle. John kept the music and the holler going for what seemed like minutes. His performance was a crowd and judge pleaser, and he won over his arch-rival. As Robertson left the scene of the contest, someone asked, "Eck, did John outfiddle you?" Eck answered, "Hell, no! He didn't outfiddle me. That damned old man Wills outhollered me!"

Fiddling was common to all of the English-speaking Americas. In his history of the "Grand Ole Opry" Charles Wolfe tells the story of Mellie Dunham from Maine, who was considered by many to be the world champion fiddler in the mid-1920s. Uncle Jimmy Thompson, a southerner, had been declared America's champion barn-dance fiddler following a competition in Dallas, so Dunham challenged him. "He may have defeated 86 opponents in the Dallas contest," said Dunham, "but they were all southerners, and they don't know as much about barn-dance fiddling in that section as they do 'down in Maine.'" (The challenge wasn't accepted.)

Instrumentation has long defined country music, and nowadays a twanging steel guitar, not a fiddle, can turn virtually any performance into country. That defining twang derives not from a southern source, but from Hawaiian performers. A "classic" instrument in Europe, the guitar was well established in music from the lowland South before it made its way into the mountains. Railroad workers, most of them black, penetrated the highlands late in the nineteenth century; they brought their music, introducing not only strong rhythms but new types of melodic picking. By 1894 Sears advertised seven guitar models—most cheap— making the instrument widely available. Then via vaudeville at the turn of the century the Hawaiian instruments and "sliding steel" styles of play were adopted from performers who toured rural America. From them later developed dobros, steel guitars, and pedal steels. Mexican guitars and methods spread from the Southwest at about the same time as Hawaiian guitars appeared. Historian Bill C. Malone has pointed out, "Most of the innovative developments in steel guitar style came from musicians west of the Mississippi River." Those varied developments typify the eclectic nature of what has come to be called country.

Blacks in particular had a great impact on country guitar playing. Such stalwarts as Bill Monroe, Ike Everly, and Mose Rager (as well as, indirectly, both Merle Travis and Chet Atkins), for example, were in the thrall of an African-American musician named Arnold Shultz. He is often credited with having developed the syncopated "thumb style" of guitar picking, with its heavily accented bass, swinging tempo, and chording up the guitar's neck; and via his white disciples, Shultz revolutionized "white" country music at a time when racism and racial barriers in America were horrendous. Cantwell explains a deeper import of such contacts:

> It may be difficult for us to catch the significance of a young rural white in the 1920s taking up what the late Birch Monroe called "them old nigger blues." To seek out the black bluesman was usually a literal journey to the nether regions of society—shantytown, railroad, honky-tonk—but more significantly, a social descent which, like the descents of mythology and folklore, was made on behalf of the special powers conferred by secret knowledge.

Minstrel shows introduced another vital agent, the banjo; ironically, an instrument originally developed in Africa was spread by whites in blackface. The mandolin was adopted after the wave of immigration from Italy shortly before the turn of the century. The accordion made its way into southern music via both German and Cajun (Acadian French) music, while the harmonica ("mouth harp," "French harp," etc.) was developed in Germany.

As tastes changed and electrical amplification influenced musicians and audiences alike, solid-bodied guitars eventually became dominant. By the early 1960s writer Rich Kienzle points out, "Fiddles were . . . considered too corny by several country producers, and for a time they became casualties of the so-called 'Nashville Sound.'"

There has, in truth, been no practical limitation on instruments that can be used in country, although certainly some are more traditional than others, and various conventions rise and fall. No outfit better illustrated that truism than the zany Hoosier Hotshots ("Are you ready, Hezzie?"), movie favorites in the 1940s. They employed guitar, clarinet, bass, slide whistle, washboard, bulb horns, pots, pans, and anything else that worked to produce (in the words of their own promotional material) "a wonderful tintinnabulation heretofore unheard by mortal ears." Perhaps only the novelty of Spike Featherstone's harp in Spade Cooley's orchestra rivaled them.

In any case, during the post–World War I period technology had played a major part in country music's birth. The popularity of radio after that conflict caused a significant drop in record sales, prompting recording companies to cast about for new audiences. That resulted in the initial recording of many rural southern entertainers, black and white alike. This music, that as dogma has complained about big cities and newfangled devices, was largely brought into being by them.

Now, over seventy years later, Nashville is the seat of this music's business. It is not, however, its spiritual core: that can still be found in the lives of hard-working people everywhere, perhaps at the churches and honky-tonks, the rodeos and monster truck rallies, where they gather. And of course much of this music has indeed been countercultural, revealing rootlessness, loneliness, and more than a little desperation in the American psyche. It has not—until recently at least—been the anthem of a contented people.

If the southern diaspora energized songs and spread the audience for this commercial music in the 1920s, the Okie migration of the 1930s had a similar effect in California, and the World War II and postwar migrations were even larger and more important. But the various types of country music had enjoyed a considerable following in the Golden State even before those events occurred. It can be said to have started in the 1920s with a family of southern transplants called the Crocketts.

THE CROCKETT FAMILY

After bouncing from West Virginia to New Mexico then back to Kentucky, John and Admonia Crockett arrived in Fowler, California, with their brood in 1919. They had not been aiming at the Fresno County farming town, but when John "Dad" Crockett was offered a job there, the family settled.

This clan of displaced southerners in many ways summarized country music's beginnings. Both John and Admonia were familiar with traditional songs; their son, Johnny, remembered that his mother sang at home such songs as "Barbara Allen," "Bury Me Beneath the Willow," and "The Dying Ranger," the kind of material folk-music specialist Cecil Sharp had collected in the southern mountains between 1916 and 1918. Dad Crockett was from a musical family, and he had been a rural singing teacher in his youth. He knew instrumental as well as vocal numbers, and his repertoire was varied. He recalled that when he was a boy in West Virginia, peddlers had sold song sheets from house to house. Those pages contained words but no musical notations, allowing the peddlers to teach the tunes exclusively to paying customers.

When Sharp had visited the mountains, he had logged almost no instrumental music. Early hillbilly recordings, on the other hand, would be dominated by instrumentals. The Crocketts exemplified this apparent paradox, since Dad had played fiddle and banjo all his life at various public gatherings, as well as at home. Music scholars Anne and Norman Cohen explain that "the reason Sharp collected no instrumental music was that he was not present at, or interested in, those occasions at which instrumental music was played."

The Cohens point out that two parallel folk-music paths existed in the rural South, indeed, in rural America: an "assembly tradition" and a "domestic tradition." The former included music performed by groups of avocational musicians such as Dad Crockett at family gatherings, parties, weddings, rallies, church services, and so on; the latter tended to be performed at home by people such as Admonia Crockett, often unaccompanied: ballads, lullabies, children's songs, and the like. The assembly tradition, in particular, became an ancestor of hillbilly (thus country) music, and it was much influenced early on by various professional modes and styles. The domestic tradition has remained closely linked to the commercial music called folk.

Even in rural California musical influences were rich and varied; the Crockett kids (there had been eleven, but at least three died in childhood) were exposed to chautauquas and minstrel shows. Vaudeville was accessible in nearby Fresno. Moreover church music of various kinds was popular, records were increasingly well liked, and even such media as school and community choruses introduced varied material to the region. Dad and the boys occasionally entertained at shindigs near Fowler—the assembly tradition was alive and well there. Eventually, talented young John Crockett, Jr., called Johnny, was invited to perform on Fresno's KMJ radio. He remembered going on the radio in 1923, but newspaper accounts of his performances didn't appear until 1926. He was by then an accomplished amateur who played banjo, guitar, and harmonica, and he sang in a pinched southern style.

Johnny was an immediate hit, drawing on both the topical ("The Death of Floyd Collins") and the more traditional ("Bury Me Not on the Lone Prairie") songs but avoiding "high art" or Tin Pan Alley numbers. An article in the November 6, 1926, issue of the *Fresno Bee* announced, "John Crockett, cowboy balladist, was back on the air with his usual grist of old-time numbers and received numerous requests for others. Valley fans who may have old-time ballads hidden away in scrap books and would like to hear them on the air are requested to send them to *The Bee* radio department, and they will be turned over to the singer." Such an appeal reveals why much early country music remained a celebration of old times and traditional values nationally. It was a countercultural (or counter-*mass*-cultural) expression even then, pitting "Turkey in the Straw" against "Yes, We Have No Bananas."

Eventually, Johnny coaxed his brothers Albert, Clarence, and George—then Dad (who'd been the most reluctant)—to join him on the air. Like most early "hillbilly" entertainers, the Crocketts were throwbacks to popular music's nineteenth-century roots, for they played stringed in-

The Crocketts: Albert, Sam, Elnora, Alan, George, Mother, Dad, Johnny. Only Sam wasn't a family member. Photo by Monroe, Hollywood. Courtesy of Norm Cohen.

struments and continued performing mainly what were being called "old familiar tunes." By 1927 the family had introduced their sister Elnora, only six years old, to their show, and they had developed so large a following that they were referred to as "radio favorites."

Another article in the *Bee* reported, "Dad Crockett and his 5-stringed banjo, John and Clarence Crockett, all of Fowler, were on the air with numerous old-time songs and novelty numbers. They specialize in western ballads and will be glad to sing any song treasured in family scrapbooks if it will be forwarded to the *Bee* radio dept." Once again, the repertoire sounds like a summary of most early country music: whatever plain folks liked.

Despite the publicity, the Crocketts were not paid for their broadcasts. Eventually, though, they began appearing in local theaters, initially in blackface as the Crockett Minstrels. Johnny later recalled that that was the first time the family had ever received wages for performing.

By 1928 they had moved on to Los Angeles, where they appeared on KNX for $40 a week—big money when contrasted with the fact that they made nothing on KMJ-Fresno. After they substituted for a no-show at the Hippodrome Theater, their career accelerated, and they became part of a six-day Southern California theatrical circuit. By 1931 they were in New York City, where they landed a nightly program on WABC, about the same time Tex Ritter and Ray Whitley began hosting the "Barn Dance" on rival WHN.

Eventually, the family recorded for Brunswick and Crown, joined a national vaudeville circuit, performed in several movies (including the Jeanette McDonald and Clark Gable hit, *San Francisco*), and even provided the sound track for some Walter Lanz cartoons. Folios and books of their songs were published. During World War II, Johnny Crockett would become a significant songwriter, contributing such hits as "You Were Right and I Was Wrong" for Roy Rogers, and "My Heart Belongs to a Stranger" for Johnny Bond.

By then most of the family had returned to Fowler. They'd had a good and unexpected run and can be credited as California's first local country-music stars. They also exemplified one of the oldest traditions in country, the musical family that eventually became professionals doing what they'd have done anyway but more of it and for pay.

In the end they had pride in their work and wonderful memories. Johnny Crockett recalled in 1966 that the first time they'd performed at the Forum Theater in Los Angeles in the late 1920s, the manager had warned them in advance that he allowed no encores. As was common at the time, when the live entertainment was completed, a movie screen descended and the feature film was immediately shown. After the Crocketts concluded, the screen was indeed lowered and the film started, though fans kept cheering and demanding more music. The manager finally relented and had the screen run up so the family could perform an encore.

Country music has been doing that in California ever since.

The increasing numbers of Californians who owned radios in the mid-1920s could barely discern familiar tunes rasping from ultra-low-fidelity speakers: Johnny Crockett and the Crockett Cowboy Singers from KNX in Los Angeles. Old-timers recalled that at first all they heard was something a little like music. "You had to listen real close before you caught on to what they were doing," said J. K. Johnson, a musician born and reared on California's Central Coast late in the last century. "We had a crystal set, and mostly things just kind of buzzed." Little did anyone suspect that those buzzes announced a revolution in popular music.

California's economy was booming after World War I; thus rural folks could afford crystal sets. Oil, agriculture, tourism, and of course movies, among other lures, drew migrants to the state, and automobiles eased their travel. Because settled and contented people did not tend to move West, California gathered more than its share of seekers. Many of them were poorly educated, if ambitious and driven; some were unrealistic, and others were escapists. If many sought to join the modern world, others sought to escape it.

This decade was also shadowed by the effects of the Eighteenth Amendment—Prohibition—as well as behavior that defied old-fashioned morality: flaunting sex, digging jazz, and seeking fun for its own sake—*"What's got into these younguns?"* There followed of course, in this essentially conservative society, a compensatory rise in moral outrage, in religious fundamentalism, and even in nativism, the latter often favored, ironically enough, by poorly educated nonnatives who had brought their prejudices with them.

Historian Lawrence Levine has noted that "the central paradox of American history . . . has been a belief in progress coupled with a dread of change; an urge toward the inevitable future combined with a longing for the irretrievable past." Both California's stereotype and many of country music's themes were products of that paradox.

By the 1920s the Golden State hosted a considerable population of rurally identified folks, so what would come to be called country music found an immediate audience. Technology, in the guise of radio and records, had played a major part in the new genre's birth. In California as in many other regions those media served to connect folks in an increasingly disconnected society, as nineteenth-century communities and values were breaking down, and erstwhile rural folks increasingly found jobs in cities. J. K. Johnson recalled that "we all knew the same songs in those days. At picnics and fiestas, we played the same ones. Later we'd hear them on records or on the radio. They were a sort of a glue that kept us together."

The first country-music radio programming began in the South: WSB-Atlanta is credited with initiating it when the station broadcast Fiddlin' John Carson on September 9, 1922—nine months before the same artist cut his first record. On January 4, 1923, WBAP in Fort Worth, Texas, produced the nation's initial barn-dance show, featuring a Hawaiian band and an old-time country fiddler. It didn't take California long to become involved; John Crockett remembered that he was invited to perform on KMJ that same year.

At first, country-music radio programs were all live, the most spectacular and enduring being the barn-dance format—musical variety programs in the tradition of nineteenth-century medicine or minstrel shows. One index of fan demographics is that the first program to become a major favorite was the "National Barn Dance" broadcast from powerful WLS-Chicago, which began in April of 1924. The longest-running of the barn dances, the "Grand Ole Opry," debuted on November 28, 1925, as Nashville's "WSM Barn Dance." Neither of these programs paid their entertainers at first; that novel notion emerged later. But they did allow the performers to promote themselves, their records, and their song sheets.

In 1926 an established performer, Harry "Haywire Mac" McClintock, started a program on San Francisco's KFRC, the state's first country show in a major outlet. The next year, Len Nash and his Original Country Boys were broadcasting from KFWD in Los Angeles, so California's two major metropolitan areas boasted popular country-music programs in the late 1920s. By the end of the decade, KFI in Los Angeles also featured hillbilly music on its "Saturday Night Jamboree." Bands such as "Sheriff" Loyal Underwood's Arizona Wranglers and Charlie Marshall and his Mavericks, both of whom favored western-influenced dance music, had also become popular in Southern California, where the population was growing rapidly. Because station wattage was then unregulated, thus often powerful, much of the state could listen to variations of country music.

During the first few years it was recorded, this "hillbilly" music was dominated by the performances of southern whites (while southern blacks were then being heard on "race" records). One pioneer in recording the music of both groups, Ralph Peer of Okeh Records, didn't realize at first that in those southern musicians he had discovered a treasure. Much music performed by whites then was distinct; it favored stringed instruments, especially fiddles, and a wailing, nasal style of singing. Peer said upon hearing Fiddlin' John Carson cut country's first commercially successful disc on June 14, 1923, that he considered him "pluperfect awful."

➤   ◄ ➤   ◄ ➤

High Voice, Low Voice — Country Voice

Although he couldn't know it, Peer was responding to a highly stylized nineteenth-century, southern singing technique, often described as pinched and nasal. Some scholars think it may have evolved as the vocal equivalent of the wail and whine of fiddle music or perhaps of bagpipes or other kinds of pipes.

Today, with pop orchestration eclipsing traditional instruments and styles, scholar W. K. McNeil argues that "the only connection modern, commercial country music has with folk music is in the style of singing," and one enduring stereotype of country music is that its singers employ that constricted, moaning, nasal delivery. Certainly in the past full-voiced singers were an exception.

The vocalizing of bluegrass master Bill Monroe has come to epitomize "breaking out" to some. Scholar Robert Cantwell discusses Monroe's "tonsil-busting pitches" and his tendency to employ that range to achieve "the high, lonesome sound" that some consider the epitome of southern singing.

Cantwell also reveals that Monroe "in riding from show to show would attempt to sing the songs of one performance a half-tone higher for the next. This is not high singing for its own sake," he argues; "rather it is an effort to preserve the morally grounded tension between the vocal powers and the demands the singer makes upon the voice." Indeed, Monroe could sound strained at worst, crystalline at best, and his voice could even lead Cantwell to "wonder if it is not a musical equivalent of that characteristically romantic effect produced by the conjunction of beauty and terror called the Sublime." Whew!

Despite influential high duets by Buck Owens and the late Don Rich, California has encouraged deeper, more worldly voices. Perhaps illusions of innocence had long since been stripped from the southwesterners who provided the core of the state's large country community, so the earthy pragmatism of baritones, even bassos, had been readily accepted. Tex Williams, Ernest Tubb, Ernie Ford, Tex Ritter, Stoney Edwards, Merle Haggard, Dave Alvin, and Country Dick Montana, among others, have all employed deeper ranges in their performances, far from the reedy tenors of bluegrass (and southern myths) in their songs. Williams, for instance, was a kind of mirror image of Monroe in that he had worked to *lower* his voice.

Vocal styles remain very much an issue in this musical world, for the high southern pitches, vocal constriction, and nasalization may stem from deeper causes. According to musicologist Alan Lomax, agricultural societies seem to favor higher pitches; the constricted vocal styles tend to mirror the severity of a culture's sexual proscriptions. Attempts to curtail bawdy urges in the South may therefore account for the persistence of those tight, "overcontrolled," sometimes nasal singing styles employed by many country wailers.

Sublime, indeed.

◄ ►   ◄ ►   ◄

Despite his distaste for Carson's singing, Peer sent to Polk Brockman in Atlanta a thousand discs of Fiddlin' John performing "The Little Old Log Cabin in the Land" (a vaudeville favorite) and "The Old Hen Cackled and the Rooster's Going to Crow" (probably a minstrel song). Peer considered the recording "so horrible" that he didn't even bother to assign it a catalog number. Only a couple of days later, though, "Brockman got me on the phone and said, 'This is a riot, I gotta get ten thousand copies down here right now.'"

Although those two southwestern fiddlers mentioned earlier—"Eck" Robertson and Henry C. Gilliland—had recorded for Victor the year be-

Okeh Records in the 1920s sought a broader audience with the "Old-Time Pieces" and "Hill Country Music" of Fiddlin' John Carson and Henry Whitter. From the Gid Tanner Artist File #NF1996, The Southern Folklife Collection, Wilson Library, The University of North Carolina at Chapel Hill.

fore, Fiddlin' John's record can fairly be considered commercial country music's start. Its success led to a talent search. Frank Walker of Columbia Records recalled, "I rode horses into the woods to find people who were individualistic in their singing and who could project the true country flavor."

Carson followed up with another successful platter featuring "You Will Never Miss Your Mother Until She's Gone" and "Papa's Billy Goat." That recording led the astute Brockman to hire a young woman to transcribe Carson's words and music; he wanted to copyright traditional songs and issue sheet music to enhance revenues. Irene Spain, who did the transcribing, explained in a 1965 letter to folklorist Judith McCulloch: "Poor John couldn't make a record unless he was a little more than half drunk, and he always had to have a 'jaw-breaker'—a candy ball about half as big as a golf ball—in his mouth, and he would roll that around while singing. His words were so muddled up at times that we had almost to guess what he was saying to get them on paper." Jawbreaker and all, country music was on its way, and within four years, a total of 104 million so-called hillbilly records would have been pressed, although many had nothing to do with hills or billies.

The new music's initial nationwide hit was "It Ain't Gonna Rain No More," recorded by a Chicago artist named Wendell Hall in 1923. By 1925 country had its first million-selling hit and its first major pop crossover success, "The Prisoner's Song" by Vernon Dalhart. He was a Texan with light-operatic training, who was recording in New York. Dalhart—his actual name was Marion Slaughter—became this music's first superstar on discs; in those more casual days, "he often recorded the same song for as many as 10 or 12 labels, usually under the 135-odd pseudonyms he used," reports writer Charles Wolfe, who goes on to point out that "in 1925 he dominated the best-seller chart as no singer—including Garth Brooks—has since." During his career, the many-named Texan would record and release an astonishing 5,000 numbers.

Along with Dalhart's pop appeal, two other major tracks of this music appeared in late July and early August of 1927. Peer was on one of his recording tours of the South when he stopped at Bristol, Tennessee, and ran newspaper ads to lure local acts. Entertainers of all kinds auditioned, including some who were or would be well known, such as Ernest and Hattie Stoneman and Henry Whitter, as well a number of important amateurs, including Blind Alfred Reed, and the Tenneva Ramblers. But what made the Bristol sessions special was the appearance of two acts. One encapsulated elements of the past and helped popularize the myth of this music's mountain roots; the other shaped the music's future with African influences.

On August 1, Sara, Maybelle, and A. P. Carter appeared at the furniture store where recording equipment was set up. "He's dressed in overalls and the women are country women from way back there," Peer reported. "They look like hillbillies. But as soon as I heard Sara's voice, that was it. I knew it was going to be wonderful." The Carter Family would become the most important exemplars of mountain traditions in this music's history. One of them was also an adroit entrepreneur; after taking credit for traditionals printed as sheet music, A. P. admitted, "Well, maybe I didn't write them, but I *wrote them down*."

Mountain music, always one interesting root of this genre, has never come close to dominating country, but the Carters gave it a great boost, and some commentators have since been pointing toward it as the music's essence, if not its genesis. By the end of the 1920s mountain-style string bands, such as the Crocketts or the Skillet Lickers (featuring Riley Puckett, Gid Tanner, Clayton McMichen, and Fate Norris) would reign commercially. But that soon changed due to the second major performer who appeared in Bristol.

Jimmie Rodgers, a skinny, white Mississippian who slouched in with his own string band, augured the future. He sang in a variety of styles, some of which altered country music forever; his "blue yodels," for instance, employed black techniques without disguising them. "He was an individualist," Peer recalled. "He had his own style . . . singing nigger blues . . . ," thus making explicit the cultural cross-pollination of music that had occurred principally in the lowland South. In no small measure as a result of Rodgers's influence, the next decade would see far more rhythmic and jazzy music—pointing toward the forthcoming rise of western swing.

Jimmie is also often credited with triggering an increased emphasis on vocalists rather than string bands, which would also characterize country's next decade. "The Singing Brakeman's" performances so impressed later male vocalists that nearly everyone in the 1930s seems to have emulated him to some degree. Jimmie Davis, Elton Britt, Ernest Tubb, and Gene Autry all copied Rodgers, breaking away from earlier hillbilly stylings. Later, suggests writer Bob Millard, "Cliff Carlisle's blues dobro on a Jimmie Rodgers' session put the Hawaiian steel guitar on the road to its ultimate honky-tonk sound." Jimmie's wardrobe also brought cowboy hats and western trappings—perhaps western yearnings—to prominence in this musical world. In the next decade many country artists would abandon their bib overalls and straw hats for boots and Stetsons.

More than a few country entertainers in the 1920s still employed vaudeville, minstrel, or medicine-show modes and guises, so they featured broad, bumpkin humor in their repertoires; they also chose names like the Kentucky Wonder Bean, the Skillet Lickers, the Cumberland Ridge Runners, the Coon Creek Girls, the Arkansas Woodchoppers, the Fruit Jar Drinkers, and the Hillbillies. The Hillbillies were the first group to appear in a movie; they are credited with—or blamed for—the not-always-positive use of the term "hillbilly music" to describe this emerging musical world. In Stockton during the late 1920s, Logan Laam's Happy Hayseeds—then recently transplanted from Oregon—partook of this tradition. Dr. Humphrey Bate and the Possum Hunters, who didn't appear on radio until 1925 but who had been together since 1903, was the first band on the "Grand Ole Opry." It featured two banjos, a guitar, a fiddle, a "doghouse bass," sometimes a cello, along with Dr. Bate on harmonica, thus illustrating how idiosyncratic country instrumentation could be even then.

The dobro played by Cliff Carlisle may actually have been one of the Golden State's major contributions to country music in the 1920s. A six-string, wood-bodied guitar with a vibrating metal resonator, it was developed in this state by the Dopyera (also spelled Dopera) brothers—John, Rudy, Emile, Bob, and Louis. The dobro successfully amplified sound without electricity; pioneer guitar-maker Victor Smith claimed it could deliver five times more tone than could a standard instrument. Although it was eventually displaced by electric steel guitars in most bands, it today remains a major feature in many bluegrass and "old-timey" groups.

As a result of the innovative Smith's work, the Dobro Company (journalist Stuart Kellogg explains that the name was "a play on 'Dopyera,' 'brothers,' and the Czech word for 'good'") introduced an even more important innovation in 1929, an electric Spanish-style guitar. Smith remembers, "I took some metal grindings and put them on a piece of paper. I then took a magnet and placed it directly under the metal grindings. These stood straight up and danced around." After thinking the matter through, he experimented with a system that passed vibrations from guitar strings through a magnetic flux to a magnifier, and, as he recalls, "sure enough, it came through the amplifier loud and clear." Imperfect as that first version was, it foreshadowed the future of country music.

Through all this, the West continued contributing fans, plus some of its own unique musical spirit, especially cowboy (and fake cowboy) songs, hobo tunes, and labor lyrics. All of these, like most of country's other roots, had national corollaries, real or imagined. Actual cowboy songs, like actual cowboy life, had long been a fascination in American popular culture, part of an interest in occupational folkways. In 1908 a working cattleman named Nathan Howard "Jack" Thorp had published a collection of numbers he claimed to have heard in the bunkhouse and on the trail, *Songs of the Cowboy.* Two years later folklorist John A. Lomax published *Cowboy Songs and Other Frontier Ballads.* A third collector, John I. White, was a prominent performer of both cowboy and hillbilly songs from the mid-1920s on—he wrote and performed the classic "Little Joe the Wrangler." However, despite the work of Thorp, Lomax, and White, not many actual cowboy songs made their way into country music.

The heroic cowboy image, on the other hand—much shaped in popular culture—had a great impact. Everything from Ned Buntline's dime novels to Buffalo Bill Cody's wild west shows had created a powerful figure in the nineteenth century. After World War I increasingly popular movies, such as those starring Tom Mix, presented western guises much closer to Buffalo Bill's flamboyant shows than to history. Those simple, gunsmoke-filled, often moralistic films apparently satisfied an existing interest, perhaps an existing need, so a large audience quickly developed for them.

Musicians quickly caught on, and as early as 1923 Otto Gray, an Oklahoma rancher, "pioneered the commercialization of cowboy music," reports music historian Bill C. Malone. That year Gray took over a group called the McGinty Cowboys and changed its name to the Oklahoma Cowboys. They attired themselves in western-style clothing and traveled in a customized automobile—a precursor of the elaborate buses used by so many entertainers to this day. This slick group set a new standard for popularity and promotion in its time, claiming in one press release to be "riding, roping, shooting, bronco-busting cowboys, and musicians as well." They were certainly musicians.

Western influence would soon be enhanced by a new kind of Hollywood cowboy. By 1927 audio equipment improved and outdoor action films became possible. Some filmmakers experimented with innovative uses of sound tracks and in the process created the singing cowboy, a figure that would dominate the next decade. That unlikely character emerged of course from films that successfully combined two already popular genres, the musical and the western. These in turn contributed to the accelerating legacy of western garb on country singers (and on their fans), but hindsight now also makes clear that horse operas affected far more.

For one thing, they eventually shaped the music itself and spread variations of it to every hamlet within reach of a "picture show"—which is to say most of the nation—considerably broadening country's fan base. They thus presaged the music's widespread acceptance during World War II. All the kids who sat through Saturday matinees became potential listeners to country music, in part because they responded to the western material—mostly contrived—that transcended and thus expanded the music's earlier image.

Of the silent-screen cowboys who managed the none-too-smooth transition to talkies, Ken Maynard is credited with having become the first singing cowboy in the 1929 film *In Old Arizona*. From its beginning, commercial country music had been popular in the rural West, in part because there was so much rural West to be popular in and also because the music projected resistance to the increasingly urban modern world. Moreover, many of the Golden State's new migrants after World War I were from the Midwest and Southwest, established country-music turf. As a result Maynard was able to tap an existing store of tunes when he became a crooning cowboy. Later, composed ("contrived," some say) cowboy songs would dominate movies.

The handsome Maynard's major appeal, though, came from the trick riding and roping skills he had developed as a performer for both the Kit Carson and the Pawnee Bill wild west shows. He was arguably the nation's leading western film hero before he ever sang on screen. Film historians George N. Fenin and William K. Everson describe his musical work this way: "Songs in Maynard's films were never introduced for their own sake, and they were integral parts of his films. . . . Maynard had a pleasant voice and frequently accompanied himself on the fiddle. Songs in his westerns were usually sung around the campfire . . . , introduced logically to provide moments of relaxation between melodramatic action." Ken could, in fact, sing and yodel; his voice was of the southern type, constricted and nasal; and he played a passable country fiddle, too, bracing it in the crook of his arm, not against his chin.

Although the cowboy image certainly dominated, many songs long popular in the West retained strong hobo and prolabor flavors, two other offshoots of what is called occupational folk music. The careers of Goebel Reeves and Haywire Mac McClintock were much closer to western real-

The first singing cowboy, Ken Maynard. From the Gid Tanner Artist File
#NF1996, The Southern Folklife Collection, Wilson Library, The University
of North Carolina at Chapel Hill.

ity than were horse operas, and both developed substantial California followings.

Reeves, a native of Sherman, Texas, was called, among other things, "the Texas Drifter" during his career, and he did indeed drift. The son of a music teacher and a state legislator, he had learned musicianship at home. He was also called "the Yodeling Wrangler," and he had picked up the rapid vocal moves in and out of falsetto called yodeling from a vaudeville professional named Al Wilson. (In general, vaudeville performers seem to have introduced that Swiss technique to rural westerners.)

Goebel was both familiar and comfortable with the cowboy mystique early in his life, and like many young men of his generation he also developed an interest in hoboes, the "bindle stiffs" who rode the rails. By the second half of the nineteenth century the railroad had provided mobility for many working people, offering the possibility of becoming "ramblers." Reeves determined to take advantage of that and to sing about it, too. There was, as it turned out, a considerable market for hobo songs in the 1920s, in part because of the commonality of the experience. There was then no dishonor in young, unmarried men riding the rails from one migrant job to another; it was often viewed as a rite of passage. In 1921 Reeves himself went "on the bum," becoming a troubadour. Early in his travels he even met an apprentice entertainer in New Orleans, none other than the future "Singing Brakeman," Jimmie Rodgers.

As was true of many other early singers, Reeves recorded using a variety of names (Johnny Fay, Bert Knowles, George Riley, etc.) and titles (the Yodeling Rustler, the Broadway Rustler, the Broadway Wrangler, etc.). He also had radio programs everywhere from California to Nova Scotia and appeared on both WLS's "National Barn Dance" and WSM's "Grand Ole Opry." His repertoire and style helped broaden the appeal of country music in California, and he eventually relocated to and remained in Bell Gardens near Los Angeles.

Haywire Mac McClintock was, like Reeves, not only a great favorite in the Golden State but also a member of the Industrial Workers of the World (IWW or Wobblies), for whom he traveled and entertained early in the century. His repertoire featured both cowboy and hobo tunes (he once published a book entitled "Mac's" Songs of the Road and Range), but he also brought to the stage a considerable body of labor songs from the celebrated Little Red Songbook of the IWW. It was not long before commercial country music would flee from such rebellious statements and develop its present, none-too-critical stance.

Mac, also like Reeves, lived the life of drifting troubadour for a time, literally singing for his supper. What became his most famous song, "Hallelujah, I'm a Bum," originated before the turn of the century; in it he produced not only a Wobbly anthem but also a blending of labor and hobo themes. He also wrote another hobo classic, "The Big Rock Candy Mountain," about homosexual predators in hobo camps (although many listeners seemed not to understand its subject). And he was of course a pioneer radio performer of such songs in California. Scholar Archie Green recalls, "An old timer once told me that when Mac played on the "Blue Monday Jamboree," the streets of Modesto were so deserted that a man could fire a shotgun down the street and never hit a soul." J. K. Johnson agrees: "Oh, Mac, he was just the best. We never missed him if we could help it."

During the 1920s country music in this state was discovering what it

California favorite Harry "Haywire Mac" McClintock. His hobo and labor songs
would eventually go out of vogue. From the Gid Tanner Artist File #NF1996,
The Southern Folklife Collection, Wilson Library, The University of North
Carolina at Chapel Hill.

could be; at that point, it couldn't be a quick route to riches. The genre that
had first been recorded in the South and that drew upon assorted music
long popular with white working people nationwide immediately took
on class overtones that still persist. Most performers on the West Coast, as
in the South, originally harkened back to styles and numbers developed
in the last century: minstrel shows, medicine shows, vaudeville tunes,
gospel music, and so on. A number of enduring controversies appeared
that early, too: Country-pop stylings already troubled conservatives; black
influences disturbed some white fans; and a few traditionalists complained about singing cowboy movies introducing western and fantasy
elements. "Countrier-than-thou" had already emerged as a stance.

This was particularly the music of hard-working people who felt ex-cluded from high culture and who took pride in their "plain folks" roots, folks who often yearned for old days and old ways. Throughout California in the 1920s, at barn dances and urban house parties, at church socials and picnics, fans heard and harmonized with old familiar tunes—the heart of this new commercial music—those melodies as comfortable as old jeans.

Gene Autry owned the next decade because he shaped the image of the singing cowboy, and that image in turn shaped what came to be called country-and-western music. Gene achieved a degree of commercial popularity previously unknown by any "hillbilly" entertainer because he moved well beyond that concept, and he spread his version of that music to countless listeners previously untouched by it. As writer J. R. Young points out, Autry "represented the first popular commercialization of country music on a grand and sweeping scale."

When Gene's signature was added to the Hollywood Walk of Fame, he became one of the very few honorees to receive five stars—one each for his work on stage, records, television, radio, and film. It was a fitting tribute, because he had become one of America's most versatile and important entertainers and a defining vocalist. Writers Charles Hirshberg and Robert Sullivan concluded in 1994 that Autry's approach led to country "smoothing its edges, becoming slicker and more cosmopolitan, a process that has continued to this day." He helped invent the modern country sound.

Orvon Gene Autry was born in Tioga, Texas, in 1907. He began his career as a child soprano singing in the choir of his Baptist preacher grandfather's church. When he was a teenager, his family relocated to Ravia, Oklahoma. One summer when he was still a schoolboy, he joined the Fields Brothers' Marvelous Medicine Show—singing, acting, promoting. He also sang at a nightclub "for whatever the collection plate yielded, generally about fifty cents a night."

Following high school graduation, Autry found work with the St. Louis & Frisco Railroad, where he became a relief telegrapher. (Years later, his friend John Wayne—the erstwhile "Singing Sandy" in a musical movie series—publicly kidded Gene: "You're lucky I couldn't play a gie-tar or you'd still be pounding that telegraph key back in Oklahoma!") In 1928 Autry used his railroad pass to travel to New York City, where he contacted Johnny and Frankie Marvin, Oklahoma boys who had become popular entertainers there. Although Gene didn't achieve stardom during that visit, he began the process that would lead to his eminence. He was encouraged by New York bandleader Nat Shilkret, who gave him a letter of recommendation. Remembers Autry, "I used it to wrangle a radio show over KVOO in Tulsa. I was billed as the Oklahoma Yodeling Cowboy, backed up by Jimmy Wilson's Catfish String Band. Meanwhile, I had gone back to my job as a relief operator working up and down the Frisco Line. The idea of paying for radio talent had not yet caught on in the Southwest."

The young singer recorded his first hit in 1931, "That Silver Haired Daddy of Mine," which he cowrote with Jimmie Long. Eventually Gene would write almost 300 other songs, including standouts such as "Be Honest with Me," "You're the Only Star in My Blue Heaven," "Tweedle-O-Twill," "Tears on My Pillow" (the latter two with Fred Rose), and the classic "Back in the Saddle Again" (with Ray Whitley).

As "Oklahoma's Singing Cowboy," he also joined the dominant "National Barn Dance" on WLS-Chicago in 1931, and that was a big boost indeed. Gene recalls, "No matter what they say today about Nashville, the *Barn Dance*, out of Chicago, was the granddaddy of country music," and Chicago was the national hub of the music then. Autry was also given a daily show, "Conqueror Record Time," on the same station, and he began recording for the Conqueror label during that period. Soon he released his famous version of "The Death of Jimmie Rodgers."

On the radio program he was supported by old friends Frankie Marvin and Smiley Burnette. Those and other associations—plus the style he developed on that show—seem, in retrospect, to have been essential in Gene's career. Years later the star recalled other key influences. "Between the three of them . . . [Johnny] Marvin, [Arthur] Satherly, and Ann Williams, they finally got it through my ornery skull that instead of doing poor imitations of all the popular singers of the day, I should stay in my own backyard and sing the songs I knew best." He never received better advice.

Conqueror Records was then controlled by the American Record Company, headed by Herbert Yates, who also presided over what would become known as Republic Studios. The exact series of events that led to Autry's movie career is in dispute. Producer Nat Levine explained that Autry (along with Frankie Marvin and Smiley Burnette) was hired to support Ken Maynard. Gene himself asserts that when Levine needed money to finance a movie, Yates told him, "Nat, I'll give you the money, but on one condition. We have a fellow who sells a helluva lot of records for us. . . . It would be worth your while to take a look at Gene Autry." The star added, "To get financing for his picture, Nat Levine would have looked at a singing kangaroo."

His early films were actually forerunners of the formula that would lead to his prominence. After appearing in the serial *Mysterious Mountain* (1934) starring Maynard, Gene sang in a Maynard feature entitled *In Old Santa Fe*. Green says the former telegrapher "stole the picture" from the star. In 1935 he was cast in *The Phantom Empire*, a twelve-chapter serial in which he played a character named "Gene Autry," a cowboy singer who broadcast from his Radio Ranch. As fate would have it, the ranch sat above a subterranean kingdom that featured ray guns and warriors wearing variations of Roman armor. "Autry," the character, survived a series of near-disasters in the story that combined science fiction, westerns, and dashes of crime thrillers and historical romances, with plenty of action. In retrospect, the serial seems more closely related to the Flash Gordon series that would soon follow than to the Hopalong Cassidy or Lash LaRue westerns. In varying degrees Gene's movie career continued to be marked by the use of fantasy.

This was no accident. "To offset expected criticisms that this new brand of musical western was a travesty of tradition," film historian William Everson reveals, "Republic set them in their own never-never land, placing them quite apart from other Westerns." Although not a conscious aim, these fantasies jibed with the escapist sentiment of that grim decade; audiences loved them.

Autry's first starring role in a feature was in *Tumbling Tumbleweeds*, a fast-moving story highlighted by the title song and "Ridin' Down the Canyon" (a duet with Burnette, who cowrote it with Autry), two numbers that would become western classics. It was an auspicious beginning, with Joseph Kane directing and Armand Schaefer producing. Says critic

Don Miller, "A better start for a new cowboy star, and a new western series, couldn't have been hoped for."

Once Gene began crooning on the screen, Schaefer discovered that songs, instead of interrupting the story and making audiences lose interest as he had feared, actually could be used to further the plot. They had the effect of moving what was inherently escapist—the shoot-'em-up western—even further into the realm of imagination: fully orchestrated ballads could be sung at lonesome campfires, with banks of violins and a chorus of voices backing the singer. "By 1936, the musical content of his pictures had been expanded until it almost overwhelmed the traditional western action," observes another film historian, Kalton C. Lahue.

Some of Gene's more than 100 movies would feature not only songs but versions on a major theme of that time: big-city styles and values pitted against rural ones (gangsters in snap-brim hats, driving convertibles, and occasionally carrying tommy guns, chasing or being chased by Gene and his posse); rural folks inevitably won these movie encounters. Bankers and lawyers, rather than highwaymen, were the villains in many of these films, which also broke with the usual girls-in-distress heroines, presenting instead independent young women who held their own with the star. Gene himself said of his films, "the endings were always happy and the plots often implausible."

When asked to name his favorite among his own Republic movies, Autry named *South of the Border* (1939). "Yes, I guess I liked the songs in that one," he added. The movie, which can stand as an example of Autry's unique vehicles, was set in the modern West, and included foreign agents, counterspies, and submarine bases, along with reluctant vaqueros who were convinced by one of Gene's songs to help with a cattle drive.

Autry's own skills as a thespian were at best rough; writer Alva Johnson recalls, "The fact that he couldn't act was at first considered a negligible flaw, later an asset. . . . Autry has the kind of awkwardness and embarrassment that audiences like." In fact Hollywood types never did figure out what made this star so popular, and often they spoke of him in condescending terms.

But he certainly could attract viewers, and he could sing. Bill C. Malone asserts that Autry "became the first great singing cowboy of the silver screen, thereby introducing country music to the largest audience it had ever enjoyed," and Wade Austin also credits Autry not only with popularizing the idea of country singers as cowboys but also with making the guitar a favorite avocational instrument; "remember the Sears Gene Autry model?" Adds music historian Robert Shelton, "The revolution that Autry had effected . . . virtually made the name 'Western' synonymous with the music of the Southern rural areas."

In his films and public appearances, Gene rarely attired himself as a working buckaroo; instead, he was clothed in costumes that the flamboyant Buffalo Bill or Tom Mix might have admired, and subsequent generations of country entertainers have imitated that. A publicity photo from the 1930s shows him in an unsullied white Stetson contrasted with his black-and-red shirt with white piping, polka-dot neckerchief, and creased slacks tucked into ornate boots. Wrote clothing historian Tyler Beard,

> By 1950, a large portion of Gene's Hollywood home was being used as closet space. Hundreds of multicolored, custom inlaid boots by Lucchesi, Rios, Olsen-Seltzer, and Charlie Garrison lined the walls. Stetson hat boxes in rows were stacked to the ceiling, and closets burst at the hinges full of hundreds of embroidered shirts and suits in an array of colors, styles, and designs that solidified Gene's position as top-dog clothes horse in the world of western wear.

His collection included outfits by the renowned tailors Rodeo Ben, Nathan Turk, Viola Grae, and a youngster named Nudie Cohen, among others.

In most ways Autry defined horse operas. His songs, like those in "high" operas, were not meant to project reality but to evoke the spirit's joyful flight or, conversely, its swoop into sorrow and everything in between. Only rarely were they intended to actually elicit folk expression, and audiences understood that. As another film historian, Jon Tuska, says, "However ludicrous the Autry Fantasy may appear to us today, its impact on Westerns in general and the thinking of those times was immeasurable." The historian especially extols the humane and revisionist portrayal of American Indians in Gene's later films.

Labeled "King of the Cowboys" by Republic Pictures, Autry did sing numbers in his films that ranged from old-time hillbilly lyrics to genuine folk songs, but new western songs closely related to Tin Pan Alley dominated. The contrived, commercial nature of most of those numbers and

Gene Autry with his Melody Ranch band, featuring (lower right) Merle Travis
and Johnny Bond. Photo by James L. Murphy. From the Gid Tanner Artist File
#NF1996, The Southern Folklife Collection, Wilson Library, The University of
North Carolina at Chapel Hill.

also of some action in his films led to much consternation from traditionalists. Shelton recalls a parody of dialogue in Autry's films: "Them
bandits have beaten mah mother, ravished mah girl, burned down mah
house, killed mah best friend and stolen all mah prize cattle. Ah'm agonna
get 'em if'n it's the last thing ah do—but first, folks, ah'mn agonna sing
ya a little song." Old-time cowboy star Buck Jones, who had appeared in
a few western dramas himself, complained that Autry's movies gave the
impression that "all you need to stop an Indian or a rustler is a loud voice
accompanied by a hillbilly band." But Gene's voice was far more than
loud, and his accompaniment a long way from hillbilly. He had that in-
dispensable characteristic of great country singers—*sincerity*. Autry remained apparently unaffected by his own success, and audiences believed him.

In the late 1940s he moved to Columbia Pictures, where he formed his
own production company and improved the quality of his movies. But by
then the popularity of horse operas was slipping. He still hosted a weekly
radio program and was traveling seven months a year to make public appearances in addition to acting in six films annually. Always an exciting

"live" performer, Autry appeared at fairs and rodeos, where he sang more country songs than Tin Pan Alley inventions, captivating audiences with his friendly, down-to-earth demeanor.

The popularity of horse operas continued eroding in the early 1950s, then they were gone. Gene remembered wistfully,

> There were no farewell toasts, no retirement dinner with someone handing out a pocket watch for twenty years of faithful service. Actually, nineteen years, between the release in November of 1934 of [In] Old Santa Fe, when I made my first appearance with Ken Maynard, for Mascot, until Columbia released my last [Last of the Pony Riders] in November of 1953. It just kind of slipped up on us. I don't recall ever saying that I had quit, or that I would never make another motion picture.

An astute businessman as well as a remarkable entertainer, Autry moved into television just as it began to gain major appeal. His Flying A Productions was not only responsible for Gene's own popular half-hour television program (launched in 1950), it also produced "The Range Rider" (starring Jock Mahoney), "Annie Oakley" (starring Gail Davis), "Buffalo Bill" (starring Dick Jones), "Champion" (starring the horse of the same name), "Death Valley Days" (featuring Ronald Reagan for a spell), and "Cavalcade of America." These shows had a great impact on early commercial television but by no means as great as Autry's previous effect on motion pictures and music.

In 1956 his "Melody Ranch" radio show went off the air, but it returned shortly thereafter as a television program on KTLA in Los Angeles, where it remained a favorite for seven years. Among program regulars were Johnny Bond, the Cass County Boys, Carl Cortner, and Billy Mize. Gene's connections in Hollywood as well as in the country-music world provided the show with a marvelous guest list.

Autry's recording career meanwhile not only produced country and-western hits but also such pop classics as "Rudolph the Red-Nosed Reindeer," "Here Comes Santa Claus," and "Peter Cottontail." Autry sold millions of records, as well as many millions of matinee tickets. Through it all, he remained direct and unassuming, precisely the kind of man who so appealed to "plain folks." Tuska summarizes, "Autry's massive appeal as a modest cowboy troubadour leading a uniquely charmed life, a musical magician who could turn darkness into light, sorrow into happiness, tarnish into splendor, a Pied Piper able to control men and alter the course of world events by means of a song, is the most tremendous single occurrence in the history of American Western cinema."

Gene's old pal Alex Gordon says, "He really wanted kids to grow up and emulate the heroic doings of his and other westerns, and follow the cowboy code. . . . [He is] the living example of the modern pioneer American spirit." The secret of Autry's enormous success was no secret at all: he believed in what he was doing, and as a result his audience believed in him.

In 1930 Glen Rice, the manager at radio station KPMC in Los Angeles, conducted an elaborate publicity campaign claiming that he had discovered a small village of primitive folks living in log cabins near Beverly Hills. Amazing as it seems, some listeners swallowed his story. Rice then announced that he had invited a few of the bumpkins to the station to entertain and—after an interval to build interest—the Beverly Hill Billies arrived.

Leo ("Zeke Craddock") Mannes, Cyprian ("Ezra Longnecker") Paulette, Aleth ("Lem H. Giles, H. D. [horse doctor]") Hansen, and Tom Murray were talented musicians, and their gentle parody quickly developed a huge following. By January of 1931, Rice claimed that 779,000 fans had seen the band perform. Variations on country music soon became so popular in Southern California that another station countered with the "Hollywood Hillbillies," while yet another built a show around the remarkable Stuart Hamblen. With several changes of personnel—including the addition of Elton Britt and perennial favorite Hamblen—the Hill Billies' popularity endured until late in the decade, fitting symbols for the innovative, if desperate, tone of the 1930s.

During this vital period country music shed its narrow southern identification and increasingly became an acknowledged emblem for all of rural America, especially in the Midwest and West. The music in California was, as Jonny Whiteside has written, "free from the traditional constraints which ruled the Bible Belt and quickly grew to explore artistic ground forbidden to its southeastern cousins." If the 1920s had established country music in California, the 1930s firmly established California in country music.

During the decade's first summer Jimmie Rodgers recorded several songs in Los Angeles, including "In the Jailhouse No. 2," "My Blue-Eyed Jane," "Pistol Packin' Papa," and "Blue Yodel No. 9." The yodel featured another star of historical stature, Louis Armstrong, on coronet; a rare black-white collaboration, it is one of the great early fusions in American popular music. The impress of Rodgers early in this decade was profound, for his adoption of black styles helped shape the music's future. This is not to say that African modes were its defining characteristic, but they became, thanks to Rodgers, major elements of its texture. In fact black and white music from the lowland South had long braided, each influencing the other. As *The Illustrated History of Country Music* explains, "Nothing in traditional American music is as white as it might seem, or as black."

Rodgers also brought the music explicit southwestern qualities. He was most popular in that region, especially Texas, where he made his home. His emergence marked a radical veering from the hillbilly image that had previously dominated this music, tilting it toward an area that was home to musical styles ranging from cowboys performing buckaroo ballads to the hot jazz of what came to be called the black territory bands. As a result the most significant musical addition from the southwestern style would be its African-influenced rhythm, with drums or a driving bass as an integral component, one that distinguished it clearly from the string-based, melody-dominated groups of the Southeast. Southwestern modes would eventually energize California's country style.

The nation had "busted" as it entered the 1930s and slid into a horrendous economic slump: the Great Depression. California by no means escaped the effects of the national economic collapse. In 1932, 200,000 more barrels of oil were produced daily in California than could be sold; agricultural revenues—$750 million in 1929—fell to $327 million in 1932; movies lost $83 million that year, and tourism dried up. A fifth of Los Angeles County's population was by then on relief, and San Francisco's unemployment rate reached 25 percent. California was the state to which many hopeful migrants fled, so it not only became a major setting for singers and bands but also received a considerable influx of potential country fans and performers thanks to the so-called Okie migration during those hard times.

As a result of the steep economic fall, the 1930s became a decade when the entertainment industry had to reconfigure itself. After selling

A later incarnation of the Beverly Hill Billies: Charlie, Clint, Jad, Mirandy, Lem, Ezra, and Gus. Courtesy of Kern County Museum. Used by permission.

104 million records in 1927, sales dropped to an appalling 6 million units in 1932. Radio of course surged again not only because it was relatively economical but also because technology had much improved its sound; the music it broadcast actually began to sound like music. Movies meanwhile offered escapist adventures at decreasing prices—old-timers remember door prizes, free popcorn, even cash "bonuses" to lure customers, and of course the Hollywood star system was by then in full swing.

Rural and urban dwellers alike scraped pennies together to watch, among other things, the low-budget wonders called horse operas. Although California had a lively (if little known) "western" history, nothing in its past prepared the public for the impact of singing western movies. There were many reasons for the popularity of horse operas, but foremost was the symbolic power of the cowboy image, which had come to embody many things Americans wanted to believe about themselves.

The imaginary cowboy had already drifted well away from reality in the late nineteenth century as Americans, increasingly citybound yet still intrigued by the frontier, sought a hero with whom to identify. Buffalo Bill Cody seemed to embody him, and his celebrated wild west shows did much to shape the national image of buckaroos as adventurers rather than as hired hands on horseback. In his shows Cody, using his own name, played a fictional version of himself, just as Gene Autry and Roy Rogers would later objectify themselves in cinema. Bill's many fancy costumes would, indirectly of course, later be reflected in the grandeur of getups favored by commercial country singers.

A less prominent yet parallel tradition also emerged in dime novels and western shows: the cowgirl. Mountain Kate, Bess the Trapper, and Hurricane Nell were all figures who equaled their male counterparts in nineteenth-century popular fiction; when Lucille Mulhall, Calamity Jane, and Annie Oakley began to embody equality in nonfiction books and wild west shows, a popular ideal developed. The famed sharpshooter Oakley, in particular, a star of Buffalo Bill's wild west show and involved in an enduring marriage-of-equals with fellow sharpshooter Frank Butler, became a cultural icon. Scholar Camille Paglia calls her "a great, liberating archetype from America's pioneer past."

The cowboy myth came to stand for all that popular culture in the nineteenth and early twentieth centuries piled on it—William S. Hart to Tom Mix to Ken Maynard to Gene Autry and beyond. Taking into account the simplistic yet apparently irresistible power of that figure, it seems unremarkable that rural folks identified with it.

Horse operas became big business indeed in the 1930s, and movie studios were falling all over one another trying to find singers and actors for their cowboy offerings. The confusion of southern and western in music continued, and music historian Robert Shelton has observed that "the late 1930s and early 1940s saw the transformation of Hollywood into a mecca for country musicians, comics, and all identified with country music." Woody Guthrie moved to Los Angeles late in the decade, and he found dime-store cowboys crowding the sidewalks. The music being played in Southern California then "didn't bear the vaguest resemblance to the real cowboy ballads that Woody knew, like 'Sam Bass' or 'Buffalo Skinners,'" points out biographer Joe Klein. "With all the yodeling and barbershop quartet harmony, it sounded more like Switzerland than Texas."

Some of the movies seemed that remote, too. Among other things, though, they did demonstrate that there was more than one way to sing well. Hollywood bigwigs seemed unable to comprehend why a Gene Autry, a Roy Rogers, or a Tex Ritter could be so popular, while full-voiced singers in cowboy clothes flopped. Studio bosses were generally in the cultural thrall of the European "fine arts," and their mistake was in not recognizing that Autry and the others were working in a distinct, parallel tradition that emphasized sincerity instead of volume or vibrato.

The actual style of songs in horse operas was neither "hillbilly" nor "classical" nor even traditionally "western." Scholar Thomas F. Johnson points out that "two changes occurred almost immediately: vocal style and stanza pattern were altered to fit the more generally popular Tin Pan Alley format." National audiences did not favor the nasal, constricted vocalizing that then characterized most southern styles, and of course what Johnson describes as "educated northern art singers" sounded phony and affected to the "plain folks Americans" who made up the bulk of these films' audiences.

The greatest singing cowboy Autry slid between extremes. He had begun as one of the seemingly endless string of Jimmie Rodgers imitators, with a high, nasal delivery, but in the movies he dropped his register, did away with nasality, and usually employed an unconstricted style. In fact he successfully sang in a variety of manners; the one he finally settled on would become the model for virtually every singing cowboy who followed and would also liberate many country singers from narrower southern styles. To be a country crooner, or so went an old saw, you needed three things: acute melancholia, nasal congestion, and a guitar. Gene Autry changed that, and if broadening styles had been his only accomplishment, he would still be a major figure.

The new kind of western song he sang brought both country and city tunesmiths to the movies in the 1930s. What developed was a soft-focused (maybe an unfocused) version of the West that had little to do with reality but that revealed another version of the pastoral longing of urban dwellers, perhaps, or of Depression-era escapism. As John I. White observed of the classic "Home on the Range,"

> Thanks largely to the sudden growth of radio broadcasting, in the early 1930s America discovered and took to its heart what it thought was a genuine folksong. As the haunting, comforting strains "Where seldom is heard a discouraging word / And the skies are not cloudy all day" miraculously came out of the air the country somehow felt that it had a good thing going, stock market crashes and depressions notwithstanding.

Many of the best new songs came from easterners. For example, "I'm an Old Cowhand"—a great parody song—was the creation of New Yorker Johnny Mercer, and "The Last Roundup" by Bostonian Billy Hill has of course become another standard. One of finest songwriters was Bob Nolan, who sang with the most influential group of the time, the Sons of the Pioneers. He wrote such memorable numbers as "Cool Water," "Tumbling Tumbleweeds," and "Why, Tell Me Why."

Hugh Cherry, a country music disc jockey and historian, says, "Bob Nolan is to western music what Zane Grey was to the western story." The poetic Nolan, a native of New Brunswick, Canada, did much to establish in music the romantic, often landscape-inspired image of the West and as a result to broaden country music. His approach to western material had been shaped, he said, by his move at age fourteen from Boston to Tucson. Nolan was, moreover, a student of poetry, especially Shelley, Keats, Byron, and Burns; and he admitted to copying their styles, seeking to adapt them to desert themes.

Romantic songs such as those written by Nolan, Hill, and Tim Spencer became standard fare in horse operas, and no one performed them more effectively than the band in which Nolan and Spencer performed. Critic Robert Hilburn points out that "few groups have ever dominated a particular musical field the way the Sons of the Pioneers . . . dominated western music." So prevalent were the Pioneers that Whiteside says their "canny synthesis of familiar themes and contemporary perspectives . . . represented the field's greatest artistic leap since Jimmie Rodgers."

Formed in 1933 by Nolan, Missourian Spencer, and Ohioan Len Slye as simply the Pioneers, the unit soon added Texans Hugh and Karl Farr and became the Sons of the Pioneers. Eventually Lloyd Perryman from Arkansas also joined them. The band was in the right place at the right time and was hired by radio station WFWB in Hollywood, where it captured an immediate audience. In 1935 the Pioneers became only the third West Coast unit signed by Decca Records. Moviemakers soon became aware of them, and they were cast in a 1935 Liberty Studio film, *The Old Homestead*; an appearance in Gene Autry's first feature film, the 1936 *Tumbling Tumbleweeds,* followed. They were then hired by Columbia Studios to provide music for a series of westerns starring Charles Starrett.

The Pioneers sang some of the era's greatest songs, including "Tumbling Tumbleweeds," "Cool Water," "I'm an Old Cowhand," and "Roving Cowboy," moving the content of country music distinctly toward the West. Eventually Slye would be renamed Dick Weston, then Roy Rogers at Republic Pictures, and Nolan would become what film historian Jon Tuska describes as "virtual second lead" in most Charles Starrett films. Slye/Weston/Rogers later convinced his former partners to join him at Republic, where they became fixtures in his movies.

Young Len Slye had originally headed West in an old Ford pickup in 1929, done ranch work in New Mexico, then arrived in Tulare in 1931 to toil as a migratory fruit picker. Six years later he began his ascent to movie stardom. In fact 1937 was a signal year for singing westerns because Autry, who was voted the number-one western star that year, broke with Republic Pictures, and Rogers was hired to replace him. Roy recalls that his "discovery" came when Sol Siegel, who knew him from the Sons of the Pioneers, literally tapped him on the shoulder one day and said, "Roy, we've been testin' for a new cowboy. We tested 17 different guys, and we're lookin' for a musical singing cowboy to start a new series. And you never entered my mind until you walked through that door." Rogers concludes, "They liked the screen test, and they signed me. . . . I was there 14 years."

Autry complicated matters by returning to Republic's fold, giving that studio two major singing cowboys. Gene's films were consistently granted larger budgets than Roy's. The latter's films enjoyed fewer frills but stronger story lines, and he became a solid actor. During his tenure with the studio, Rogers would be dubbed the second "King of the Cowboys."

Like Autry, Roy wore what can only be called dude cowboy clothing in most movies, engaged in fast-action fisticuffs with dark-hatted villains, rode a beautiful horse (a palomino named Trigger), and sang; but his films were otherwise distinct from Gene's. Observes Jon Tuska, "Ultimately, because there was no underlying fantasy about Roy's person, as there was about Gene Autry, he remained merely a wholesome, likable man who sang and performed and had great camaraderie with the Pioneers and who, invariably, embodied the impulse to make beautiful westerns."

Eventually Roy was outfitted in duds even fancier than Gene's. Rogers explained those fancy costumes, saying that after his boss Herbert Yates had seen *Oklahoma* on Broadway, "He . . . put out a memo that from then on my films were to be made in the mold of *Oklahoma*. He wanted musicals more than Westerns from me." No one knew the extent to which the very appearance of the country-music world would be changed by costumes like Roy's and Gene's. When this decade began country musicians and singers—the overwhelming majority of whom were male—tended to wear suits and ties or varieties of bumpkin hillbilly costumes. But the influence of cowboy movies, especially horse operas, changed that; clothiers became important components in this musical world.

Rodeo Ben of Philadelphia—who operated "The East's Most Western Store" and who later both designed Wrangler jeans and pioneered the use of snaps on western shirts—provided clothes for Tom Mix, William Boyd (Hopalong Cassidy), Autry, and Rogers. His catalogs made western wear available nationwide and exponentially increased America's dime-store cowboy population. He was by no means the only provider of fancy buckaroo gear, though. Viola Grae, for example, the most famous embroiderer of western clothing, began her Los Angeles career during this decade, when she provided garments for another singing cowboy, Rex Bell, among others. Literally scores of lesser-known clothiers and tailors found western wear a hot item as the 1930s progressed.

Most important was Nathan Turk—"N. Turk" read his label—who, according to Whiteside, "originated the extravagant rodeo stage wear which soon became synonymous with country music." Turk was a fine tailor in the 1920s before he turned to western wear, something he first did to provide apparel for riders in the annual Rose Bowl Parade. Before long his garments were worn not only by riders but also by movie stars, and singing cowboys attired in his gear could be seen on theater screens na-

"Sincerely Dick Weston" (aka, Len Slye; aka, Roy Rogers). Gerald Haslam Collection.

Hugh Farr, Bob Nolan, Tim Spencer, and Len Slye—the Sons of the Pioneers. From the Gid Tanner Artist File #NF1996, The Southern Folklife Collection, Wilson Library, The University of North Carolina at Chapel Hill.

tionwide. Celebrities like Ken Maynard, Mix, and Autry wore it. Singers and musicians followed, and eventually clothing historian Tyler Beard would write, "There is not one name in the country music world who did not own something by Turk."

The hot colors and innovative embroidery employed by Ben, Grae, and Turk initiated the process that turned hillbillies into cowboys, cowboys into fops, and established a standard of attire that has rarely been questioned since. As Beard summarizes, "Throughout the 1930s and '40s, western movies probably had more to do with creating the western wear market and establishing western as a style than any other influence."

When it came to scripts, just as when it came to costumes, Republic Pictures knew a good formula when it saw one. Many parallels developed between pictures by Autry and Rogers. Like Gene, with his comic sidekicks Smiley Burnette and Pat Buttram, Rogers had as his pal the shaggy, mumbling, and memorable George "Gabby" Hayes, who was eventually replaced by Pat Brady. Roy's later films not only featured the Pioneers but also occasionally Foy Willing and the Riders of the Purple Sage, favorites on the "Hollywood Barn Dance."

He also benefited from the considerable talents of Dale Evans, who would later be his wife. Roy found in Dale a strong costar, and Yates would allow the then-novel pairing to continue in most of Roy's films after 1944. Like Rogers, she acted well, usually playing variations of the nineteenth-century's idealized cowgirl. She also sang solos as well as duets with Roy, and as a songwriter she contributed the western classic "Happy Trails," which became her husband's theme song.

Although Rogers was a major movie star and a fan favorite, he did not have nearly as great an impact on country music as did Autry or the Pioneers, except perhaps to edge it a bit farther west. His most successful country-western record was "Blue Shadows on the Trail" (backed by his old group), and in the 1970s he reached the country chart with records of "Lovenworth" and "Hoppy, Gene, and Me."

The roll call of others who tried (or who were tried by studios) as singing cowboys included Tex Ritter (seventy-eight movies), Ray Whitley, Jimmy Wakely, T. Texas Tyler, Eddie Dean, Monte Hale, Rex Allen, as well as pop and classical singers like Ken Curtis, George Houston, Cliff Edwards, Gene Austin, James Newill, Bob Baker, Smith Ballew, Dick Foran, Fred Scott, Jack Randall, and even Jimmy Dodd (later to be the chief Mouseketeer on television's "Mickey Mouse Club").

Before coming to Hollywood, Ritter had been credited with stimulating a fad for cowboy music in New York early in the 1930s and with
bringing western material to pop charts. A college-educated native of
East Texas, he was an expert on cowboy music. Tex had performed four
western numbers in the 1931 Broadway production of *Green Grow the
Lilacs*. Over the next few years he would star on "The Lone Star Rangers,"
a radio program at WOR in New York; then he cohosted with Ray Whitley the WHN "Barn Dance." Eventually—probably inevitably—he landed
in Hollywood. In 1936 he made *Song of the Gringo*, the first of his many
movies.

Tex's vocal equipment was special, a resonant baritone with an occasionally hyperactive vibrato that had the power to move listeners. "His
rough-hewn voice suggested authority and authenticity unmatched
among singing cowboys," asserts music historian Douglas B. Green.
"Though he was not a great singer, he was an extraordinarily effective
one."

Ritter also brought believability to movie roles; he looked like a
buckaroo, not a slick leading man. He was often cast in low-budget
movies, some of which included stock footage dating back to World
War I. Many a matinee-attending kid came to realize that countless
wagon chases and stampedes were employed in one class B western after another. Even musical scores were sometimes recycled in those in-
expensive films. Nevertheless the talented Ritter triumphed, especially
as a singer. By the mid-1940s, his records became chart favorites, with
songs like "Jingle, Jangle, Jingle," "Jealous Heart," and "There's a New
Moon over My Shoulder." The first country singer to be signed by
Capitol Records, he was also the first person inducted into both the
Cowboy Hall of Fame and the Country and Western Music Hall of
Fame; the Academy of Country Music honored him with its Pioneer
Award in 1970.

Another gifted country musician who tried movies at about that time,
Ray Whitley, had been Ritter's cohost on the WHN "Barn Dance" and
had even been a regular entertainer at the prestigious Stork Club early in
the decade. Although successful in several short movies, Whitley did
not achieve Tex's prominence in feature films; he was never placed on
the track to stardom but became a kind of perennial sidekick. His career
extended from *Hopalong Cassidy Returns* (1936) to *Giant* (1956), but Ray is
most remembered as a musician, singer, and songwriter. Among the

best he wrote are such classics as "Back in the Saddle Again" (with Autry), "Ages and Ages Ago," and "I Hang My Head and Cry" (with Fred Rose).

The list of significant country artists in films, like so many other lists, might actually begin with Jimmie Rodgers. In 1930 he appeared in a ten-minute short entitled "The Singing Brakeman." Many others appeared in short subjects or made cameo appearances in features (Ernest Tubb, Jimmie Davis, Wesley Tuttle, Lulu Belle, and Scotty Wiseman among them); still others turned up in cheap motion pictures that were little more than abridged concerts (Cowboy Copas, Eddy Arnold, Tubb, etc.). Tuttle contributed a memorable, if uncredited, performance when he recorded most of the yodels for *Snow White and the Seven Dwarfs* (1936). Both Roy Acuff and Red Foley later appeared in forgettable horse operas, while Tex Williams eventually made a popular series of fifteen musical shorts called "Tales of the West."

Hindsight now makes clear that Hollywood horse operas affected country music far more than anyone at the time realized; the content and style moved West, became slicker, and broke down regional barriers. The attire of what had previously been called hillbilly performers was so altered that by the late 1930s a photograph of the cast of the "Wheeling Jamboree," broadcast from WWVA in West Virginia, reveals fifteen of twenty performers attired in western clothing. Even the music's name reflected those things. By decade's end it was becoming known as "country and western." At the same time entertainers from all over the nation were attracted to Hollywood, and as a result that town became a major center for this increasingly popular music.

Although movies dominate the image of the decade, radio and records were also of great importance. Country music's reach was becoming wider and wider as the home states of so many singing cowboys illustrated—the Pioneers, for example, were from Ohio, Missouri, Texas, Arkansas, and New Brunswick. Radio was the prime reason for that. Barn-dance programs proliferated in the 1930s, especially in the Midwest, from which WLS's "National Barn Dance" was broadcast nationally (WLS was owned by Sears Roebuck & Company, and its call letters stood for "World's Largest Store"). *The Illustrated History of Country Music* calls that program "the reigning barn dance of this era," and it was the reason that Chicago was considered country music's most important locale during the decade.

Such "unlikely" locations as Philadelphia, New York, Kansas City, and Hollywood also boasted popular barn-dance shows in the 1930s. Peter Potter's "Hollywood Barn Dance" was a strong entry, benefiting from the
abundance of "western" talent—such as those "Swiss" yodelers who so
bugged Woody Guthrie—then looking for movie roles in Southern
California.

Variety shows such as the "National Barn Dance" and the "Grand Ole
Opry" became radio staples by the end of the decade, not only in small
towns but all over the country after both were picked up by NBC. Some
consequences of these developments were unforeseen, as Edward Morris
explained in an essay in *Country: The Music and the Musicians*:

> Radio did far more than merely spread country music . . . ; it affected the
> very nature of the music. The new, sensitive carbon microphones of the
> mid-1930s changed singing styles, moving them away from the older,
> piercing singing of Vernon Dalhart to the quiet, modulated, intricate har-
> monies of the Blue Sky Boys. Subtlety and dynamics were now possible. . . .
> The personality of the singer became important.

Local performers as well as national figures took advantage of those
changes. Remembers San Fernando's Wesley Tuttle, "just about anybody
could go down to a radio station, and they'd put you on the air."

During that decade, too, an even more pervasive phenomenon evolved:
disc jockeys. At first, broadcasters employed records—most of which
were embellished with warnings against unauthorized play— as "fillers"
if at all; every early radio fan remembers, " . . . and now for a brief in-
terlude of prerecorded music for your listening pleasure." In fact what
were called transcriptions—performances of all kinds captured on six-
teen-inch acetate discs that were not sold to the public—were far more
common than commercial discs on radio. They offered entertainers and
stations alike great flexibility. Moreover, the long-standing rivalry between the radio and recording industries had led to considerable mutual
mistrust, each side suspecting that the other might gain a commercial
advantage.

The move from transcriptions to spinning commercial records by disc
jockeys eventually benefited both businesses. In the mid-1930s, WNEW-
New York's Martin Block is credited with having coined the term "disc

jockey"; he developed a program called "Make Believe Ballroom," in which he used records to emulate the station's live dance-band programs. As Hugh Cherry explains, "Others, all over the nation, played records on the air, but Block was the first to become an important personality in this pursuit."

Randy Blake on WJJD in Chicago is thought to be the first major country disc jockey. His station had a wide reach, and his program, following a pattern that would become common, was sponsored by products that told you how the music's audience was viewed: fertilizers, patent medicines, baby chicks—a kind of latter-day version of old-time medicine shows. So successful was this radio disc spinning that many credit it with improving sales to the point that new recording labels were able to go into business.

Another radio innovation of the 1930s had a great impact on this music in California and the Southwest. In 1931 the first of the so-called X-stations began broadcasting from Del Rio, Texas. By 1938 there were eleven frequencies on the boundary with Mexico, plus one in Windsor, Ontario. Many performers who were or would be significant in California worked on X-stations: Cowboy Sam Nichols, Doye O'Dell, Walt and Cal Shrum, among others. XERB in Rosarito Beach blanketed California with country music most days, Mexican tunes most nights. The unregulated wattage—XERB boasted a 150,000-watt clear-channel signal—sent transcriptions, records, and live performances of music across the western United States. In fact, preceding its general use, transcription technology can arguably be said to have come into its own on the border

Musicians and singers were by no means the only folks to take advantage of radio's great pool of patrons; among the most entertaining were fundamentalist preachers ("UnlessUH! youUh! believeUH! in the Lord-UH! youUh! willUh! beUH! castUh! into the pitUh!"), hustlers of unproved medical cures ("Dr. Brinkley's goat gland operation," for instance, or the Pickard Family's "Peruna Tonic"), and promoters of some of the weirdest products ever sold ("I'm offering you a glow-in-the-dark statue of Jesus to protect you in the night!" or "This perpetual-motion machine has been suppressed by the government, but it cannot be stopped!"). More than a few late-night listeners found themselves intrigued by the voices and claims from below the border, and more than a few who had not previously listened to country music came to enjoy it, although tunes at times seemed to be only brief interludes between end-less commercials.

During this period, too, brief radio shows, often only fifteen minutes and featuring perhaps one performer or one band, were popular on lo-cal stations in the Golden State. They were usually assigned to "farmers' hours" or "milking time," predawn, when it was assumed that only early-rising rural folks would be awake. As the decade progressed, though, recognition of the music's widening appeal led to more and more convenient hours of broadcasting. Saturday night eventually became the assigned time nationwide for much barn-dance programming. As a result of all these innovations, country radio thrived during the 1930s.

A sense of how lively the Golden State's country radio scene became in those years is revealed in the experiences of Rubye Blevins. Teenager Rubye had migrated to California from Arkansas in 1928. She won a tal-ent contest in 1930 and was soon performing on KMTR's "Breakfast Club" in Hollywood. During that period she also sang in a duo with her brother Ken on nearby KFVD. Eventually she earned a spot on Stuart Hamblen's new "Family Album" program on KMIC in Inglewood. There she was joined by Ruthy DeMondrum and Lorraine McIntire; they formed a trio and toured for a time with world champion cowboy Monte Montana. The trio began to call themselves the Montana Cowgirls. By the time she returned to Arkansas to visit her family in 1932, Rubye had changed her name to Patsy Montana. Two years later she recorded "I Want to Be a Cowboy's Sweetheart," the first million-selling record by a female country singer, her career having been energized by early radio in California.

Even more important was Hamblen himself, arguably the state's most popular country radio personality from the mid-1930s until television began its domination nearly two decades later. At KMTR in Hollywood in 1934 his morning "Covered Wagon Jubilee" dominated the market, and his "Lucky Stars" afternoon show on the same station was also number one. He also appeared on a live western music review on KNX radio.

Stuart's ability to land jobs so easily in Southern California also indi-cates how lively the western music scene was, which would contribute to the evolution of the music's name to country western. Before long Ham-blen moved to KMIC, then in 1932—the year "My Mary" made him a recording star—to KMTR, where clothier Sam Hoffman began a twenty-

The cast of Stuart Hamblen's "The Family Album," 1930–31. Front row (left to right): Vince Engel, Lorraine McIntire, Ruthy DeMondrum, Rubye Blevins (Patsy Montana); second row: Skipper Hawkins, Norman Hedges, Hubert Flatt (Ken Carson); back row: Sue Willie, Hamblen. From the Gid Tanner Artist File #NF1996, The Southern Folklife Collection, Wilson Library, The University of North Carolina at Chapel Hill.

one-year sponsorship of Stuart. In 1938 Hamblen again moved, taking Hoffman's sponsorship with him to an even larger station, KFWB in Hollywood.

All those things developed despite Hamblen's reputation as a wild man. The strapping Stuart later admitted that during those years, "I'd always been a rough man, but my big problem was not being able to leave the booze alone. . . . I just loved to fight too, and I suppose I got thrown in jail a few times. I remember old Sam Hoffman. . . . every time I'd get into trouble, Sam'd have to come and bail me out. He never could understand why I did those things. But I guess I was the only cowboy he knew."

Country music was everywhere, even at a service station. The crew from Stuart
Hamblen's 1934–35 programs included (front row, left to right) Wesley Tuttle and
Skeeter Hubbard; second row: Darol Rice, Jim Gummo, Frank Liddell, Vince Engel;
back row: Cliffie Stone (Cliff Snyder, Jr.), Joe Espetallier, Herman the Hermit
(Cliff Snyder), Hamblen. From the Gid Tanner Artist File #NF1996, The Southern
Folklife Collection, Wilson Library, The University of North Carolina at Chapel Hill.

By 1938 the erstwhile Texan's band included Cliff (Herman the Hermit) Snyder, a banjo-playing comedian. When Snyder's bassist son, Cliffie,
joined the group shortly after graduating from Burbank High School in
1935, Stuart dubbed the talented youngster "Cliffie Stonehead." The
young man eventually became known as Cliffie Stone, California's first
native-born country mover and shaker.

Hamblen recorded for many companies. In 1934 he and Jimmie Davis
were the first country singers signed by Decca, and he enjoyed a number
of top-10 records with his own songs, including the wonderful ballad
"(Remember Me) I'm the One Who Loves You." Throughout his association with Decca, Stuart's songs were also crossover favorites. Executives

at Decca understood early the possibility of country-pop (later called "countrypolitan") hits, releasing in 1934 a Bing Crosby version of Al Dexter's western smash, "Pistol-Packin' Mama." The label also raided other major labels for talent, signing Guy Lombardo's orchestra, the Mills Brothers, and Crosby, then acknowledged the Great Depression by lowering its price for records to 35 cents, less than half what rivals were charging. That forced all prices down, and suddenly general record sales once more soared.

During this decade California's most famous modern migration was under way, but the southwestern migrants called Okies could rarely afford records even at Decca's price. In the long term they would provide plenty of fans for country music, but until World War II heated up the Golden State's economy they were often desperate. One of the many myths surrounding country music in California is that, to quote Kern County historian Richard Bailey, "The Okies brought it." Wrong. The Okies entered a state with a well-established country-music community; however, an antimigrant campaign late in the decade did create an association between them and the music they most favored. As the migrants were demonized, so was "Okie music."

The displaced folks who were called Okies came not only from Oklahoma of course but from across the Great Plains, north and south: the Dakotas, Nebraska, Kansas, Louisiana, Missouri, Texas, Arkansas, and Oklahoma, especially the last four states. "I never even knew the word," remembers Texas-native Buck Owens. "There were signs up in stores and stuff, 'No Okies allowed in the store.' . . . Well, I knew I wasn't from Oklahoma, but I knew who they was talking about."

The migration intensified in the second half of the 1930s. During that period Madera County's population grew by 35 percent, Monterey County's by 36 percent, San Diego County's by 38 percent, Tulare County's by 38.4 percent, Kings County's by 38.5 percent, Yuba County's by 50.3 percent, and Kern County's—Bakersfield is the county seat—by a whopping 63.6 percent.

Not until 1938 did the general public became sharply aware of southwestern migrants. First, floods swept large portions of the Central Valley. Suddenly reports and photographs of the plight of desperate migrants dominated newspapers, reaching everyone. Also, the Agricultural Adjustment Administration cut the state's cotton acreage by over a third that year, intensifying poverty by lessening opportunities for work. Welfare rolls, both federal and local, swelled, and the enduring sweetheart relationship between corporate agribusiness and townsfolk began to fray.

Conservative forces, such as the California Citizens' Association and the Associated Farmers, many of whom had at first taken advantage of the glut of cheap labor, hatched plans to counter the "invasion"; in 1938 the CCA organized a major campaign against the migrants. Ostensibly a spontaneous organization of taxpayers, the CCA's actual backers included twenty-seven oil companies and six banking and investment firms, so it had considerable clout. Among its activities was the circulation of a petition demanding that no more relief be distributed to migrants and that the government "aid and encourage the return of the idle thousands" to their home states.

For people already battered by poverty, illness, and dislocation, the social discrimination they suffered was painful indeed. At first the Okies tended to find only menial work in California, often having to follow crops or accept bottom-of-the-barrel labor, if they found jobs at all. Farm Security Administration settlements, called "government camps" by residents, came to represent those hard times to outsiders. By the late 1930s, though, the camps had become the focus of the increasingly shrill anti-Okie campaign. Big agribusiness and related organizations especially disliked the FSA settlements for reasons that were principally economic: the camps limited growers' traditional ability to exploit migrant labor. For the migrants themselves, the FSA communities could be havens from the misery and humiliation of ditch-bank camps and "Hoovervilles" (as informal encampments were called).

Wherever migrants gathered—in towns, in camps, or in Hoovervilles —music offered cultural comfort, and it transcended literacy. The FSA camps, for example, hosted regular dances and other musical events such as talent shows. More common were casual, postdinner sessions, folks singing familiar songs, sharing common values. Woody Guthrie tells of watching people walk from all over a squatters' camp to hear two girls sing. "It cleared your head up," he reported, "that's what it done, caused you to fall back and let your draggy bones rest and your muscles go limber and relax."

Tough times remained for most migrants until World War II's prosperity relieved economic pressure. As historian Carey McWilliams pointed out, "Three wars in the Pacific within the span of a single generation accomplished wonders for most Californians, including [John Steinbeck's] Joads." The war in fact not only reinvigorated exhausted incomes and rearranged the nation's social order, but also and most importantly it restored faith in America's promise.

One product of the Great Depression, with its attendant political radicalism, was the performance of what came to be called "folk music," a socially conscious (or some would say self-conscious) version of old-time styles. Politicians such as Henry Wallace—whistling in the economic dark—had declared this the "Century of the Common Man." In the 1930s, writers, painters, and even "serious" composers responded. George Gershwin produced his remarkable "folk" opera, *Porgy and Bess* (1935), for example, and Aaron Copland wrote an exceptional series of "folk"-influenced ballets: *Billy the Kid* (1938), *Rodeo* (1942), and *Appalachian Spring* (1944).

In the 1930s the work of folklorists such as John and Alan Lomax, B. A. Botkin, and Charles Seeger produced, as writer Joe Klein so well phrases it, "an exhilarating, almost giddy discovery; America had a culture." Indeed it did, and everything from New Mexican Hispanic *modismos* to the prison songs of African-American Texans became worthy of study. Hillbilly music was another area of interest; like the rest, it was often squeezed into a leftist political frame. Seeger, for example, suggested that American musical tastes had been manipulated to ensure class differences: "Fine art" music was an affectation of the ruling classes; pop music was a watered-down version of that fine art material, mere "crumbs from the table of the rich and powerful," the product of capitalism. A number of scholars sought to recover "classless" music.

A musicologist, Seeger was a major theorist in the rise of "progressive" folk music. One of his contributions was a scale—"Folk-Hillbilly-City-billy-Concert"—to classify the level of sophistication. He pointed out that once singers like Molly Jackson or Leadbelly became professional, they tended to move from Folk to Concert (where the big money was) in a hurry. This "new" music, which emerged from some of the same roots as country, was inextricably linked to the politics of the time. Because it was supposedly of common people, the music was considered inherently proletarian (thus "progressive"). Beliefs as questionable as the innate progressiveness of folk buoyed sanguine fans in cities.

➤   ◄ ➤   ◄ ➤

Country or Not?

Rarely can the moment be pinpointed when a person becomes an icon, but Woody Guthrie was an exception. On March 17, 1956, in New York City's Pythian Hall, a concert to benefit the ailing Guthrie's children drew a who's who of "progressives," and, as biographer Joe Klein has accurately asserted, that marked the beginning of Woody's "canonization."

Woodrow Wilson Guthrie's roots were hardscrabble. In his inimitable style, he once described his hometown, Okemah, Oklahoma, as the "singingest, dancingest, walkingest, talkingest, laughingest, yellingest, preachingest, cryingest, drinkingest, gamblingest, fist-fightingest, shootingest, bleedingest, gun-, club-, razor-carryingest of the oil boom towns."

As a result of a series of family tragedies, including his mother's hospitalization with Huntington's disease, an incurable, hereditary disorder, Woody and older brother Roy were cut loose in 1927. Eventually, a seventeen-year-old Woody ended up in Pampa, Texas, in 1929. There he came under the thrall of his uncle, Jeff Davis Guthrie, a jack-of-all-trades, who "was . . . the finest country fiddler in the panhandle. . . . he'd won several contests to prove it." Jeff gave his nephew a guitar and also helped Woody learn the mandolin and fiddle. With two friends, young Guthrie eventually formed the Corncob Trio, and he also began writing songs.

Sources don't agree about when Woody made his first trip into California. Although married, he hoboed and sang on the road for a while in 1936. On one visit he "toured" the Central Valley, spent several weeks in Turlock with an aunt, and had to trade his sweater for a plate of beans in Tracy, then was run out of town. More importantly, during those years he was deeply moved by the plight of migrant Okies with whom he identified: his people. He had in fact endured a sample of the disdain they were suffering when he visited the Golden State.

Woody, who had an unusual gift with language, was in the process of becoming a supreme lyricist, though he wrote in a down-home style, frequently setting his words to the tunes of earlier favorites. He also began employing an old African-American style of song called "talking blues"—rural patter songs—that had been popularized on the "Grand Ole Opry" by Robert Lunn (the "Talking Blues Man").

Guthrie arrived in Los Angeles in 1937, and his career as a professional entertainer began in earnest, thanks to his cousin Jack who talked their way onto a radio program on KFVD there. Rodeo rider Jack dominated; his western songs fit well with California's country music at that time. Woody, also in the mode of that period, played the comic sidekick.

Later the duo added the talented Maxine "Lefty Lou" Crissman to their show. Then Jack quit, leaving the program in Woody's hands. Cowboy songs gave way to a considerable addition of mountain ballads, gospel songs, and hillbilly numbers. During this time he wrote one of the most memorable of California songs, "Do-Re-Mi," in response to the unconstitutional "Bum Blockade" that the Los Angeles police had mounted to limit entry into the state.

In 1939 Cisco Houston and Will Geer persuaded Guthrie to try New York City. Leaving his family behind, Woody moved in with Will and Herta Geer there. The East Coast hosted a lively folk-music scene then, and Guthrie joined Pete Seeger and others on the circuit. He was soon "discovered" by Alan Lomax and invited to Washington, D.C., where his famous Dust Bowl ballads were recorded by Lomax for the Library of Congress in 1940. Later released by the musicologist, they have been called by some the first "concept" album. They have also become a major basis for Woody's subsequent fame.

Another myth about country music in California is that Guthrie was a leading figure: not true. He certainly wrote some wonderful songs, but he remains far more celebrated among "progressives" than among country-music fans. This is not intended to denigrate Woody but simply to place his achievements in perspective; he had little impact on country, but he became a force in the commercial folk movement. He did not bring proletarian music to country audiences; instead he brought a down-home style to proletarian audiences. His reputation grew in the city and on the campus, not on the farm or in the honky-tonk.

◄ ►   ◄ ►   ◄

Throughout this period, a hybrid music was brewing in the Southwest. Its direct lineage has been traced to the late 1920s and early 1930s when a number of white bands in Texas, Oklahoma, and Louisiana were influenced by African-American contributions such as Dixieland and other jazz, as well as emerging styles of big-band dance music. Those southwestern whites were in fact swept up by some of the same forces that would produce a Benny Goodman, an Artie Shaw, or a Tommy Dorsey. Guitarist Merle Travis explained the new form this way: "'Western Swing' is nothing more than a group of talented country boys, unschooled in music, but playing the music they feel, beating a solid two-four rhythm to the harmonies that buzz around their brains. When it escapes in all its musical glory, my friend, you have 'Western Swing.'"

Bands sprang up all over the region during the developmental stages of this phenomenon, and an uncoordinated but parallel progression occurred. Literally scores of musical groups were formed from San Antonio to Oklahoma City to Shreveport. "The repertoires varied from city to city, but basically, it was the same sound," points out music writer Cary Ginell.

The Light Crust Doughboys, an organization that in the early 1930s included Bob Wills, Milton Brown, Herman Arnspiger, Durwood Brown, and Sleepy Johnson, is usually considered the seminal band in this style. By the middle of that decade, however, many Doughboys had departed to form their own groups. One of those, Milton Brown and his Musical Brownies, was for a time regarded as the region's best. It featured virtuoso jazz fiddler Cecil Brower and the trombonelike licks of Dunn on electric steel guitar, and it seemed more a jazz ensemble with country roots rather than vice versa. The leader's death in 1936 ended its reign. But by then what was being called country jazz was an established musical form, and California welcomed it.

This music once more made explicit African influences on country music, for it was a far stretch from beat-deficient traditional Anglo-Celtic music. Explains fiddler Johnny Gimble, "J. R. Satwell [who played fiddle for Adolph Hofner] said, 'A man ain't no better than his rhythm section.' . . . So we'd just bring a good rhythm section and ride the crest of the wave." White players from the Southwest took melodic and rhythmic insights from their black neighbors and toted those modes across the tracks to receptive audiences, especially in the Golden State.

Many of those jazzy country kids experimented with instruments unusual or new to country music: clarinet, drums, bass, piano, accordion, and saxophone, among others. Bob Wills successfully added drums to his band, and soon, over the protests of traditionalists, they were widely used and a hot "boogie beat" crept into the music. Electrical amplification became important, too. As early as 1929 the Stromberg-Voisinet Company had advertised an amplified guitar, and Adolph Rickenbacher's "Frying Pan" was being played in some swing and jazz combos.

Les Paul, known as "Rhubarb Red" in his country-music days, figured prominently in the refining of the electric guitar. An inveterate tinkerer, he was unhappy in the 1930s because his instrument couldn't be heard over the din in noisy nightclubs. As a result he perfected the use of the electromagnetic pickup originally developed by Victor Smith for the Dobro Company to amplify a steel-strung acoustic guitar. About then the Gibson Company introduced an electric Spanish-style guitar, the ES-150, that soon became identified with jazz greats such as Oklahoma's Charlie Christian. With a low-tech arrangement that worked, Bob Dunn electrified his Martin O-series acoustic guitar in 1934 (some historians say it was 1935) while playing with Milton Brown's Brownies: "A Volu-Tone pickup was mounted over the soundhole, and a wire ran from the pickup to a small, nondescript amplifier," explains writer Rich Kienzle.

Even more important was *how* the new instruments were used: Dunn not only amplified his guitar, but "the Martin's strings had been raised to permit Hawaiian-style playing," what has come to be regarded as country's defining "twang." That was only the beginning; soon the style of the music itself changed, with "take-offs"—jazzy individual improvisations —becoming standard fare. Dunn and later artists such as Leon McAuliffe, Clell Summey, Jimmy Wyble, Cameron Hill, Benny Garcia, and Johnny Weiss produced hornlike riffs with their steel guitars.

Amplification became central to yet another major development of this decade: honky-tonk music.

In California during the late 1930s and '40s many low-rent beer joints or saloons in areas where blue-collar men worked or gathered were southwestern enclaves. Like the tents and storefront churches that also arose, they were centers where migrants such as a new band called the Maddox Brothers and Rose could feel comfortable. If white gospel songs migrated via churches, beer joints brought their own modes of musical expression.

Historically, honky-tonks (defined by Webster's as "a cheap nightclub or dance hall, a dive"; the name is likely African in origin) were associated with the East Texas oil fields, and before long oil field towns in California hosted beer joints that could have been plucked directly from the Lone Star State, and so did agricultural communities, as well as the outskirts of most cities. The music, as Michael Bane points out, "took a little bit of this and a little bit of that, a little bit of black and a little bit of white, juggled it all together and came up with music just loud enough to keep you from thinking too much and to go right on ordering the whiskey."

The young Maddoxes honky-tonkin'. Courtesy of Jonny Whiteside.

Its white pioneers—Ernest Tubb, Al Dexter, and Floyd Tillman, in particular—employed a strong, danceable beat. California honky-tonks frequently offered four-piece bands on weekends (electric guitars increasingly slicing through crowd noise), and jukeboxes during the week. These lively "dives" continued to grow in importance during the next decade, but in the late 1930s they provided apprenticeships for many future country-music stars.

The development of jukeboxes is acknowledged to be a "major reason for the revitalization of the once nearly moribund record industry," according to *The Illustrated History of Country Music*. They certainly allowed those enclaves of blue-collar and southwestern culture to open all over rural California late in the decade. Many of them were "juke joints," with no band at all, but featuring western swing and honky-tonk records to accompany beer and dancing and fighting.

During the 1930s country music moved well away from the nineteenth-century styles and songs that had at first dominated it. One reason was that old material was exhausted by the growing demand for more music, so new tunes and new styles were produced. The barn-dance radio shows that proliferated and spread this sound nationwide were increasingly built around charismatic individual singers rather than string bands and medicine-show shenanigans. Those programs were especially popular in the Midwest and the East where more people owned radios.

In this decade the music of the West—"Coast country"—with its openness to new forms and innovations, began to differ sharply from the music of the South, and California became the national center for country music by the late 1930s. While some traditional groups such as Roy Acuff's Smoky Mountain Boys or the Carter Family certainly did thrive, another vision of the future was signaled by western swing, singing cowboys, the birth of a boogie beat, and the raw beginnings of honky-tonk. What was locally called "western music" was attracting an increasingly heterogeneous audience in this state. Add to those changes the various technical innovations of the period, and this economically and socially difficult junction in the nation's history looms as one of country music's most creative. California was in the middle of it then and would stay there for a long time.

Bob Wills—of English, Irish, and Cherokee extraction—was a Texas native, and one reason he liked the Golden State after he had seen a bit of it was the similarity of some locales there to the region where he had been raised. The Great Central Valley, in particular, he recognized as a comfortable enclave. That territory was full of folks happy to pay to hear and dance to good music, so the Texas Playboys filled dance halls from Pumpkin Center in the South to Del Paso Heights in the North. Retired oil worker Lee "Brownie" Brown recalls, "He could sure pack 'em in. Wasn't nobody else like ol' Bob."

There sure wasn't. As much as any entertainer, he represented the independence of the West from the South in matters musical. After Wills had retired, many speculated on whether his band the Texas Playboys had been country musicians at all. If country means only southern songs or, narrower still, acoustical mountain music, the answer is certainly no. But if this is music produced by rural folks and appreciated by rural folks (among others, that is), then Bob Wills was, to quote William Ivey, former executive director of the Country Music Foundation, "one of the few great innovators in country music."

In 1968 Bob was voted into the Country Music Hall of Fame. As his biographer Charles Townsend remarks, he was honored in "a musical field of which he never felt he was part." Why did he feel that way? First, southern illusions and limitations still ruled the music when Bob came of age, and Wills was to the fiddle and the cotton patch born—pure country as a person. But his band moved beyond accepted categories and sounded much more like the jazzy dance ensembles of his time than like previous country groups. As the Playboys' steel guitarist Leon McAuliffe revealed, "I can't think of a country artist we ever listened to and learned their tunes. We listened to Benny Goodman, Glenn Miller, Louis Armstrong, and [Bob] Crosby." Dixieland was a major influence; yet Wills never abandoned his Stetson or his country fiddle, and his music always included a dynamic merging of styles.

Like so many major country artists, he was the product of a musical family. His father John Wills was a first-rate frontier fiddler from a family of frontier fiddlers. Young Bob (called Jim Rob then)—as well as his talented brothers, Johnnie Lee, Billy Jack, and Luke—learned music informally in the southwestern tradition, sharpening skills at hoedowns and dances. As a musician he can be said to have served an apprenticeship rather than having received training. He certainly experienced hard knocks, too, and they served him well. He became tough in a tough business.

He became a consummate showman, moving about the bandstand, chanting and pattering in his peculiar way, sawing his $5,000 fiddle, so he and the Texas Playboys eventually left a distinct mark on the Golden State's music scene. Like a dancer, Wills provided a visual style as well as hot music. His band was loaded with excellent soloists, some of whom became stars in their own right: McAuliffe (whose "Steel Guitar Rag" was a classic), singer Tommy Duncan, drummer Smokey Dacus, pianist Al Strickland, plus a string of fine fiddlers, such as Tiny Moore, Johnny Gimble, Jesse Ashlock, Joe Holley, and Louis Tierney. Bob himself never lost his common touch, though, and country folks understood that he was *them* and he had made it.

Although Bob was a down-home country fiddler who called his first group the Wills Fiddle Band, his Playboys nevertheless employed many instruments that broke with country-music traditions: drums, piano, and a horn section that shocked conservatives. He had picked cotton with many blacks as a kid in Texas before World War I, and he recalled that they "generally always had trumpets and guitars, and I will never forget how well they played them." Writes his biographer Townsend, "Years after this experience, he combined the frontier fiddles his family played with the instruments Negroes played in those cotton shanties" to produce the Wills's sound. Bob also developed perspective on race relations in the border South, echoing a vintage minstrel line, "dark skin raise the cotton,

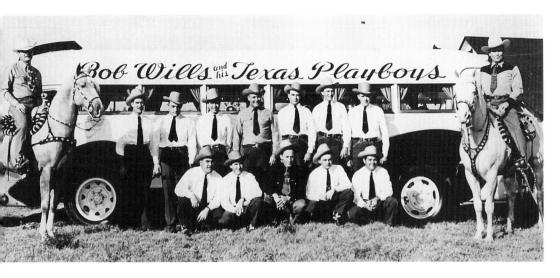

Bob Wills (mounted right) and his Texas Playboys during his California years.
Courtesy of Kern County Museum. Used by permission.

white man gets the money," in his and Duncan's classic "Take Me Back to Tulsa" (1941).

Many a fan of big-band jazz was won over to the Playboys' innovative offerings, because, as Dacus put it, "Bob's music included a great deal of improvising. . . . Bob Wills would not allow music to be put into a strait-jacket." The Texas Playboys characterized a period during which dance jazz dominated. Because his music ruptured old limits and stretched ideas about what country music could be, it also appealed to a much wider audience, not just to California's migrant southwesterners and southerners. It did, however, give enormous pride to those transplants who had so recently been disdained: "We needed a hero," says Merle Haggard, "and Bob was certainly that and more."

Wills and the band also appeared in movies, starting with a 1940 Tex Ritter vehicle entitled *Take Me Back to Oklahoma*. Biographer Townsend reports that "the movie was a typical Saturday western or shoot-'em-up. Wills had some lines in it, and it was obvious before he spoke half a dozen of them that he would never win any Academy Awards." Characteristic of the make-believe world of those movies, a great chunk of it was given over to what amounted to a Texas Playboys' (or a five-instrument version of them, anyway) recital: four lively songs concluding with "Take Me Back to Tulsa." Although the action was set in a time and place without electricity, Leon McAuliffe was still able to "take it away" on his electric steel guitar. The Playboys eventually appeared in thirteen other features, plus two short subjects designed to highlight their music. The movies exposed Bob and his music to an even larger, more diverse audience than he had ever enjoyed before.

In 1943 Wills had to dissolve what many consider to be his greatest band, so that many of its members—including the leader—could enlist in the military. "I was not a very good soldier," Wills later acknowledged. "They didn't like me, and I didn't like the army." Many stories of Bob's military experiences circulated. For instance, former Texas Playboy Eldon Shamblin, who was an officer during World War II, told Merle Haggard about a visit to his old pal at the induction center.

> As Eldon walked around the corner of a building, who did he meet but this awful-looking person coming down the steps. The old Western Swing King was recovering—and none too well—from a terrible hangover. The clothes he had been issued were too damn big, and there was a bunch of tags hanging all over him. Eldon said he "looked like a man between pukes." Finally Eldon said, "Well, Bob, I don't know what to say to you." Bob just flipped back and said, "Well, Eldon, just don't say a fuckin' thing." And he walked away.

Once out of the army, barrel-chested Bob had one of the longest tenures on top of any country-western performer in California. He was discharged in 1943 and decided to make the state his base of operations. What makes this especially important is that, according to Townsend, "the years from 1943 to the early fifties were Bob's best." During September of 1943, the band began radio broadcasts on KMTR-Los Angeles each weekday, then played at the Mission Beach Ballroom in San Diego on weekends. He and his wife settled in the then-bucolic San Fernando Valley, where they could enjoy their horses and live privately.

As early as 1940 Bob and the Playboys had been in such demand that he began to encourage his talented brothers to form spin-off bands. The first group was built around Johnnie Lee, who went on to record such hits as "Milk Cow Blues," "Rag Mop," and "Peter Cottontail." Luke Wills and the Texas Playboys No. 2 (later, Luke Wills and his Rhythm Busters) followed in 1947. Based in Fresno, it featured Shamblin and Junior Barnard and was recorded by RCA. Youngest brother Billy Jack, who had succeeded Tommy Duncan as Bob's lead vocalist and who had also written the lyrics to the classic "Faded Love," formed a Sacramento-based group in 1949. Spotlighting fiddler-mandolinist Tiny Moore (with whom Wills had written "Lily Dale"), Billy Jack and his Western Swing Band were major Northern California favorites, often playing rhythm-and-blues–influenced numbers that anticipated rockabilly. The band was recorded by both Four Star and MGM.

In June of 1945 Bob and his wife Betty purchased and moved to the Triple B Ranch outside Fresno. The Fresno Barn became his base of operations, and he settled into the growing but still rural town. Wills brought in forty mares and seven stallions, then purchased a nearby dairy and installed his in-laws as its managers. The band leader and his favorite horse Punkin were soon prominent figures at rodeos and parades all over the state.

The Wills's ranch became popular for band members, too, and many of them helped build fences and stalls. Betty, Bob's wife, remembered that her husband "wanted to retire on that place. That's when he hated to go on the road. When we had that place, he wanted to stay so bad. We had a lot of good times out there." One of the most memorable was when Bob had to deliver their second child because they could not get to a hospital in time. Townsend observes that Wills "was probably happier while he lived on his Triple B Ranch at Fresno than at any other time after he left Tulsa."

During that period, too, the band's radio presence widened due to "transcriptions" recorded in Oakland for Tiffany Music and sold to radio stations all over the country, taking the Texas Playboys' unique sound to more and more listeners. The late 1940s (and early 1950s) were also a period when the Wills band regularly recorded in Hollywood, and his records reached a wider audience due to the proliferation of country disc jockeys.

As Wills's stardom continued growing, he became "Mr. Southwest." Merle Travis recalls, "You'd be surprised how many people say, 'Hey, I went to school with old Bob Wills.' It was always 'Old Bob Wills.'" When Travis asked Wills what he did when folks claimed to have gone to school with him, Bob replied, "I get down close to them and say, 'Don't say that too loud. I never went to school.'"

In 1947 Wills purchased the Aragon Ballroom just outside Sacramento and changed its name to Wills Point. He moved his family there; it was a compound that included apartments (where some band members and their families lived), a large swimming pool (called "Del Paso Plunge" by locals), and a small amusement park. His radio broadcasts over 50,000-watt KFBK-Sacramento were heard all over the West. By then the band had gone through many changes of both personnel and instrumentation, and the only member of the original Texas Playboys still with him was vocalist Tommy Duncan. In 1948 Tommy left to form his own band, the Western All Stars.

The Wills family continued to reside at their Sacramento compound off and on throughout much of the early 1950s, alternating principally with a house in Amarillo, Texas. Public taste changed during that period, with more and more folks watching television—Bob had his own television show in Los Angeles during 1955—while fewer and fewer attended dances. On June 15, 1956, the Wills Point Ballroom burned down; Bob sold the remaining property and never lived in California again.

As a boy young James Robert Wills had traveled with his dirt-poor family across Texas in covered wagons, picking cotton along the way to pay for the two-month journey. Eventually he recorded best-selling records, made successful movies, and his band's appearances broke attendance records in ballrooms and dance halls all over the West, helping make California the national center of country music in the 1940s. And of course he ended up in the Hall of Fame himself.

It was quite a journey.

PENNGROVE, 1994

Main Street, the parade route, fishhooks a total of two blocks from Old Redwood Highway to Adobe Road. Four other short streets comprise the remainder of tiny Penngrove, population 893. A railroad track slashes diagonally across the parade route, and the old wooden buildings on both sides are wedges: two feet wide on one end, fifty on the other; folks don't waste space here.

Fifty miles north of San Francisco, this farm town has no sidewalks, but some yards do have horses, goats, geese, and cows. Everyone picks their mail up at the post office on Main Street—no home delivery. Today that roadway is jammed with residents and tourists alike as one of Northern California's popular small-town Independence Day celebrations begins, fire truck sirens wailing.

We've positioned ourselves slightly above the street on a sloping vacant lot next to the judges' stand—a flatbed trailer parked across from one of the wedge-shaped buildings, the one housing Kelly's Bar. On that long trailer sit the judges: five men and two women wearing American-flag shirts. Across the street, an upstairs window above Kelly's Bar is open, and a large, white dog rests, chin on extended legs—eyes, paws, and nose clustered like coal chunks.

As the fire trucks pass, but before the grand marshal appears in a shiny pickup, a thoroughly lubricated spectator puffing a twelve-inch cigar lumbers by us. He is wearing what appears to be a large lampshade on his head, and he has a can of beer jammed into each back pocket.

"That guy's set if there's a drought," grins Bernie.

As usual the parade features the color guard from nearby Two Rock Coast Guard Station, horses, old cars, shiny trucks, and kids scrambling for tossed candy. Other children in costumes are frolicking on a flatbed pulled by a bright green 1946 John Deere tractor. A 1912 seed-spreader, restored and painted bright red, draws cheers; then a comic drill team in pseudo-Italian-army uniforms stumbles its politically incorrect way past the judges, loud

83

laughter in its wake. (Later, the Italian army marches en masse into Kelly's for further maneuvers.)

The crowd livens—a few street dancers begin to boogie—when the Saddlerack Band, perched on another flatbed (much hay is grown and transported locally), plays a hot version of "Take Me Back to Tulsa" as it passes. "They're really good," says Pam, and the assembled throng seems to agree. A surge of applause follows the band up the street.

After Clo, the Clover-Stornetta Dairy's cow mascot, another drill team—business-suited stockbrokers and accountants, their briefcases at order arms— two bikinied young women on the running board of an old Chevrolet, and 4-H kids with pygmy goats, louder applause once more rolls up the street. On yet one more flatbed Cisco and the Kids are playing "Six Days on the Road."

"They're good, too," says Alex.

Kat, grinning, asks, "Is country music a cottage industry around here, or what?"

"Yeah," I reply, "and the cottage is called the Twin Oaks Saloon."

Literally following the parade, watching where we place our feet on the unswept route so recently traveled by many horses, we wander to the nearby park. There a long line wends its way toward deep-pit barbecued beef or grilled chicken, potato salad, and beans, and a small white bandstand fills with Sal Sage and his Sage Gang. Greetings are exchanged, especially with the good old boys hovering near the beer booth: "Hey, Sal! Try to do a decent job for a change, will ya."

Another calls, "Hey, that Gina gets prettier every year!" and the lone woman on the bandstand smiles.

"You just get blinder, Tony," responds one of the musicians from beneath a ten-gallon hat.

Sal Sage laughs. He's a short, compact, middle-aged man. He has paid his dues, and in this part of the state he is well known, playing everything from wedding receptions and wakes to honky-tonks and these large public gatherings.

Band members josh back as they tune their instruments. Occasionally they exchange serious remarks with one another—"Do you have an extra pick?"

I ask a man wearing a "Penngrove Social Firemen" T-shirt if the elaborate bandstand is historic. He grins, "Naw. Looks like it, but it isn't"; then he takes another swallow from his beer. "We tossed it together back when they had the Bicentennial."

Suddenly, a steel guitar is twanging, and the voice of Sal Sage quiets potato-salad-filled mouths. "Way down yonder in the Indian nation. . . ." The guitar and fiddle that back him are professional, and Sal's singing is, too. He employs no southern drawl, but the instrumental solos could be straight from Nashville or Los Angeles.

Diners bounce at the long picnic tables as they eat, and several children begin dancing on the cement slab before the bandstand—swirling, falling, giggling. Soon adults join them, just a few at first, then more. "Hell, Wally, you never could dance!" shouts one of the beer booth habitués.

SAL SAGE
GINA GAYE
AND THE SAGE GANG

P.O. Box 282
Penngrove, CA 94951
(707) 795-7198

Sal Sage and Gina Gaye. Courtesy of Sal Sage.

"Sioux City Sue" brings the jitterbuggers out, old and young, with few graying no-touch couples of middle age; that generation appears to have been almost skipped here. "The Auctioneer's Song" stops dancers, with many folks standing in front of the bandstand. It is clearly a favorite, and the Penngrove Social Fireman says to me, "Old Sal's an auctioneer, too, you know."

"Pretty versatile," I answer.

"He trains horses, too."

The dancers swing back into action when Sal launches his next number: "When my blue moon turns to gold again.... "

"He local?"

"Been here for years. And old Sal's even been in the movies and TV commercials, too."

"I'll be darned."

The singer launches another number: "Roly Poly, daddy's little fatty...."

"Old Sal's pretty damn good, isn't he?" says the Social Fireman.

"Yeah, he is."

"He sings better'n two-thirds of the guys you hear on the damn radio."

I merely nod. Sal Sage, and the hundreds of local entertainers like him who liven affairs at Yreka or Porterville or Escondido, represents the heart of country music in California. His connection to folks is direct, a fact he illustrates when he alters lyrics in midsong to include the names or attributes of friends in the audience. The beer booth boys explode with laughter each time he does that.

By now the grassy area around the bandstand is crowded with even more dancers—a classic country shindig with little girls being twirled by grandfathers, and adolescent males being dared to dance with their mothers. Around the beer booth, billed caps and cowboy hats are slightly askew as the afternoon wears on.

"I'm from San Francisco originally," Sal tells me later. "I got interested in horses and roping when I was a kid—you know, the Cow Palace used to really be the Cow Palace in those days," he grins. "Anyway, that kind of led me to western music, and that's what I tend to play, western not southern. And I've got a nice roping arena over at the place," he adds.

Sal pauses, removes his gray Stetson to reveal a tan pate, then grins, "It's been a good life," he says. "Nowadays, if I play some small thing, some party or reception or something like that, I just take a synthesizer, so I'm a one-man band. That's a great invention," he smiles. "But for big deals like this, I bring the whole band—they're all local; Gina lives right over there," he points toward a lane north of the park, "and we all have a big old time."

After another pause, he says, "You make a lot of friends in this business. Over the years I've seen two generations around here, and I've played most places in the Bay Area—John DeMarco's 23 Club in Brisbane near the Cow Palace, that was a real favorite. I was a regular at the Twin Oaks, too." The singer sips his coffee, then repeats, "It's been real good."

The key figure in the West Coast's unexpected domination of country music during World War II wasn't a musician at all, but an astute disc jockey named Burt (also spelled Bert) "Foreman" Phillips. He had noticed that the movie industry in Southern California was attracting a remarkable gang of musicians and that war-related industries were also concentrating tens of thousands of workers with money in their pockets. Then he figured out how to bring musicians and fans together, developing a circuit of dance halls and assembling bands for each.

He began with the Los Angeles County Barn Dance at the Venice Pier Ballroom in 1942 and soon leased the Town Hall Ballroom in Compton, the Plantation in Culver City, the Baldwin Park Ballroom, and, for a while, the Riverside Rancho, too. Major acts such as Roy Acuff, Ernest Tubb, and Bob Wills were imported to supplement house bands led by such stand-outs as Ray Whitley, Al Dexter, Ted Daffan, Spade Cooley, and Hank Penny. Foreman's "western" dances were a huge success, and this perceptive businessman even arranged to accommodate two audiences of workers by switching bands when swing-shift workers came off the job.

Carolina Cotton, who performed with Spade Cooley's orchestra in those days, recalls:

> We used to finish a dance with Spade and then get in the car real quick, and then they'd take us out to what they called a Swing-Shift dance out at the beach. We alternated country with pop—with Glen Gray, Stan Kenton. Swing music. So we'd alternate back and forth with them. . . .
>
> It'd be like three o'clock in the morning. I can't remember what time we quit at the Riverside Rancho, probably one. And then we'd drive out to the beach and do theirs until probably five. It took a rugged constitution. Lots of vitamins, lots of raw liver.

Merle Travis noted, however, that Phillips didn't understand the music that made his "ballrooms" so popular. "I don't think I'll ever forget the time that in a conversation with Hank [Penny] he told me that Foreman had said 'I don't want any of this Western Swing!' Foreman had a sign painted, and it hung on the wall for all musicians to see. The sign read: STICK TO THE MELODY." Writer Gerald Vaughn suggests that Foreman's stress on melody, while appropriate for listening music, missed the point: "A dance band hopes to make people *move*, not stand and listen, so the emphasis has to be on beat, rhythm, syncopation." Ironically the melody-versus-rhythm fuss harkened back to the roots of this music when Anglo-Celtic songs stressed melody, while African-influenced music was strongly rhythmic.

Travis's buddy Penny, a notably independent bandleader, was eventually ordered by Phillips to fire jazzy sidemen Jimmy Wyble (guitar), Harold Hensley (fiddle), and Noel Boggs (steel). Hank discussed it with his band, then returned and said, "Write out four pink slips and put my name on the fourth one. Thank you very much." Then he left, never to return. Whatever music Phillips may have wanted, he got western swing, the music he may have named, and it got him a huge, eclectic crowd with many folks who had previously considered "country" to be a synonym for "hayseed."

World War II and its aftermath, rather than musical disagreements, dominated this decade in California as elsewhere. When hostilities broke out the Great Depression faded, and increasingly military enterprises began to flourish in the state. Closely related—and still thriving—was the birth of "high-tech" industries. Furthermore, as historian Carey McWilliams explains, "the West did not *convert* to war production for there was nothing much to 'convert'; what happened was that *new* industries and *new* plants were built overnight." Richmond, San Pedro, Vallejo, Sausalito, and Oakland, for example, became the sites of sudden shipyards.

During the international conflict, some 15 million people found war-related jobs, and 16 million others joined the military. Six million women entered the work force. Partly to cash in on the boom, migrants in jalopies again sputtered west over Routes 66 and 40, this time toward wartime jobs on the coast. Economist Davis McEntire argues that the "drought-depression-impelled movement of the 1930s . . . only set the stage for the much larger movement to come," so this was in a sense the second half

The Spade Cooley Band, 1942. Kneeling in front are (left) promoter Burt "Foreman" Phillips and Cooley. Back row (left to right): unidentified, Happy Perryman, Gene Haas, Rocky Stone, Polly McKay, Dick Roberts, George Bamby, unidentified, Tex Williams, Ralph Thomas. From the Gid Tanner Artist File #NF1996, The Southern Folklife Collection, Wilson Library, The University of North Carolina at Chapel Hill.

of a two-stage migration. In the Bay Area 29 percent of all wartime new-comers came from Texas, Oklahoma, Arkansas, and Louisiana. The state's population in 1940 was 6,900,000; only two decades later, it would soar to 15,650,000.

There was also considerable internal migration within California during that global conflict—farm laborers left the Central Valley for coastal cities where better jobs in war-related industries could be found. Migrant

George Watson explained, "We moved to Oakland and worked in the shipyards for two years and saved every dime we could lay our hands on." His family then returned to the valley and bought a farm. Of course when country-music fans relocated, they took their music with them. Honky-tonks, juke joints, and dance halls sprang up near plants and military bases. "Richmond was *really* hot then. There and Santa Monica was the hottest places goin'," remembers bandleader Bill Woods.

Many shindigs were initially tribal gatherings of southwesterners. Soon, however, they expanded to include heterogeneous audiences as military service mingled diverse young people and as more and more Californians were lured by swinging country bands. Historian Marilynn Johnson points out, "In 1944 alone, [Bob] Wills' band played in Oakland four times, selling out the Oakland Civic Auditorium to capacity crowds of more than 19,000."

The shipyards and military bases in the Bay Area had provided many fans for Bob's appearances, and more than a few local groups sought to imitate his style. None succeeded in doing that, but several developed their own considerable followings: Ray Wade and his Rhythm Riders, in particular, were a major beneficiary of the boom in jazzy country music. Based in Maple Hall in San Pablo, the band was, reports writer Al Turner, "an immensely popular act on the West Coast in the early/mid forties." Wade's vocalist Johnny Texerra later formed his own successful band, and it drew fans to Rafael's Club in San Francisco throughout much of the decade. Dude Martin's band continued enjoying a large following in the area, and he later relocated to Los Angeles where in the 1950s he became a radio and television favorite.

As might be expected, many part-time units were formed to satisfy this new market. Elwin Cross and the Arizona Ramblers was an important band in part because Cross hired two future stalwarts, Bill Woods and Dave Stogner. Woods later formed his own Texas Stars and Stogner started the Arkansawyers. Those two groups, along with Leo Stevens and the Ozark Playboys, became popular indeed; yet they were really semiprofessional operations where future professionals were serving apprenticeships. Some of those "part-time" ensembles were able to become full time and successful: Bud Hobbs's band, for example, had a national hit with "Louisiana Swing."

The story of young Bill Woods was perhaps more typical than Hobbs's. Bill was working as a boilermaker, first for Kaiser, then for U. S. Steel,

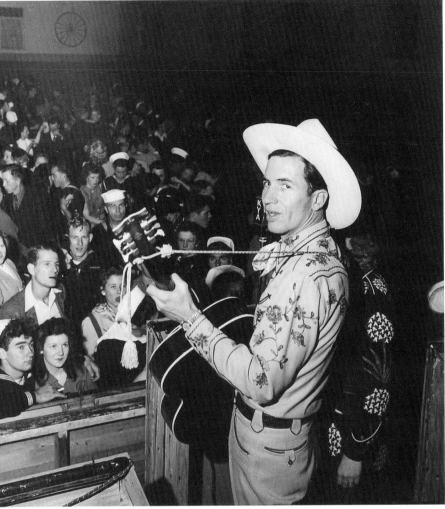

Dude Martin and fans at Redmond Hall in Richmond, 1943. Photo by Dorothea Lange. Copyright the
Dorothea Lange Collection, The Oakland Museum of California, City of Oakland. Gift of Paul S. Taylor.

when Cross gave him his first job in a band. After he formed his ensemble, they played not only at local clubs but also for bond drives: "The
boss'd give us a couple hours off to play at this shipyard or that one. We'd
be on the same stage with big stars. One time even Lana Turner! Not too
bad for a kid from Visalia." After the war he would become a professional
musician and enjoy a long and noteworthy career, as would his friend
Stogner.

Carolina Cotton, for a time billed as "The Yodeling Blonde Bomb-shell," performed with the bands of Martin, Wills, and Cooley, then later became a successful actress in western movies. She offers some sense of those hectic war years when, as a San Francisco schoolgirl, she became a musician:

> The only reason I did music is because when the war was on, they kept drafting all the musicians, and they [the bands] had to have seven people with union cards. I was one of the only kids at a dancing school who played ukulele for one of the Hawaiian numbers, so therefore I got my musician's card.
>
> But . . . I didn't get the card until they said, "Well, can you play?" And I said, "Sure I can play." You know, what's a kid going to say. So they [Dude Martin's band] hired me to play, just because I had a union card. Nobody's going to draft me. So I played bass; in fact I played bass for Spade Cooley for awhile, until he got a real bass player. I played bass, I played guitar. I played steel guitar. I played drums for a very short time. And I played steel guitar for a very short time. I can't play anything. You know, you just do it. You don't stop to consider how. You just do it.

Redmond Hall in Richmond rivaled Maple Hall as the main Bay Area venue, and clubs such as John's Half-Barrel, Craby Joe's Big Barn, and Mc-Fadden's, all in Oakland, hosted appealing country scenes. So popular had western swing music become that dances were scheduled at Alvarado and East Shore parks every week. Remembering the shindig at East Shore Park, Helen Vaughn told Johnson, "the place was always packed. . . . we often ran into other people we knew from the shipyards." Country dances linked the old and new cultures for migrants, while attracting longtime Californians as well.

Many social taboos had earlier been weakened when nuclear families broke down during the Depression (by 1940, for example, at least 1,500,000 wives had been deserted), and wartime conditions exacer-bated that. Sexual roles underwent radical alteration; in the aircraft in-dustry, for example, 40 percent of the work force in Southern California was female. Despite considerable harassment of the crudest kind, women established themselves as valuable employees and thus began the chain of events that would eventually alter professional and social possibilities in the culture. Single women and men filled the honky-tonks and dance halls and so did married ones; they became the subjects of country songs. Some whites also found themselves toiling alongside nonwhites for the first time—and a few whites, at least, began enjoying the music played by those nonwhites, too. This despite the fact that de facto segregation was common in work situations and that blacks in particular were consigned to low-paying, dangerous jobs.

The wartime migration of southwesterners certainly had a greater impact on music and musical tastes in California than had the earlier Dust Bowl ingress, because this time far more transplants found decent jobs. As a result they had money to spend; they could afford to buy records, attend dances, drink at honky-tonks, play jukeboxes, and patronize radio sponsors. That new commercial clout led virtually every radio station to add a cowboy or hillbilly show to its format. Red Rowe and his Ridge Runners could be heard daily on 50,000-watt KMPC-Hollywood; Murrell, Tex Williams, and Tex Ritter were featured on that same station's "Palace Barn Dance." Carolina Cotton was a disc jockey on Long Beach's KGER, KXLA in Pasadena boasted a show with the peripatetic Williams, while ABC began a Saturday night network show from Southern California that featured Shug Fisher and Jack Rivers. Cliffie Stone was also rolling by then with shows on two Los Angeles stations, KXLA and KRKD. Bandleader Bill Woods summarizes, "Oh, radio was big then. *Real* big. It just got everything goin'."

Country did not fade from the Bay Area. Cal Shrum's Rhythm Rangers were regulars on KYA-San Francisco. Later Shrum hosted a barn-dance show and was a disc jockey at KEEN-San Jose. The popular Ray Wade also had a radio show on Oakland's KWBR, and KVSM in San Mateo would follow with Red Murrell. The "sophisticated" Bay Area's flowering led Janie B. Hamilton to write in *Tophand* magazine, "It hasn't been so many years since Hillbilly and Western programs were a real scarcity out here. . . . Boy, OH BOY, it's a different story now! Turn the dial just any hour of the day or night and by recordings, transcriptions or live talent, you'll get a good old time program of OUR KIND of music." Furthermore, by 1949, KXLA-Pasadena became what most experts believe was the first all-country radio station in the nation.

Given the breakdown of many traditional taboos and the attendant rambunctiousness of entertainers in the 1940s, it's not surprising that suggestive titles and lyrics would creep into country music, and during that decade they caused a great fuss among those trying to protect the genre's "family-and-faith" image: "Pussy, Pussy, Pussy," "Let Me Play with Your Poodle," "Wham Bam Thank You Ma'am," "Get Yourself a Redhead" ("She's at home in bed all right / But brother, she ain't asleep . . . "), and "The Freckle Song" ("She has freckles on her but [*pause*] / I love her just the same . . . "), among others, outraged self-appointed censors.

More shocking, to naive fans at least, many musicians have acknowledged that liquor and pills—especially benzedrine ("bennies"), what some called "truck-driver specials"—cut a swath even then and that marijuana use was not unknown. Many performers seem to have taken pills in those hectic days. This may have been particularly true of western swing musicians because of their demanding schedules, as well as their association with the subculture of West Coast jazz. Hank Penny, whose band would make that jazz connection explicit with a recording of "Hillbilly Bebop" in 1949, however, points out that even ostensibly staid Nashville wasn't immune to drug use. He recalls the time Red Foley and most of his band joined a recording session there, and "one of them silly musicians slipped some bennies in the Coke bottle Red was drinkin' from. Later Red says, 'Man, I didn't sleep for a week.'"

Those were nickname-cluttered days, too, so a curious aside to the music was the rich variety of monikers that country musicians brought to California. Deuce Spriggens, Smokey Rogers, and Tex Williams, for example, made up a singing trio (invented by Spade Cooley) known as "Okie, Arkie, and Tex"; although the handles were not necessarily geographically accurate, Spade knew his audience, and the group had a great following among transplanted southwesterners. Those names had nothing on the ones boasted by Boots Harris, Booger Red Arnall, Slumber Nichols, Hi Pockets Busse, Dusty Taylor, Cactus Soldi, Muddy Berry, Spike Featherstone, Happy Perryman, Rocky Stone, Dude Martin, Porky Freeman, Tiny Moore, Sleepy Carson, Red Murrell, Skeeter Abrams, Cottonseed Clark, Speedy West, Slim Duncan, and Ramblin' Jimmie Dolan. Clearly in this profession, as in wrestling and real estate, a colorful—thus memorable—nickname has been considered an asset.

Nudka Cohn, a Russian native whose name was misspelled "Nudie Cohen" on his immigration papers, certainly boasted a label that might qualify for the list above. The soon-to-be-famous tailor moved to Los Angeles in 1940. The trend toward western-style clothing was already well

Hank Penny. From the Gid Tanner Artist File #NF1996, The Southern Folklife
Collection, Wilson Library, The University of North Carolina at Chapel Hill.

under way then, and Cohn, a one-time maker of G-strings for strippers,
almost blew his first major country-music assignment to outfit Tex
Williams and the Western Caravan. As Tyler Beard relates, "Nudie took
measurements and recited them to his assistant, who was not entirely
sober at the time. Leg lengths got chest measurements, and the short of
it was that none of the costumes fit. Nudie had to remake them."
Williams was Cohen's special benefactor, and the costumes were indeed
remade. In the four decades that followed, Nudie's Rodeo Tailors would
become the world's—and of course country music's—most famous pur-
veyor of colorful western wear, as well as a show business institution.

Some of the nicknames actually on that list are associated with folks
who developed significant local followings in the Golden State but didn't
"hit" nationwide. Porky Freeman, for example, a popular sideman with
bands headed by Texas Jim Lewis and Red Murrell, was a pioneering

guitarist; he recorded "Porky's Boogie-Woogie on the Strings" for a small Southern California label, Morris Lee, in 1943. It became a major regional hit. Writes Kienzle, "GIs played it constantly on jukeboxes, and copies were worn out faster than they could be replaced. In fact, the problem got so bad that a special 45 with the tune on both sides had to be issued."

Small labels, such as Morris Lee, proliferated in this decade. Zeke Clements, a member of the "Grand Ole Opry," came to Southern California in 1945 and launched Liberty Records (later called Blazon), which would feature Paul Howard and his Arkansas Cotton Pickers, Curly Williams, and Clements himself. The Rodeo label (later called Coast) was the "western/western swing" arm of Peerless-Disco, a company founded in Mexico in 1924. Its distinguished list boasted Ray Wade and his Rhythm Riders, Walt Shrum and his Colorado Hillbillies, Jimmy Walker and his Western Stars, Idaho Call and his Sun Valley Cowboys, and Boots Faye. Oakland-based Westernair was owned by Cal Shrum and recorded members of his band the Rhythm Rangers—Dusty Taylor, Jack Gross, Stan Boreson, as well as Benny Olsen's Rancho Serenaders. Black and White Records released work by Clement, Rudy Sooter, and the country parodies of Rody Erickson and his Dude Ranch Boys. The list could be much longer.

Joyce "Red" Murrell, whose first recording had been on the Morris Lee label, was a jazz lover who'd played with swing and Dixieland bands in his native Missouri. He switched to western music after hearing a hot group that included Spade Cooley, George Bamby, Deuce Spriggens, and Gene Hass playing at Lyle's Frontier Lounge in Santa Monica in 1940. Three years later he attracted the attention of Cliffie Stone, who in turn invited him (along with Freeman and Billy Hughes) to play on the "Dinner Bell Roundup" radio program on KXLA. Eventually, Murrell joined Texas Jim Lewis's stellar Lone Star Playboys (with Merle Travis, Fiddlin' Kate [Margie Linville], Vic Davis, Charlie Linville, and George Bambi); as vocalist for that group in 1945, he became the first country singer to perform at the Hollywood Bowl. His own outfit the Ozark Playboys, which featured a fine female singer named Terry Temple, was formed shortly after that appearance. The next year *Tophand* magazine not only called it Southern California's most improved band but also presented Red with its award for best bandleader.

Murrell himself described his band as a "Spike Jones–type," wide open, entertaining, and certainly one of the state's most popular. The group cut many records, the best-known of which was "I'm Sick and Tired of You Little Darlin'," a parody of the "Little Darlin'" craze that was sweeping country-music radio stations. As the popularity of the big ballroom appearances began to wane, Murrell, like many other musicians, moved to radio. After stints as a disc jockey at San Francisco's KYA and San Mateo's KVSM, he became a Bay Area fixture from 1958 to 1974 at San Jose's KEEN, arguably the most popular country station in that region of the state.

Despite the belief that the Okie migration had turned Bakersfield into a country-music mecca, in 1945 pioneer bandleader Bill Woods, who was by then playing at the Rhythm Rancho, a small club there, remembers that "there was only one western show on radio, and that was from 12 to 12:15 with Bob Wills. That was all the radio show there was. . . . It was transcribed." Other than its proximity to entertainment-rich Los Angeles, the Kern County town was not much different from others in the Central Valley and by no means dominant.

That region's hottest act, the Maddox Brothers and Rose from Modesto, had been on hold while three of the brothers served in the military during the war; they returned and soon the group was again very popular. As a result, Modesto—also the home base of Al Brown and his Alabamans—can be reasonably considered the core of country music in the valley at that time. The area from Sacramento to Bakersfield—likely because of its large Okie population—supported many local country acts, some of them very good indeed. Dave Stogner's western swing band, the Sagebrush Serenaders, Woods's Orange Blossom Playboys, and Brown's ensemble, among many others, filled the Red Barn in Sacramento or Growers Hall in Stockton, the Uptown Ballroom in Modesto or the Pumpkin Center Barn Dance in Pumpkin Center. Variations of western swing dominated, although how it was played differed considerably from band to band; and the hard-driving hillbilly version by Stogner's group, based at the Fresno Barn (or "Big Barn"), was then developing a substantial fan base. Meanwhile radio stations such as KGDM in Stockton, KTRB in Modesto, KMJ in Fresno, and KFBK in Sacramento also kept the music alive.

In Bakersfield during World War II, "The Blind Troubadour" from Alba,

Texas, Leon Payne, had a program on KERN-AM. Eventually a regular on "Louisiana Hayride" and the "Grand Ole Opry," Payne became a song-writer of note as well as a singer and would create two hits for Hank Williams—"They'll Never Take Her Love from Me" and "Lost Highway" —and a country classic he recorded himself, "I Love You Because." As a re-sult, he was the first major figure whose name would be associated with Bakersfield.

During the late 1940s the Kern County town was slowly and imper-fectly growing to accept the music that would one day bring it promi-nence, just as it was slowly and imperfectly growing to accept the people with whom it was locally identified. But the effects of the dual migration would become evident in Bakersfield by the end of the decade when all-country KAFY radio was popular, and virtually every other station in town had country-western shows. Tex Butler's band (featuring George French and Eugene Moles) attracted dancers to the Blackboard. "Things was really startin' to jump then," says Woods.

Western swing remained the key ingredient. "Hey," remembered Ba-kersfield native Jim Fix, "it was the best music going." The expanded fan base resulted in the fact that favorites like Wills and the Texas Playboys at-tracted larger California crowds than did the mainstream bands of Harry James, Tommy Dorsey, and Benny Goodman. When Wills relocated here in 1943, he and the Playboys were acknowledging how important the Golden State had become to this music and how important the music had become to the Golden State. Country-music historian Malone notes that during those years "the most vigorous region for live country perform-ances may very well have been California."

While the most important ingredients in this rise were demographic and economic, the lure of what was variously called "Okie jazz," "Okie swing," "country jazz," "western jazz," and finally "western swing" was considerable. Ironically Phillips is credited with helping popularize the enduring term when he labeled his star act, Spade Cooley: "The King of Western Swing."

The Southeast meanwhile produced few, if any, significant swing bands. Perhaps as a result some commentators—apparently seeking a static definition of the music—have claimed this western style wasn't country at all. Eventually, though, explains biographer Charles Townsend, "the distinction between western swing and country music was blurred.

Trade magazines, disc jockeys, record companies, and historians made little or no distinction between them." What actually occurred of course was that western swing had become a prominent addition to the many types of music gathered under the title "country," another of its branches.

Southern musical traditionalism was challenged as never before during this decade. The introduction of new instruments, for example, especially riled old-timers; many of them (forgetting the variety of contraptions in early hillbilly bands) insisted that country music meant only acoustic strings. In the 1930s Hank Penny led the Radio Cowboys, one of the first and the hottest of the western swing bands in the Southeast. He recalled that Charlie Reel of the "Grand Ole Opry" said, "We sure would like to have you come on the 'Opry.' . . . There's not but one thing that's stopping us from giving you the spot." When Penny asked what, Reel told him, "If we give you a spot, you would have to have Noel Boggs play a Hawaiian guitar; we could not allow an electric instrument on the 'Grand Ole Opry'—that would not work." The feisty Penny suggested that Reel hire Acuff's Smoky Mountain Boys instead, then walked out. Five years later, electric steels were common on the "Opry."

Perhaps an even sillier example of this resistance to innovation occurred when Bob Wills and the Texas Playboys were finally invited to play on the "Opry" following World War II. According to writer Ken Griffis, officials insisted that Wills hide the group's drums behind a curtain. Bob, bold as a gopher snake, placed Smokey Dacus and his drums in the band's front row. Western swing was pointing toward a national future, while traditionalists continued gazing back at their versions of a southern past.

Another innovator, Oklahoman Spade Cooley, became Bob Wills's major rival as the most popular bandleader in California. He had arrived in Los Angeles in the mid-1930s, and he had found work in clubs, saloons, and some movies, too. His reputation as a musician continued growing, and finally Foreman Phillips urged him to form his own ensemble. He did, and by 1942 Spade's orchestra was a major regional favorite.

Hollywood-native Joaquin Murphey (often spelled Murphy) was a stalwart in Cooley's group. His instrument the pedal steel, originally called the Gibson Electroharp, had been developed by John Moore for the Gibson Company in the 1940s. Other companies soon built their own versions of this new device. It altered sounds and opened new possibilities. Writer Nick Tosches describes one,

It stood on four legs like an insect and had up to four separate eight-string necks. A complex system of cables, pulleys, and rods connected to foot pedals (and later knee pedals) enabled the guitarist to weirdize the pitch of individual strings and to make chords and voicings that none had heard before. . . .

Pedal steels were harder to master than conventional guitars. Men sat at this strange shining tool, their fingers gleaming with metal.

According to Merle Travis, Murphey was "way ahead of his time" on the pedal steel. An exciting soloist for Cooley, Joaquin developed a loyal following during that decade, as did Leodie Jackson, but a transplanted, innovative Missourian named Wesley Webb "Speedy" West probably had more to do with the emerging California style. West had relocated to Los Angeles in 1946. Two years later he bought the second pedal steel guitar built by the famed Paul Bigsby and became a major session musician in Southern California, recording over 6,000 records with 177 singers in a five-year period. His performances led critic Richie Unterberger to call Speedy "one of the greatest virtuosos that country music has ever produced."

Eventually, West played with both Spade Cooley and Hank Penny's bands. His work on two 1952 recordings, "Waiting in the Lobby" by Hank Thompson and "Song of the Old Water Wheel" by Slim Whitman— both featuring Speedy's high-volume runs—is credited with alerting the entire industry to the possibilities of the new instrument. Again the Southeast took note, and pedal steel solos there became more prominent and a bit more jazzy—more *Californian*, in fact.

Speedy's frequent partner in crime was Georgian Jimmy Bryant, who joined him in "The Flaming Guitars" duo to create such hot instrumentals as "Whistle Stop" and "Stratosphere Boogie." Bryant, who had taught himself to play the guitar while recuperating from a war wound, was one of the first to employ a Fender Telecaster (then called Broadcaster) and to grasp its remarkable potential. He had drifted to Los Angeles after his discharge from a military hospital and played in clubs, where West originally heard him.

Jimmy, much influenced by the postwar jazz renaissance, eventually joined the cast of "Hometown Jamboree" and was signed by Capitol Records. Like West, he played countless recording sessions in the 1950s.

During the next decade Bryant wrote the Waylon Jennings hit "The Only Daddy That'll Walk the Line" and recorded five albums for Imperial. He and Speedy also recorded a reunion album in the 1970s. Jimmy's introduction of jazz-oriented solos to country cuts remains his enduring legacy, a style that helped differentiate California's country music from the Nashville variety. No one has topped his artistry.

Another innovative guitarist (and remarkable songwriter) eventually performed on Foreman Phillips's circuit, Merle Travis. He is justly identified by Bill C. Malone as "one of country music's most brilliant and multitalented entertainers." Writer Jonny Whiteside calls him an "all-around genius." Merle, a Kentuckian, moved to Los Angeles in 1944 and after scrambling for a time caught on with Ray Whitley's band. In 1946 Capitol signed Travis, and his first session led to a double-sided hit: "No Vacancy" and "Cincinnati Lou." For all his brilliance as a performer, and he is still considered by old-timers to have been the finest guitar picker of the era, Merle's phenomenal songwriting made him a legend.

His list of hits seems endless: "Sixteen Tons," "Dark as a Dungeon," "Divorce Me C.O.D.," "So Round, So Firm, So Fully Packed," "I Am a Pilgrim," and so on. Wesley Tuttle remembers that Travis wrote seventeen songs in one night. "He was fantastic," says Tuttle. "He could write a new theme song for a radio or television show in ten minutes." A particularly memorable instance occurred on March 26, 1947, when old pal Tex Williams arrived at Merle's San Fernando Valley home and explained that he desperately needed a hit for a recording session scheduled the next day. Travis, who was painting a fence at the time, had previously seen Tex perform a talking-blues number on stage, so he composed—almost literally not missing a stroke on the fence—what would become Capitol Records's first multimillion seller, "Smoke! Smoke! Smoke! (That Cigarette)." Writer Rich Kienzle calls this "the song that legitimized both Tex Williams and Capitol Records . . . an American standard that transcends all musical categories."

Tex Williams had departed from Cooley's orchestra when Cliffie Stone offered him a recording contract with Capitol Records. A number of his fellow bandsmen joined him, among them Cactus Soldi, Spike Featherstone, Pedro DePaul, Deuce Spriggens, and Smokey Rogers. They called themselves the Western Caravan, a partnership with everyone sharing profits. The band soon opened at the Redondo Barn, then moved to a converted skating rink (located between Los Angeles and Glendale) called the Palace Barn. They filled the Foster Park Ballroom in Ventura, the Harmony Park Ballroom in Anaheim, and the American Legion Hall in Placentia. They even packed the Aragon Ballroom in Chicago. From the start, this was a strong ensemble, and their music—"Artistry in Western Swing," for instance—was exceptional.

Tex had recorded several honky-tonk classics written by Travis, such as "No Vacancy," "So Round, So Firm, So Fully Packed," and "Divorce Me C.O.D.," but it took "Smoke! Smoke! Smoke! (That Cigarette)" to catapult the Western Caravan to their pinnacle. Williams remembers that producer Lee Gillette had told him when he heard the number in rehearsal, "This is the one we've been looking for." How right he was. The chorus featured Williams, Spriggens, and Rogers—who had constituted the popular "Okie, Arkie, and Tex" singing group for Cooley's orchestra—as well as Cliffie Stone on bass. This number sold nearly 2 million copies and topped the country chart for sixteen weeks; it even crossed over to earn number one on the pop chart for six weeks. The Western Caravan eventually disbanded in 1957, and country-music authority Rich Kienzle refers to it as "the cutting edge of West Coast swing acts."

As a result of hosting so many innovative musicians, as well as the concurrent development of West Coast jazz and the cross-fertilization that ensued, Coast country became distinct, "hot, upbeat, and full of risk taking," points out Whiteside. Writer Al Turner, on the other hand, suggests that three characteristics set the Golden State's western swing apart from the Southwest's in the 1940s: tightly orchestrated arrangements, the use of accordions, and the influence of singing cowboys. In any case, the abundance of work in Southern California lured more and more musicians there, and they formed a distinct community, everyone seeming to know everyone else. Penny had come to the Golden State in 1945 in response to a letter from old chum Travis. Merle took him to the Sunset Rancho in Hollywood to see Spade Cooley's band, and Hank recalls, "They were something else. I'd never seen or heard any other group do what they did with that great fiddle section, playing from written arrangements." Shortly thereafter the jazzy Penny was himself fronting that band for Phillips and had become an established—if controversial—figure in the local musical community. Woody Herman called him "The Hip Hick," and Hank's upbeat records such as "Steel Guitar Stomp," "Bloodshot

Eyes," or "Little Red Wagon" became hits. Penny would make the transition to television and remain a musician, comic, club owner, and outspoken persona for years to come.

Like Hank, other members of the unique subculture in those halcyon days lived strange, inverted lives—working late, sometimes seven nights a week, sleeping most of the day, traveling from venue to venue, and conducting their personal and business affairs within the limits of their sometimes exhilarating profession. When they socialized it was usually with other musicians and their families, many of whom were old friends from other parts of the country. Word of mouth became more important than trade newspapers among them when jobs were open, and many sidemen, it seemed, played with almost every band in the area—and of the era—at one time or another.

When this decade began, there were only three major record labels nationally: Columbia, Victor, and Decca. During the 1940s, however, fifteen companies, including the big three, plus two founded in California—MGM (1945) and Imperial (1947)—maintained offices on the West Coast, principally in the Los Angeles area. Capitol Records, yet another California creation, was the most successful newcomer. Music store owner Glen Wallichs, famed songwriter Johnny Mercer, and producer Buddy DaSylva formed it in 1942, and eventually the circular Capitol Tower at the corner of Hollywood and Vine Streets would become the center of the recording industry on the West Coast. Writer Gene Lees calls it "an innovative and tremendously creative company that gave a great lift to American music."

Capitol's initial country success, "Jingle, Jangle, Jingle," by Tex Ritter in 1942 established the label as a force. In 1944 Capitol hired Lee Gillette as A&R (artists and repertoire) man for its country division, and he soon followed the lead of Ralph Peer and Frank Walker, touring the South with portable recording equipment in search of new acts and recording, among others, young Chet Atkins, then a fiddler. Gillette continued as head of the country division until 1950—producing such artists as Merle Travis, Jack Guthrie, Wesley Tuttle, plus Williams and the Western Caravan. That year his friend Ken Nelson replaced him. As Kienzle accurately observes, Lee "set in motion a direction that produced innovative country material in the 1940s and paved the way for Ken Nelson's triumphs in the 1950s and 1960s."

Tex Williams and the Western Caravan, 1948, country music's nickname champs. Front row (left to right): Joaquin Murphy on steel, Spike Featherstone on harp, Muddy Berry on drums, Pedro DePaul on accordion, Williams, Deuce Spriggens on bass. In back: fiddlers Rex Call, Max Fidler, and Cactus Soldi, guitarists Benny Garcia, Smokey Rogers, Johnny Weiss, and Ossie Godson on vibes. From the Gid Tanner Artist File #NF1996, The Southern Folklife Collection, Wilson Library, The University of North Carolina at Chapel Hill.

Tex Ritter. Courtesy of Kern County Museum. Used by permission.

TEX RITTER

Gillette had benefited particularly when Capitol hired Cliffie Stone as a consultant. Stone, explains music writer J. R. Young, "was known as a man who could make careers. He proved that at Capitol almost immediately as a talent scout, helping land Tex Williams, Merle Travis and a few years later, Tennessee Ernie Ford." After taking over Capitol's pop division in 1950, Gillette is credited for moving the music toward the merging of country and pop styles—creating countrypolitan—before Atkins and Owen Bradley did the same thing in Nashville.

The duets of Jimmy Wakely and Margaret Whiting ("Slippin' Around," "'Til the End of the World," etc.), as well as some of Wakely's singles ("One Has My Name, the Other Has My Heart," "I Love You So Much It Hurts Me," and so on), were strong precursors of the current pop-style sound. Gillette's work at Capitol during the late 1940s thus contributed in no small measure to the growth of a "mainstream" country music. *The Illustrated History of Country Music* summarizes, "Musical divisions blurred as it became the first country music sound created in a somewhat sophisticated and growing urban environment for both pop and country audiences. California, it might be said, spearheaded the first commercial movement in modern country music."

Pop or Country or Both?

Given the amorphous, eclectic nature of the various types of music lumped together under the title "country," it really isn't surprising that pop techniques and material would early become mingled in it. "The Prisoner's Song" by Vernon Dalhart in 1925 had of course been "soft" country sung by a man with light-operatic training, and it sold over a million copies—many of them to pop fans. Not nearly as soft but equally popular with noncountry fans was Jimmie Davis's "You Are My Sunshine" (1940); in that case pop fans moved toward country.

"Countrier-than-thou" is as old as the music; purists fussed when established stars like Gene Autry ("You're the Only Star in My Blue Heaven" in 1934) or Eddy Arnold ("What Is Life without You" in 1947) moved into countrypolitan modes. Some seemed not to notice that this was a two-way street: Bing Crosby, for example, regularly included country-western songs in his shows, and between 1933 and 1949 he placed fourteen country songs on pop charts. According to Douglas B. Green, "The occasional crossover did have the effect of continuing the trend that Autry and his fellow cowboys had begun: the de-yokelization of the country song among non-country fans. The seeds of acceptance among a wide public were beginning to sprout, slowly but surely paving the way for the nationwide acceptance of the country music that was to come."

Arnold, a member of Pee Wee King's Golden West Cowboys, became Nashville's classic crossover singer, lingering on pop charts for years, while he also managed to remain a best-selling country singer. "The Tennessee Plowboy" described his music as "Heinz 57: a little country, a little pop, and a little folk, and it all goes together."

Part of what's called the "countrypolitan" problem is terminological: First, "pop" is a title, not a description (ironically, nowadays country *is* America's most popular music). Second, who defines exactly what's "country" and what's not? At the extremes— Grandpa Jones singing and strumming his banjo, say, as opposed to Frank Sinatra crooning to the accompaniment of Nelson Riddle—that's an easy question to answer. But when borderline musicians, such as Wakely or Arnold or even Autry perform, who's to say? Perhaps even more importantly does it matter how the music is defined if listeners enjoy it? What we know now is that Dalhart and Autry, Arnold and Wakely were pioneers of what has become the dominant track in this music; just ask Garth Brooks.

◄ ►　　　◄ ►　　　◄

By the late 1940s a few commentators had begun to use the term *hard country* to describe styles undiluted by pop influence. Capitol covered all bases then, producing soft and hard country and most everything in between. It's a good thing the company did, too; music writer Kienzle reveals that, "in 1947, the Capitol bosses could be certain of profit from just one area: the country division." Billy Liebert, who was musical director of Stone's "Hometown Jamboree" and who played piano and accordion on hundreds of Capitol sessions, adds that late in the decade the company's country division had become vital indeed. "Capitol overextended themselves," he explained.

> They were a new company, they were growing, spending all this money in the pop field, and they were having success, and all of a sudden that dried up. And the only people that were selling any records—Merle [Travis] had three or four songs on the charts at one time, and it didn't cost anything to do a country date. . . . I think union scale was $33 to do a record date for four songs. And the country music department at Capitol saved their ass.

Recording during the 1940s was shadowed by two strikes called by James C. Petrillo, president of the American Federation of Musicians, the first in 1942–43, the second in 1948–49. New technology threatened old patterns, and Petrillo asserted that the increase in numbers of radio disc jockeys, plus other recorded-music programs, as well as the proliferation of jukeboxes, were putting musicians out of work. He insisted that record companies create a fund to compensate union members. Eventually, the companies agreed, but the impact of the strike on country music during this big-band era was considerable. For instance, leaders had a tough time keeping large ensembles together. Worse, still, a number of the best versions of various bands went unrecorded; for example, the Texas Playboys' largest unit—twenty-two musicians—never cut a song. On the other hand some recording companies sought to "beat the ban" by having artists record virtually their entire repertoire before the prohibition went into effect. Rose Maddox told Whiteside, "We went in ever'day for two weeks, so we had records coming out for the entire time the strike was, and the union couldn't do anything."

Movie music continued playing, too, and during this decade horse operas remained important California contributions nationally. One of the best of the later singing cowboys was Wakely, with over seventy movie appearances. He had ventured west from Oklahoma City in 1940, part of the Jimmy Wakely Trio with Johnny Bond and Dick Reinhart (who had recently replaced Scotty Harrell). After struggling for a time in tinseltown, the three eventually joined generous Gene Autry's "Melody Ranch" radio show. In 1944 Jimmy began starring in his own series of movies for Monogram Studio. He not only became a noted cowboy actor but, by the end of the decade, was also one of the nation's most popular vocalists.

Johnny Bond, who remained on the Autry show until it was canceled in 1956, was a guitar virtuoso and singer, a solid record seller from the 1940s to the mid-1960s and also an important composer ("Cimmaron," "Tomorrow Never Comes," "I Wonder Where You Are Tonight," etc.). He, like Red Murrell and a few other standouts, was something of an anomaly in that he did *not* come from a musical family. Eventually Johnny appeared in over a hundred motion pictures, nearly always as a sidekick or as part of a singing group. He had begun his musical career with a 98-cent ukulele in Oklahoma, much in the thrall of Jimmie Rodgers, and ended up soloing with his guitar at the Hollywood Bowl. Like so many other standouts from the Midwest and Southwest, he settled in the Golden State, raised his family here, and remained for the rest of his life.

When Bond and Wakely ceased performing as Autry's backup group on the "Melody Ranch" program in 1942, they were replaced by Eddie and Jimmie Dean. That duo had served a long apprenticeship on the radio and had, like Autry, been in the cast of WLS's "National Barn Dance." Eddie became the more prominent of the two, appearing in several Tex Ritter westerns and singing with Foy Willing's Riders of the Purple Sage. He was also featured on Judy Canova's popular radio show.

According to writer Ken Griffis, in 1944 Judy's brother Pete talked Eddie into starring in the first color western picture *Song of Old Wyoming* filmed the next year. "The cost of production—$35,000. The new color film was a great success, making for the producers over a million dollars for the first three [films] released." Eventually Eddie starred in twenty cheap westerns for Producers' Releasing Corporation and Eagle-Lion Studios, but his real strength was as a singer and songwriter. He contributed two country classics—"One Has My Name, the Other Has My Heart" and "I Dreamed of a Hillbilly Heaven." Eddie eventually performed at such slick Southern California nightspots as Ciro's and was even the subject of a comic book. He eventually became a fixture in Southern California's country-music community.

The last major singing cowboy Rex Allen was an former rodeo rider from Arizona and another distinguished alumnus of Chicago's "National Barn Dance." He managed to bring a country feel to a big baritone voice, something no one else ever pulled off. Beginning with *Arizona Cowboy* in 1949, Rex often wore clothing so extravagant as to appear clownish, yet he managed a convincing screen presence. His attire was not an accident; several of Rex's early scripts had been intended for the flamboyant Roy Rogers, then Republic's top cowboy. Many of Rex's films were also shot in color, which emphasized his gaudy duds. Allen came along as the horse opera's popularity was riding off into the sunset, and not even Slim Pickens as his sidekick could help much. Later, though, Allen's famous voice narrated many Disney nature movies, so he remained prominent in Hollywood.

The professional environment within which the talented Rex Allen and other later singing cowboys worked was in many ways grim. Writes film historian Kalton Lahue, "Increasing costs, shrinking markets and television were taking their toll. . . . and despite the use of reissues with new films as a means of filling out a season's series, stock footage used in place of shooting new sequences, and other economies to reduce costs, the end of the road was in sight for the B western."

By 1949 a Buffalo Bill–type wild west show called the Western Hall of Fame Annual "Hoss Opera" toured the West Coast. It featured an all-star cast—Roy Rogers, Dale Evans, Ken Curtis, Hoot Gibson, Rex Allen, Carolina Cotton, George "Gabby" Hayes, the Sons of the Pioneers, Lash LaRue, Forrest Tucker, Monte Montana, Andy Devine, and Allen "Rocky" Lane. Still, the heyday of "hoss operas" was passing even as they toured in the nineteenth-century-style show, and matters seemed to have come full circle.

In the 1940s Hollywood also introduced and promoted its first successful singing cowgirl, Judy Canova. In 1939 Dorothy Page had starred in a series of three singing westerns, and Patsy Montana had made a couple of films, too, but Judy topped them. Like many women entertainers in those days, she had begun in a family singing group, then progressed to radio where her strong voice was a favorite. She made her way to Broadway but achieved her greatest fame in the movies, where she became the major female moneymaker for Republic. Perhaps more importantly, however, notes writer Robert K. Oermann, "her remarkable evolution from small-town hayseed shows to Hollywood stardom is a barometer both of country music's transformation into a truly national phenomenon in the 1930s and of women's strides forward within the genre." That circuitous route was probably necessary to achieve any acceptance in the notoriously male-dominated country-music business.

If the gifted comedienne Canova often harkened back to hillbilly styles despite her cowgirl clothes, the equally gifted Patsy Montana continued during the same period to sing cowgirl material, appearing at rodeos and other shows with the likes of Autry, Rogers, and the Sons of the Pioneers. In Montana's long career she, more than any other entertainer, embodied the cowgirl image.

The social upheaval caused by World War II radically expanded the lure of country music. Many GIs or war workers learned to love what was commonly called "shit-kicker" music. (For many years, Armed Forces Radio would open the day with a country-music disc jockey program,

109

"Hillbilly Reveille.") When the international conflict finally ended, things did not get back to "normal"; they got back to something new. Columnist George Will has pointed out, "In 1940, most Americans were renters, most households had neither a refrigerator nor central heating, 30 percent lacked inside running water, coal fueled most furnaces and stoves, wood was the second-most used fuel. More than a fifth of Americans lived on farms, less than a third of which had electric lights and only a tenth had flush toilets. In 1945 most households did not have a telephone." Before the war the idea of company-paid retirement had also been novel, and the average workweek was closer to fifty than forty hours. If you weren't white, jobs of any quality were tough to find; sexual roles were tightly defined.

The postwar situation was more promising. While housing tracts offering "No Down Payment for Vets" caught everyone's attention after the war, the greatest shift was attitudinal: many people began to think of their lives in new ways. Only a few years after V-J Day, the cultural rupture that resulted from the war would become increasingly obvious as, for example, black Americans and some whites, too, refused to accept racial segregation. And when a sharecropper's son had become a combat hero or a migrant laborer's daughter had become a shipyard shift foreman, they often rejected the prewar social order that had relegated them to low rungs and reduced opportunities.

This was especially true if they had used the GI bill to pursue educations. Following the conflict, droves of veterans, many of whom likely could never have attended college otherwise, achieved higher education thanks to the GI bill, and as a result they rearranged American society. Recalls one beneficiary, Senator Daniel Inouye of Hawaii, "Within half a decade, the bill lifted the intellectual level of the United States by quantum leaps."

A music many considered unintellectual—honky-tonk—at that time came to reflect the discomfort some folks experienced as a result of all these changes. Like the honky-tonks themselves, it had always been about margins, and the continued importance of such "dives" in the Golden State became especially obvious in communities where war-related industries had earlier lured workers: San Diego, San Pedro, Richmond, Vallejo, and others. In fact the wartime clubs and their customers also helped create new followings for country music in the decades that followed. Honky-tonks had of course been prominent—if not necessarily honored—institutions earlier in places where oil and agriculture had attracted migrants.

At that time some critics said the honky-tonk scene was reflective of a coarsening of country music. Predictably traditionalists decried this variation, too; drinkin' songs and cheatin' songs in particular upset them. However, some numbers at least brought deeper implications to their lyrics. In 1942 Ted Daffan's "Born to Lose" had become a honky-tonk anthem at a time when more southwesterners than ever before were heading West in search of jobs. "Born to Lose" became one of the most telling songs in country-music's history, because it evoked a sense of powerlessness felt by those who were not rising in the society. World War II had led to a loss of innocence (or a lessening of hypocrisy, perhaps) and to more direct musical expressions of harsh social realities. The content of honky-tonk lyrics had early veered from previous forms of country music; it was much less concerned with Mother's Bible—traditional stuff—than with dislocation, adultery, divorce, and drink.

In truth, at the time Phillips's dance halls were thriving, many other venues also successfully featured country musicians. While there were plenty of dives in Southern California, what might just as fairly be called country nightclubs also arose there. The Painted Post ("Where the sidewalk ends and the West begins")—owned at various times by Ken Crisman, Hoot Gibson, and Hank Penny—featured top local talent (Wesley Tuttle led the house band). So did Pop's Willow Lake, Cowtown, Valley Ballroom, Cowshed Club, Dick Ross's Ballroom, and Dave Ming's 97th Street Corral. The Palomino in North Hollywood, which became arguably Southern California's most famous country nightclub, was opened by the versatile Hank Penny and Armand Gautier in 1950. Whiteside calls it "one of country music's most fabled venues, the commercial and social focal point of Hollywood's country set." Reflecting Penny's musical eclecticism, the club hosted Monday night jazz sessions at the same time it was considered to be the West's top country booking. It went on to endure many fads and changes in musical taste, but "western jazz" brought it its initial popularity.

Before the Palomino the top venue was the Riverside Rancho, a magnet for the expanding community of country entertainers in Southern California. Operated by Marty Landau, the Rancho's vast 10,000-square-foot dance floor was complimented by a restaurant and three bars. More to the point, however, Whiteside reveals, "the Rancho's regulars were working up a distinct, groove-oriented West Coast sound"—the hot beginnings of what would become the California Sound. That music was certainly popular in the Golden State, even if its name was contrived. Recalls Travis,

> At this time the phrase "Western Swing" was a household word. Spade Cooley had recorded "Shame, Shame On You." Tex Williams had recorded "Smoke! Smoke! Smoke! (That Cigarette)." Al Dexter had had a million seller on his "Pistol-Packin' Mama" record. Bob Wills was heard on every jukebox with his "San Antonio Rose." T. Texas Tyler was doing well with his "Remember Me (When the Candlelights Are Gleaming)." It was practically impossible to wedge your way into the Palace Barn where Red Murrell and his band were playing. A mile down the hill was the Riverside Rancho. You were lucky to find a ticket on a Wednesday night. Tex Williams and his Western Caravan were playing there.

Country saloons thrived during the 1940s, and when the dance halls began to whither in the next decade, the clubs and honky-tonks still sold beer and blared jukebox hits all week, then often offered live bands on weekends. Bandleader Bill Woods recalls,

> While I was at the Blackboard, see, the clubs were getting stronger and better, bigger and better. And guys that had five bucks to spend, they could come in there and dance all night and drink a beer or two for fifty cents a beer or whatever they paid, or a shot of whisky for a dollar. . . . And they could take their girlfriend in there. Where if they went to a dance, it'd cost them all of that, and they'd have to hide their bottle out in the car. So it was eventually coming to a close for ballrooms.

As the 1940s faded into the 1950s significant bands continued to appear all over the state: Floyd Hodges and the Texas Tornadoes in Fresno, Smiley ("Give Me a Red Hot Mama and an Ice Cold Beer") Maxedon in Tulare, Tommy Hays and the Western Swingers in Bakersfield, Billy Jack Wills and his Texas Swing Band in Sacramento. Recalls Don Plank of Woodland,

> After I got back from overseas, I'd see Billy Jack Wills and his boys at Madison Town Hall one weekend, then at Plainfield Station in Woodland the next

one, and at Dunnigan Town Hall on the next one. Mostly it was the same crowd that was just following the band.

Later, I'd call old Billy Jack to book him for the Elks or the American Legion, and he'd say sure thing, and his people'd post signs up everywhere. He always filled whatever hall you had with folks from all over and put on one hell of a show.

Following the war, country-music action actually picked up statewide as travel restrictions eased. Woods points out that after V-J Day, when he left the Richmond area, one of his best jobs was at the Fresno Barn ("That was the number-one spot there. Everybody knew where the Barn was"). In those years, California also became part of the "Cornpone Circuit" followed by major southern entertainers—eventually bringing in such acts as Hank Williams, Little Jimmy Dickens, and Lefty Frizzell. Promoters had to sell many tickets to pay for famous touring acts, however, so large halls were favored. The competing honky-tonks with their jukeboxes or local bands made their money, as Woods pointed out, selling drinks. Eventually—perhaps inevitably, as Woods also pointed out—the large venues began to lose money.

It has become common of late to blame television for the demise of the ballrooms—"TV picture comes in and kills your halls," asserts bandleader and promoter Jimmy Thomason—and the growth of that electronic medium was indeed far from blameless. Ignored in that explanation, however, is the more important fact that the circumstances that had led to the rise of the dance halls were themselves abnormal—the products of social disruption caused by a war. Nightclubs were and would again be the norm.

One of the most famous California country-music clubs—and still a popular nightspot—John DeMarco's 23 Club in Brisbane (an unincorporated area between San Francisco and South San Francisco) opened in 1941. This big-time honky-tonk attracted a significant following from the nearby Hunter's Point shipyard during the war. Guitarist-trumpeter Jimmie Rivers described it as a spot where "the dancing starts at nine and the fights start at ten." Many young men attending Bay Area colleges in the 1940s and '50s thought that attending a Saturday night soiree at "The 23" was a daunting rite of passage, and it often was.

Probably because property values were lower and complaints from neighbors fewer, many country bars tended to be located in "combat

Guest singer Al "Pistol-Packin' Momma" Dexter performs with Ray Whitley's Rhythm Wranglers at the Los Angeles County Barn Dance in 1943. Identifiable from left are Tex Ann Nation, Whitley, Dexter, Muddy Berry on drums, and Tex Atchison on fiddle. From the Gid Tanner Artist File #NF1996, The Southern Folklife Collection, Wilson Library, The University of North Carolina at Chapel Hill.

zones" on the outskirts of towns. Waterloo Road on the edge of Stockton— it featured the locally renowned (or infamous) House of Blue Lights and Georgie's Playhouse, among other dancin' and drinkin' establishments— was a prototypical California combat zone. Educator Leo Ruth from Chico also recalls that the 1073 Club just outside his hometown could live up to that combat zone designation on occasions; "it could be pretty heavy on the combat part," he recalls. It's also true that many honky-tonks never ceased to be Okie joints, in the peculiar California use of "Okie," especially in the eyes of longtime residents. In a sense that's exactly what they were, proudly so: Tex's Barrel House, the Pioneer Club, Okie and Arkie's, the Feedlot, J. D.'s, the Wagon Wheel, the Texahoma Club, and the Corral all advertised with their names a rural bent and an allegiance to migrants from the Southwest. Writes historian James N. Gregory,

> The name out front said "Pioneer Club." A dark and dingy bar near the end of Arvin's commercial strip, it was a place respectable residents made a point of avoiding. The clientele was mostly male, mostly farmworkers.

Its unsavory reputation was probably deserved. Drinking was not the only activity the premises condoned. Men went there to play pool, gamble at cards, flirt with the handful of women present, and, with some frequency, to fight.

Every San Joaquin Valley town had its Pioneer Club by the end of the 1930s, though sometimes one had to scout the lonely outskirts to find it.

Musician, songwriter, tavern-keeper "Okie" Paul Westmoreland, who settled in Sacramento after beginning his career in Los Angeles, understood that his nickname announced pride in his roots; he carried it with dignity not arrogance and captured a vast following of equally unbowed southwesterners plus plenty of Californians (then called "prune pickers") lured by his warm, down-home personality. He ended radio ads with a patented "Tell 'em Okie Paul sent ya, heah!" Westmoreland, more importantly, wrote "Detour (There's a Muddy Road Ahead)," which became a hit for Jimmy Walker, Spade Cooley, Wesley Tuttle, and Jack Rivers and his Muddy Creek Cowboys (featuring Tommy Sargent). That all those sides were evaluated by Billboard's "folk music" reviewers testifies to the continuing confusion of names for this music.

Okie Paul had arrived from Oklahoma during the Dust Bowl migration, and his life in the Golden State, like that of many other musicians, shifted between field work, defense work, and music, principally in the Los Angeles area during World War II. He then moved to Sacramento, and by 1946 he had his own record label, San Antonio, as well as a fifteen-minute radio program. In the next decade, as he explains, "I opened me a beer joint [The Detour Inn] and got behind the bar with my guitar and sold beer and sang." By the mid-1950s, he had become a regional institution, homey as a butter churn, and enjoyed up and down the valley's considerable length.

T. Texas Tyler was another important transplant to California. He had earlier served a long apprenticeship in everything from pool halls to beer bars in the Southwest. The Arkansas native, who understood the symbolic power of that contrived "Texas" label, had an unusual career. Although he sang honky-tonk songs, most of his hit records were based on traditional numbers: "Deck of Cards," "Black Jack David," and "Remember Me (When the Candle Lights Are Gleaming)." His version of Woody and Jack Guthrie's "Oklahoma Hills"—earlier a hit for Jack—was also a top recording for 4 Star.

When Eddie and Lorene Dean joined Hal Blair in 1946 to write the honky-tonk classic "One Has My Name, the Other Has My Heart," no one in Nashville would record it. The composers then turned to a California label, Crystal Records, and in 1947 a much larger California company, Capitol, released Jimmy Wakely's version with Margaret Whiting singing harmony. This song about adultery became a major crossover hit, opening pop doors, too, for cheatin' songs.

Honky-tonk music also contributed to changes in the instrumentation in country. The string bass and drums and later the amplified bass guitar all provided strong rhythm, but electrically amplified lead guitars dominated. In that sense, honky-tonk paved the way for both rockabilly and rock and roll's domination by the same instruments. Those amplified guitars were a great help to musicians trying to be heard over the din of boozy conversations and occasional battles.

Pioneer rockabilly Carl Perkins observed that in honky-tonks, "You have to learn to defend yourself even with a Fender guitar. . . . I love them solid-body guitars." Drummer Henry Sharp recalled, "We were playin' for a bunch of hard-workin' people, and they'd get out there and some guy popped off at this guy's wife, he'd probably hit him. It was just one of those things."

Bandleader Bill Woods remembers that Bakersfield's Blackboard (which for a time was labeled the "Black Board") could be "pretty rough. . . . You could count on three or four fights every night, and there were a couple of killings while I was there. They'd get ahold of that firewater and flex their muscles." Sometimes, though, the clubs' rough reputations outstripped their realities; Buck Owens points out, "People would talk about the Blackboard who'd never been there [and] who was just tellin' stories."

By the 1940s, at any rate, as Michael Bane reports, "the honky-tonk had become a southern institution on a par with southern belles and mint juleps"; the same could have been said for the Golden State. As a result it is no surprise that Joe Maphis, the wondrous guitarist whose career is clearly associated with the development of what came to be called the California Sound, wrote the defining honky-tonk song, "Dim Lights,

Thick Smoke, and Loud, Loud Music" after a night in Bakersfield's dim, smoky, loud Blackboard.

A shift in the lengthy career of Stuart Hamblen illustrated yet another steady tributary to the state's country scene: sacred music. A notorious boozer and brawler, Hamblen was one of three publicized converts (the others were mobster Jim Vaus and Olympic athlete and war hero Louis Zamparini) at Billy Graham's famous 1949 Los Angeles Crusade, which drew 350,000 people. In fact the major convert that year was probably Graham himself. According to biographer Marshall Frady, when the eight-week tent meeting began, Billy was "little more than just another spirited but obscure young gospel-slinger among all the other free-lance evangelists." Thanks in no small measure to the remarkably enthusiastic Hearst newspapers' coverage of that Los Angeles revival, he was converted to a national figure and has remained one.

Hamblen, a preacher's son, certainly needed conversion. During the war, for example, a blackout was in effect on the coast, and Hamblen—reportedly under the influence of firewater—one night shot out street lights until police restrained him. His barroom brawls and drunk-driving citations were the stuff of legend, yet the big Texan had nonetheless paid professional lip service (literally in this case) to religion by squeezing gospel songs into his performances and even hosting ostensibly religious programs, often, as he admitted, with booze on his breath. After his re-birth in Christ, however, he soon wrote a hymn, "It Is No Secret (What God Can Do)," that became a top-10 hit, plus two others—"Open Up Your Heart and Let the Sun Shine In" and "The Lord Is Counting on You"—that became standards. He also—like many other aging country stars—actually changed his life.

Early in the following decade, Hamblen also wrote two other major hits, "(Remember Me) I'm the One Who Loves You" and "This Ole House," and he even ran for president in 1952 on the Prohibition Party ticket. He lost, but he and his wife Suzy, who cohosted various programs with him, would remain major figures on California's country-music scene until their retirement in the early 1960s. In 1971 they returned for another decade of prominence on radio KLAC every Sunday morning with "Cowboy Church of the Air."

Wesley and Cliffie

Two of California's first country-music stars, Colorado-born Wesley Tuttle and native son Cliffie Stone, emerged in the 1930s, matured in the 1940s, and endured longer than most of their peers.

Tuttle, a resident of the San Fernando Valley who had only two fingers on his left, guitar-strumming hand, began playing on the radio with local bands such as Jimmy LeFevre and his Saddle Pals, Sheriff Loyal Underwood and the Arizona Wranglers, and Jack LeFevre and his Texas Outlaws in the early 1930s. He became a significant recording artist in the next decade when he had hits such as "With Tears in My Eyes" (a *Billboard* number one), "Detour," and "I Dreamed That My Daddy Came Home."

His successful records didn't make him rich. "We weren't making much in royalties in those days"; although major pop artists were receiving 4 cents or 5 cents a record, Tuttle explains, "we were getting half a cent or a cent royalty per record. Merle's [Travis's] first records, 'No Vacancy,' 'Divorce Me C.O.D.,' and my 'Detour' and 'With Tears in My Eyes' were all made at a flat rate, $100 a side. We were unknown artists."

Eventually he would be featured—sometimes with his wife Marilyn—as a television personality on Stone's "Hometown Jamboree" as well as "Town Hall Party" and would host the "Foreman Phillips' Show" until he retired in 1957 to become a minister.

Of his relationship with Stone, Tuttle once said, "whenever I needed a bass man, naturally I'd use Cliffie, because he was the best." He was the best at many things, as it turned out. As composer, bandleader, singer, comedian, even as an executive at Capitol Records, the Burbank native was perhaps the Golden State's most important country-music personality in the 1940s and '50s. Certainly, he was its busiest, and he stayed close to home, yet still managed to become a figure of national importance.

The son of banjoist "Herman the Hermit" Snyder, Cliffie broke in on Stuart Hamblen's "Covered Wagon Jubilee" in 1934. He launched his career as a disc jockey that same year—on KFVD's "Wake Up Ranch" five mornings a week—and during that period he made a lifelong commitment to this music. By the mid-1940s, he probably knew the country scene in Southern California as well as anyone, so it was logical for Capitol Records to hire him in 1946 as a consultant in its "folk and hillbilly artists" section. Cliffie changed the department's name to "country."

A number of his own singles were successful, but more importantly he had a great sense of talent. He brought to Capitol such stellar artists as Travis, Hank Thompson, Leon McAuliffe, Tennessee Ernie Ford, and Tex Williams. Collaborating with some of these entertainers, Stone also became a songwriter of note. He has been assigned at least partial credit for country classics such as "New Steel Guitar Rag," "No Vacancy," "So Round, So Firm, So Fully Packed," "Sweet Temptation," and "Divorce Me C.O.D." Finally, Stone's variety show, "Hometown Jamboree," debuted in the late 1940s and became a Saturday night ritual with families in the Los Angeles area. It remained on the air for ten years and featured a virtual who's who of West Coast country.

◄ ►   ◄ ►   ◄ ►

In the South during that same decade, Bill Monroe and his Blue Grass Boys were creating something close to a musical counterrevolution, completing a process begun late in the 1930s. With his guitar-picking brother Charlie, mandolinist Bill had formed an innovative duet early in the Great Depression, but the actual realization of bluegrass was achieved by Bill's 1945–48 Blue Grass Boys. That band—Lester Flatt on vocals and guitar, Chubby Wise on fiddle, Howard Watts on bass, and Earl Scruggs on banjo—produced what one wag called a "new old-time" music based on up-tempo, high-pitched acoustic runs and Bill's high-harmony vocals with Lester. The leader's mandolin and Scruggs's banjo demonstrated that those instruments could dominate as fiddles once had. To some, bluegrass music seemed to be the antithesis of honky-tonk and western swing, but writer Dave Samuelson has suggested it could be "considered country music's equivalent of jazz." This innovative return to the acoustic string band found an immediate audience.

In the late 1940s developments in Dixie began altering the balance of country, now a national music. First, the ever-popular "Grand Ole Opry" (much improved thanks to the vision of Jim Denny and Jack Stapp) on radio station WSM finally achieved superiority over the "National Barn Dance" at Chicago's WLS. Then the forming of the [Roy] Acuff–[Fred] Rose publishing company led other publishers and record companies to open offices and studios in the Tennessee town. Later Jim Denny and Webb Pierce opened Cedarwood Music in Nashville, while Denny's booking agency there came to control many major stars.

In the next decade the development in Nashville of the disc jockey–led Country Music Association reinforced the Tennessee city's centrality. Reports music historian Philip H. Ennis, "The Hollywood-based motion

picture industry and the large southern California country music establishment . . . lost out in the process." The reason they lost out is that
Nashville needed country music more, wanted it more, and certainly
cared more about it. Hollywood was growing bloated with and blasé
about entertainment businesses. The mainstream entertainment industry
in California seemed little concerned over the intense rivalry between
country musicians here and those in Tennessee.

For two decades California-based entertainers had more than held
their own, but in 1949 all of them were eclipsed by the emergence of the
greatest of honky-tonk singers and writers, Hank Williams. His remarkable catalog of songs was written for Acuff-Rose, and on June 11, 1949,
he joined the "Opry." How dominant was Hank? Explains *The Illustrated
History of Country Music*, "the country charts were dominated by West Coasters from 1945 to 1949—that is, until the coming of Hank Williams."
Like Jimmie Rodgers before him, Hank was a fulcrum upon whom major periods in this music balanced. Scholar Mary Bufwak summarizes his
accomplishments well: "From 1947 to 1953 Hank Williams took the
honky-tonk sound that had developed in the drinking and dancing establishments of the East Texas oil fields to national audiences. . . . It was
filled with the emotional intensity of displaced people and returning
war veterans. Cries of loneliness were carried in the vocals and in the steel
guitar." Hank became, among other things, the bard for postwar people
who hadn't quite settled: the drifters, the yearners.

As the decade ended, anxiety once again began to rise in America; the
Cold War and nuclear threats moved to center stage. Nevertheless the
1940s saw the Golden State rise to the top of country music, which enjoyed its largest, most varied audience ever in the state as more and better music was being produced. Wartime demographics had much to do
with this, gathering large, heterogeneous audiences to West Coast venues
where western swing ruled and attracting many talented musicians from
elsewhere.

Country's appeal grew so much in the 1940s that many in California
didn't seem to notice that Nashville was in the process of assuming musical primacy. The Southern California scene in particular was so rich in
entertainment that country music constituted no more than a small slice;
in Nashville, Tennessee, country became the whole pie. As a result, many
would come to believe that had always been this music's capital.

The rise and fall of Spade Cooley is a representative California tale, embody-ing the best and the worst of country music here. It also mirrors trends that led to western swing's widespread popularity in dance halls and ball-rooms, its translation to television, and the eventual heavy encroachment of pop styles into this music.

Donnell Clyde Cooley was a poor boy who rose high, partook of his rewards, then tumbled tragically. When he murdered his wife Ella Mae in 1961, his accomplishments as an entertainer were suddenly obscured by his horrible crime and the sensational reporting that followed. He moved from entertainment legend to tabloid monster and died before a prom-ised pardon, but his musical legacy remains significant indeed.

An Oklahoma native, young Cooley traveled with his family, first to Oregon, then to Modesto, as they searched for better opportunities. "I was born poor and raised poor," Spade later commented. Like Bob Wills, he was the son of a country fiddler and had played in square dances from the age of eight. While in Oregon his father struck up a friendship with a local music teacher, who in turn helped hone young Donnell's skills. One-quarter Cherokee, Donnell also attended Chimawah Indian School, where he studied both cello and violin. As a result, he was unusually well trained for a country fiddler.

In Oregon, then in California, young Cooley played at dances and hoedowns, earning only a dollar or two for a night's work during the De-pression. During days, he was a farm laborer, while nights he sought mu-sic gigs. Encouraged by local responses to his playing, he traveled to the Los Angeles area seeking a club job. No luck. Eventually, he returned to Modesto and was hired at a small club for $15 a week. It wasn't much, but it sure beat sweating in the fields. He earned something else then, too. According to writer Rich Kienzle, "One night in a poker game he won three straight flush hands, all in spades, and won himself a nickname as well."

In 1934 (or 1937, stories conflict here)—married and a father—he again ventured to Southern California, arriving with 6 cents in his pocket. This time his luck was better. He worked in clubs and saloons in the area with local acts, including the Sons of the Pioneers. He met and hit it off with Len Slye, a former member of that group, who was then being transformed into Roy Rogers. Soon Spade was Roy's stand-in and was acting in B westerns.

Primarily, though, Cooley played with various bands in the area—most prominently the Jimmy Wakely Trio—and he even sang briefly with the Riders of the Purple Sage. All the while his musical reputation grew. Soon he was a favorite at recording sessions. Remembers another Rogers, Smokey, composer of "Shame, Shame on You" and one of the top musicians of the period, "Spade was the first fiddle player called." Cooley also fronted small groups at various clubs. Smokey recalls, "He could take a mediocre two or three guys and make 'em look like a million dollars."

The great flowering of country nightclubs and dance halls that occurred with the influx of soldiers, sailors, and war-industry workers during the 1940s seemed to present unlimited opportunities. Cooley, who could provide down-home music with a swing beat that resembled the popular big bands of that era, was quickly a favorite. For a time he was featured with various ensembles at the Venice Pier Ballroom. Foreman Phillips heard Spade perform and proposed that he form his own band; by 1942 his group was a hit at Venice. The next year Cooley broke with Phillips and leased the 10,000-square-foot Riverside Rancho for himself. When even that couldn't hold his crowds, Spade leased the biggest hall in the area, the Santa Monica Ballroom. He filled it, too.

Cooley's persona was a major reason for that success. He seemed to dance as he directed his band, and his own solos were consistently impressive. Writer Ken Griffis points out that Spade's "fiddle sounds were decidedly different from anything previously heard in country and western music." With the addition of standouts like Smokey Rogers, Tex Williams, and California-born jazz-style steel player Earl "Joaquin" Murphey, the ensemble—Cooley called it his orchestra—virtually defined western swing for many in Southern California, but among themselves the musicians called their music "Indian jazz."

By then the leader was in the habit of referring to virtually any male as "son." "How are you, son?" he might say to an old pal or an unknown fan. According to Merle Travis, when the marvelous Murphey was auditioning for the orchestra, "He played the best he could and he got so worked up at the end that he fainted. Spade said, 'Son, I'd like to use you, but I don't know. . . . How often do you faint?'"

Cooley was also known as an easy touch, a man who had made big bucks, who would make bigger ones before he was through, and who was always generous. His manager Bobbie Bennett recalls, "He didn't ever want to displease anyone. No matter what they asked, he answered, 'That's a deal, son.'"

Spade was a man deeply troubled by jealousy, too, and he could be a hard drinker, ornery when drunk, a trait Spade reportedly shared with Bob Wills, among many others in the business. "He was a Dr. Jekyll and Mr. Hyde–type person," says Bennett. Like many other jealous men, Spade was a reputed womanizer, a trait that doesn't set him apart from many of his fellow musicians. Speaking off the record—*always* off the record, it seems—country star after country star acknowledges, often in titillating terms, the easy availability of sex. Handsome Spade was said to have been particularly attractive to women.

In 1945 the Cooley orchestra recorded "Shame, Shame on You" (with Tex Williams on vocal), the Smokey Rogers tune that would become their theme song; it was the year's top country record. Shortly thereafter, after his first marriage ended in divorce, Spade wed vocalist Ella Mae Evans. His music meanwhile continued moving further away from traditional country. This was especially true after 1946, when orchestra stars Williams and Rogers left to form their top-rated band the Western Caravan.

Cooley reorganized, and his new group was a dance music ensemble complete with brass and reeds. Writer Kienzle elaborates: "The sound became smoother and may have brought pop music fans into the Cooley camp, since only fiddles and steel guitar distinguished it from any other big bands." Johnny Gimble, a fiddler with Bob Wills, has observed that "western swing got pretty organized," and it can be said that Spade's orchestra epitomized that variation. Employing the Gimble definition, it must also be said that the Wills band played something different from Cooley's group, a jazzier "Texas swing."

Spade's sidemen added instruments—dual accordions (played by George Bamby and Pedro DePaul) and harp (played by Spike Featherstone)—that were by no means common in country bands or mainstream swing bands. Along with those three Smokey played banjo as well as guitar, and Spade added three or four other fiddlers to the group. It eventually grew to twenty-five musicians, probably the largest country ensemble of all.

In 1950 Cooley signed with Decca Records, but as writer Al Quaglieri points out his orchestra's "overwrought recording bore little resemblance to the spirited country swing of their earlier heyday." Over the years, too, the band was gifted with vocalists such as Tex Williams, Carolina Cotton, and Rex Williams. At one point later in his career Spade even tried an all-female orchestra; exactly how he "tried" them was of course the subject of much humorous speculation.

No one disagrees that Cooley was broadening and softening the image of West Coast country, while considerably expanding its audience. Some sense of the musical synergy going on in Southern California is revealed by jazz singer Dorothy Rae, then a popular vocalist in Los Angeles area nightclubs. She recalls that Spade heard her and invited her to join his band. "He said he'd rather teach me to sing country than teach music to a country girl," she chuckles. "So I did that for a year and had a great time singing country tunes for part of the evening and then getting together afterward for jam sessions." She adds, "Spade had some great jazz musicians in his band."

During that period, too, Cooley continued to appear in western movies, but now his entire band joined him. Explains writer Bruce Henstell, "In these films the hero just happened to have a friend, played by Cooley, who just happened to have a band out on the prairie all set and rarin' to let loose with a few tunes at a convenient pause in the story line. A reviewer once wrote: 'In the picture but not in the plot was Spade Cooley.'" The bandleader's movie experiences not only provided him with more visual recognition to a future television audience but also made him comfortable before a camera.

Spade always cut a dashing figure on stage. Speedy West, who played pedal steel for the group, reports, "He was outstanding, I believe as good a showman as I ever saw hit a stage as a bandleader. He was not comical

Spade Cooley, Tex Williams, and Smokey Rogers, 1943. From the Gid Tanner
Artist File #NF1996, The Southern Folklife Collection, Wilson Library, The
University of North Carolina at Chapel Hill.

or anything. He had spirit, he had poise. He had lots of enthusiasm, a big
smile on his face, and he jumped from one side of that stage to another,
constantly wavin' that fiddle bow and then pointin' it at the audience and
wavin' it at the band as a baton." "There was *nobody* dressed as sharp as
him," adds Hank Penny. Spade owned a hundred hand-tailored suits,
thirty-six pairs of boots, and a yacht to wear them on. He had come a
long way from dirt farming, and many of the fans who assembled to enjoy his music felt they had, too.

Cooley's down-home public manner made him something of a character in Los Angeles. When he bought himself that yacht, it proved something of a mystery to him and, as Henstell reports,

In his first few weeks of fitful sailing Cooley managed to fall off the boat, losing a camera and wrist watch; bash in the boat's side and sink it in Santa Monica Harbor; put its sails up upside down; and, finally, smash it into the Hyperion outfall.

"But I'm a-gettin' the hang of it now," he said, folksying it up for the press. "I bought me some books on navigation. . . . Heck, this sailin's easy. The man showed me where the wheel was and what button to push. That's all I need."

Soon his ease before cameras, his colorful attire, and that down-home persona would pay large dividends. Spade's showmanship came to the attention of a genius of early television, Klaus Landsberg, who was directing KTLA, the first commercially licensed station in Los Angeles. Cooley's ballroom appearances had long been virtual variety shows with many soloists and guests. It was not difficult to convert that to a television show, "The Hoffman Hayride." Popular Dick Lane ("Ol' Leather Britches") was his announcer and straight man. Combined with bumpkin humor by Penny and enough good music to enthrall viewers, "Your Fiddlin' Friend," as Spade was then called, emerged as the top television figure in one of America's major markets.

The leader often attired himself in his trademark shirt adorned with musical notes and clefs, while his band members wore paneled blouses with dark spades on the chests; they seemed just right for a visual medium. Writer Norman Corwin has pointed out that the introduction of radio had been a revolutionary event, while television seemed to be an extension of movies; Spade apparently understood that. Henstell further observes, "Los Angeles loved Spade Cooley, and in the late 1940s, 75 percent of the receivers in Los Angeles were tuned each Saturday night to "The Hoffman Hayride." Called the Ed Sullivan of the West Coast, Spade featured such "country" guests as Sarah Vaughn, Frank Sinatra, and Jerry Lewis on his show. "The Hoffman Hayride" was awarded Emmys as Los Angeles's top local program in both 1952 and 1953.

The leader's fame became national, and predictably major networks soon came calling. Penny saw a deeper dimension of Cooley in his response to them: "I remember his refusal to move his TV program from the local network to one of the major networks, because he felt a loyalty to the local station for giving him a start. He could have made a lot more money by the move, and I respect a person who will do something like that." In light of the sad events that followed, Penny's observation suggests the complexity of Spade's character.

By the middle of the 1950s, however, even Cooley's popularity began to wane as new tastes such as rockabilly emerged, as networks rather than local presentations continued their climb to prominence, and as Lawrence Welk began to dominate the Los Angeles market. Spade officially retired in 1958, performing only sporadically thereafter, and he started building a huge entertainment center, called Water Wonderland, in the Tehachapi foothills of the Mojave Desert northeast of Los Angeles. As had become Cooley's style, it was a flamboyant project that was to include an amusement park, a ballroom, and three artificial lakes. During that period, too, he suffered his first heart attack.

Spade also had a luxurious ranch built in remote Willow Springs for his wife and two children. A second heart attack followed, and shortly thereafter problems in his marriage became public. Bobbie Bennett explained, "He virtually kept her [his wife] a prisoner." The couple separated, and he announced his decision to file for divorce. Ella Mae returned, hoping for a reconciliation, but what actually followed ruined several lives.

After a meeting with business associates on April 3, 1961, a drunken Cooley beat his wife to death. The horror of the crime was compounded by the fact that he called their fourteen-year-old daughter home from a friend's house and forced her to witness the final stages of his brutal attack; she would later offer damning testimony at his trial.

To some Spade's fierce deed seemed to undo all the positive things that he had previously contributed, including his considerable part in overturning California's negative stereotype of Okies. It seemed to be a betrayal not only of his wife and children but of country music itself, and as his manager recalls, "Entertainers in the field . . . were very harsh as far as he was concerned." Rich Kienzle agrees that "he got little support from his fellow western performers."

During the trial he wrote to his children Melody and Donnell, Jr., "Today in court they will fight to take my life. I want you to know that no matter what happens to me, I love you both with my heart and soul. You can't help it if I love you—even more than I ever did before—you see, I loved your mother with all my heart." Spade was convicted and sentenced to life imprisonment, and he suffered yet another heart attack. As a result he was sent to the department of corrections' medical facility at Vacaville.

There he became a exemplary prisoner, instructing other inmates in music, and he was noted for his generally cooperative behavior. He even led an inmate band. In another letter to his children, he wrote, "It may be asking too much to be your daddy again, but I pray every day and night that God will let you know someday that I have been sick for some time"; the context made it unclear if he was referring to his drinking, his temper, his heart disease, or all of them.

In November of 1969, not long before he was due to be paroled, he was allowed to perform at a "Grand Ole Opry Spectacular" benefit concert in Oakland. Playing with many of his old cronies there, he entertained a crowd of 3,000. "He did the first show," recalls his son, who was twenty-one years old at the time. "He went backstage to sign autographs, and I went with him. He collapsed and died in my arms."

Red Murrell, who was in the band that backed Cooley on that night, said he believed Spade had elevated western swing to its highest level. "Not only was Cooley himself an accomplished musician (a violinist, not a fiddler . . .), but he introduced many innovations through his orchestra and established them by virtue of his showmanship."

Hank Penny remembered, "Not long before his death, Spade had said to me, 'Son, do you think that I would be able to get out of prison and get back into show business?' I said, 'Spade, I have no doubt about it.' Now I was kiddin' just a little bit, because I knew that people would give him a hard time and make his life extremely unhappy."

Cooley never had to find that out.

"Town Hall Party," televised locally each week from Compton and broadcast nationwide as "Western Ranch Party," illustrated the abundance of
country talent in Southern California during the 1950s. One 1957 show,
for example, supplemented the distinguished regular cast—Johnny Bond,
Wesley Tuttle, Joe and Rose Lee Maphis, Les "Carrot Top" Anderson, the
Collins Kids, Skeets McDonald, Tex Carman, Fiddlin' Kate, and the singing
host, Tex Ritter—with three guest stars: Ray Price, George Jones, and Tex
Williams.

That remarkable gathering of talent would have stopped traffic almost
anywhere; yet in Southern California it hardly merited a nod. More and
more entertainers had continued streaming to the Golden State after
World War II, for it remained America's primary destination. But because
the Los Angeles area's surfeit of pop culture buried them, many country
musicians and their numerous fans still felt like outsiders.

In 1950 Lee Gillette, the California architect of countrypolitan music,
moved to Capitol Records's pop division, and Ken Nelson took over
country recording. Nelson would leave a remarkable legacy, due in part to
his instinct not to overproduce artists, allowing them to sound like themselves. "You hire a person for what they can do," he later explained. "If
you infuse yourself into every record, they're all gonna be the same." He
was moving in almost the opposite direction of Nashville's increasingly
intrusive producers, and by the end of the decade his work at Capitol
considerably energized the label's country division.

Instead of slipping into a recession following World War II, the 1950s
California in which Gillette and Nelson worked had embarked on sus-
tained economic growth. Only two decades later, the state's economy

would be the eighth most productive on Earth. Returning military veterans and their families, many of them from other parts of the country, enriched the population. "Young, productive, highly skilled, and eager for success," report historians Richard Rice, William Bullough, and Richard Orsi in *The Elusive Eden*, "they gave the state a transfusion of new blood and great energy." Due to Cold War pressures the defense and aerospace industries continued growing until they rivaled agribusiness, entertainment, tourism, and oil as the state's "peacetime" leaders.

At the same time the children of earlier migrations were now taking advantage of California's educational opportunities, matriculating to universities, and beginning the process that would make them movers and shakers in the state's dynamic society. Some of them at least would not be farm laborers or oil field workers; they would be owners and bosses, legislators and artists. But their enhanced credentials would begin to produce a generation gap within the families of some erstwhile migrants: "School don't teach you ever'thing."

The state's ongoing population boom, too, brought physical changes most evidenced by the increase in construction of houses, schools, and (perhaps most important of all) freeways. Southern California in particular became an automotive society in the 1950s, with suburbs sprawling in all directions. When television joined that postwar mix, luring more and more neighbors indoors, some residents complained of a breakdown of community. Discontent among intellectuals was intensifying, too, triggered not only by that lost sense of community but perhaps even more by the result of international nuclear threats and national red baiting. Artists and academics, who had in large measure conformed to wartime demands, now found themselves particularly at odds with middle-class conformity.

Discontent also flared in that frustrated segment of the working population that had not managed to advance even during the heated wartime economy. Country's most powerful voice of blue-collar dissatisfaction, Hank Williams, came from the South in the late 1940s and dominated the music in the early 1950s. He captivated fans in California as he had on the "Louisiana Hayride" and the "Grand Ole Opry."

The war's shock waves still reverberated during his brief career, especially among those folks who resented having largely missed an elevation in educational or socioeconomic level. Military service and war-related jobs in distant places had also cut the umbilical cord for many individuals, and that led to legions of drifters soaking up beer in honky-tonks that reminded them of home, shades of the earlier rural diaspora. Williams's music epitomized the dark side of the postwar experience, a sense not only of having left roots behind but also of having been left behind by society.

So important did Williams become that a 1994 article by Charles Hirshberg and Robert Sullivan in *Life* magazine arbitrarily ranked the "100 Most Important People in the History of Country"; Williams was number one because he "wrote the rules for what everyone since 1950 has considered true country."

Ironically this quintessential country singer and writer also contributed many crossover songs; pop vocalists had great success with Hank's numbers. Major impulses to "go pop" had surfaced in both Nashville and Hollywood in the late 1940s, as exemplified by the rise of Jimmy Wakely. His success (like Eddie Arnold's in the South) then prompted country-music executives to reach for a more general audience by adopting a "softer" approach to recordings. But not without protests.

Self-appointed purists had fussed when established stars like Vernon Dahlart, Gene Autry, Red Foley, Slim Whitman, Wakely, and Arnold moved toward pop. They complained louder when pop vocalist Patti Page had a blockbuster hit with Pee Wee King and Redd Stewart's "The Tennessee Waltz" in the early 1950s or when San Francisco's Rusty Draper confused definitions with lively crossover hits like "Freight Train." Some even complained when Tennessee Ernie Ford recorded his version of Merle Travis's "Sixteen Tons" in 1955. According to scholar Douglas B. Green, "The occasional crossover did have the effect of continuing the trend that Autry and his fellow cowboys had begun: the de-yokelization of the country song among non-country fans. The seeds of acceptance among a wide public were beginning to sprout, slowly but surely paving the way for the nationwide acceptance of the country music that was to come."

But more important disruptions were then in play. Social upheavals that had begun during World War II evinced themselves in increasingly high profile as old forms of suppression or habitual behavior were ignored or defied. Everything from white kids listening to what had previously been "race" records to the growing cult of beat writers and poets to the organized Negro resistance to segregation bespoke the surge of change. This isn't the only way things can be, rebels asserted. Youngsters even freed themselves from family radios (and from their parents' control) when transistors and radios in their own autos allowed them to indulge their private inclinations.

Meanwhile the uncompromising performances of Williams, Lefty Frizzell, T. Texas Tyler, and the Maddox Brothers and Rose, among others, remained exceedingly popular in the state because, unvarnished, they touched universal truths. Honky-tonk variations, especially as performed by the demonstrative Maddoxes, helped release white bodies from traditional notions of decorum as surely as Pentecostals had earlier been freed from high-Protestant conventions; more and more younger white artists began to behave on stage like the lively Maddoxes.

In fact how singers moved became an issue. Many blacks of course, like many "holy rollers," had long ignored the body-spirit dichotomy, so they were pioneers in this aspect of the postwar musical revolution. In southern juke joints and nightclubs, Negro artists had been playing and singing and dancing to a form of music that came to be called rhythm and blues ("dancin' blues, man, dancin' blues," explained singer Tee Dixon). And in many white honky-tonks, variations of a closely related hard-driving and danceable music that would become rockabilly was heard. The African influence in rockabilly was of course nothing new to country; earlier stars such as Bob Wills and Jimmie Rodgers were arguably *more* overtly black in their styles. What may be most surprising about rockabilly is how *white* it remained, "sung by redneck wildmen" recalls Larry Nelson, a youthful fan in those days.

For white kids in the Golden State early in the decade—a period of bland popular music ("How Much Is That Doggie in the Window?" "Shrimp Boats Are Coming," "Three Coins in the Fountain," etc.)—delicious validations of their own emerging sexuality could first be heard on those "race" records: the heat of Big Joe Turner in "Cherry Red," the Dominoes delivering "Sixty-Minute Man," or Little Richard's explosive "Tutti Frutti." Ironically rhythm and blues was more acceptable than country to middle-class white kids then because listening to it was considered rebellious, not "Okie."

A group of white country singers and musicians in Memphis, strongly influenced by upbeat gospel music, adopted rhythm-and-blues styles to express their own powerful feelings. The result was rockabilly, the seeds of rock and roll, a strongly rhythmic music that confounded definitions in a label-bound business. In 1956, for example, Carl Perkins's "Blue Suede Shoes" climbed to number two on the pop chart, two on the rhythm-and-blues chart, and two on the country chart. Jerry Lee Lewis's "Whole Lot of Shakin' Goin' On" managed number one on both country and rhythm-and-blues charts and number three on the pop chart.

That tangling of categories disturbed traditionalists, but there were more threatening dimensions to this sound; as *The Illustrated History of Country Music* points out, "What made rockabilly such a drastically new music was its spirit, which bordered on mania. . . . Country music had never known such vehement emotion." Rockabilly was also sung by "white trash," rather than the music's increasingly gentrified aristocrats in Tennessee. "There was a real class thing going on in the music then," recalled an anonymous, middle-aged fan at the Johnny Otis Red-Beans-and-Rice Festival in Santa Rosa in 1995. As such, rockabilly might be seen as one aspect of the social upwelling (especially the white underclass's rise) during and after World War II, just as was the youth culture.

A musical civil war broke out by mid-decade, with rockabilly and rhythm and blues energizing the emergent teenage community. The postwar baby boom and relative affluence contributed to the youth culture's coalescence, but changes in perception were most important. The concept of "youth" as a distinct stage between childhood and adulthood was relatively new in the United States. Earlier in this century rural citizens in particular went to work young, married young, procreated young, and died young.

For members of the growing middle class, however, the development of a subculture of often-discontented adolescents in the 1950s seemed to be a matter of more youngsters, more money, and more leisure. Goals and imperatives endorsed by the older generation were no longer sacrosanct to kids listening on their own radios to programming aimed at them. Recalls singer Neil Young,

Originally I wanted to become a farmer. I was planning on going to agricultural college and getting my own farm. I was going to raise chickens at the beginning. Then eventually branch out into a full farm. I started seri-

Lefty Frizzell. From the Gid Tanner Artist File #NF1996, The Southern Folklife
Collection, Wilson Library, The University of North Carolina at Chapel Hill.

ously working on this project when I was about ten years of age. I even got
the chickens and set up a coop.

But then something unexpected happened. I heard Elvis Presley for the
first time.

The lightning rod in all this was Presley. Music writer Greil Marcus
argues that "no white man had so deeply absorbed black music, and
transformed it, since Jimmie Rodgers." *The Illustrated History of Country
Music* counters by arguing that Presley was actually a product of that
braided black-white affinity rather than white usurpation of black music and that he "derived the bulk of his music from country and pop

sources." His performance style was much influenced by rhythm-and-blues artists.

What did Presley himself think of these matters? "The colored folk been singin' it and playin' it just the way I'm doin' it now, man, for more years than I know. Nobody paid it no mind till I goosed it up." He told Bob Festavan, "My stuff is just hopped-up country."

The young truck driver had cut a demo record at Sam Phillips's Memphis Recording Service, and Marian Kreisker MacInnis, who managed the small studio, sent a tape of the unknown singer to her boss. She later explained, "The reason I taped Elvis was this: over and over I remember Sam saying, 'If I could only find a white man who had the Negro feel, I could make a billion dollars.'" Although he didn't immediately realize it, Phillips had found his singer, and *somebody* would indeed make a billion.

Presley's magic seemed as much linked to his inherent sensuality as to his "blackness," his Pentecostalism, or his redneck roots. Not just any singer could have accomplished what he did. Marcus asserts that Elvis was "a kind of necessity . . . existing in every culture that needs to produce the perfect, all-inclusive metaphor for itself." Along with Presley, Johnny Cash, Roy Orbison, Carl Perkins, and Jerry Lee Lewis endured as major stars, and other rockabillies such as California-connected Wanda Jackson, Eddie Cochran, Gene Vincent, and Ricky Nelson also enjoyed considerable success.

Most movers and shakers in Tennessee did their best to ignore this latest progression in country music. Along with Jim Reeves, Elvis was named the top new country artist of 1953 by *Billboard* magazine, but he was granted only one appearance on the "Grand Ole Opry." Writer Bob Millard asserts that Elvis and the other rockabillies "blasted a hole in country music big enough to drive a pink Cadillac through. Country's establishment rejected him as fast as it could."

The consequences of that rejection were, as it turned out, far more harmful to traditional country music, especially in the South, than to Presley. "Losing the majority of rural youth, and subsequently a string of radio outlets to . . . rock 'n' roll," points out Millard, "country music nearly didn't recover." To regain popularity, producers promoted what came to be called the Nashville Sound, which pushed country performances toward pop-oriented audiences. Producer and guitar ace Chet Atkins told writer Nicholas Dawidoff, "I don't know if there is such a thing as Nashville Sound. We took the twang out of it. . . . What we did was, we tried to make hit records. We wanted to keep our jobs." They accomplished that, but according to writer Chet Flippo, they also "thoroughly emasculated country music."

Some in California weren't having any of it. On the evening of April 10, 1957, the state and rockabilly enjoyed a public wedding when Ricky Nelson lip-synched his own recording of "I'm Walkin'" on the nationally broadcast "Adventures of Ozzie and Harriet." Teenager Nelson was in the thrall of the rockabillies, especially Carl Perkins, whom he called "my idol." Rick's older brother David remembers the two of them singing in the echoing—thus flattering—confines of a bathroom at home, and biographer Joel Selvin asserts that "Southern rock & roll stung Ricky. 'Blue Suede Shoes' changed his life." If so, young Nelson was typical of his generation in California. Unlike other kids, though, Ricky could do something about it.

The exact route that led to his musical debut was largely dictated by Nelson's father Ozzie. The casual, bumbling dad played by the senior Nelson on the family's television show was virtually the opposite of the real man. Ozzie Nelson was an astute businessman who had been a popular bandleader and who possessed a special understanding of show business. He was also more than a little controlling. "If you want to sing," he told his son, "if you want to make records, there's a right way to go about it."

As a result of Ozzie's knowledge and clout, Ricky enjoyed a debut like no other. The father arranged for his son to be recorded by Verve (with major sidemen like Merle Travis and Earl Palmer), singing a cover of Fats Domino's "I'm Walkin,'" plus "A Teenager's Romance" and "You're My One and Only Love." Ricky himself had considered cutting a Hank Williams song, but Ozzie's choices prevailed. The first two of those recorded numbers were released as the youngster's initial sides after his singing debut on the television show, and the impact of that earlier television performance was immediate and overwhelming. Both songs vaulted onto the national charts and remained there for five months, selling more than 700,000 copies. Rarely had a beginner enjoyed such success; never had one enjoyed such exposure.

Nelson's musical career was certainly energized by the introduction of his numbers on the national television show and by the preexisting popularity he brought to his new pursuit. As a result his string of hits was long and eclectic, with a surprising country tilt, including Hank Williams's "My Bucket's Got a Hole in It," Johnny and Dorsey Burnette's "Believe What You Say," Sharon Sheeley's "Poor Little Fool," and his own "Travelin' Man." By 1958 he was accompanied by the powerful rockabilly guitar of James Burton, by the country strumming of Joe Maphis, and by bassist Joe Osborne. Some of his songs "were as raw as anything coming out of Memphis," argues music writer Michael Bane. Ricky—that nice, clean-cut boy on television—was able to bring rockabilly into homes that had not previously tolerated it.

Predictably Nelson's California and show business base led many people to consider him a fake who had enjoyed a backdoor entry into recording. Thus they did not recognize how good he was becoming. By the time his third and fourth records were released, "he was," writes Selvin, "no longer a Hollywood imitation of rock & roll but was beginning to sound like the genuine article." California rockabilly had its own star.

➤   ◄ ►   ◄ ►

Hank and Eddie

In Southern California in 1954 two unrelated white singers named Cochran, Hank and Eddie, teamed up. Mississippi-native Hank and Oklahoma-native Eddie were living in Bell Gardens when they joined forces. Hank had been a regular at the Riverside Rancho—as a customer, not a performer—and the two may have met there. Eddie had come of age in the Golden State, since his family relocated in 1949 when he was eleven. When the duo joined forces, teenager Eddie was backup guitarist behind aspiring vocalist Hank. The two eventually became the Cochran Brothers and were big favorites in the Los Angeles area, playing everything from store openings to county fairs.

They recorded two country singles ("Mr. Fiddle" and "Guilty Conscience") in 1955 but moved to rockabilly after seeing Elvis Presley perform in Dallas. Their next record ("Tired and Sleepy" and "Fool's Paradise") was described as "frantic, country-based rock." In 1956 the duo broke up, and Hank headed back into traditional country music as singer and composer, performing at such undistinguished venues as the Fort Ord Noncommissioned Officers' Club before he began to gain some recognition after becoming a regular on the "California Hayride" television show in Stockton. Eventually he moved to Nashville, and while his singing career never took off he wrote a string of hits that made him a premier songwriter: "Make the World Go Away," "Don't Touch Me," "I Want to Go with You," "Don't You Ever Get Tired of Hurting Me?" and (with Harlan Howard) "I Fall to Pieces."

Eddie, on the other hand, was destined to become one of rock-and-roll's tragic tales of great promise and early death. In 1956 he sang "Twenty Flight Rock" in the classic rock movie *The Girl Can't Help It,* made the charts with a teenybopper ballad "Smoochin' in the Balcony" the next year, then became a major star with the chart-topping "Summertime Blues" in 1958, a song he cowrote with Jerry Capheart.

A pioneer of overdubbing, he followed that classic record (in which he played and sang all parts) with another multitrack hit, "C'mon Everybody," then with "Somethin' Else," both of which made the charts in the United States and became hits in Britain, where he was a major influence on the rock scene. He also appeared in two other movies, *Untamed Youth* (1957) and *Go Johnny Go* (1959). By 1960 he was a signal figure in the youth-driven rock scene. That spring he toured Britain, and on April 17, a day after appearing at the Bristol Hippodrome, he was killed—at only twenty-one—in an auto accident that also injured his fiancée Sharon Sheeley and his buddy Gene "Be-Bop-a-Lula" Vincent.

As a songwriter Cochran's wry revelations of teenage life during that period of the emerging youth culture rivaled Chuck Berry's. He was also ahead of his time in studio techniques, but he is best remembered as a gifted guitarist and a dynamic performer. *The Encyclopedia of Rock* asserts that he was "probably the most widely talented rock star of the fifties."

◄ ►　　◄ ►　　◄

For a decade or more before Ricky Nelson's first record, the Maddox Brothers and Rose had been performing protorockabilly—a hot, blended music with no regard for labels. As Fred Maddox explained, "We was always about ten or twelve years ahead of ourselves, but it was just a-happenin', so we just let it happen." So did other established West Coast performers such as Wynn Stewart and Ferlin Husky, as well as emerging artists such as Glen Glenn (né Glen Trout), whose "Everybody's Movin'" made the charts; Jackie Lee Waukeen Cochran, who recorded for Decca; and especially the popular Collins Kids, television favorites whose "wholesome, all-America looks made them the perfect ambassadors of the new rockabilly style to a country audience," points out writer Richard Carlin.

Lorrie and Larry Collins joined the cast of "Town Hall Party" in 1953 after moving west from Oklahoma. Raised there on a dairy near the tiny town of Pretty Water, the kids came with their parents to California after eight-year-old Lorrie had won a talent contest in Tulsa. She and her younger brother served an apprenticeship that allowed them to change as the music changed, grow as it grew; they were already professionals by the time rockabilly had a name. Bouncing Larry became a hot guitarist, a protégé of Joe Maphis, and he played his own version of Joe's double-necked instrument. Pretty Lorrie was a teen heartthrob with genuine gifts as a vocalist, so the act soon transcended the "cute kids" category as they belted out everything from country traditionals to hard-core rockabilly.

When Lorrie and Ricky Nelson became romantically entangled late in the decade, fan magazines loved it. As Lorrie remembers,

> We just had a lot in common because of our youth, the music business, country music, and he admired a lot of the people that were really good friends of mine. It was taking him out of "Ozzie and Harriet" into the music business, and that's where I think he really wanted to be. . . .
>
> As young as we were, how do you know what you feel? But at that particular time, I guess we really loved each other a lot.

Nelson's biographer Selvin refers to Lorrie as "the first real love in his life." As luck would have it, she would soon marry flamboyant promoter and manager Stu Carnall ("The Baron of Bellflower") and leave the business, while Nelson would remain in it for the rest of his life.

A year before Ricky's first record, unknown Corky Jones had released a rockabilly side, "Hot Dog," on Pep Records; Corky would eventually become famous using his real name, Buck Owens. In California rockabilly and honky-tonk, both of which influenced the later Owens style, were integral parts of the region's less conservative musical mix. Local television programs and clubs were thriving; bandleader Bill Woods, who worked both venues then, recalls, "We played it all, whatever they called it—rock, country, jazz."

The beginnings of what came to be called the California Sound began to coalesce then, a unique West Coast honky-tonk style that subsumed rockabilly and was driven by amplified instruments—especially by Fender Telecasters. More than a few Californians in this decade still identified country music with the distinctly southern, hillbilly offerings of old radio favorites like the "Grand Ole Opry," but thanks to the popularity of television shows all over the state, many more folks were developing a taste for the increasingly distinct California version of country, although they preferred not to frequent actual honky-tonks to hear it.

About then more local disc jockeys also found themselves playing cuts from independent labels to avoid the Nashville Sound's blandness. Country disc jockey shows had proliferated since the end of World War II for two reasons: hundreds of new permits for radio stations were issued by the Federal Communications Commission, creating a legion of outlets without network affiliations. They in turn filled much of their airtime as inexpensively as possible. Second was the impact of television; nearly every radio program that could be converted to the visual medium in those early days was, so radio suddenly had time to be filled as it struggled to retain or find listeners. Disc jockeys proved to be the answer.

Whether widely known like Jolly Joe Nixon or struggling for recognition like young Buddy Mize, disc jockeys certainly played a major role in expanding the music's popularity. The availability of portable radios and improved radios in cars lured larger numbers of younger fans to recorded songs and to the local radio celebrities who bantered and spun records. For a while at least kids could telephone their requests to disc jockeys and hear not only favorite songs played but familiar names mentioned as well.

Many of those jocks in California did something both Jack and Woody Guthrie had done earlier; they employed a down-home patter and even hayseed images as they became "radio personalities." Foreman Phillips became popular in Southern California in the 1940s; "Squeakin' Deacon" Moore on KXLA in Pasadena developed a national reputation with his antics. Well-known entertainers such as Red Murrell (especially during his sixteen-year stint at KEEN in San Jose), Hank Penny, Stuart Hamblen, T. Texas Tyler, Wesley Tuttle, and future recording great Tennessee Ernie Ford ("the ol' pea picker") also spun records at one time or another. At one point KXLA featured a sparkling lineup of Stone, Moore, and Ford on their twenty-four-hour country-music format.

Owner and manager Lowell King of KXLA in Los Angeles was a national leader. He hired a stellar group to play country records, not only Stone, Moore, and Ford but also Joe Allison, Charlie Williams, and Biff Collie. After King's death in 1959 many of those folks joined the staff of KFOX in Long Beach when Bing Crosby Enterprises turned it into a major country station, replacing KXLA as the area's alternative voice. It featured such luminaries as Allison, Dick Haynes, Lee Ross, Cliffie Stone, and the redoubtable Squeakin' Deacon. KFOX even lured the nationally renown Hugh Cherry west from Nashville.

In 1954, concurrent with the celebration of the Grand Ole Opry's anniversary in Nashville, the Country Music Disc Jockey Association had been formed. It was only natural that with lively folks like Tennessee Ernie, Texas Tiny, and Squeakin' Deacon spinning discs in this state, jocks here would soon become part of that new class of celebrities called "radio personalities." That in turn begat a Federation of Country Air Personalities, and it led to the Country Music Disc Jockey Hall of Fame.

In 1958 the Country Music Disc Jockey Association metamorphosed into the Country Music Association. Headed by Jo Walker, the association became the music's most effective public relations arm, pushing for all-country stations and generally elevating the music's image. This Nashville-based organization also performed the paradoxical feat of creating the impression that country was more southern than was true, while at the same time encouraging the pop movement, which would further break down regional barriers. Reported *The Illustrated History of Country Music* in 1995, "It took only some impressive public relations by the . . . Country Music Association to steal Hollywood's thunder entirely and create the impression that Nashville had always been at the center stage of country music."

Okie Paul Westmoreland remained a favorite disc jockey in the Central Valley; he captured listeners throughout the region from his Sacramento base, where he had started with a fifteen-minute morning radio program. In fact music programming, both recorded and live, remained especially popular in the state's agricultural heartland where Westmoreland offered both types of shows. Bandleader Harley Huggin enjoyed a large part of the Fresno market but was rivaled by Don Hillman. Another bandleader

Smiley Maxedon was especially popular in Tulare County, while Bill Bates, the station's owner, spun discs at KTRB in Modesto. Kern County was dominated by Jimmy Thomason, Bill Woods, and Cousin Eb Pilling (who on weekends entertained at the Pumpkin Center Barn Dance with his band the Squirrel Shooters). The growing popularity of country music can be illustrated by Thomason's schedule at KAFY-Bakersfield in 1951: 6 to 7 A.M., 12 to 1 P.M., 7 to 8 P.M., and 9 P.M. to midnight; he did everything but wash windows.

Bandleader Dude Martin had relocated to Southern California, and he hosted a popular live-music program, "The Roundup," on KFI. His Roundup Gang became a hot band in the southland; it featured the comedy of the versatile Hank Penny and the singing of Sue Thompson, a Missouri native who had been raised in the Golden State. Thompson's unique, almost childlike voice would produce pop hits for her in the 1960s, but in the 1950s she cohosted with Martin, by then her husband, a country television program in Southern California. After divorcing Dude, Sue married Penny and eventually, like so many Southern California entertainers, relocated to Las Vegas. Her most memorable country records were a series of duets with Don Gibson.

To the north Black Jack Wayne enjoyed a considerable following in Sonoma County, then later in the Bay Area. Also popular in the Bay Area were Long Horn Joe's Cowboy Hit Parade (KROW-Oakland), Foreman Bill's Rhythm Rodeo (KYA-San Francisco), Eddie the Hired Hand's Hillbilly Hit Parade (KLS-Oakland), and the Cactus Jack Show (KLX-Oakland). Don Cox would become a headliner in San Jose, but Cottonseed Clark was equally prominent in that market. These people, with many others, had considerable impact. Merle Haggard recalls that when he was just starting in music in the 1950s, "we tried to play like anybody who had music on the radio."

Eventually top-40 programming—repeating the same group of popular recordings over and over—arose as an aspect of what was called "format radio," scheduling adapted to the tastes of specialized markets, including potential fans of country music. Omaha broadcaster Bill Stewart claimed that he and colleague Todd Storz concocted this practice after noticing that bar patrons played the same songs over and over on a jukebox. As the decade wore on traditional live-music radio shows faded. The reality was that sleepy musicians who had worked in a club the night before were not always in top form for daytime performances; phonograph records spun by jocks, on the other hand, were convenient and of consistent quality, even if *how* a record managed to make the top 40 remained a mystery to most.

When television networks began searching for vehicles to attract wider audiences in the mid-1950s, country music was one they explored. ABC tried "Ozark Jubilee," featuring Red Foley, in 1955. It "set the tone for all country music TV shows: easygoing host, cornball comedians, and oh yes, country singers," Ken Tucker wrote in Kingsbury and Axelrod's *Country: The Music and the Musicians*. The large country-music community in Southern California about then began to televise barn-dance shows: Cliffie Stone's "Hometown Jamboree" (called "Dinner Bell Roundup" earlier when it was on radio); "Hollywood Barn Dance," hosted now by Cottonseed Clark and Foy Willing; and "Town Hall Party," emceed by Tex Ritter. The last was an immediate local favorite as a three-hour program, and half-hour segments of it were retitled "Western Ranch Party" when they were broadcast nationwide. It had been originated by William Wagnon, Jr., in 1952 after he purchased the large Town Hall dance venue in Compton from Foreman Phillips. "Town Hall Party" took full advantage of Southern California's abundant talent pool and of its audience, too. In 1953 Texan Lefty Frizzell, then perhaps the hottest male country vocalist in the nation, relocated to La Cañada and joined the cast.

Cliffie Stone's "Hometown Jamboree" debuted in 1948, and viewing it became a Saturday night routine for families in the Los Angeles area, many of whom had no previous interest in "Okie music." It remained on the air for ten years and featured a virtual who's who of West Coast country's best: Ernie Ford, Merle Travis, Wesley Tuttle, Eddie Kirk, Molly Bee, Jimmy Bryant, Dallas Frazier, Speedy West, Billy Liebert, Gene O'Quinn, Red Sovine, Harold Hensley, Billy Strange, Bucky Tibbs, Jeanne Black, Joanie O'Brien, Tommy Sands, Polly Bergen, Ferlin Husky, Skeets McDonald, and Cliffie's father, Herman the Hermit.

Arkansas-native McDonald had moved to Southern California in 1951 and auditioned with Stone at KXLA. He was immediately accepted for "Hometown Jamboree"; then Ken Nelson signed him at Capitol Records. Skeets was a honky-tonk singer whose style came to resemble Lefty Frizzell's, complete with drooping octaves and split syllables, and for a time Capitol saw him as a possible rival to that dominant performer. Although McDonald never achieved Lefty's level of success, he did produce some memorable records—"Don't Let the Stars Get in Your Eyes," "I'm Hurting," "Wheel of Fortune," and others, and he remained a television favorite. Eventually he joined the cast of "Town Hall Party" and switched his recording contract to Columbia, where "Call Me Mr. Brown" in 1963 was his biggest hit. As country music moved toward pop stylings, Skeets remained true to his honky-tonk roots.

By the end of this decade television had become a dominant musical venue. Because it was a visual medium, more and more California entertainers began to attire themselves as the Maddox Brothers and Rose always had, in gaudy pseudowestern gear. The flamboyant attire of Spade Cooley, in particular, showed he understood the appeal of eye-catching clothes. He also understood that he was reaching an audience well beyond country's traditional base.

A change was also afoot back in Nashville. In 1950 Cowboy Copas and Little Jimmy Dickens brought outfits from Nudie Cohen to the "Grand Ole Opry." Nudie's widow, Bobbie, told Jonny Whiteside, "They were so influential there for us. So we made a trip out there and just knocked them dead with the clothes. Later, Hank Williams called Nudie and asked him to come back, because he and Audrey wanted some clothes. . . . Hank's buried in one of our suits, the white one with musical notes." Soon other major entertainers in the South began to attire themselves as flamboyantly as many California performers long had.

Meanwhile back in the Golden State many other entertainers were involved in that continuing enlargement of country music's audience. Veteran Smokey Rogers bridged the media gap by dominating both the radio and television scenes in San Diego, and singer Doye O'Dell, who wrote one of California's most popular country songs, "Hey Okie!" hosted a local television show in Los Angeles and won two Emmys in the 1950s. Also important were Dave Stogner, Chester Smith, Del Reeves, and Black Jack Wayne; the list could go on and on. Most of those participated in country music on a variety of levels, and some names, like Cliffie Stone's, seem to appear on every list: entertainers, promoters, disc jockeys, producers—you name it. (Power has often been concentrated in this business, with folks such as Cliffie, Ken Nelson, and Buck Owens eventually exerting enormous clout.)

JIMMY THOMASON SHOW
Channel 23, Bakersfield

Jimmie Addington Enterprises
P.O. Box 1921
Bakersfield, California
Fa 3 - 0541

Jimmy Thomason—promoter, performer, disc jockey, television host—with
one of his television bands. Front row: Eugene Moles sits to Thomason's
right; back row (left to right): Al Brumley and Jimmy Phillips. Courtesy of
Kern County Museum. Used by permission.

Wayne, who was a performer, a promoter, a booking agent, a songwriter, a label owner, and of course a popular television host in Oakland,
was not quite in the Stone-Nelson-Owens league but was important
nonetheless. By the 1960s he had become a major West Coast talent bro-
ker. He didn't start there; early in his career, Wayne and his band, the
Gamblers, played at a Santa Rosa nightspot called the Squirrel Cage. Former patron Ed LaFrance told writer Gaye LeBaron that they "would play
a few tunes and if things got dull he'd whip out these .45 pistols he car-

ried loaded with blank cartridges and squeeze off a couple of blanks at people driving by." Later in his career Black Jack may have wished he had kept his pistols as the business grew increasingly impersonal—the domain of bookkeepers and attorneys.

More than a few so-called prune pickers still had not become entirely comfortable with their Okie neighbors; some still believed the negative stereotypes that had been encouraged by the antimigrant campaign of the late 1930s. But when pleasant, attractive men and women began appearing on television screens, singing familiar hymns, sometimes poking fun at their own roots, often introducing their families, an inevitable reevaluation began. Performers such as Illinois-native Cousin Herb Henson or Texans Jimmy and Louise Thomason in Bakersfield helped erase the sense of "otherness" that still plagued the music in some circles. They played on a smaller stage than Stone or even Stogner in Fresno but were equally important in their region. As scholar Philip H. Ennis has observed, "Even though the 'Grand Ole Opry,' the 'National Barn Dance,' and the ten or so other major network country shows were at the top, there were still hundreds of shows on local, independent stations, constituting a large country music pyramid." At the base of that pyramid local talent was celebrated and personal audiences developed. Some of those locals soon became national.

Because gifted performers were still streaming into California, a disc jockey–musician–booking agent like Bill Woods in Bakersfield encountered his fair share. He recalls,

One time Chester Smith—he could really sing—and Hazel Howser they came to my radio record show in KPMC and Chester he said they had this little demo record he was takin' to L.A. hopin' to find somebody to give 'em a contract. Well, I told Chester to play that demo for me right there in the studio, and it was real good . . . 'Wait a Little Longer, Please, Jesus' it was.

As soon as I went off the air, I called Ken Nelson down at Capitol and set up an appointment for Chester and Hazel to meet him. Well, Ken signed them right up. Chester was to make seven or eight singles . . . seculars and gospels both.

Del Reeves he was another story. One time I booked Chester at the Blackboard, and he brought this new guy—Del Reeves—with him. Del did a good job, so I started booking him, too. I helped him get his first contract with MGM Records because he could sing, Del. He's had some big hits, and he's still a regular on the 'Grand Ole Opry.'. . .

Then there's ol' Ferlin [Husky]. He's a character and another real talented guy. I went and asked the station manager if we could get him a program of his own, and the manager he said, 'If you can go out and sell some time for him, I'll give a him show.' Two days later he had a show.

The country-music scene in Bakersfield, as elsewhere in California of course still endured old prejudices. Asked if country musicians had a poor reputation then, Owens recalls, "We were looked down on pretty bad." He adds, "deservedly so most of the time. There were lots of musicians who had no discipline about them whatsoever." Buck himself represented a new breed that would eventually turn negative assessments around. "He wasn't a big talker," remembers Bill Woods. "He didn't drink; he didn't smoke. He was just a nice kid." But for a while, even the nice kids like Owens were overshadowed by lingering demonization created in the earlier anti-Okie campaign.

A "combat zone" east of town on Edison Highway remained a hub for Bakersfield's country music, and Chester Avenue north on the route toward Merle Haggard's adjacent hometown of Oildale began to host a series of popular clubs in the 1950s. There were many wild stories about events on Edison Highway, and fiddler Jelly Sanders tells one: Railroad tracks ran parallel to that road, and Sanders reveals that after young Herb Henson was hired to play piano at the Clover Club, the band took a break one night, and Herb disappeared. "Know what he'd done? Walked across the road over there and caught a freight train. Made it to Illinois." "Rough as those joints were, he probably got *chased* to Illinois," suggests a former patron, Peter Epp, Jr.

Maybe because the lively Herb was missing from the Clover Club, the Lucky Spot became the most popular nightclub on Edison Highway. It featured Tex Marshall (Woods calls him "the best club singer I ever heard"), then later Johnny Barnett led the band. Most local musicians played there at one time or another. Says Merle Haggard, "The Lucky Spot was the top place in town then, and Johnny Barnett was a very important name."

Some musicians who performed in those locales—Ralph Mooney, Roy Nichols, and Owens, in particular—are credited with having developed what came to be called the "Bakersfield Sound," which cut through honky-tonk smoke and chatter with high-pitched, wailing pedal steel runs, staccato finger picking on Telecasters, and up-tempo bass accompaniment, all often enhanced by vocal "high duets" similar to those of bluegrass singers.

That wailing pedal steel was often played by Mooney, an Oklahoman who toured with Skeets McDonald in the early 1950s but who is most noted for his work with Wynn Stewart's band. There Ralph's high-pitched driving style established a major component of California's musical distinctness. He had actually built his own pedal steel guitar in the late 1940s, and, reports Rich Kienzle, "Leo Fender borrowed Mooney's instrument to study it and gave him a Fender model." Ralph certainly figured out how to use the Fender model, and he contributed his unique sound to accompany three major figures who themselves contributed to the new sound: Stewart, Owens, and Haggard. Although he was not a bandleader, Mooney was certainly a master musically.

With Chuck Seals, Ralph wrote "Crazy Arms," recorded by Ray Price in 1957. "The song was a hit of major proportions for Price," notes Bill C. Malone, "a refreshing reassertion of hard-core country music at a time of rockabilly ascendancy, and a vehicle for the introduction of Price's shuffle-beat sound into country music." That shuffle beat, so-called because of a danceable rhythm produced by a shuffling drum cadence and an electric walking bass underlying melodies with four beats to a bar, would itself become a component of the emerging Bakersfield version of the California Sound. As is so often true in the arts, cross-fertilization brought riches.

Roy Nichols was another peerless contributor to the distinctness of West Coast country. Reported Tommy Collins, "I have not seen his equal among people playing lead guitar." Few have, for this prodigy—born in Arizona but raised in Fresno—began his professional career two weeks before his sixteenth birthday when Fred Maddox heard him play on the show of Fresno disc jockey Barney Lee. He was hired by the zany Maddox Brothers and Rose, a gig that lasted eighteen months. Fred Maddox told Whiteside that on New Year's Eve 1950, "I dressed up as old Father Time goin' out, and we had Roy get into a diaper (he didn't want to do it). I carried him on stage, as the New Year was comin' in!"

Nichols rarely wore a diaper again in a career that extended until his retirement in 1987. Along the way he played with the bands of such luminaries as Smiley Maxedon, Lefty Frizzell, Herb Henson, Johnny Cash, and Wynn Stewart. With his Telecaster, Nichols developed some distinct techniques, such as his string-bending style. As Robert Price describes it, Nichols would bend the guitar string, strike it, then relax it, thus lowering the note. With James Burton he is also credited with "chicken pickin,'" a single-string technique with spicy, staccato bursts.

In 1966 Roy was the first sideman hired when Merle Haggard formed the Strangers. In that outstanding band he combined with pedal steel ace Norman Hamlet to produce another hard-driving variation of the California Sound. Nichols remained with the Strangers until his retirement, and his legacy on records and in the memories of fans remains great. Says Rose Maddox, "He could play anything. Every guitar picker in the country wanted to play like him, but none of them ever compared."

Bringing in the Talent

Beginning in the 1930s, but especially in the 1940s and '50s, local promoters spread country music by booking performers into halls, auditoriums, and clubs all over the state. Some, like Foreman Phillips, Cliffie Stone, Stu Carnal, Black Jack Wayne, and Steve Stebbins, became well known in their own right, but virtually every town of any size had its impresario or gambler, since many lost everything when crowds didn't provide enough gate receipts to cover guarantees.

Jimmy Thomason—performer, disc jockey, entrepreneur—brought big-name talent into many venues in the Bakersfield area. He made and lost considerable money in the process, and his memories give some sense of the scene there in the late 1940s and '50s:

Beardsley Ballroom ... had been a pop dance hall. They sold it to some people, and they come down and wanted me to put a western band in there every Saturday night, so I did. I put a western band in Beardsley on Saturday nights. During the week, I booked talent in. I brought in [Bob] Wills. I brought in T. Texas Tyler. I brought in Hank Williams.

I had the first show in Harvey Auditorium, with Hank Snow. And they presented me with an award out there, in 1950 or '51, I think. . . . Then I put on a lot of shows in Harvey.

Beardsley Ballroom. It was a hot spot, a beautiful country dance hall. Then, Beardsley Ballroom burned—that was in 1950—burned to the ground. With $5,000 worth of my equipment and clothes. I had just bought my first western suit . . . from old Nudie [Cohen] down in Hollywood. And every damn bit of it burned up in Beardsley. . . .

But any rate, that was in '50. So I moved from there to Rainbow Gardens and continued the same thing in Rainbow Gardens. . . . When Lefty Frizzell got into the picture in 1950, I booked him here for the first time.

Bandleader Bill Woods worked the same area at the same time, but he booked performers into a much smaller venue, a popular nightspot called the Blackboard. He explains the arrangements when he engaged talent:

I would book the stars, call their agents and book them for so much, see, to appear Monday and Tuesday night. And in the contract, they had to be in town by five o'clock to be on the Cousin Herb [television] Show and make a guest appearance. And for us furnishing them talent, [Herb and company] would plug that they were going to be at the Blackboard. And I would write up the ads and use the newspaper and put in a picture and this and that. So that went on, gee, a good ten years.

Although they did not often achieve high public profiles, without those promoters the course of country music in the state (and the nation, for that matter) would be far less significant. All were entrepreneurs, but some were virtually missionaries, too, putting their livelihoods on the line over and over again.

◄ ►   ◄ ►   ◄

In a pattern that was common statewide, many musicians had to hold nonmusical jobs to supplement their incomes or to produce the core of those incomes. As the appeal of country music slowly expanded, though, a rise in earnings allowed a number of previously avocational musicians to become full-time performers. Not that anyone grew wealthy playing locally; Bill Woods laughingly remembers that sideman Buster Simpson's little brother Red—who would one day become a major songwriter—said, "'When I get big I'm gonna be a big star like you guys.' And we were making ten bucks a night playing at the Clover Club and doing radio free for the publicity." By the early 1950s Owens was paid $75 for six nights a week at Bakersfield's Blackboard, and if he played Sunday afternoon he received another $7.50. "You're talking 82 bucks. $82.50. I could dang sure live on that," he says.

That economic improvement resulted because the music's fans were themselves now enjoying steady jobs and discretionary funds. Merchants soon learned that advertising on what were called country-western radio programs was effective, so more and more disc jockeys—many of them musicians—spun that music all over the state. But this was really television's decade. From his Bakersfield base Henson dominated the television market in the southern San Joaquin Valley. That area was then being called the state's "Bible belt," and gospel music was a significant part of Henson's repertoire as it was of most country entertainers. But Herb really believed it. Bill Woods, the son of two ministers, recalls that Henson once called him aside and admitted that he and his wife had been unable to conceive. "Brother Woods," he asked, "I wonder could you pray over us?" Bill did that, and before long Mrs. Henson was pregnant. Several children later, Cousin Herb again approached the preachers' son and said, "Brother Woods, that prayer you said worked real good, but I wonder could you turn it off now?"

The genial Henson was noted for welcoming gifted amateurs to his show. An Oklahoma native named Ronnie Sessions, for example, started on the "Trading Post Show" as a nine-year-old. He went on to record for MCA Records and to place ten songs in the top 10 in a career that lasted until 1987. Then there were Woody Wayne Murray and Bobby Adamson, called the Farmer Boys from Farmersville by Henson; they had begun singing along with phonograph records in that small Tulare County town. They honed their skills by performing locally and finally were "discovered" by Cousin Herb, who invited the duo to perform on his daily television show.

The Farmer Boys had both moved to California from Arkansas as kids. Perhaps as a result their singing was more southern in unity, diction, and style than most others heard on the Henson show. The young men became special favorites with viewers and were signed by Capitol Records's Ken Nelson at Henson's urging. Many of their high-energy numbers, such as "Onions," "Flash, Crash and Thunder," "Charming Betsy," and "Humdinger"—all of them featuring such exceptional "Trading Post" instrumentalists as Nichols, Woods, Owens, Hamlet (also from Famersville), and Lewis Talley—sold well in California. The boys never developed a strong national reputation, though, and their career faded in the 1960s.

Herb Henson, himself, was a neighbor to his Kern County fans, meeting them on the street, in church, at the fair, anyplace viewers considered him to be simply good ol' Cousin Herb. A hokey comedian, a passable singer, and a solid musician, Henson was also, to quote fiddler Jelly Sanders, "one of the best pitch men that I have ever worked for in my life." Most of all, like Stone and the Thomasons, Cousin Herb was an endearing personality, frequently funny and never pretentious.

Longtime fan Charlotte Epp smiles as she recalls, "He was sure full of the dickens." She recalls especially a show when Henson, touting cars for longtime sponsor Leo Meek, smacked the hood of one and left a prominent dent. After a moment—background laughter could be heard from the set—Herb examined the dent, then grinned into the camera and said, "Ol' Leo'll give you a *real* good deal on this one, folks."

The Cousin assembled an extraordinary group of performers for the "Trading Post" show, and they set the stage for Bakersfield's prominence a decade later. Among the program's early regulars were Woods, Mize, Carlton Ellis, and Johnny Cuviello. Later Nichols, Fuzzy Owen, Eugene Moles, the Farmer Boys, Jelly Sanders, Lewis Talley, plus Buck and Bonnie Owens became part of the crew. Many went on to important careers in the business. Owen, for example, would later not only run Tally Records with his cousin, Talley, at the time Merle Haggard began recording there, but he would also manage Haggard and cowrite with Fern Foley "Apartment #9," 1966's song of the year.

Pretty Bonnie Owens was a particular favorite on the "Trading Post Show." She both soloed (her version of "I Want to Be a Cowboy's Sweetheart" was especially popular) and sang duets with Fuzzy Owen, while her former husband Buck Owens played guitar, confusing gossips in the audience. Bonnie's utterly unpretentious demeanor and easy grin seemed to charm everyone. She of course later married Haggard, who by then was managed by Fuzzy—this sounds too much like a soap opera to be real.

Born in Blanchard, Oklahoma, as Bonnie Campbell, this enduring figure had married Buck at age sixteen in Arizona where her family migrated. The couple had two children but divorced in 1953. Both Bonnie and Buck saw some hard times. She worked as a carhop before Henson

Cousin Herb Henson's Trading Post cast in the late 1950s: Henson, Johnny
Cuviello, Billy Mize, Jelly Sanders, Bill Woods, Dallas Frazier, Carleton Ellis.
Courtesy of Kern County Museum. Used by permission.

hired her for the "Trading Post Show." Over forty years later she remains
among the most personally popular vocalists in the business.

The first national hit from the area was Jean Shepard and Ferlin
Husky's "A Dear John Letter" in 1953. Shepard, a frequent guest on the
early "Trading Post Show," had been born in Paul's Valley, Oklahoma, and
her family had moved to the Visalia area when she was ten, so she had a
strong local connection. In high school she had formed an all-female
band, the Melody Ranch Girls, that specialized in western swing. Pretty

Jean Shepard. From the Gid Tanner Artist File #NF1996,
The Southern Folklife Collection, Wilson Library, The
University of North Carolina at Chapel Hill.

Jean, only five feet, one inch tall, was a sight to behold as she played a bulky bass. She recalled, "My mama and daddy hocked every stick of furniture in our home to pay for my bass fiddle. It cost $350. . . . Back then, $350 would have bought a whole house full of furniture."

She had appeared on Jelly Sanders's radio show on Porterville's KTNV as a schoolgirl and was already well known in the San Joaquin Valley when Hank Thompson heard her sing and used his influence to finagle a tryout for her with Capitol. She recorded a number called "The Crying Steel Guitar Waltz" but almost didn't manage a major label for her second disc, the million-selling "A Dear John Letter" duet that made her California's first major female recording star since Patsy Montana. Later in 1953 she and Ferlin had another top-10 hit with their sequel "Forgive Me John."

Her partner Husky, who then lived in Bakersfield, was a man who took the premise that you can reinvent yourself in California to an extreme: The former disc jockey from Missouri became three persons. Calling himself Terry Preston and his band the Termites, he had played at country venues all over the San Joaquin Valley. He frequently used yet another name and persona during that period, the hilarious bumpkin Simon

Ferlin Husky. From the Gid Tanner Artist File #NF1996,
The Southern Folklife Collection, Wilson Library,
The University of North Carolina at Chapel Hill.

Crum, to gain his first contract at Capitol Records, and he initially recorded using that name.

After "A Dear John Letter" he abandoned the Terry Preston moniker, and his Termites became the Hush Puppies. Four years later, as Husky, he rerecorded in Nashville a song he had originally cut as Preston, this time with Ken Nelson producing it. "(Since You're) Gone," was one of the year's great country hits. He later suggested that the difference between recording in California and in Tennessee was that "when I rerecorded it in Nashville in 1957 . . . , I used an echo chamber and a choir, a group of singers. The first time [in California] it was just me, a drummer and a couple of guitars." The following year, Simon Crum, his enduring alter ego, enjoyed his first hit, "Country Music Is Here to Stay." The versatile Husky (who also spelled the name Huskey) had left Kern County soon after his first two successes with Shepard, but both their impacts continued to be felt there because those two performers had proven that local artists could reasonably aspire to national prominence.

There was a third or fourth and fifth party involved in "Dear John Letter." Its writer was Johnny Grimes, a locally prominent figure who went by the professional name of Hillbilly Barton. According to Bill Woods,

"Lewis Talley, he traded a motor scooter to Hillbilly Barton for that song. Can you imagine that?" (Other versions of the story have Talley trading a Kaiser automobile for the song.) Talley then sold half of it to his cousin Fuzzy Owen for $150. When the big bucks began to roll in, however, that motor scooter didn't look like such a bargain, and Billy Barton, who was under contract to American Music, threatened to sue for one-third of all profits. "So they came over to my house," Woods recalls. "They was cross-ways with each other over it . . . [but] they finally got things straightened out." The attribution for "A Dear John Letter" from that time on included Talley, Owen, and Barton.

Another Bakersfield resident, Tommy Collins, confirmed that local folks could make it big. The handsome former Marine was such a fixture on California television, especially on the shows of Cliffie Stone and Herb Henson, and in California nightclubs during the 1950s that many fans assumed he was a Bakersfield native. Actually he was from Oklahoma City (his first band was called the Rhythm Okies), but he had lived with Husky in Bakersfield. Signed by Stone for Capitol, Collins became the initial Kern County–identified artist to perform on the "Grand Ole Opry." (Young Buck Owens went along as an accompanist.)

Tommy recorded mostly his own songs and performed with a livelier sense of humor than nearly all of his peers on hits such as "You Better Not Do That" (featuring Buck on guitar) and "You Gotta Have a License" (with Bill Woods on fiddle and Husky on guitar), both slightly risqué numbers that became big California favorites. He would also write the marvelous "Roots of My Raising," recorded by Merle Haggard in 1976.

The interrelationship between the music scene in Bakersfield and the one in Los Angeles became so intimate during the 1950s that they could reasonably be viewed as the two parts of single whole; the former was considered rawer, more "Okie." Many musicians traveled back and forth with such regularity that only their friends knew for sure in which community they lived. Clubs in the two areas exchanged acts and so did radio and television shows. But access to the recording industry—then as now the rocket to national fame—was centered in the metropolis to the south.

Joe and Rose Lee Maphis, who lived in the southland, performed all over the state and were particularly popular in Bakersfield. Of Joe's musicianship, Merle Travis said, "He plays any instrument but he can play a

Tommy Collins. Photo by Schaeffer, Hollywood. Courtesy
of Kern County Museum. Used by permission.

guitar the way you'd play a fiddle, you know, hoe-down on a guitar just
as fast as you please, and never miss a lick." Like so many of his peers, Joe
was the product of a musical family; he had started playing professionally
at square dances with his father in his native Virginia when he was only
ten years old. At sixteen he began a radio career that extended to Sunshine
Sue Workman's "Old Dominion Barn Dance" and, eventually, to the "National Barn Dance" itself.

Rose Lee, a Maryland native and also an excellent musician, had her
own radio program when she was only fifteen; she was known then as
"Rose of the Mountains." The two met on the "Old Dominion Barn
Dance" in 1948, married, and moved in 1952 to California, where
Johnny Bond and Travis recommended them to Foreman Phillips; they became regulars on "Town Hall Party." Their personal appearances, with
solid vocals as well as picking, soon guaranteed a sellout at nightspots all

over the state. The Maphises, called "Mr. and Mrs. Country Music" in California, traveled 100,000 miles a year entertaining.

In the 1950s the emerging Mosrite of California guitar company in Bakersfield began issuing Joe Maphis model guitars, which led to a spate of imitators, but no one ever duplicated the Maphis style, especially his patented twin-necked guitar. And when television began to supplement radio as a major medium for country, Joe and Rose Lee were among the entertainers who made the transition seamlessly. Early in the 1960s an ailing Cousin Herb Henson would ask the Maphises to cohost the "Trading Post Show" with him, and they accepted, although they never broke their link with the Los Angeles area. They continued to tour and record until the mid-1980s.

Southern California had long boasted many country-music nightclubs—scattered from San Bernardino to Santa Monica to San Diego—and musicians obtained abundant work there. The region's early Anglo settlement had absorbed so many Midwesterners and southwesterners that a "country" market had been in place there from the 1923 birth of this music. This fact was often unacknowledged, perhaps due to the attention being given the oddball fringe there.

The large, eclectic audience for country music continued growing in the region during the 1940s and '50s, and it in turn attracted migrant musicians and also developed native-born (or at least California-grown) stars. "Oh, L.A. was hot," admits Bill Woods. "There was plenty of studio work down there, and club work, too. There weren't any big labels here in town [Bakersfield] at all. You had to go down there to work for one of those." Jelly Sanders says that he stayed in Bakersfield in the face of offers to relocate to Southern California or move to Nashville because "I was a family man. . . . So I raised my kids up where they'd be in a good environment."

Billy Mize, one singer and bandleader associated with Bakersfield, made the journey to Los Angeles and remained there. Few performers on the Herb Henson television show cut a more dashing figure than the handsome Billy. A star high school athlete, he had grown up loving country music. "My main influence . . . was Bob Wills. I knew every song that Tommy Duncan had sung." His own career had begun when his father brought a guitar home from his furniture store and told Billy he could keep it if he learned to play it. He learned.

Mize had arrived in Bakersfield with his family (including younger brother Buddy, later a successful songwriter in Nashville) when he was a high school senior. To his delight he found himself in a country-music hotbed. He soon began playing and singing with Bill Woods and his Orange Blossom Playboys, had his own local disc jockey show, then joined Henson when the "Trading Post" began airing on television. "It started off with Bill Woods, Cousin Herb, and myself," he recalls. That was September 26, 1953, shortly after Jimmy and Louise Thomason's initial "Western Jamboree" (also called the "Jimmy and Louise Thomason Show") telecast on KAFY-TV became the first local daily country-music program.

In 1955 Mize appeared on Hank Penny's television show in Los Angeles. It was a prescient moment, for Billy would soon return to Los Angeles and perform on "Town Hall Party," "Country Music Time," and the popular "Cal Worthington Show." Billy would become an entertainer who dominated a major market but never quite became a national star. Eventually he would win Grammys for best local and regional television programs, would host the nationally syndicated "Gene Autry Show," plus his own syndicated "Billy Mize Show," and record a few chart records, but his enduring fan base remained rooted in the Los Angeles area.

Arguably the most influential figure who developed in that urban churning was Wynn Stewart, a native of Missouri. He was among the first to combine honky-tonk and rockabilly styles powerfully; only the Maddox Brothers and Rose preceded him. Stewart had migrated to Southern California with his family in 1948 when he was fourteen. He was an entertainer even before the move, and he soon formed a band in Los Angeles, becoming locally prominent. In 1950 Intro Records in Hollywood signed him, and his recording career was launched. In fact Wynn had a knack for assembling remarkable bands, and as early as 1953 he was joined by Roy Nichols, Ralph Mooney, and Bobby Austin, an exceptional gathering of talent. The next year Capitol became his recording label, and he scored hits with "Keeper of the Key" and "Waltz of the Angels."

Eventually his band would feature not only Nichols, Mooney, and Austin but also Helen Price, George French, and Jim Pierce. It was one of the best, making forays into the hard-driving rockabilly-and-honky-tonk style that would later be perfected by Buck Owens and the Buckaroos and come to be called the California Sound or the Bakersfield Sound. Moreover Wynn's singing technique would also be reflected in the voices of Owens, Haggard, and Bobby Durham, among others.

Late in the 1950s, after moving to the Jackpot and Challenge labels, Stewart recorded a rockabilly hit, "Come On," as well a series of successful duets with fellow Missourian Jan Howard. Of the duets Richard Carlin has written, "Stewart's normally aggressively honky-tonk personality [was] somewhat toned down by the choice of kissy-poo material." Wynn's top individual hits with Jackpot were "Wishful Thinking" in 1959 and "Big Big Love" in 1961. Two years later he and his band, which for a time included Haggard, became regulars at the Nashville Nevada Club in Las Vegas. He also hosted a local television show and worked as a disc jockey there.

After signing again with Capitol, Wynn enjoyed his greatest commercial success in 1967, the distinctly non-honky-tonk "It's Such a Pretty World Today," which remained on country charts for twenty-two weeks. In 1976 this enduring talent would savor one more top-10 single with "After the Storm." Wynn Stewart's impact on California's brand of country music looms larger than his list of hits might suggest; he was a defining performer whose style is still echoed throughout the industry, especially in California.

In the vast and churning population of the Los Angeles area, Mize and Stewart found audiences whose sense of displacement was far more intense than in the rural Bakersfield region. They also found other fans with a taste for slicker presentations, likely due to Hollywood's influence. Many savvy viewers wanted their country entertainers to retain authenticity without bumpkin self-parody.

The music business as a whole in Southern California was still growing, too. The founding of a music publishing company, Vidor Publications, by Johnny Bond and Tex Ritter, for example, opened doors for Los Angeles–based songwriters, although it never rivaled the major Nashville agencies such as Acuff-Rose. Vidor did ultimately come to control the impressive Delmore Brothers' catalog ("Blues Stay Away from Me," "Freight Train Boogie," "Brown's Ferry Blues," etc.), and it also hired a future songwriting superstar named Harlan Howard, who was then toiling in the Golden State.

California would temporarily leapfrog past Tennessee in country pop in the late 1950s as a result of the career of a one-time disc jockey on KXLA, Ernie Ford. By then ensconced in California, where he would live for the rest of his life, Ford's varied records, especially "Sixteen Tons" in 1955–56 (which sold over four million copies), made him a major force.

◄ ►   ◄ ►   ◄ ►

The Ol' Pea Picker

California's first nationwide country television star was Tennessee Ernie Ford, "the ol' pea picker," born in fabled Bristol in the Volunteer State. He first performed in California over San Bernardino's KFXM-AM as a GI during World War II. After his discharge from the military, he returned to the radio station but was soon hired at Pasadena's KXLA-AM, thanks to the influence of Cliffie Stone, who recalls being impressed by newscaster Ernest Jennings Ford on the San Bernardino station. The news was followed by something called the "Bar Nothing Ranch," featuring a wild, hillbilly disc jockey named Tennessee Ernie. "The unique thing that he did was to sing along with [the records] in harmony. Then, during the chorus instrumental of the record, he would switch to the lead part. During the entire show, there were farm animal sounds: ducks quacking, pigs squealing, cows mooing, horses whinnying, dogs barking and so on." Stone didn't yet realize that the newscaster and the disc jockey were one and the same.

In any case both "Ernies" soon livened the air from KXLA. The switch to that more influential station also led him to a slot on Stone's "Dinner Bell Roundup" and later the "Hometown Jamboree." Ernie brought a rich voice and some training from the Cincinnati Conservatory of Music, as well as enough sense not to overwhelm his material. Stone, who eventually became Ford's agent, also recruited him for Capitol Records.

In the ol' pea picker's first year with that label, 1949, he managed one top-15 record, three top 10s, and a number one ("Mule Train"). The following year Ernie again hit number one with "Shotgun Boogie." At that time, the talented comedian remained a radio personality in Southern California. He also seemed to be the right man in the right place at the right time; his robust deliveries were seen by many fans as an antidote to the growing power of rockabilly and rock and roll. His deliveries, while rich, always remained distinctly country. Over the years, as he became more and more a

Tennessee Ernie Ford as a bumpkin radio disc jockey. From the Gid Tanner
Artist File #NF1996, The Southern Folklife Collection, Wilson Library, The
University of North Carolina at Chapel Hill.

favorite with pop audiences, Ford would be urged to drop the "Tennessee" appellation, but he always refused. He was who he was.

In retrospect Tennessee Ernie now can be credited with several important contributions to country music. With songs like "Country Junction," "Shotgun Boogie," and "Smoky Mountain Boogie, he was, for example, a significant contributor to the surge of boogie tunes that livened country in the late 1940s and early 1950s and that paved the way for rockabilly. Moreover Ernie was also a major—some say the major—factor in spreading southern white gospel music to a general audience; his 1957 album *Hymns* remained on the *Billboard* chart for nearly six years. In fact he was also perhaps the first major country star to focus on album sales rather than those of singles, presaging contemporary marketing.

Ford's full voice also made him a logical crossover performer, and from his cover of Frankie Laine's hit "Mule Train," through his blues-influenced "I'll Never Be Free" duet with Kay Starr, to his unforgettable version of Merle Travis's "Sixteen Tons," Ernie regu-

Ernest Jennings Ford, the name Tennessee Ernie used for his "straight" work.
From the Gid Tanner Artist File #NF1996, The Southern Folklife Collection,
Wilson Library, The University of North Carolina at Chapel Hill.

larly graced pop as well as country charts. Lee Gillette chose to remain Ford's producer even after leaving the country division at Capitol; he knew a major star when
he heard one.

Stone recalls that Ernie had sung "Sixteen Tons" on the live daily television show
Cliffie hosted from Hollywood's El Capitan Theater, and "within the next few days,
over twelve hundred letters came in about that song." Stone put them away, and when
Ernie was recording a cover of Ernest Tubb's hit "You Don't Have to Be a Baby to Cry"
at Capitol six months later, Cliffie showed the letters to Gillette. The latter decided that
"Sixteen Tons" would be the single's B side.

Wesley Tuttle credits Gillette, whom he calls a genius, with coming up with an
opening that helped make Ernie's version of the Travis song such a winner. "Gillette
would come in with an idea . . . that's how he did 'Sixteen Tons.' Ernie [Ford] was saying
'Let's do it about this tempo, boys' [snapping his fingers]. And Lee, sitting in the control
room said, 'Hey, Ernie—stop the band and you sing that first sixteen bars, with just

you and your fingers.'" In no small measure because of the exposure offered by that record, the former disc jockey began hosting "The Ford Show" on prime time for NBC in 1956. In that setting, too, he proved to be a big winner, easy to work with and flexible enough to blend with a variety of other performers; Rich Kienzle aptly suggests, "*The Ford Show* paved the way for every other country singer who successfully hosted a network show." Increasingly a popular guest star on the shows of others, Ernie followed the NBC program, which he left in 1961, with a daytime slot from San Francisco for ABC.

The current widespread acceptance of country entertainers owes at least part of its existence to the talented Ford. As Kienzle astutely summarizes, "Mainstream America may have had a stereotyped notion of country singers as ignorant, uneducated rubes, but Ford demolished that image.... He was the ideal country artist to make the move to national TV."

Ernie's soft-yet-genuine country style broke down many barriers, and he pioneered the performance of this music in such prestigious mainstream locales as the Thunderbird in Las Vegas, the Copacabana in New York, and the Palladium in London. He was inducted into the Country Music Hall of Fame in 1990, a year after the Nashville Network had produced *50 Golden Years*, a retrospective of the Bay Area resident's career. By then it was clear that Ernie's approach to country music and his television style had been much closer to what the future was bringing—from Glen Campbell and Barbara Mandrell to Garth Brooks and Trisha Yearwood.

◄ ►   ◄ ►   ◄ ►

Some older forms of music (and imitations of older forms) also became popular late in this decade in the so-called urban folk revival—actually the first time that this music had ever reached a large, general audience. Historian James C. Cobb wryly observes, "The movement was in essence another idealistic attempt to celebrate a genuine, undiluted, and therefore of course nonexistent culture of 'the folk.'" Aficionados originally loved this music because they perceived it as countercultural—celebrating ethnic perspectives, minority beliefs, and regional integrity rather than the bland popular culture of the time. Unfortunately, it, like country, had become commercial as soon as it became fashionable, something many of its fans chose to ignore.

In 1952 Folkways Records issued the landmark *Anthology of American Folk Music*, featuring such early hillbilly acts as Uncle Dave Macon, Buell Kazee, Dock Boggs, Clarence "Tom" Ashley, and the Carter Family. Folk purists still considered contemporary performers beyond the pale, but those traditional acts certainly reached listeners who would have turned up their noses at "country-western" music. This and other albums of the time are the likely source of a belief among some fans that somehow the Carters, Doc Watson, Bill Monroe, or *someone* represented "real" country music, while everything else was "just" commercial.

In 1958 the Kingston Trio, a San Francisco Bay Area group, recorded "Tom Dooley," which energized the marketable boom; there was big money to be made in them thar "traditionals." Dave Guard, Bob Shane, and Nick Reynolds were college students when they met in the mid-1950s. They formed the trio and after singing at student hangouts eventually moved on to perform at San Francisco nightclubs. In 1958 Capitol released their first album *The Kingston Trio*, which contained "Tom Dooley." Four years later Stephen Fiott would write in *Sing Out!* a magazine by no means friendly toward commercial music, "It remained for yet another group to bring folk music up to its true place in America. This group was the collegiate Kingston Trio. With them, folk music rose up and up to great heights."

A virtual renaissance of story songs also followed "Tom Dooley," with a string of genuine country performers reaching folk and pop audiences with their versions of these traditionals. The great commercial success of Marty Robbins's "El Paso" and Johnny Horton's "The Battle of New Orleans" especially infused new vitality into the old genre. Folk music thus commercially revitalized the careers of some traditional country performers: the Carter Family, the Stonemans, Ashley, Jimmy Driftwood, and Jean Ritchie, among others. Moreover, because it was now called "folk," many people could at last admire what until then they had denigrated. New listeners brought a combination of curiosity and condescension to this supposed discovery of their pasts. Roni Stoneman remembers, "They'd say, 'Do you play that folk music?' I said, 'Well, I guess we do—we're folks, ain't we?'"

This new rush of interest, however, disturbed many old-line, often left-wing, fans of folk music, who felt their special "progressive" world had been invaded by capitalists, some of whom in turn had begun copyrighting arrangements of traditional songs long in the public domain. During this folk revival, too, Woody Guthrie—by then debilitated by Huntington's disease—finally achieved wide recognition as his songs were acknowledged to be the special creations they were, and his life was viewed as legendary. Moreover a new generation of folk singers and some younger country performers, too, began to sing Woody's creations.

The years 1950 to 1959 represented another busy, varied period for this music in California. Country here again veered sharply from the South's offerings, and audiences continued growing as radio and television carried it to new fans. Nashville nevertheless rose to national prominence early in the decade and managed to remain there even though the era was dominated by the rise of rockabilly and by the youth culture it symbolized or ignited. Rock would quite literally rock the musical world, creating a counteruniverse of its own. In California attractive performers such as the Collins Kids, Ricky Nelson, and Eddie Cochran lured youngsters otherwise unimpressed by country music. To them the new stuff wasn't "Okie"; it was the future, and perhaps it was independence, too.

To understand why many longtime fans of country music consider Nashville's pop-influenced incarnation of it to be terminally bland, one needs only to listen to forty-five-year-old recordings by the Maddox Brothers and Rose. These precursors of rockabilly and cowpunk were arguably the most original, most outrageous, most entertaining of all California-based performers. They were also forward-looking, trying virtually everything, but they always remained undeniably country. Although the country-music establishment has paid far too little attention to this exciting band, other musicians hold them in awe. Rockabilly Roy Campi, for example, recalls, "They were the definitive hillbilly, boogie woogie, western swing, rockabilly, country gospel band. . . . they were the most wonderful band I've ever seen. Absolutely amazing. They had so much comedy and showmanship, like a medicine show kind of vitality."

The Maddox Brothers and Rose, like so many other acts in country, were the product of a musical family. Hard times had pushed the sharecropping Maddoxes off a farm near Gadsden, Alabama. In 1933 the family—Charlie, Lula, and their five children (ranging in age from five to seventeen)—sold their belongings for $35, then began trudging, hitchhiking, riding the rails across the country toward California. "Mama had always read these books, these western novels about California, the West, the Golden West," Rose explained, "where you can go and just pick gold off trees, and she *believed* that." Of the trip west itself, Rose said, "We was exposed to danger, but the railroad people took care of us because we were a family, and there wasn't any families riding the rails at that time. It was just migrant workers and hoboes and things like that."

The Maddoxes arrived in Oakland on April 11 of that year. Perhaps as a result of their mother's faith in the California dream, they actually panned gold for a spell without any great success. Eventually they became, according to brother Fred, "fruit tramps. . . . We followed the apricots, grapes, lettuce and other crops . . . but our home base was Modesto."

While they moved from labor camp to trailer court to ditch-bank settlement during those lean years, Fred noticed how much working folks appreciated music. He told journalist Gary Girard, "Around the camps I used to see some of the people form up little musical groups and begin playing before the crowds at the camp and people would throw money at them in appreciation. That gave me an idea." Fred had especially been inspired by Logan Laam and the Happy Hayseeds from Stockton. "They had played for this rodeo in Modesto, and they got $100 for doin' it. And I thought, 'My God!'"

Then while the family was picking cotton between Tipton and Earlimart, seventeen-year-old Fred had his vision. As he later explained it to writer Jonny Whiteside,

> It was November, an' colder'n the dickens. We's pickin' cotton an' Cliff an' Cal an' Mama was way ahead of me. I had about 10 pounds in my sack, an' I just sat down on it, started thinkin'.
>   They all looked around, said, "What are you doin'?"
>   I said, "I'm a-thinkin' . . . "
>   "Well, what're you thinkin'?"
>   "I'm a-thinkin' we oughtta go into the music business."

The family agreed, and they headed back for Modesto.

Fred was himself no musician, but his brothers Cliff and Cal had frequently entertained around campfires. Those two would play, Fred decided, and he would be their manager. Bill Woods recalled, "ol' Fred, he had more guts than a slaughterhouse, and the gift of gab." He used both to convince a Modesto furniture store owner, Jim Rice, to sponsor the as-yet-nonexistent band on KTRB, the local radio station. Fred would be the announcer, but the sponsor wanted the group to have a girl singer. Fred replied that they had one, although they didn't, not that he was aware of, anyway. Little sister Rose was eleven years old then, too frail to pick cotton, but "I was forever just singing at the top of my lungs just as loud as I could," she remembered.

Fred's said, "you could hear her 10 miles a-singin' at home. Rose'd wash the dishes and you could hear her just bellerin' out them songs." Rose turned out to be talented indeed, and when their radio show finally aired, the ingenue not only "bellered" songs but also read many of the commercials.

The group's real manager was Lula Maddox, called Mama by her kids. "Independent and domineering, Lula had a high spirit and fierce drive," writes Whiteside. They had followed her vision west, and eventually they would follow it to musical stardom. Manager and booking agent Jack Mc-Fadden, who would get his start scheduling for the Maddoxes, later called Lula "the Queen of the Pocketbook," and went on to say, "Mama Maddox was a great lady. I wish I could have worked with her some more."

After many seasons of dance halls and honky-tonks and television appearances, little sister Rose would be assessed by the astute Bill C. Malone this way: "Her performances with her brothers made her one of the most beloved and highly regarded singers of the fifties. Her energetically emotional, open-throated style strangely suggested the influence of both the honky-tonk and the country church."

The final ingredient in the original band was Fred himself, its erstwhile manager. He told Girard, "At first I played the 'juice harp' which I tapped as I held it between my teeth." Eventually, though, he found the instrument that came to be identified with him. He had seen a bass fiddle being played by a sideman in Arky Stark's Hillbillies, so he made a deal with Rice: "I asked him to give me a bass fiddle and I would pay $10 down and $10 a month, and he did." Fred never learned to tune the fiddle. "The first time I even touched the instrument was the day it arrived, and the next day I played it on the radio."

"I never heard anybody else play bass like that, and he was good too," guitarist Roy Nichols recalls. "Fred will tell you himself that he don't know no chords, he just goes up and down, slappin'." That wasn't his only contribution. The gift of gab that got the band started in the first place became standard fare on their shows, the bass slapper kidding and kibitzing on stage. "Fred is one of the funniest entertainers on the bandstand that I've ever heard," said Woods, who had heard quite a few. In many ways Fred set the group's frenetic pace. "We always put on a show," Rose recalled, "the antics and stuff. I mean it just wasn't us up there pickin' and singing. It was something going on all the time."

Their first radio program in Modesto was broadcast during "farmers' hours," 6:30 A.M. to 7 A.M., and they were an immediate sensation, receiving over 1,000 letters from fans. Eventually they performed an evening show, too. As was true of most radio bands, the only payment they received then was free publicity boosting appearances at everything from honk-tonks to store openings, from dance halls to rodeos.

The latter were especially important. "Weekends, there was usually a rodeo nearby," Rose recollected, "and we'd go into the town where it was being held, pick out a bar, go in and ask the owner if we could set up and play for tips. Well, they was gettin' free entertainment, so of course they said yes. Every bar in town had somebody playin' in it. The towns were loaded with cowboys and people there for the rodeo." They became big hits along the valley's rodeo circuit—Oakdale, Clovis, Bakersfield, Red Bluff, and the rest.

In 1938 the group entered the State Centennial Band competition. They took first place in a fifteen-band field and were awarded a sixty-four-station radio hookup with the McClatchy network. By the next year the Maddoxes had become a favorite from Washington to Arizona, broadcasting twice a day and playing, it seemed, nearly everywhere.

Although they could and did perform in almost any setting, especially the dance halls that were so popular in the state, the gang's sometimes lusty lyrics, their sometimes bawdy antics, and their always danceable music made them special favorites at honky-tonks. In those rowdy settings, their performances were uninhibited. Rose likes to tell about the time she was singing Johnny Horton's hit song "Johnny Reb" when a beef broke out near the front door of the Blackboard in Bakersfield, "and while I was singin' that 'He fought all the way . . . ' that fight went down the Blackboard right straight in front of the stage and all the way through," a visual aid for the lyrics.

Ultimately, though, success caused the Maddoxes to up their price, and only larger venues could host the crowds necessary to pay them. At the same time honky-tonks, dance halls, and even auditoriums were cultural centers for poor, displaced southern whites and remained as such well into the 1950s. Today it's difficult to imagine how important a group like the Maddox Brothers and Rose was to erstwhile migrants. It's also difficult to recall the prejudice they suffered. Rose reflected, "All of your sophisticated, upper-class . . . so-called upper-class . . . people looked down their noses at us. And . . . when we went into the music business, they . . . still looked down at them Okies . . . playin' that Okie music." Down-home entertainers such as Rose and "the boys"—who never departed from their hot hillbilly roots—were beacons of pride, perhaps of hope, in an otherwise grim period.

World War II interrupted the lives of the Maddoxes as it did the lives of so many others. Fred and Cal were drafted, and younger brother Don volunteered for military service. All of them saw action; Fred, for example, fought on Saipan and Okinawa. Cliff, who suffered from rheumatic fever, was deferred from military service, and baby brother Henry was too young to serve. Rose meanwhile stayed active, playing bass and singing for Arky Stark and his Hillbillies, then performing at Dave Stogner's Saturday night barn dances in Fresno. During that period, too, she tried unsuccessfully to convince Bob Wills to hire her. As Whiteside tells the story, "The last time she saw him Rose got so angry she nearly blew up, telling him, 'When my brothers get back from the service, we're gonna start up again and put you out of business.' Wills often retold this story, always saying in conclusion, 'And you know something? They damn near did, too!'"

After Cal, Don, and Fred were discharged, the group once more developed a radio program, this time on KGDM in Stockton. Fred remembered that they made their first postwar club appearance in Salida at the Blue Moon Cafe, hardly the big time, but it began the process of rebuilding their momentum, and it was a treat for local folks.

Country music on the West Coast had gone through a revolution during the war, with the profound influence of western swing. After the Maddox Brothers and Rose reorganized, said Fred, "Cliff wanted us to keep that beat, 'the ole hillbilly beat' we called it; I said, you've got to have somethin' they can tap their foot, or dance to, or to make 'em *feel* it. And me and Cal was a-doin' that other beat, but Cliff he was older, set in his ways. Me an' Cal said, 'We gotta have that!' It just came to us and we stuck with it." The band "shifted into higher gear," writes Whiteside, "leaning more toward a whimsical honky-tonk feel, with a heavy, manic bottom end—the slap bass of Fred Maddox."

Famed guitarist Roy Nichols, who started his career with the Maddoxes (Fred was his legal guardian), says, "They played hillbilly music, but it sounded real hot. They played really loud for that time, too, and I'll say this, it was okay for them to do it, where it wouldn't have been okay for someone else to try and get away with it. Now, Henry's mandolin was a lot of the hot feeling, plus the bass behind it."

Henry was know as "Friendly Henry," reportedly because he never smiled and would descend from the bandstand to duke customers he thought were ogling his sister. Add to such events Cal's frantic falsetto cackle, Don's trunk of props (that might produce a wig one time, a squirt gun the next), Fred's signature cry: "Yes sir, that's my sister!" echoing through the hall, their eclectic repertoire, and Rose's continuing ascent as a major singer, and it's little wonder fans found this group unforgettable: they put on a show, not just a concert.

But there was another element in their impact on audiences. Said drummer Henry Sharp, "I think your appearance on the stage is about 50 percent of your show. The Maddox Brothers and Rose proved that. They dressed with those loud western clothes . . . and they were called America's most colorful hillbilly band." The Nathan Turk getups sported by the Maddoxes were more than loud, they were extraordinary: bright red blouses, for example, with rhinestone musical notes across the back and chest, and plenty of gold and silver piping, with trousers to match. Rose sported a sunflower-yellow satin blouse with large red blossoms and green stems on the sleeves and small ones along the buttonholes, worn with a bright red, yellow fringed skirt that boasted elaborate yellow flowers embroidered thigh high, as well as a red fringed and flowered vest. Words don't do this costume by N. Turk justice; it was, according to clothing historian Tyler Beard, "one of the most incredible western stage outfits to ever come down the pike." Tennessee Ernie Ford was more pithy: "Their costumes make Liberace look like a plucked chicken."

In 1947 the group's reputation soaring, Rose and her mother traveled to Southern California to see if they could arrange a recording contract. "We went to Decca and R.C.A. and all them, none of the bigwigs was in." Finally, she said, "Me and Mama came out of Capitol and I said, 'Let's go over in Pasadena and see 4 Star Records. They've got T. Texas Tyler and he's goin' great.'" The bigwigs at 4 Star listened to the transcriptions of performances the women had brought, then decided they wanted to sign Rose but not her brothers.

The Maddox Brothers and Rose: Fred, Henry, Rose, Gene LeMasters (?),
Cal, Don. Courtesy of Kern County Museum. Used by permission.

Rose told them, "I don't believe you can get it that way." Her mother
telephoned Fred, the band's leader. His answer was direct: "They can't
have her without us." The company signed the entire group, a move it did
not regret.

"We went in and cut over a hundred songs for 'em," recalls Nichols,
"one right after the other." The group's first two records for 4 Star were
"Sally Let Your Bangs Hang Down," the provocative tune that dated back
to their early radio shows, and Woody Guthrie's "Philadelphia Lawyer."

Both were hits, but the band realized little profit from them; 4 Star was infamous for not delivering royalties. "We received only union scale for our recording time and no royalties," acknowledged Fred. "We wanted on records so bad, and they were sharp, and we were dumb hillbillies and [we] also wanted the publicity."

Although the Maddoxes over the years played on many radio programs, arguably their most important one came about during the 1948 recording strike. Don Pierce of 4 Star arranged for Polo Juaquez, a disc jockey at powerful XERB in Rosarito Beach, to play the group's transcriptions for fifteen minutes a night and to announce their forthcoming appearances. The tremendous reach of that border station led Whiteside to observe, "Those nightly XERB broadcasts were instrumental in breaking the Maddox name outside of California." Without XERB, he continues, "they might have remained a West Coast act."

Veteran promoter and bandleader Jimmy Thomason remembers the gang from that period: "I booked them in here—they were strictly a show band. . . . When I first come here in '48, I booked them in Shafter at the Veterans' Hall. And I had played them in Pumpkin Center. They were hot radio-wise, with their records. And as a result of that, I booked them into the spud festival in Shafter [in 1949]. Very, very hot. Very hot."

In 1949 the band made its lone appearance on the "Grand Ole Opry." The Maddoxes performed in their startling garb and with their usual antics. "Their appearance was almost as usurpers, a pack of wild Okies bent, it seemed, on violating every canon of WSM conduct," Whiteside reports. The band performed its first truly national hit, a sacred song entitled "Gathering Flowers for the Master's Bouquet." Despite their wild reputations, the Maddoxes consistently and effectively sang gospel numbers. In any case, they were not invited back to the Opry, but they later became regulars on the "Louisiana Hayride" on Shreveport's KWKH and appeared on its packaged tours with the likes of Elvis Presley, Marty Robbins, and Sonny James.

Although they changed their record company to the far more prestigious Columbia, they could not change the direction of American entertainment. Eventually economics shifted, and individual performers rather than groups became the mainstays in country music. Rose, who had her own personal contract with Columbia along with the group's, fit the new mold perfectly, so she, along with Cal (and Mama, ever the boss), left the group. As arguably the finest female singer of the period, she was invited to become a regular on the "Grand Ole Opry" in 1956 but became entangled in internal politics there and left. Her records during that period featured many styles and types of songs—most notably, her own brand of rock and roll—and in 1959 she was signed by Capitol after Columbia had released her.

The boys hung on for a time as the Maddox Brothers and Retta, with Don's wife Loretta Graham taking their sister's place, but in 1959 the group disbanded. They had had a great run, remaining unrestrained and innovative at a time when popular music was being engulfed in blandness, but eventually the road grew too long and life away from home became too much. No other outfit has ever threatened to take the place of the Maddox Brothers and Rose. As Whiteside summarizes, "The artists influenced by the family were amazingly numerous and varied, and the Maddox impact was so strong that it continued to echo through country music for decades after the breakup."

Older brother Cliff, who had earlier left the family group to form his own band the Rhythm Rangers, had died in 1949. Henry and Don purchased a farm near Ashland, Oregon, and relocated there with their families and their mother. Fred, always the livest wire, "stayed in the business as long and as actively as he could," explains Whiteside, "continually burnishing his reputation as a local legend with fresh conquests and tomfoolery." At one point he operated three nightclubs in Southern California, booked top acts into them, and performed at them himself, all at the same time, while managing to hold disc jockey jobs, too! His energy level remained amazing, and he also toured with various acts. A performance with Rose in a 1991 KCET-Los Angeles television special, "Bakersfield Country," one of his last, was vintage Fred: lively and fun. He was one of a kind.

Malone has summarized well the unlikely careers of those wild Okies from Modesto, who became one of the most entertaining acts in the history of American music: "Although Rose Maddox's career soon surpassed that of her brothers and extended well past their retirement, her deserved success should not obscure for us the considerable achievements made by this family of musicians. They conveyed a spontaneity and zest for life and music that is rarely displayed among country musicians today."

Rose and Cal of course remained on the show business circuit, and she went on to become an enduring star in a notoriously fickle firmament. Always an outsider due to her West Coast base and her independent ways, she presaged the proud and autonomous female entertainers of today in many ways. Malone notes that "Rose Maddox was one of several women who began to compete favorably with men in the postwar years."

By 1961 she and fellow Nashville outsider Buck Owens had two of the year's biggest hits with "Loose Talk" and "Mental Cruelty," confirming her as perhaps the top female country singer of the time. Not until 1996, however, was Rose even nominated for a Grammy (for her *$35 and a Dream* album). That disc was titled for a number that David Price wrote after reading her biography. Rose explained, "He told me the next day that he decided my life would make a good song." The result—composed more than sixty years after the Maddox family departed from Alabama—was "$35 and a Dream."

After having been in frail health for many years, the "bellerin'" little sister died in 1998. Although Rose had been granted a square on the Country Music Hall of Fame's Walkway of Stars, she was never inducted into the hall itself and neither was the family group in which her career started. "And don't *that* tell you somethin' about the politics in this music," says Bill Woods. Country music lost one of its unique and accomplished performers, and too few people in the business seemed to notice.

California's country scene was in an uncertain position early in the 1960s. Since Nashville's successful promotion of itself as this music's one and only true home, performers in the Golden State were being increasingly marginalized, while fewer and fewer performers were migrating west. Yet by the end of the decade country music here was once more big indeed. Credit for that resurgence goes largely to two singers originally from the Southwest, Buck Owens and Glen Campbell, and to a producer from the Midwest, Ken Nelson.

Also important was that some rock and roll, which had started as such defiant music, lost its Little Richard–Jerry Lee Lewis–Elvis Presley edge and moved toward softer pop styles, so the hard-driving country offered by Owens and Wynn Stewart in particular emerged as a new sound of rebellion. Herb Pedersen of the Desert Rose Band recalls that the incendiary performances of early rhythm and blues and rockabilly were followed by "Frankie Avalon and the Italian crooners. Sappy stuff. People started switching over. I switched over."

Owens and Campbell gave California a one-two commercial punch in the 1960s that was rivaled only by the resurgence of Johnny Cash who, ironically enough, had moved his family to the state in 1959. "I fell right into the Southern California life style and made believe I was enjoying it," he wrote in *Man in Black*. He added, "I even developed a taste for vodka, wine, and beer. I found that you can cultivate a taste for anything as long as you keep on tasting." Although it would be more accurate to refer to that mode of behavior as "a" rather than "the" Southern California lifestyle, there is little doubt that Cash adopted it. In 1961 the family relocated to the Ventura area and remained there until Cash—his marriage coming apart—began residing in Nashville between tours.

WYNN STEWART

Wynn Stewart. Courtesy of Kern County Museum. Used by permission.

In fact he was on tour much of that period, and he was—by his own admission—on drugs much of that period, too. Several near-fatal episodes turned the singer around, and by 1967 his "most Californian" album *Johnny Cash at Folsom Prison* was spectacularly successful. The next year he married June Carter, and the following year he gained his own ABC television variety show. He had continued producing hits despite his problems in the course of the decade, but his personal life had neared the bottom before he began to put himself back together.

The talented threesome summed up country music nationwide in the decade: Cash, the erstwhile rockabilly turned southern iconoclast; Campbell, the epitome of countrified pop; and Owens, the Telecaster clarion of the hard-country Bakersfield Sound. The other major California story was the prominence of Bakersfield's image. Riding the success of Owens, the Kern Country town was suddenly called "Nashville West," but another journalistic innovation, "Buckersfield," was closer to the truth. Bakersfield came to stand for Buck's successful, independent approach in the face of country pop from both Nashville and Hollywood.

What was really happening in the 1960s, though, was a bit more complex and considerably more revealing. The Golden State's grandiose myth had barely tolerated Bakersfield and had largely ignored country music, but its reality embraced both. Not until the 1960s did the nation's media finally acknowledge California's eminent position in the world of what some still called hillbilly music. To make that concession, however, journalists also had to reluctantly recognize "the other California"—the nonstereotypical sections where so many hard-working Californians actually lived: Arvin and Downey, Yreka and Richmond, Bell Gardens and Bakersfield—the latter a prosperous city long-vilified within the state by cliché-loving journalists and entertainers. It was perhaps predictable that the media, awakening from their collective nap, would assign centrality of a supposedly bumpkin music to a supposedly bumpkin locale: Bakersfield became Nashville West.

It did indeed then shelter a country cluster. According to writer Paul Hemphill the community hosted about 200 musicians, 35 songwriters, 10 music publishing companies, 5 studios, 3 recording labels, 2 booking agencies, and an assortment of lively nightclubs in the late 1960s. In 1965 the area produced its own native-born star Merle Haggard. Another Bakersfield product, Dallas Frazier, won song of the year from the Country Music Association in 1967 for "There Goes My Everything," while Owens and the Buckaroos continued bulldozing the decade.

During the 1960s, too, Bakersfield's Mosrite of California was producing 1,000 guitars a month—single necks, double necks, even triple necks—and developing its own Mosrite Records. Owned by brothers Semie and Andy Moseley, Oklahoma natives, it was not the only guitar manufacturer in the area then. Standell, Grugget, and Hallmark had local shops, but Mosrite dominated; and such stars as Campbell, Little Jimmy Dickens, Barbara Mandrell, Ronnie Sessions, Tommy Duncan, Joe Maphis, and Don Rich all played its instruments.

Was the country-music balance shifting to the West? In a word, no, but the Kern County seat was on a roll then, and writer Martha Hume revealed both a misunderstanding of history and a sanguine projection about the future when she observed

> In contrast to its contemporary country cousin, the Nashville Sound, music made in Bakersfield was rawer, incorporating the steel guitar of pickers like Ralph Mooney, and also more rhythmic, including many elements of rockabilly music. The success of musicians such as Owens and Haggard marked the first time that country music produced in California became popular on a national level, and that success in turn marked the beginning of the end of Nashville's complete hegemony over the production of country music.

The music was indeed distinct, but it was not even close to being California's first national success. And Nashville still dominates this music, yet Bakersfield did come to symbolize western resistance to Tennessee's corporate control and cookie-cutter music.

Along with that story, another important one was developing in this state as the 1960s progressed: the powerful musical merging called California country rock, which had been earlier heralded by the songs of Ricky Nelson. *Bright Lights and Country Music* thrust Nelson into the country-music mix in 1966, and his autobiographical song "You Just Can't Quit" hit the top of California's country-radio charts. The following year Rick (no longer Ricky) formed the Stone Canyon Band around the talents of Randy Meisner, and he began work on another good collection, *Country Fever*. Impressive as Nelson's performances were, much of the public seemed stuck on his teenage rock-and-roll image. Nelson and the band cut three more country albums during the decade—*Another Side of Rick* (1968), *In Concert* (1969), and *Rudy the Fifth* (1969).

Like many musicians in the 1960s, he was suspended between rock and country, between old and new, but unlike most others, he was trying to prove—to himself, mostly—that he was the genuine goods, something most of his musical peers accepted as fact. Said Kris Kristofferson, "[Rick was] a musician and a troubadour because he was *in* it."

During this period showmanship became central with the widening influence of rock and roll, and youth culture became an international phenomenon—music and fans, attire and conduct, often interchangeable from concert to concert, location to location. Then, as now, kids often

Johnny Cash (left), during his California stay, with Herb Henson. Courtesy
of Rick Henson. Used by permission.

sought immediate gratification; music, sex, and drugs could provide that.
Country music didn't embody this excitement early in the 1960s, although the rumblings of its own brand of rock and rebellion could already be heard.

This was an especially exciting decade in California's country music,
but a troubling one in society, with heroes assassinated, dreams shattered,
and disturbing questions raised. On November 24, 1962, California was
declared the nation's most populous state; an index of how things have
changed is that the event (or "pseudoevent" since no one knew for certain if it was actually true) was much celebrated.

In the Golden State as in the nation seeds of change sown in World
War II bore social consequences: civil rights, women's rights, environmental activism, student rebellion, the antiwar movement. The state,
like the nation, was painfully tested. The youth culture began asserting
itself politically. For instance, when the House Un-American Activities
Committee—increasingly seen as a government witch-hunt—convened

in San Francisco in 1960, hundreds of students protested. They were met with police clubs and high-powered spray from fire hoses. The placid public asked, "What's *wrong* with those people?"

Four years later, the regents of the University of California, who defied a 1963 Supreme Court decision and restricted on-campus political activity, triggered the Free Speech Movement at the Berkeley campus. Eventually student protests were generated across the country, especially after 1968 when the U.S. war in Vietnam increasingly polarized the nation: "What's *wrong* with those people?"

With its large, heterogeneous population, California had endured a history of racism dating to the decimation of native peoples. The Golden State's cities tended to be as segregated as their southern counterparts; Los Angeles in fact was called one of the two most segregated cities in the nation in the 1960s. In November of 1964 the Rumford Fair Housing Law, which forbade racial discrimination in real estate transactions statewide, was overturned by California's voters, who passed Proposition 14. Although the state supreme court later reversed it, that measure revealed that a racist core remained intact here. Less than a year later the crowded black ghetto in the segregated Watts area of Los Angeles exploded into a week-long rebellion, and many whites expressed both outrage and bafflement: "What's *wrong* with those people?"

Before long the supposedly docile Hispanic minority began to follow the example of a navy veteran named César Chavez, who had joined forces with Filipino-American Larry Itliong to form the United Farm Workers of America. In cities and on campuses the term "Chicano" came to represent a new Latino militancy. Eventually Chavez initiated an effective boycott of table grapes, and many in the majority asked: "What's *wrong* with those people?"

Historian James J. Rawls has written that a key factor in California politics in the 1960s "was the emergence of vividly colorful but startlingly eccentric new varieties of fanaticism at both ends of the political spectrum." Zealots like the Red Guerrilla Army and Venceremos on the left, the John Birch Society and the Posse Comitatus on the right, seemed increasingly to sum up this turbulent time. The educational gap that had first appeared a decade earlier became dramatic—student protesters (many rock fans) frequently on the left, blue-collar counterparts (many country fans) frequently on the right—both sides convinced of their po-

Fresno favorite Dave Stogner (right) with his band, featuring songwriter Red
Simpson (left) on piano and Norman Hamlet (second from right), future
leader of the Strangers, on steel. Courtesy of Kern County Museum. Used
by permission.

sition's righteousness. Antiwar activism in particular was dramatically on
the increase as the decade closed, and country music's response was
increasingly right wing. In 1966 *Billboard* magazine explained that "since
the first of the year, well over 100 Vietnam [War] records have been
released . . . a dozen making *Billboard's* country charts."

By then Kris Kristofferson, an iconoclastic former Pomona College
student who had been an army helicopter pilot, had contributed the
counterjingoistic "The Viet Nam Blues" recorded by Jack Sanders. The
state's strongest example of a political lyric, though, was Merle Haggard's tongue-in-cheek "Okie from Musokogee," and his later, mean-
spirited, "Fightin' Side of Me." More important, perhaps, was that most
of country radio cast itself as a conservative bastion in opposition to students and liberals, to rock and folk music, which were identified with
leftist positions. Stations began referring to country as "America's music"
or "all-American music," and it came to be viewed as patriotic by im-

plication: it was identified with flag decals on hard hats and, from the point of view of many liberals, with political naiveté, too.

In the midst of this national pugnaciousness, another small battle was being waged as Buck Owens defied the South's grip on country music. In 1965 his famous "Pledge to Country Music" ran in Nashville's *Music City News*:

> I shall sing no song that is not a country song.
>
> I shall make no record that is not a country record.
>
> I refuse to be known as anything but a country singer.
>
> I am proud to be associated with country music.
>
> Country music and country music fans made me what I am today.
>
> And I shall not forget it.

Buck's pledge seemed simple: in California we're sticking with the real deal, no matter what you folks're doing.

That year Buck also released his *I've Got a Tiger by the Tail* album, and by then he pretty much had the country-music world by the tail as well. Meanwhile the bosses in Nashville continued their move toward the dubbed and overdubbed recording of muted instruments, of background singers, and of pop-style vocals. Owens and the Buckaroos, on the other hand, cut their records live, and their sharp, up-tempo sound was driven by Buck and Don Rich on Fender Telecasters: their mutant honky-tonk much influenced by rockabilly.

Some traditionalists, though, were already peeved at Owens because he had also released his version of Chuck Berry's "Memphis" in 1965, a song that they had classified as *not* country. In fact, Owens was open-minded and perceptive enough to recognize the country–rockabilly–rhythm-and-blues–rock-and-roll continuum and to understand that Berry's work was a product of that association. "Listen to the lyrics [of 'Memphis']. If they're not country lyrics . . . the melody—if that ain't a country melody," he pointed out. "The only thing was, a black man was singin' it. A black man who I was a big fan of."

To no one's surprise both overt and covert racism were thriving in the country-music world, and Buck might have roiled the water even more if he had added that Berry was also a black man who had acknowledged be-ing much influenced by country music. Owens, unlike many—perhaps most—of his peers, recognized the ignorance of those who refused to acknowledge the country roots of rock and the black roots of country. He later cut a dynamite version of Berry's "Johnny B. Goode," covered the Coasters' "Charlie Brown," and revived "Hot Dog," his own first rockabilly song from 1956.

In 1961 Buck recorded two hit duets with another notably independent West Coast singer, Rose Maddox: "Mental Cruelty" and "Loose Talk." Two years later the duo struck again with "Sweethearts in Heaven." But with his fifteen consecutive *Billboard* number-one recordings between 1963 and 1967 Owens overwhelmed the southern establishment. (A grudge lingers; he has rarely been given his due there and was not inducted into the Hall of Fame until 1996, long after many performers of much less accomplishment were honored.)

The Country Music Association meanwhile continued to grind out press releases that lauded the countrypolitan Nashville Sound In 1964, however, Californians intensified the regional rivalry when Eddie Miller, Tommy Wiggins, and Chris and Mickey Christensen formed the Academy of Country and Western Music (now the Academy of Country Music). While the Country Music Association was, as Jonny Whiteside notes, "the insiders' club, made up of song publishers and record executives," the new group welcomed fans, performers, and anyone else. "In its early years," according to the organization's own history, "the Academy sought not only to interest the general public in the appeal of the music, but to demonstrate to other industries the value of using country music in their advertising, and its celebrities as spokespersons."

In 1965 the Academy of Country Music began presenting its annual music awards, and the group had the effect of highlighting West Coast entertainers. Among the winners were Owens as male vocalist, and Bonnie Owens as female vocalist, Haggard as new male vocalist, the Buckaroos as touring band, Biff Collie as disc jockey, Billy Mize as television personality, and Roger Miller as man of the year. Scrambling to catch up, the Country Music Association launched its own awards show two years later with a much narrower voting base, and only one California act, the Buckaroos, was honored. The rivalry between Tennessee and the Golden State had intensified during those years, and the competing awards shows made it clear to the public that more than one locale and style were central to country music.

The Academy of Country Music's 1967 winner for male vocalist was Glen Campbell, whose soft-country style troubled many West Coast purists. Successful country-pop recordings had not only been produced in California but were still being produced in the state, so Nashville was by no means alone in diluting this music. Capitol had originally accented modern arrangements, including some extravagant string backgrounds that preceded the Nashville Sound by a decade. The differences between pop and country musical categories became less distinctive, and the number of listeners grew as companies recorded artists backed by arrangements that could have been written for Frank Sinatra or the Andrews Sisters. Much of the expanding urban audience readily accepted pop-flavored music, as commercial appeal overrode country traditionalism. Since the 1940s, under the aegis of Lee Gillette, Capitol Records had taken the lead in developing what might be called a middle-of-the-road sound, one that initially featured many duets with pop and country singers: Kay Starr and Tennessee Ernie Ford, Dinah Shore and George Morgan, the Andrews Sisters and Ernest Tubb, Margaret Whiting and Jimmy Wakely (a curiously consistent pairing of female pop stars with male country stars).

Gillette's successor as country-music boss at Capitol Records was Ken Nelson, who produced both hard and soft styles. In 1967, for example, Capitol's Hollywood facility released records by Arkansas native Campbell and by a native of Mississippi who had grown up in Palm Springs, Bobbie Gentry. Campbell's "Gentle on My Mind" and Gentry's "Ode to Billie Joe" (which she wrote) both shot to the top of country and pop charts. Most of Gentry's successes after "Ode to Billy Joe" would come in duets with Campbell. Their 1968 album *Bobbie Gentry and Glen Campbell* earned gold records for the artists and produced chart singles with their versions of previous Everly Brothers' hits, "Let It Be Me" and "All I Have to Do Is Dream."

Campbell was an established musician and singer when he had been signed by Capitol in 1962. He had skillfully played rhythm guitar and had sung harmony with many artists and groups, including Haggard's band the Strangers. For a time he had even filled in for Brian Wilson with the Beach Boys and also played with the Champs (of "Tequila" fame). In his first solo efforts at Capitol, Glen floundered with inappropriate material. "Finally," he recalls, "I worked out an arrangement with Al DeLory where I could do a couple of songs of my own choosing on each session."

Bobbie Gentry and Glen Campbell. From the Gid Tanner Artist File #NF1996, The Southern Folklife Collection, Wilson Library, The University of North Carolina at Chapel Hill.

In 1967 he broke through with the John Hartford song he had touted to his bosses, "Gentle on My Mind"; it was the first of a string of triumphs with soft-country vocal hits. By 1968—after two gold records, plus awards for album of the year, male vocalist of the year, television personality of the year, the Country Music Association's entertainer of the year, three Grammys, and more—the Arkansas native was the nation's top-selling recording artist, displacing even the Beatles. He also hosted the award-winning network television show the "Glen Campbell Goodtime Hour" from 1969 to 1973.

Glen was not a pop star poaching into country but—like Ernie Ford—a man with deep country roots. He was also, to quote writer Hemphill, an example of "the ones who *respect* Ernest Tubb but don't want to *be* Ernest Tubb*.*" In fact Campbell seems in many ways a prototypical country singer. He was born and raised on a farm near Billstown, Arkansas, close to the corners of Louisiana, Texas, and Oklahoma. The product of a large, musical family, he received his first guitar when he was seven years old, a $5 Sears Roebuck model. With his seven brothers and four sisters, he sang in the choir of the Church of Christ, and he occasionally sneaked a listen at a livelier Pentecostal church. At fourteen Glen left school and toured Wyoming with Uncle Boo Campbell's three-piece band, then joined the western swing band of another uncle, Dick Bills, in Albuquerque. Four years later he formed his own ensemble Glen Campbell and his Western Wranglers. "I'd make as much playing at Coon Holler on Friday and Saturday as I could make picking cotton or gathering corn all week," he remembers, "and I didn't like looking a mule in the rump."

In 1960 Campbell drove with his wife and a small trailer full of their belongings to Los Angeles, where he found studio work. He also played at clubs and honky-tonks and appeared on local television. Capitol signed him two years later, and his skill as an instrumentalist was featured on a series of albums. Five years later, though, "Gentle on My Mind" made him a star.

Campbell's performances on various Jimmy Webb songs—"By the Time I Get to Phoenix," "Galveston," "Wichita Lineman"—came to define the West Coast countrypolitan of the day. The singer himself observed that "Webb's stuff is a little bit Country. But it's like John Hartford says, they have to quit writin' about 'You broke my heart so now I'm gonna break your jaw.' . . . Actually, I don't like to segregate music. . . . It's like when I record, I don't aim at anything. I just find a good song and do it like I want to, and if country fans gripe or pop fans gripe, I cain't help it."

Although his great success enhanced the national acceptance of this music, it also made him an enduring target of resentful traditionalists. For those who didn't appreciate the affable Arkansan's pop version of this music—and who chose to forget the gaudy outfits worn by "Hank Williams, Hank Snow, Hank Thompson, and Hank Hank," as one wag put it—his 1975 record of the year and gold record for "Rhinestone Cowboy" summarized the ills of West Coast countrypolitan. Ironically most of the real rhinestone cowboys were parading around Tennessee.

John Hartford, who wrote Campbell's first great hit, was himself a performer and writer of considerable skill. He had also experienced both the Nashville and the Southern California scenes, having recorded his first five albums in the Tennessee city, then subsequent ones in Hollywood. He suggests why so many artists were attracted to California in the 1970s. "I had a constant fight on my hands in Nashville. I was constantly told to 'be careful you don't turn off that country audience.'" In California, though, "you have a bigger palette to work with . . . people who can give you a strictly Nashville sound if you want it, but they can also digress with you." Hartford understands this musical world: "There's a lot of fantastically real country music and there's a lot of bullshit." Distinguishing bulls from bullshit is often a tough task.

Author John Grissim described the Hartford-Campbell-Webb songs at one point as the "California Sound . . . a blend of pop and pop-Country which has brought down on Hollywood the wrath of Country purists." Of course another California Sound thrived as an antidote to the version Grissim defined. At the time Gentry, Hartford, Campbell, and Webb were riding countrypolitan high in Los Angeles, just north in the honky-tonks and beer bars of Bakersfield (where Campbell himself had served part of his tough apprenticeship) that Telecaster-driven Bakersfield version of the California Sound was picking up steam. In some circles, though, honky-tonk itself had grown unfashionable. As Bill C. Malone explains, "The style that had once dominated country music ran counter to the crossover impulse and threatened the respectability that the country industry was trying to attain. Honky-tonk music was too 'country' and too reflective of seamy barroom culture to attract that broad audience that country music was trying to win."

For many California fans, though, the twanging electric guitars of honky-tonk remained the core of country music in the late 1960s; much from Hollywood and Nashville sounded like elevator lullabies. Journalist Tony Scherman has predicted that "a century from now, honky-tonk will probably be considered the classic country-music style," despite—or because of—its ability to discomfort some listeners. "The titter of sophisticates may only reflect their discomfort with honky-tonk's directness, their embarrassment at so naked an emotional display," adds Scherman.

Back in the early 1960s on the heels of the rejection of rockabilly by country traditionalists, honky-tonk's national appeal had begun to wane, especially on the airwaves where disc jockey discretion was swept away by national playlists, which sought to create hits, not merely to recognize them; pop-rock styles dominated there. Top 40 can be said to have limited listeners' choices, signaling the end of those call-in request shows that old-timers so loved. "It all got too damn slick on the radio" says Ken Johnson of Apple Valley, but he adds, "we could go to Juanita's in Rosamond and hear Bill Woods or Woody Murray, stuff that disk-jockeys'd forgotten."

Ken Nelson wisely promoted parallel country tracks at Capitol—"soft" (Campbell, Gentry, etc.) and "hard" (principally Owens and the Buckaroos). The latter were allowed to record in Buck's Oildale studio, then Capitol packaged and released the records with few if any changes. The producer said of the Bakersfield area, "It was much different than Los Angeles. It was more Okie, you know. . . . I got a lot of talent out there." As it turned out Capitol produced a string of successes with both countrypolitan and what was being called the Bakersfield Sound.

◄ ►   ◄ ►   ◄ ►

Excerpt from a conversation between Ken Nelson and Buck Owens in the presence of Richard Chon—Bakersfield, June 1, 1995:

Ken Nelson: Well the thing I remember about you, you kept asking me to audition you to sing. And I don't know if you remember this or not, but I was like, "Yeah, yeah, okay. Get away from me boy" [laughs]. You bugged me, see.

Buck Owens: You always were so nice to me. You always had me do sessions no matter what they were.

Nelson: That's right. But, anyway, finally one day I said, "Well, okay come on in and we'll audition you." And if I remember rightly, which I think I do, you went in and you started to sing and I cut you off after about sixteen measures, and I said, "Okay, that's it." And I think you came out figuring that's it; he's gonna turn me down. But I said, "No. I'll sign you."

Owens: You remember this? I remember something like this. We were doing a Farmer Boys' session.

Nelson: Yes.

Owens: And we was about halfway through it. You said, "Buck, did you sign with anybody yet?" And I said, "Nope." And I said, "I have a thing with Columbia."

Nelson: Don Law. I remember you saying something about that.

Owens: So you said, "Well we'll finish this session and we'll go up to my office." I said, "Okay," because I said I'd like to think about it. So we did a couple more songs and we came out, and you said, "Let's go to my office." And we went up to your office and you put this contract [in front of me] and said, "Okay here." And I said, "Ken"—I remember this distinctly—I said, "Ken, you remember I said I wanted to think about it?" You said, "It's been an hour and a half. How long does it take you to think about it?" So you know what I did? I signed it right there. Never had a better deal in my life.

Nelson: I remember also in Chicago, your contract was up, and I brought a contract with me. And I hadn't read it closely before I brought it . . . and Scotty, who takes care of the business, had put a clause in there where you would have to sign over half of your songs . . .

Owens: Twenty-five percent.

Nelson: . . . the royalties. And I took a pen and crossed it off and said, "Forget it."

Owens: I said, "Ken, what's that?" And you said, what you actually said was, "I'd like to know what that is, too. I don't understand it." And you took your pen out and scratched it through. But that was standard for legal.

Nelson: The record companies did that a lot. And as a matter of fact, let's just say some A&R men would have practically all the royalties signed over to them. Because they would tell the artist, "This is the promotion. You're going to be able to promote yourself. This will get you out on the road. You'll be able to make money." Gosh, that used to get me mad. That was wrong.

Owens: And you heard stories about those people all the time. But we never heard one story about you.

Nelson: You couldn't.

Owens: Cause you didn't do it.

Nelson: I never did it. No sir.... Another thing at the time, artists were charged for their recording sessions. And if an artist wasn't making enough money, he owed the company and the businessman would come in and say, "What's this? Get rid of him." And I lost some good artists because of that. But anyway, your first couple of records or so didn't sell too much, and you were in the hole, and they came to me and said, "Why don't you get rid of him." And I said, "No way."

Owens: I'm glad you did.

Nelson: Oh, no. I said, "No way." I remember Royal Gilmore as the head of A&R, he came to me and said, "Dump him." And I said, "No way." Because I just had faith in you.... I didn't sign you because, man, you're going to be fantastic. No, I signed you because you had talent.

Owens: You loved to sign people that had their own songs. their own sound. We was talking today, you said, "You know, if they had the songs and they had the sound and knew what they wanted when they come in there"—we're talking about how you produced.

Merle and I was talking about it on the phone last night, how you produced. Merle said to me, "You know, if we hadn't have gotten with Ken Nelson, you and me might never have gotten to be ourselves."

◄ ►   ◄ ►   ◄ ►

Young Merle Haggard's second recording in 1963 on Bakersfield's Tally Records, "Sing a Sad Song," written by Wynn Stewart, climbed onto the national charts. His follow-up, "You Don't Have Very Far to Go" on one side and "Sam Hill" on the other, also charted. Then in 1965 Hag cut Liz Anderson's "All My Friends Are Gonna Be Strangers" and cracked the top 10. Capitol Records bought his contract from Tally's Fuzzy Owen and

Lewis Talley. Merle, by then an established performer in California, had scored not only as a soloist but also with a series of sterling duets with Bonnie Owens (their only rivals as a duo in the state were the lively Johnny and Joni Mosby).

Anderson also provided Merle's first number-one song in 1967 "I'm a Lonesome Fugitive." Haggard had almost missed that landmark song by Liz. She "came to a show we were doing in Sacramento," Merle recalls. "She said she had some songs, but I wouldn't have listened if it hadn't been for my brother Lowell. It turned out she had six hits in her pocket." More importantly her songs provided an important lesson for Haggard as a songwriter, who had earlier scored with tough drinking numbers like "Swinging Doors" and "The Bottle Let Me Down." He had not much mentioned his prison background up to that time, although it would have resonated an old theme in country music. "I'm a Lonesome Fugitive" burst on the scene just when the public's fascination with outlaws had once again been stimulated, principally by Johnny Cash. Suddenly here was a real former convict, and the allure grew more intense.

For Haggard as a songwriter it was a galvanizing moment; Anderson's songs

> kind of opened up a whole trend of songs, such as "Branded Man" and "Sing Me Back Home." It gave me thought for writing. It gave me direction for writing. You see, what it was, with that song, I was really and finally some way or another come together—musically and image-wise. I mean, it was a true song. I wasn't trying to shit nobody, because long ago I had made the decision not to try to hide my past. But then I found out it was one of the most interesting things about me.

A quick learner, Merle refused to be imprisoned, as it were, by the bar songs and prison songs with which he enjoyed early success. He had eight more number-one hits in the two years that followed, and a song that didn't reach that peak, "Today I Started Loving You Again," has become a standard. Among other classic numbers from that period was "Mama Tried." His albums such as *Strangers, Sing Me Back Home,* and *Swinging Doors* established the young Californian as an exceptional talent.

Merle's award-winning band the Strangers was at the same time beginning to challenge the Buckaroos as the best in the business. Its personnel at one time included as alternating lead guitarists Roy Nichols and James Burton, plus Glen D. Hardin on piano, Ralph Mooney on steel, and none other than Glen Campbell on rhythm guitar and singing harmony—a group of all-stars. Moreover fans at Hag's live performances heard a band, a singer, and a songwriter unwilling to remain trapped in any single groove. One set might offer a playful version of Tommy Collins's "Shade-Tree (Fix-It Man)," followed by Hag and Red Simpson's heartbreaker "You Don't Have Very Far to Go," then close with Anderson's "All My Friends Are Gonna Be Strangers." By the end of the decade he and his band constituted a major musical force.

Nineteen sixty-nine turned out to be remarkable for Haggard, for it saw the recording of such exemplary singles as "I Take a Lot of Pride in What I Am," "Mama's Hungry Eyes," and "Workin' Man Blues." Nevertheless a lesser musical effort dominated: "Okie from Muskogee," which Merle cowrote with band member Eddie Burris. It captured a huge "silent majority" market and made the former convict an icon to that unhappy, conservative constituency.

One of the most unusual and perceptive responses to Merle's new political image came from *People's World*, the American Communist Party's newspaper:

> If Merle Haggard is a conscious right winger, then so are a lot of other people in the U.S. The straight fact is that Haggard represents in a public way the resentments and aspirations of the southwestern working people, who have an importance greater than their numbers.
>
> . . . Haggard is the son of Okie parents who rode their running boards to the promised land during the Depression. He worked in the oil fields near Bakersfield. From the nothingness that is the lot of working people in a capitalist society, he has managed to become a star in a type of music that is both a glorification of that nothingness and a cry against it.

Haggard's sung poetry had by then begun to stimulate considerable interest among so-called progressives and intellectuals, and "Okie from Muskogee" hit them hard, leading to a left-wing backlash. Nevertheless many younger musicians and songwriters remained enthralled by his lyrics and music, and for good reason, as it turned out.

As the 1960s progressed, a number of pioneering country artists were

growing long in the tooth and weak in the voice, while too few Merle
Haggards, Loretta Lynns, and Charley Prides were emerging to replace
them. At the same time commercial forces were continuing the process of
smoothing—or neutering—country music. Scholar Philip Ennis summarized matters this way:

> A double crisis occurred in country music. First, Nashville's major stars
> were aging. . . . The other difficulty was that many of country's new stars
> were minimally country artists. Anne Murray, Olivia Newton-John . . .
> John Denver, Glen Campbell, Jimmy Dean, and others like them had clearly
> diluted the traditional country vocal quality, its instrumental distinctness,
> its lyrical content—so much so that the blurring of the boundary between
> pop and country music threatened to divide country into a museum wing
> at the Ryman Auditorium in Nashville and a pop wing anchored some-
> where between the executive offices of the major record companies and
> their television studios.

Largely ignored in discussions of this music then was country's commercial cousin, folk, which extended its popularity well into the 1960s.
A significant reason for the continued interest in it seems to have been the
desire to escape (or at least feign escape) from the crassness of commercial popular culture; some fans sought to find white cultural expressions
at a time when other ethnic voices were becoming popular and when
racism and defiance were dominating images, especially from the South.
This movement also reflected a continuing desire for songs with substantial subjects and themes; as folk's prominence grew, it also became a
major component on pop charts.

Folk music's popularity broadened during the decade, with considerable television exposure on programs such as "Hootenanny" and the
"Smothers Brothers' Show." Conservative country music was showcased
principally on the perennial "Grand Ole Opry" in the South, while the revived "Melody Ranch"—starring Johnny Bond and Billy Mize on Gene
Autry's KTLA in Los Angeles—was California's principal choice. This period represented folk music's high tide, while conservative country's
general influence seemed to be waning.

One variation of folk expression, protest songs, became central to the
Civil Rights and antiwar movements of the time. Californian Malvina

Reynolds emerged as a favorite writer of them, and her "Little Boxes" was perhaps the benchmark for this subgenre. A former professor, she had begun penning lyrics in the late 1930s. By the 1950s everyone from the Almanac Singers to Pete Seeger were singing her words, and she was acknowledged to be a major writer. When "Little Boxes"—a commentary on look-alike suburban houses and on society—appeared in 1964, Reynolds (born in 1900) became not merely the "Singing Grandmother" but a mature and clever voice of reason and resistance.

Like country this music was of course composed of many subgenres—British ballads, the blues, prison songs, labor lyrics, and others—and another Californian, Joan Baez, seemed capable of singing them all. She had stopped the show at the 1959 Newport Folk Festival when she made her big-time debut. Despite her peerless position among female singers and the tremendous popularity of her albums, the young woman's outspoken liberal politics prompted many disc jockeys to avoid playing her recordings for years. She was considered the left wing of country folk music. Not until 1971, when she recorded "The Night They Drove Old Dixie Down" in Nashville, did she enjoy a top chart hit.

Baez was raised in Redlands and graduated from Palo Alto High School. Her Mexican-Irish ethnic blend was typical of many people living in the Golden State. She was also the product of a turbulent time, so her views and actions upset many conservative fans of country music. Unlike most other high-profile social critics during those years, however, she saw and pointed out the weaknesses of all sides.

As it turned out a good many country fans resented folk's academic and leftist tilt, and most folk fans disliked country's "regressive" social and political connotations, but that didn't keep artists from successful crossovers: Johnny Cash cut "It Ain't Me Babe," while Buffy St. Marie recorded "I'm Gonna Be a Country Girl Again." Bobby Bare had a hit with "Four Strong Winds," while Baez offered her version of "Blue."

In 1967 the man considered by many to be the dominant force in American popular music in the 1960s, Bob Dylan, alienated folk fans when he entered neowestern ranks and performed with amplified instruments on his *John Wesley Harding* album. Two years later he recorded the landmark *Nashville Skyline* album that included a fine duet on "Girl from the North Country" with Johnny Cash. These albums are credited with having loosened the prejudices of pop critics so that they began to offer their approvals of various blendings of country with other kinds of music.

Dylan's influence on country lyrics was a benefit of the folk explosion. Although he never developed a significant following among its fans and few of his songs had any impact on its charts, many country singers and songwriters were much affected by his creations. Dylan himself had been impressed by Woody Guthrie, as his writing revealed. In the 1960s and '70s Bob's influence brought a new kind of social realism, as well as new forms of poetics to country, as exemplified in the works of Kris Kristofferson ("Sunday Mornings Coming Down"), Tom T. Hall ("The Year That Clayton Delaney Died"), and Dick Feller ("Some Days Are Diamonds [Some Days Are Stone]").

Rock and roll, the national major musical force, drew upon both rockabilly and some folk roots and led to the creation in California of what came to be called country rock. A precise definition of what evolved is difficult because rock itself was so varied. Youthful players of that time were part of the first generation for whom rock and roll had become the primary popular music; their interpretations of *all* song styles, then, were colored by the energy and rebellion originally found at rock's core. Without blinking they could return to roots music—honky-tonk, for instance— while bringing with them rock's shrieking electric guitars and up-front showmanship.

Throughout the 1960s the boundary between rock and country grew less distinct in some music. That blending of course led labelers to another problem: What *was* this stuff? What should they call it? Redneck rock? Progressive country? Country rock? A *new* California Sound? In his book *The Heart of Rock and Soul*, Dave Marsh probably makes the wisest choice by simply ignoring categories and allowing the music itself to direct his picks for the 1,001 best singles ever recorded. His choices included ample representations from Buck Owens and Merle Haggard, and the author asserts that Owens "was probably the greatest country artist of the 1960s, and certainly the one most influenced by rock and soul."

Whatever else was true in the tangle of labels, the state that had welcomed and refined the youth culture's music from the start became a powerful nexus of rock, country, and folk in the late 1960s, as can be illustrated by its "newgrass" (sometimes aptly called "blewgrass") connection. At that time and well into the following decade many variations of the music Bill Monroe and the Blue Grass Boys had developed were being played as remedies to Nashville's and Hollywood's pop impulses. As banjoist Eddie Adcock pointed out, "Bluegrass is one of . . . [the] other kinds of music that Nashville can't control." With its firm rooting in traditional southern styles, bluegrass featured sounds inherently opposed to heavily produced countrypolitan cuts. Everyone, from the "old-timey" Hotmud Family in Ohio, to the youth-oriented Earl Scruggs Revue (featuring Earl's three sons), to the David Grisman Quintet's jazz-bluegrass fusion in California, spoke of independence from commercial concerns. This was a "music-first-popularity-second" movement.

Bluegrass festivals during those socially tumultuous years offered one of the few settings where rednecks, hippies, and many folks in between, as well as their music, mingled. Neotraditional acoustic sounds might have seemed to be antithetical to electric rock and roll, but young musicians, especially in Southern California, rejected musical stereotypes. In the innovative tradition of Owens—who would himself record bluegrass hits such as "Ruby" and "Roll in My Sweet Baby's Arms"—they were by then experimenting with string bands, jug bands, electric bands, with any bands that worked and several kinds that didn't.

The Kentucky Colonels (earlier called the Country Boys and Three Little Country Boys), for instance, had begun performing in 1954 and eventually appeared on such major venues as "Town Hall Party" and "Hometown Jamboree," presenting lively traditional arrangements that developed a distinct following. Exposure on major television programs originating in the Los Angeles area—the "Beverly Hillbillies" and the "Andy Griffith Show"—demonstrated that this southern form could appeal to a wide audience indeed. In the 1960s they became celebrities in such prestigious settings as the Newport Folk Festival. After the band dissolved, cofounder Roland White went on to join Country Gazette, an enduring bluegrass favorite, while his brother Clarence moved toward rock.

Perhaps a more significant bluegrass unit on the West Coast was the Dillards, originally from St. Louis. They became regulars on Andy Griffith's network television program for three years in the early 1960s, on which they portrayed the Darlings, a family of stereotypical hillbillies who could not function well in town but who could certainly play bluegrass. Bill C. Malone credits them with having "introduced Ozark humor and sophisticated musicianship to a national audience." The Dillards recorded for one of the big folk labels of the time, Elektra, and played at most of the West's top folk venues.

In some ways their experience was roughly parallel to that of other experimental country groups because the Dillards were sharply criticized by purists when they added drums and electronically amplified instruments, shades of Bob Wills and his not-so-hidden drummer. Founder Doug Dillard eventually left the band in 1968 and formed—with Gene Clark and Bernie Leadon—an experimental folk-rock and bluegrass group called the Dillard and Clark Expedition. The original Dillards didn't fold; with the addition of guitarist and banjoist Herb Pedersen and drummer Paul York, it continued as a force in what came to be called "progressive" bluegrass into the 1970s.

In 1963 yet another collection of young musicians, this one called the Golden State Boys (later, the Hillmen), began to perform in California. The band featured Rex and Vern Gosdin—the latter is now a significant singer of hard country—Don Parmley, and Chris Hillman. Parmley later teamed with his son David and Larry Stevenson in yet another major group the Bluegrass Cardinals. Hillman went on to become a mover and shaker in three country-rock groups: the Byrds, the Flying Burrito Brothers, and the Desert Rose Band.

Many of the other neobluegrass performers moved toward newer sounds and styles without totally sacrificing traditional elements. As a result they became elements in the burgeoning country-rock scene in Los Angeles, a movement that was at first not entirely distinct from the folk-rock scene there. This movement led to a list of musical unions almost strong enough to be considered quasi-biblical "begats": The Hollies, formed in 1962, included Graham Nash. The Beefeaters, founded in 1964, included Jim (later Roger) McGuinn, Gene Clark, and David Crosby. A few months later Clark, Crosby, and Roger McGuinn joined with Chris Hillman and Michael Clarke to form the Byrds. Meanwhile innovative electric guitarist Clarence White, late of the Three Little Country Boys, joined the Byrds in 1968. In March of 1966 Buffalo Springfield got started with both Stephen Stills and Neil Young as members. Eventually Crosby, Stills, Nash, and Young emerged from those groups. The Byrds meanwhile picked up a youthful vocalist named Gram Parsons. Hillman then joined Parsons and Michael Clarke in the provocative Flying Burrito Brothers. This list could go on and on.

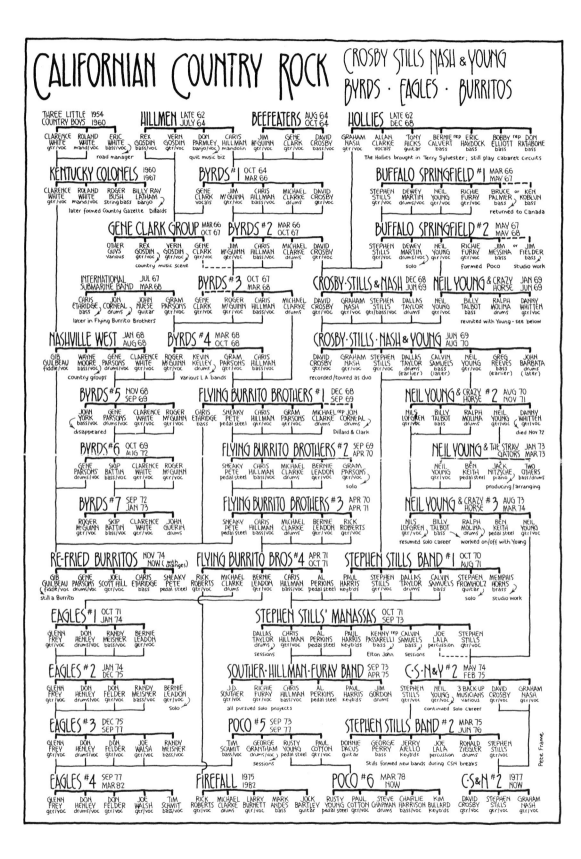

CALIFORNIAN COUNTRY ROCK

CROSBY STILLS NASH & YOUNG
BYRDS · EAGLES · BURRITOS

Pete Frame

In some ways Chris Hillman's career may best summarize the Golden State's innovative uses of country and rock in the past four decades. Born in Los Angeles but raised in rural northern California where country music was the rule not the exception, Chris learned to play guitar and mandolin as he grew up. He later became one of the many Los Angeles musicians who wore a cowboy hat but was perhaps the only one who had in fact worked on a cattle ranch. His move into the "blewgrass" scene in Southern California was natural, and he was considered to be perhaps the premier mandolin player at the time and for some time to come.

In 1964 producer Jim Dickson recruited him for the Byrds, the new band he and Roger McGuinn were forming. For that group Chris played bass, sang, and provided songs. This scene was new for all of them, and David Crosby admits he stood before a mirror trying to figure out how to hold a guitar while not seated on a stool (as he had played on the coffee-house circuit). The group's goal was to retain their folk roots while employing rock approaches—they learned to play electric instruments with late-night rehearsals at Los Angeles's World Pacific Studios and eventually strummed them well indeed—producing hits such as "Mr. Tambourine Man" and "Turn, Turn, Turn."

By the time that group recorded *The Notorious Byrd Brothers* in 1968, a definite country feeling had crept into their music. Unfortunately their internecine disputes, which even included fistfights on stage, were legendary. "We were all heading in different directions. There was a power struggle," explains Roger McGuinn. When Crosby left the unit, Hillman helped recruit Gram Parsons to replace him. Parsons in turn reinforced the country bent favored by Chris. The newly configured group traveled to Nashville and recorded an album called *Sweetheart of the Rodeo* that featured stellar steel guitar work by J. D. Maness. Malone describes it as "extremely influential and thoroughly country." Along with Dylan's *Nashville Skyline*, it is now credited with having epitomized country rock, but it also put a dent in the Byrds' following of rockers.

Songwriter-musician-singer John Hartford, then also much a part of the Los Angeles folk-country-rock milieu, told John Grissim in 1970, "Even though rock groups on the West Coast are very much into the Blue-

"California Country Rock" by Pete Frame. From *The Harmony Illustrated Encyclopedia of Rock* by Mike Clifford. Copyright ©1986 by Mike Clifford. Reprinted by permission of Harmony Books, a division of Crown Publishers, Inc.

The Byrds: Kevin Kelly, Gram Parsons, Roger McGuinn, and Chris Hillman. From the Gid Tanner Artist File #NF1996, The Southern Folklife Collection, Wilson Library, The University of North Carolina at Chapel Hill.

grass thing, there's a great deal of difference in attitude. The Byrds' *Sweetheart of the Rodeo* is really liberal-left country music, both lyrically and in the way it's presented. It's very different from the same type of music put out by someone like Ferlin Husky or Bobby Lord. . . . I tend to like the stuff the rock groups are doing because they're creative and original." Freed from constraints, country, rock, and pop were all redefining themselves and in doing so recognizing that the arbitrary barriers between them need not be respected.

Close to the rock boundary, though, some artists began reclaiming territory ceded by country conservatives in their 1950s flight from rockabilly. As mentioned above, rockabilly had become an essential part of the music scene in California, so there was no great gap to be bridged here between bluegrass, newgrass, honky-tonk, folk, and rock.

A couple of years after the formation of the Byrds, another folk-rock-influenced band coalesced in Los Angeles: Buffalo Springfield. It became for a time the southland's most popular group, featuring a sterling lineup: Stephen Stills, Neil Young, Dewey Martin, Richie Furay, and Bruce Palmer. As the house band at the Whiskey A Go-Go, the Buffs were the hottest ticket in town. Dave Marsh recalls, "In 1966 and 1967, crowds of longhairs gathered on the Sunset Strip near two clubs, the Whiskey A Go-Go and Pandora's Box, blocking sidewalks, smoking dope, spilling into the streets." Predictably the Los Angeles police responded, and what came to be called the Sunset Strip riots followed, an event examined in a song, "For What It's Worth," written by Stills and recorded by Buffalo Springfield in 1967.

This band lasted only two years, disbanding in 1968, but most of its personnel moved on to major successes. Young and Stills became important soloists after departing, then they joined David Crosby and Graham Nash to create Crosby, Stills, Nash, and Young. Jim Messina and Furay formed Poco, what some consider to be the most *country* of country-rock groups, with pedal steel player Rusty Young, drummer George Grantham, and bassist Randy Meisner. That band, with its mountain-style banjo picking, anticipated the neotraditionalist movement a decade later.

Among the most Californian units of the time was the Nitty Gritty Dirt Band, begun in Long Beach in 1966 as an imitation southern jug-string ensemble. At first called the Illegitimate Jug Band, four of its seven members—Bruce Kunkel, Les Thompson, Jimmie Fadden, and John McEun—had been born in Long Beach. Jackson Browne, Ralph Barr, and Jeff Hanna were transplants. Whatever their origins, though, these talented performers broke through when McEun's brother Bill produced their initial album *Nitty Gritty Dirt Band* (1967). They were playing what came to be called good-time music, their sound strongly influenced by traditional country.

Most of the Bay Area groups that touched country music at that time did so indirectly, via a folk-and-blues route so esteemed by beatniks and the hippies. Bob Stephens, who was a student there in the late 1950s and early 1960s, suggests that "Jack Kerouac and Gary Snyder may have had as much musical influence as anyone then. There were people from all over coming to San Francisco and Berkeley to be beatniks, complete with bongos and berets, and Pete Seeger was a king." The folk renaissance powerfully influenced Bay Area music, in no small measure because local collegiates had been enthralled by it.

During the 1960s the Bay Area hosted two outstanding bands that eventually migrated to Texas—Commander Cody and his Lost Planet Airmen (from Michigan) and Asleep at the Wheel (from Pennsylvania and Ohio)—both of which would be associated with the "revivalist" movement, due to their performances of older styles. They represent one of the few times that California, which has so benefited from transplanted Texans, sent significant country musicians to the Lone Star State. Some critics have labeled those two groups, along with a few other California-based bands such as Dan Hicks and his Hot Licks and Poco, new wave country.

Probably closer to traditional country in its music than any other major Bay Area group of the time, Country Joe and the Fish was formed by two Southern California expatriates—Joe McDonald from El Monte and Barry Melton from Van Nuys—who met at the Berkeley Folk Festival. Ironically this group's origins were as much political as musical, and the two put out their initial record with the help of Chris Strachwitz of El Cerrito's Arhoolie Records, a four-song extended play album called *Songs of Opposition*, in time for the anti–Vietnam War teach-in at the University of California at Berkeley in 1965. At that event McDonald and Melton joined other musicians to form the ad hoc Instant Action Jug Band, and navy veteran Country Joe created a classic when he sang "I-Feel-Like-I'm-Fixin'-to-Die Rag." That song placed him as far from country music's conservative thrust as possible. While Haggard was singing "The Fightin' Side of Me" (his musical version of "America: Love It or Leave It"), another Okie, novelist Ken Kesey, would assert at the teach-in, "That 'love-it-or-leave-it' stuff is bullshit. 'Love it enough to fix it' is reality."

Creedence Clearwater Revival, a country-flavored group featuring John Fogerty, was one of the many bands formed by high school kids in the Bay Area. Fogerty got together in the late 1950s with his brother Tom plus pals Stu Cook and Doug Clifford and eventually became another of country rock's shaping groups. "Lodi," written by John, remains a standard, just as Fogerty himself remains a significant performer.

It has been perhaps fitting that a merging of rock and country occurred most dramatically in California, where the initial rockabilly impulse had been little resisted and where so many people continued to live rural lives. Nevertheless country rock had little immediate impact on traditional country listeners; it distanced the West from Nashville. *The Illustrated History of Country Music* called such musical mergings "pseudo-country" and "tongue-in-cheek country," and it acknowledged that "the pseudo-country movement was by and large a product of the West Coast." The writers of that important volume, however, fell into the regional chauvinist's trap when they claimed that this music "demands . . . lifelong familiarity with Southern White culture from which country style and song spring."

California country rock and its southern cousin redneck rock (Lynyrd Skynyrd, the Allman Brothers, Bob Seger, the Marshall Tucker Band, Wet Willie, et al.) were bastard offshoots of rockabilly. Like their Memphis parent, they threatened the status quo because they represented a direction the establishment couldn't control and didn't want this inherently eclectic music to follow. As usual, fans led and "leaders" followed; later events have demonstrated country rock's great influence on what now passes for "mainstream" music.

A decade after Nashville's unwillingness to accommodate rockabilly had helped to create the separate identity and market for rock and roll, country edged toward rock and vice versa. Even the Grateful Dead acknowledged that cross-fertilization; said Jerry Garcia, "We're kind of on the far fringe of it, but we're part of that California Bakersfield school of country-and-western rock 'n' roll—Buck Owens, Merle Haggard. We used to see those bands and think, 'Gee, those guys are great.' Don Rich was one of my favorites; I learned a lot of stuff from him." *Los Angeles Times* music writer Robert Hilburn has suggested that the musical merging resulted because maturing fans "found it difficult to still relate to the intense, youth-oriented stance of rock." Rather than slide toward Tin Pan Alley tunes, they "are more comfortable with the informal country approach" where they "find mature variations on themes—rebellion, restlessness—that once appealed to them in rock."

When the 1960s in California are summarized, there are essentially four major stories: one deals with the tangle of country-rock groups; the second is dominated by folkies; the third features countrypolitan stylists. Those three all pale, however, before the fourth: Buck Owens and the Buckaroos and the rise of the California Sound. Music historian Malone acknowledges that "for several years during the sixties the music of Buck Owens and the Buckaroos blew like a breath of sparkling fresh air over the country music landscape, reinvigorating hard country enthusiasts with its sharp, clearly delineated string band sound, its high-hard har-mony, and the absence of vocal choruses." Buck's string of number-one hits not only confirmed the power of that sound but also established that Owens was then in a class by himself, and some in the South seethed. "Man," says Buck, "there were guys burning me in effigy."

Along with countrypolitan crooner Glen Campbell and gifted new-comer Merle Haggard, Owens brought the Golden State—especially Bakersfield—a prominence within the world of country music it had not enjoyed since the 1940s. Those performers managed to rattle the estab-lishment by hitting its most vital organs: wallet and ego. Owens in par-ticular was virtually redefining deep country and proving that Nashville wasn't the only place to become a superstar.

BUCK OWENS

California's unwillingness to accept southern domination of this national music was augured by Buck Owens, who perfected an exciting style and who refused to abandon his Bakersfield base. The dominant country-music performer of the 1960s, he brought the Central Valley town with him to the heights. As a result more than a few people came to believe Bakersfield had risen to challenge Nashville's power, but that wasn't the case. *Owens* had risen to challenge Nashville's power.

Although twelve of his records had already made the charts, including three number-two hits, in the spring of 1963 "Act Naturally" initiated Buck's unparalleled run of number-one hits. Not coincidentally that recording also featured a hard-driving style—Buck called it "the freight train"—that came to characterize most of his later hits. "I always had a lot of driving-type music in my bones," he later explained. "I always loved music that had lots of beat. [I] always wanted to sound like a locomotive comin' right through the front room." Apparently the public shared his taste.

Between 1963 and 1967 he released those unprecedented fifteen con-secutive number-one recordings—nineteen when both *Billboard* and *Cash Box* charts are included. He added five more number ones by 1974, with twenty-six other sides making it into the top 10 during the decade. In 1964 his single featuring "Together Again" and "My Heart Skips a Beat" did something rare indeed: the two songs flip-flopped, side A and side B switching number-one and -two positions on the charts. Few artists have ever achieved such dominance.

In 1965 Owens was on the road 302 days and nights. He played New York's Carnegie Hall, San Francisco's Fillmore West Auditorium, London's Palladium, even the White House, all a great distance from the cotton patch in which he had toiled as a child.

Buck is explicit about what inspired his considerable accomplishments. "The biggest driving force for me . . . I hated being poor. I hated wearing pasteboard in my shoes and twine for shoestrings, and I hated wearing hand-me-downs. I remember as a little kid saying, 'Boy, when I get big I ain't never gonna be poor again.'"

At least three other factors figured in Buck's great run of success. One was his songwriting associations, first with Harlan Howard, then with Red Simpson. In both cases each learned from the other and became a better composer. Even more significant was his musical connection with Don Rich. Although not booked as a duo they became a team nearly unprecedented in the history of this music, special talents that blended. The third factor was Capitol Records A&R man Ken Nelson, who preferred that artists record with their own bands rather than with studio musicians, so Buck and the Buckaroos were allowed to contribute their hard-driving, California honky-tonk style—electric in more than one sense—to his records, providing unmatched musical excitement.

Owens's manager since 1963 Jack McFadden has said, "I knew Buck was my type of artist because he was as hungry as I was." Buck grew hungry early. His odyssey started near Sherman, Texas, where Alvis Edgar Owens, Jr., was born in 1929, the second child of sharecroppers Alvis and Macie Owens. He adopted his famous nickname from a farm mule. Desperation, dust, and the Depression forced the Owens family to depart from Texas for California in 1937, but their Ford gave up the ghost in Arizona, and Mesa became home. The family tracked crops from that base, toiling along the classic route—Eloy and Gila Bend in Arizona, then up into California's Imperial and San Joaquin Valleys, then swinging back home. The Owens children enjoyed no summer vacations, and Buck made it only through the eighth grade. Of working in the fields he now says, "It was wonderful. *Today* it was wonderful. *Then* it was hot and dirty and filthy, sweaty work."

In Mesa young Owens could enjoy music from the Mexican border stations, sing gospel songs in the Southern Baptist Church, and practice the guitar chords his mother had taught him. Mrs. Owens also played the piano, and as was true for so many southwestern families music provided the Owenses some relief from a tough life. In 1945 the ambitious Buck teamed with Theryl Ray Britten on the fifteen-minute radio show "Buck and Britt" over KTYL in Mesa. In the long-standing tradition of such shows, they were paid nothing but could promote their appearances at local honky-tonks and clubs. At sixteen Buck was a professional. Eventually he and Britt added a trumpeter named Kelley, and they became regulars at Romo Buffet in Phoenix, receiving 10 percent of the gross receipts in payment.

The young musician then met Mac McAtee, a Mesa service station owner–cum–disc jockey, who was organizing the band Mac's Skillet Lickers. Then supplementing his music income by driving a truck, Buck joined Mac's band. He also met a pretty sixteen-year-old named Bonnie Campbell, who would sing for the Skillet Lickers. They married in January of 1948, and she became Bonnie Owens. Three years and two sons later, their marriage coming apart, Buck and Bonnie moved to Bakersfield. Here, too, Owens was following the pattern of many southwestern migrants, relocating to a region where kinfolk had earlier settled.

After some lean days, both became established in Bakersfield's music community. Owens credits steel guitarist Dusty Rhodes with giving him his first job at a club called The Roundup. Buck, who had scrambled for fill-in work at nightspots, recalls,

> When I first came here, I went to work out at [The Roundup] . . . there were four guys playing music out there: Dusty Rhodes, Tommy Hays. . . . But what they did was, to have me in their band, instead of them getting $10 a night—for four of them it was $40—they took $8 a night, so we all had $8 a night. I remember that.
>
> The Roundup was . . . kind of like, it was the bottom of the line. You start there; you want to get somewhere else if you can.

Owens endured that existence for a while. With other young musicians he scrambled for every penny, every gig. Billy Mize loaned him a guitar; Oscar Whittington loaned him a shirt; Rhodes let him sleep on a couch. "There were a lot of things going on in those days," Buck recollects. "Remembering them can be fun, but there were some tough times."

Eventually his reputation as a solid guitarist spread, and he was hired by the top local band at the top local club, Bill Woods and his Orange Blossom Playboys at the Blackboard. Bonnie meanwhile went her own way, first as a singing cocktail waitress, then as a regular on Cousin Herb Henson's "Trading Post," where her estranged husband also performed daily.

Buck eventually formed his own band the Schoolhouse Playboys. At the same time Ferlin Husky had played guitar on one recording session for Tommy Collins, but Ferlin and Jean Shepard suddenly hit it big with "A Dear John Letter." As a result Tommy needed another lead guitarist; Buck was his man. On Collins's first hit "You Better Not Do That," which reached number two on the charts, Buck contributed what writer Rich Kienzle calls "the raunchy twisted-note style that became his trademark." His riffs are still considered landmarks.

Ken Nelson at Capitol Records started employing Owens as a session musician and even had him play ukulele on one occasion. Buck recalls,

[The] guy says, "Can you play the ukulele? We need a little ukulele on this song." [Chuckles] "Can I play the ukulele? What, can I play the ukulele?" But I had played one a couple of times, and I remembered they were tuned like the last four strings of a guitar. So I said, "Well, yeah, I think I can." So they give me some money and told me to go down to the little old music store there on Hollywood [Boulevard] and get one. Come back. The song was called "Hawaiian Seabreeze" [by Skeets McDonald].

But it was his guitar work that truly intrigued Nelson, who says, "Buck had tremendous rhythm and he had this little style that set Tommy off, in the introductions usually."

Buck was never content to be only a sideman. Like many local performers, he cut demos and hoped. A woman named Virginia Richmond later released some of Buck's demos on her tiny Chesterfield label and unknowingly created collector's items. His first "official" discs were recorded in Los Angeles for another small label, Pep, in 1956. "Down on the Corner of Love" was well received, but independent labels, like small businesses generally, were plagued by lack of connections, so their distribution was poor. Owens later did other sessions for that company, including such solid songs as "Sweethearts in Heaven," "There Goes My Love," and his first overt rockabilly sides, "Hot Dog" and "Rhythm and Booze." Buck's Pep records clearly showed that as both writer and singer he had much to offer.

Young Buck Owens and his Schoolhouse Playboys. Courtesy of Kern County Museum. Used by permission.

That same year he met Harlan Howard, soon to become one of country's great composers, and the two hit it off immediately, collaborating on a number of songs. Says Buck, "I had a song called 'Train, You Took My Baby,' and I never could get that finished, not to my satisfaction. . . . He took it and finished it and I liked what he did. We wrote 'Daddy for a Day,' then I changed it to 'Mommy for a Day.' Kitty Wells recorded it. Became number one. And that kind of kicked it off. . . . Most of the time he wrote the lyrics and I wrote the music."

In 1957 that pair also began Blue Book Music, a business that would eventually control songs by Owens, Merle Haggard, and Red Simpson, thus becoming a major cog in Buck's corporate holdings. He explains what led him to take over the company when Harlan moved to Nashville,

The reason I started publishing is because I remember them saying, "If you write it, you take it to the publisher, he supposedly gets it exposed for you, you get half the money and he gets half." So I'm thinking now, what the hell does a publisher do? Well, he gets the copyright for you and all that. Well, can I get a copyright? Yes. Well, could I not have a publishing company? Yes. Well, then would I make the publishing money part if I did that? Yes. And would that mean I would be making twice as much? And he said, Yeah, and even a little bit more, because at that time BMI was paying the publisher an extra cent or something for [radio] play.

In 1957 Columbia Records's Don Law was interested in signing Owens, but Ken Nelson at Capitol beat him. However, Buck's first recording session at the Capitol Tower left him disillusioned. His songs "were recorded with little doo-wahs . . . kinda pop-country with this big choral group, and I thought, 'eeeee, God!'" The record went nowhere. Neither did the four other sides he recorded in 1958.

That year, on the advice of his friend Dusty Rhodes, Buck moved to Puyallup, Washington. He became involved with the 250-watt radio station KAYE and soon found himself immersed in the business, doing everything from selling ads to spinning records. This experience became another component in his education about the music business.

Buck's next session at Capitol was on October 9, 1958, and it was more to his liking, for the doo-wahs were omitted, and support came from the high-pitched steel of Ralph Mooney and the fiddle of old Bakersfield friend Jelly Sanders, as well as country journeymen "Pee Wee" Adams (drums), Allen Williams (bass), and George French (piano). He returned to Washington after recording "Second Fiddle," another of his own compositions. It became the first of his nearly eighty chart songs, rising to number twenty-four.

In 1959, still living in Washington, he added a live television show, the "Bar-K" on Tacoma's KTNT, to his busy schedule. He was joined on the program by Bakersfield pals Rhodes and Don Markham—the latter would much later become the lead horn player in Merle Haggard's band. On that program Buck put local talent before the camera, including a housewife named Loretta Lynn and a high school student named Don (Ulrich) Rich.

In June of 1959 the same group that had cut "Second Fiddle" reassembled in Hollywood to record another Owens's original, "Under

Your Spell Again"; it rose to number four on the chart. The next year the one-time Skillet Licker was named *Billboard*'s most promising country-and-western singer of the year. Buck returned to Bakersfield, and teenager Rich, whom he had hired in Washington, followed him, the real beginning of one of country's finest pairings. Explains Buck,

> I came [to Bakersfield] in June, he came in late fall. He was 18. He had graduated from high school and then he turned 19 in August, and he started to college. . . . I [had] said goodbye to him. And so he wrote me a letter and asked me if I had a job for him, and he spelled job "j-o-b-b."
>
> So I told him, "I think you're absolutely right. You need to do something else. College ain't gonna work for you." I always teased him about that. He said, "I got the job, didn't I?"

Shortly thereafter Don married his Washington sweetheart and brought her to the Kern County town. Once settled, he became part of a generous Bakersfield country-music scene that was still like a large family. For two or three years Buck and Don traveled as a team for appearances, joining house bands from date to date. Owens remembers that he was asked in 1960 to put a group together himself to play on Saturday nights at Bob Wills's old stomping ground, the Fresno Barn, and that they received 60 percent of the gate. On the edge of major stardom Owens was still a long way from wealthy: "That's what . . . the band and I lived on between '60 and about '63. That and all the little honky-tonks," he says. Don, Buck's one-man band, traveled to all appearances, and the two began to play hot duets on Telecasters.

In 1962 the early version of the Buckaroos was formed. At first Wayne Stone, Jay McDonald, and Merle Haggard joined Don and Buck; Haggard is credited with having named the band. There were inevitable shakeouts, and the group finally settled with Tom Brumley on steel, Doyle Holly on bass, Willie Cantu on drums, and Rich on fiddle and Telecaster—one of the genuinely great bands in this music's history. The Buckaroo's heart was Don Rich, its nominal leader, who played lead guitar and fiddle, allowing Owens to sing and more easily communicate with audiences. Don also sang high-tenor harmony with Buck. Those high duets came to define Buck's vocal style—indeed to define country music at its best during those years.

Rich was the sure component during Buck's great run of hits, far more than a sideman. Writer Bob Allen calls him "one of the most influential guitarists in post-war country music." Buck himself said, "Don and I made the sort of synergy where one and one don't make two. The two of us together made three."

On July 17, 1974, the duo worked on a recording in Buck's Oildale studio, then Don headed to Morro Bay for a deep-sea fishing trip. His motorcycle crashed near his destination, killing him, and Buck, who had the onerous job of telling Don's wife, was devastated. His musical career virtually halted. He told *Country Music* magazine, "When he was killed . . . all the heart went out of me. I just never got it together after that."

Their joint musical legacy remains great. "Alongside Fred Astaire and Ginger, Lennon and McCartney, Abbott and Costello, Lester and Earl, Elvis and Marilyn," asserts singer Marty Stuart, "they should clear off a space for Buck and Don because they too were a classic duo."

As early as 1966—the year he and the band had their instruments painted red, white, and blue—Buck had begun a national television career after all the local shows on which he had performed over the years. He started with his own syndicated "Buck Owens Ranch Show," originally taped at WKY in Oklahoma City. At its peak the program reached 100 markets. In 1968, which marked perhaps the most controversial phase of his career, he began cohosting the CBS television program "Hee Haw" with Roy Clark.

Based on NBC's popular "Laugh-In" and Canada's equally popular "Hot Diggity," including Gordie Tapp and Don Harron from the Canadian show, "Hee Haw" gained a large audience. In contrast with Buck's own "Ranch Show"—with its stylish southwestern rancho set—"Hee Haw" had hokey barnyard scenery, a donkey emblem, bib overalls, and leggy Daisy-Maes, which offended many old-time country fans because it tapped old stereotypes. After CBS canceled the program in 1971 and it was syndicated, its producers complained that Buck's lower-budget "Ranch Show" was too competitive in many markets.

The downside of "Hee Haw" for Owens was that a generation of viewers grew up seeing him as a television buffoon rather than as the defining musician he was. His costar Clark quickly realized that the real Owens was a long way from the image projected by "Hee Haw": "He wasn't a laid-back country boy I felt comfortable being around. He was, and still is, very opinionated, very set in his ways, very dollar conscious. If he doesn't have the first dollar he ever made, he knows where it's at." The "hardball" reality of a tough poor kid who'd made it big was belied by Buck's "softball" television role, and many long-time fans felt he had trivialized himself and, in a sense, them, too. Unsparing of himself, Owens eventually agreed: "Quite frankly, I prostituted myself for money." He left the show in 1986 and virtually retired from performing.

For a time his various businesses filled his professional life. Unlike some other country singers, Owens has never romanticized poverty, and nobody ever pushed himself harder than he did; McFadden calls him "a manager's dream." He adds, "He never missed a date. He'd play clubs, starting at 9 at night till 1 in the morning, and never leave the stage. . . . He did everything I ever, ever asked him to do and more." Buck and Jack shared a motto: "Whatever it takes."

Except for a strange, very public romance and brief marriage to fiddler Jana Jae in 1977 (it even merited unwelcome coverage by *People* magazine), throughout most of his career Buck has kept his personal life relatively private. His marriage to fourth wife Jennifer Smith has endured; moreover, his two sons by his first marriage and one by his second have become well established. He was able to provide abundantly for his hard-working parents, a point of great satisfaction. His late sister was a major cog in his businesses: "Dorothy was very instrumental," Buck admits. "Dorothy held things together." But he dismisses one local rumor, saying,

I've heard it said, more times than once, "Well, Buck would never have amounted to anything if it hadn't been for Dorothy." Well, Dorothy would be the first one to tell you that isn't true. It wasn't true. I was responsible. I brought back the money and she ran my businesses. But she never invested my money. She never bought or sold anything. She never made any policy. . . . all the day-to-day decisions, of course, she'd make.

In fact they were both astute—Buck the idea man, Dorothy the manager— and they formed a productive team and a tough one.

Buck Owens Enterprises and Buck Owens Productions are, to a degree at least, still family businesses, and this family man takes genuine pride in "being able to work with my nephews, my sons, my sister, my grand-daughter, that's very important to me."

Avoiding the bright lights has been important, too; he lives on a 160-acre ranch north of Bakersfield. Why?

> Bakersfield's my home. . . . I'm happy I still live here. I paid an awful price to live here. I could have very easily lived in Dallas or Oklahoma City, been centrally located, and not have [had] to live in Nashville. I never wanted to live in Nashville, because I thought, "Hey, you'll put yourself in there with all the rest of these people. Why do you want to do that? Bakersfield is where you belong." So I stayed.

Bakersfield seems to agree that Buck belongs. He is a leading citizen.

"Buck *owned* the '60s," summarizes his old Bakersfield boss Bill Woods. Moreover Owens and the Buckaroos came to define West Coast country, as well as the Bakersfield Sound that came to dominate California. As Emmylou Harris has said, "People have asked me to define country music. I just tell them to listen to Buck Owens and the Buckaroos doing "Second Fiddle." Journalist Jeff Tamarkin says the Buckaroos were "as tight and innovative a band as country music has ever known. . . . These guys knew how to have a ball as well as play their asses off." That sound was an almost perfect blending of many of the best elements that had entered country music since World War II, plus the genius of an open-minded, independent man. A migrant who made this state work for him, Buck Owens became the quintessential California country musician.

LOS ANGELES, 1995

"**T**his is uptown!" grins a large, balding man wearing lizard-skin cowboy boots as gray as his remaining hair. "This sure isn't like any honky-tonk I remember."

The crowd outside spills onto the street and winds around the corner, and older fans are far outnumbered by hipsters, punks, as well as yuppies because country is hot, man, and maybe a little funky, too: roots stuff. We oldsters are also a tad funky ourselves as we shuffle toward the door, excited at the prospect of seeing an enduring favorite, as well as a couple of touted younger acts new to most of us.

Within the House of Blues some of the clientele resemble extras from horse operas at Hollywood movie studios of the 1940s or '50s: young men wear bright Roy Rogers suits, and young women are attired in fringed Dale Evans skirts and vests. They mingle with Humphrey Bogart gangsters and Joan Crawford molls, while cliques of James Dean–and–Bettie Page clones hold court at sideline tables, and spiked, multicolored punks exchange reviews of dog collars there, too. In other groups young affluents—coats without ties, sockless in boat moccasins—gather and frolic.

At one front table a young man with dark hair slicked back, shoulders wide in a pinstriped suit that Clark Kent might envy, sips a martini from a stemmed glass, a large, unlit cigar in his other hand. His lady, bedecked in rhinestones, wears high heels with ankle straps and a Lois Lane suit; she, too, sips a martini with a lengthy, black, and loaded cigarette holder in her other hand. Several of us pause to stare at the young woman; we haven't seen a cigarette holder in long, long time.

Our own attire is perhaps more contemporary if not necessarily more stylish: boots, jeans, western sportcoats, and some Stetsons dominate men's gear, while women's attire is far more varied—everything from K-Mart to L.L. Bean. Most of us sidestep the throng in front and gravitate toward the rear of the room. Although a few of the older women wear vintage poodle skirts and one tall man seems to have borrowed a sequined shirt *from Gene Autry, most older fans aren't here to be seen but to listen and see.*

We are veterans of the youth culture's birth in the 1950s, drawn by memories of rocka-billy's genesis, especially by memories of Wanda Jackson in her youth, but those recollections are now tempered by the years we've lived and the dues we've paid. Despite stereotypes about our generation, several oldsters don't look like their lives have been especially easy: fading, homemade tattoos on knotted forearms and some scarred eyebrows and crooked noses hint at the rebellion during that distant decade. There is little consciously campy about us seniors, although a few of the younger spectators—already a bit tipsy—glance toward us: like, what're all those old dudes doin' here?

While many of us hurry to the rest rooms—we don't want to interrupt the main event—a local group is warming up the crowd. The lead singer winks and nods at friends in front of the bandstand and is greeted with friendly laughter and jibes. Those cold martinis seem to have warmed up many spectators.

The first of the two featured acts, Big Sandy and the Fly-Rite Boys, seems unknown to all of us senior citizens but is wildly popular with the younger set. Attired in their neo-horse-opera costumes and playing bass, drums, steel, and takeoff guitars, Big Sandy and his group don't disappoint. The boys specialize this night in variations of western swing, and the crowd is ready, jostling to the floor where 1940s jitterbug dominates. Dancers are spinning and even throwing one another. Steel guitar runs that would have made the Texas Playboys proud forty-five years earlier are followed by lively guitar picking, then a slapping bass run. The solos are uniformly exciting.

This is a band ingrained in the West Coast country tradition, and Sandy, with his acoustic guitar, really is big. His voice is as rhythmic as it is mellow, more than a little like the late Tommy Duncan's. This night he is singing mostly songs written by Robert Williams from the group's new album, and an immediate happy rapport is established with this audience: "All right, Sandy!"

The band follows "Music to Her Ears" with the rollicking "My Sinful Days Are Over," a number in the Johnny Bond–Merle Travis–Tex Williams tradition that once defined country music in Southern California. Several dancers stop to listen better to the clever lyrics as well as more of the skilled solos.

"That kid's good," says the balding man at the next table.

The intermission following the Fly-Rite Boys seems interminable (another trip to the john for us oldsters) with much schmoozing and posturing dominating the youthful action, while recorded music is played much too loud over world-class speakers. I roll up napkin plugs and put one in each ear, grumbling, "Man, these kids won't have hearing left when they get to be our age." My wife smiles and shakes her head in a semaphore that unambiguously signals "old fart."

At last Rosie Flores appears to thunderous applause. In her spangled turquoise-and-black miniskirt outfit, the singer is eye-catching, and when she bursts into song she seems

ROSIE FLORES

HIGHTONE RECORDS
220 4th St. #101
Oakland, CA 94607
(510) 763-8500

Rosie Flores. Photo by Ed Colver. Courtesy of HighTone Records.

to energize everyone. Her guitar runs, too, are fiery: Clark Kent and Lois Lane bounce before the bandstand, and so do those of us in back, although a large man behind us complains loudly, "You make better doors than windows."

After the lively Rosie completes an up-tempo medley, she introduces the erstwhile "female Elvis Presley," Wanda Jackson, and we old-timers applaud and shout. Thanks to my bad eyes or perhaps her good makeup, as well as her skillfully cut white outfit, Wanda appears remarkably youthful. "Damn!" grunts a big man my age at the next table. I know just what he's thinking. The duo bursts into "His Rockin' Little Angel," and Wanda's voice has lost little: she's still the big-volumed little gal who brought female sexuality to rockabilly in the late 1950s. The two singers exchange vocal solos, then harmonize: "I'm his rockin' little angel gonna rock him like the devil tonight..."

"I knew Wanda back in Bakersfield when I was a kid," the balding man seated at the next table with his wife and another couple says loudly.

The other man says, "Sure you did."

"I did. She came out from Oklahoma and went to my school."

The balding man's wife smiles and says, "He knew *everyone* back in Bakersfield when he was a kid," and all four laugh.

After a moment the balding man adds, "I wish those kids'd sit down up there."

219

Flores's animated mien changes midway through the set, and she announces that the next number will be dedicated to Country Dick Montana, the much-loved drummer and vocalist for the Beat Farmers, who had died suddenly in Canada earlier in the month. The crowd is suddenly silent except for a few gasps, then murmuring passes through the standing group: "Country Dick died. No shit? Oh, maaaaaan. . . ."The older customers are respectfully quiet, but at least one asks audibly: "Who was Country Dick Montana?"

Wanda says into the microphone: "I didn't know Dick, but the sadness and warm memories I've heard for him this week makes me wish I had. He was genuinely loved by a lot of good people."

"He must've been a good ol' boy," the balding man remarks to his table mates.

Sadness is palpable as Wanda and Rosie harmonize. Musical performers constitute a close-knit community, and Dick is genuinely mourned. Montana and Flores were both from San Diego, and they grew up in Southern California's punk-and-rockabilly scene; a few years back they had been in the cast of a traveling rock-and-roll musical revue called The Pleasure Barons. Rosie wipes her eyes and fights to hold her chin high. Eyes are being wiped in the audience, too.

As the number ends the singers embrace briefly, breathe deeply, then launch themselves back into rockabilly. On their duet of Wanda's "Rock Your Baby," with its mesmerizing repetition of the sexual chorus "Rock your baby, all night long," pockets of dancing break out all over the club. A few minutes later, Wanda's raw-voiced "Fujiyama Mama" virtually halts the young dancers: "That woman can rock!" At times she sounds like a female Little Richard, growling and yipping.

When the older singer returns for her encore, fans murmur, ready for more of her sensual, roots rockabilly. Instead of singing, though, Wanda launches into testimony about having been born again in Christ in the 1970s. A few older folks sitting in the rear who remember her early reputation nod and seem to be moved, but the younger customers glance at one another, then begin chatting: "What's her trip?" Although Wanda later blasts through two more numbers, her spell has been broken, and even when Rosie returns to ignite younger fans, something of the magic is gone.

When the performance finally concludes, the audience once more mills around, and that loud recorded music engulfs everyone. As they rise to leave, the woman at the next table says loudly to the balding man, "So you knew Wanda, huh? I suppose you knew that Big Sandy back in Bakersfield, too."

The man grins, then replies, nearly shouting to be heard over the recorded music, "I dated his grandma," and his wife pokes his shoulder, laughing and shaking her head.

On the dance floor Clark and Lois are spinning, spinning . . .

While Buck and Glen rode personal crests well into the 1970s, the decade was finally dominated by California's first native-born superstar Merle Haggard. The Oildale native continued exploring his own considerable talent and expanding country's stylistic and thematic boundaries as a result. He matured into a powerful creative force, shaping the future without abandoning the past.

Following his Jimmie Rodgers–tribute album *Same Train, A Different Time* the previous year, in 1970 Merle released *A Tribute to the Best Damn Fiddle Player in the World*, a paean to Bob Wills and the Texas Playboys. Haggard wrote in the liner notes, "Very few musicians can be credited with creating a type of music, but the man to which this album is dedicated did just that. It is called Western Swing." Merle eventually added former Texas Playboys Eldon Shamblin, Jimmy Belken, and Tiny Moore to his own band and improved his own fiddling skill; many of his concerts during this decade took on a distinct Wills flavor.

Haggard's work stood in high relief to what was happening in Nashville; the artistic change there was symbolized by the move of the "Grand Ole Opry" from historic Ryman Auditorium to a theme park called Opryland. In *Country Music* magazine Patrick Carr scorned "the Opry's owners substituting an artificial, tourist-pleasing version of country culture for the real thing, Disney-style." Carr continued his indictment:

> The shift to Opryland was indeed symbolic of a swerve towards new styles and customers, and away from old friends and values, across the entire landscape of the country music business. Looking back at the music itself, in fact, the loss of "soul and spirit" in the mid-70s was so dramatic that it

had the catastrophic completeness of a massive hemorrhage, as if someone—
Who? Some gang of strangers?—had sneaked up and slashed Nashville's
throat.

Hag meanwhile dazzled fans with his originality and virtuosity; he
wrote and performed not just different numbers, but different *kinds* of
them and in different manners, actually expanding the range of this music. Every great artist reinvents his or her medium, and Merle was doing
just that. On *Let Me Tell You about a Song* in 1972, for example, he offered a
spoken introduction to each tune, and the album included such Haggard
standards as "Daddy Frank," "They're Tearin' the Labor Camps Down,"
and "Grandma Harp," as well as his previously suppressed song about interracial love, "Irma Jackson."

The next year he released a Christmas album that included the remarkable "If We Make It through December"; thanks to a reserved musical accompaniment, the collection illustrated what a fine instrument
Merle's voice had become. He most commonly sang with a full-throated
delivery but was capable of constricting his voice in the southern style
and of throaty, blueslike presentations, too. In 1977 he used all of those
in the tribute album to Elvis Presley *From Graceland to the Promised Land.*

By the decade's final year on yet another exceptional album entitled
Serving 190 Proof he added to his canon several more contemporary classics
(all of which, by the way, picked up little or no radio play, but which have
certainly endured): "Foot-lights," "Red Bandana," "I Didn't Mean to
Love You," and "My Own Kind of Hat." The last, with its distinct Cajun-
style fiddle work, surprised and delighted fans who, by then, should
have expected almost *anything* from the talented Californian.

By his own admission Haggard was already having financial problems
then, and his foil, the business-savvy Buck Owens, seemed to be on an
opposite track with his Blue Book Music and other ventures thriving.
"One thing about ol' Buck," says attorney Ken Byrum, "is he's sharp and
he plays hardball." Some claim that he occasionally throws curves.

In his autobiography Haggard recalls that, desperate to repay a gam-
bling debt in the early 1970s, he had gone to Owens, whose company
then represented him. Merle asked for $15,000 against royalties for "Sing
Me Back Home." Buck offered him a deal: "Sell me half of 'Sing Me Back
Home' and I'll let you have the $15,000." Hag accepted, but "later I

A gathering of stars: Andy Griffith, Buck Owens, and Merle Haggard. Courtesy of Kern County Museum. Used by permission.

found out he'd already received a check for more than I'd asked for—all mine. It was in his desk when he was talking to me." Merle eventually sued and got his half of the song back, but he "had a hard time gettin' over that little deal and I wasn't real friendly with him for a hell of a long time." Perhaps because so many of its players have emerged from poverty, hardball—and attendant curves—often seem closer to the rule than the exception in this business.

In 1972 the Academy of Country Music's annual awards show became the first such program televised with national syndication, and Haggard was named male vocalist of the year, while a North Carolinian who had been teaching English in Southern California, Donna Fargo, was named top female vocalist. Two years later the Academy of Country Music's awards became a network presentation when it was picked up by ABC, "a breakthrough for the Academy and country music as a whole," Jonny Whiteside reports. By that year California's country, despite its own pop wing, remained closer to the bone than most of the South's; Haggard was again the winner as male vocalist, and Loretta Lynn won distaff honors. (Nashville's Country Music Association chose Olivia Newton-John as best female vocalist but did redeem itself a bit by selecting Don Rich as instrumentalist of the year.) Five years later the academy's awards show moved to NBC, where it has continued to offer an alternative view of the country scene.

The music itself retained its several tracks in California during the 1970s—principally hard country, rock country, and pop country. Haggard of course could perform any style admirably. Other children of the 1930s and 1940s had, like Merle, matured and entered the state's mainstream by this time; while many members of Haggard's generation retrenched with older styles, their own kids tended to prefer rock or pop variations. A generation gap seemed to loom everywhere, especially in politics, and not even the end of the Vietnam War early in the decade closed the chasm.

In fact politics during this highly charged period exposed most sides of California's complex society. For instance, in 1970 Jesse "Big Daddy" Unruh, a 1940s transplant from Texas, lost the gubernatorial election to Illinois-born movie actor Ronald Reagan, who had come to Hollywood in the late 1930s. Four years later the conservative Reagan was replaced by an erstwhile member of the youth culture, native son Jerry Brown, who seemed in many ways a cipher for many trends of his generation. He had opposed the war in Vietnam, favored the rights of farmworkers, promoted environmental activism, and urged people to think small—personally as well as governmentally. Brown's election also ushered in a multiethnic and sexually diverse administration unlike any other state's; among its members were Lieutenant Governor Mervyn Dymally, Secretary of State March Fong Eu, Superintendent of Schools Wilson Riles, and Chief Justice Rose Elizabeth Bird.

Before liberals could count their spoils, however, the state's notoriously inconsistent voters in 1978 reelected liberal Brown ("Governor Moonbeam" as he had come to be called) but paradoxically supported by two to one the conservative Proposition 13, the Jarvis-Gann initiative. This limitation on property taxes was actually the first shot in a tax war still being fought, one that has often pitted older homeowners against younger

THE BUCKAROOS

Country's top band? The Buckaroos with (from left) Tom Brumley, Doyle Holly, Don Rich, and Willie Cantu. Courtesy of Kern County Museum. Used by permission.

home buyers. It also marked the beginning of a steep decline of public services, especially education, and a commensurate but gradual lowering of the state's standards and reputation.

In the 1970s music in this state was as tangled as its politics. The medium had indeed become the message, so the existence of important country stars in California was considered exceptional, bespeaking Nashville's domination not only of country music as a business, but also of country music as an idea. Radio had become a particular problem, especially for country artists who lacked Nashville and major-label connections. The country-music market was largely focused on radio exposure, and those who recorded on independent record labels were doomed to receive scant airplay because tight playlist programming controlled by corporate gatekeepers reigned nearly everywhere. That meant a relatively small, select inventory of records, produced almost exclusively by a few major companies with Nashville connections, was played and replayed during the course of a broadcast day in an attempt to create successes—the top-40 mentality. Sometimes new records from well-connected artists or companies were actually assigned "hit slots" before the public ever heard them. As a result of this power to manipulate what people were allowed to hear, plus the increasing size and interrelationships of businesses and reputed buying or assigning "hit" slots to cronies—the association of radio stations and record labels became controversial.

A "blanding of the airwaves" resulted, and it affected many future musicians. Explains Phil Alvin of the Blasters, "Music in the early '70s sort of just left—we didn't really have anything." It also contributed to "regional leveling," as local labels found fewer and fewer outlets for distinct performers. As larger radio stations came to dominate they used fewer and fewer tunes from regional companies such as those that had originally introduced such standouts as the Maddox Brothers and Rose, Owens, and Haggard. National playlists featured the Nashville Sound *everywhere* it seemed, subsuming much local programming.

If by the 1970s small regional labels were not likely to gain much exposure, the success of California's first home-bred female star illustrated it *could* still happen. Sammi Smith, born in Orange in 1944, reached number one on the country charts with her version of Kris Kristofferson's "Help Me Make It through the Night," released in 1972 on the little-known Mega label. She also won a Grammy as best female country vocalist that year. Although she placed sixteen more tunes on the charts, Mega could never be certain that even such as successful an artist as Smith would allow that label to crack the disc jockey format so effectively controlled by big companies and major radio stations.

The small local stations that survived then did still tend to spin what listeners requested. On KCHJ in Delano, for example, records by Hank Williams, Lefty Frizzell, and Elvis Presley remained popular. Even disk jockeys tended to vary on those smaller stations, which often featured down-home jocks—frequently local country musicians—while smoother, if less convincing, baritones worked for nationally programmed outlets, their dialects an innocuous "network English." Observes disc jockey Hugh Cherry, "the near-automated presentation of the music on radio has helped

to facilitate a mass audience; yet in the process of gaining, we are losing."
He asserts that modern jocks and programmers "are a different breed of
cat. . . . Many of them lack awareness of country music's traditions and
heritage."

Most California musicians who claimed to play country folk or coun-
try rock in the 1970s showed little connection with the music's heritage,
although groups such as Fresno's Sweet Mill's String Band with Kenny
Hall bucked that trend, as did singers like Clovis's Jim Ringer and Santa
Rosa's Ace Atkins. The synthesis of styles and ideas that characterized
this state produced a well-known folk-rock-country nexus when the
Nitty Gritty Dirt Band reorganized and released their version of Jerry Jeff
Walker's "Mr. Bojangles" in 1970. The Long Beach group followed with
All the Good Times, their first all-country album in 1972. Then the next year
they released one of the classic sets of the country-rock blending, *Will the
Circle Be Unbroken*. The collection included cuts with Earl Scruggs, Maybelle
Carter, Roy Acuff, Doc Watson, Vassar Clements, and Merle Travis, and it
remains arguably the finest convening of old and new produced during
the period of rock ascendance. Ironically, perhaps, the *Nashville Tennessean* referred to it as "one of the most important recordings in the forty-five
years of the Nashville music business." Despite such bridges between the
old and the new, controversy over country music's continuing dilution
grew.

During this decade Barbara Mandrell's popularity came to epitomize
pop styling in this music. Mandrell was born in Houston, Texas, on
Christmas Day 1948 and was raised primarily in Oceanside, California. "I
learned to read music before I could read English." No surprise, given
that her father Irby owned a music store, and her mother Mary was a music teacher. "I could play the saxophone, the steel guitar, and the banjo by
the time I was in the sixth grade," Barbara has revealed.

The youngster's steel guitar teacher was none other than Norman
Hamlet, who for years had led Merle Haggard's band the Strangers.
"There wasn't a better teacher," she told Douglas Green. After about six
months of study her father arranged for her to play her steel and demonstrate amplifiers at a musical instruments trade convention in Chicago's
Palmer House. Joe Maphis saw her there, and shortly afterward she appeared on stage with him at the Showboat in Las Vegas. Joe recommended
her to Cliffie Stone, and soon she was performing on "Town Hall Party,"

where, only eleven years old, she became a regular. Recalls veteran fiddler Jelly Sanders, "To see a little girl sitting up there playing steel guitar. And, man, some of the improvising and everything she would do would just scare the socks off of you. Just to imagine anyone that young playing like that. She was no slouch."

Before long she made her network debut on ABC's "Five Star Jubilee," and by the time she entered secondary school Mandrell was an established professional entertainer. During Barbara's high school years, her father, a vocalist and guitarist, and her mother, who played bass, formed a country-music band with Brian Lonbeck also on guitar, Barbara's future husband Ken Dudney on drums, and Barbara on steel as well as vocals. At eighteen she married Dudney—by then a military pilot—and temporarily retired from show business.

While her husband served overseas, Barbara moved to Nashville, where her parents had relocated. A visit to the "Grand Ole Opry" prompted her to try entertaining again, and before long she was discovered by the astute Billy Sherrill, who signed her to a recording contract for Columbia in 1969. Much influenced by rhythm and blues, this blonde dynamo later placed one record on the rhythm-and-blues chart. But her duets with David Houston (such as "After Closing Time" or "Ten Commandments of Love") in particular were country, and she was asked to become a regular on the "Grand Ole Opry" in 1972.

"I think of myself as an actress," she explained. "I try to make people believe what I'm singing." In 1978 enough of them believed to make "Sleeping Single in a Double Bed" her first number-one single. She followed that with yet another number one, a cover of Gladys Knight and Rod Stewart's "(If Loving You Is Wrong) I Don't Want to Be Right."

In no time, it seemed, the lively, photogenic Mandrell became a television favorite, appearing with everyone from the Harlem Globetrotters to Bob Hope. She replaced Glen Campbell as the highest-profile country personality during the late 1970s and early 1980s, when she swept an impressive list of honors: female vocalist of the year in 1979 from the Academy of Country Music, Country Music Association, and polls by both *Music City News* and *Radio & Records*. The American Music Awards and *Cash Box* both voted "Sleeping Single in a Double Bed" the single of the year. In 1980 the Country Music Association named her entertainer of the

kaleidoscope
m e d i a

BARBARA MANDRELL

CAA
CREATIVE ARTISTS AGENCY, INC.
(615)383-8787
(615)383-4937 fax
(310)288-4545 California

photo: Dick Zimmerman

Barbara Mandrell. Photo by Dick Zimmerman. Courtesy of Kaleidoscope Media.

year, and she won the same honor a year later from the Academy of Country Music.

Despite all her honors and her successful network television variety show ("Barbara Mandrell and the Mandrell Sisters" on NBC), many country-music buffs weren't sure she retained her country roots or whether she ever had any. Ken Tucker observed in *Country: The Music and the Musicians*:

> In this [1970s] atmosphere, an experienced performer like Barbara Mandrell was able to invent a canny synthesis of both musical styles and performing personae; Mandrell was at once middle-of-the-road authentic

("I Was Country When Country Wasn't Cool," for example, was probably the least country-sounding hit ever to invoke the word "country" in its title) and attempted to be sexy in the perky way that was acceptable to the sternest country fan.

As mentioned earlier, Olivia Newton-John, an Australian pop star who was far less country than Mandrell, had been named the Country Music Association's female singer of the year in 1974. Her victory probably remains the symbolic low point in this music's pandering for a pop audience, although such pandering was by then an old habit. Traditionalists rebelled; one member of the association's board said, "I don't feel it's right that the country music industry should prostitute itself just for the sake of one hour on national television." An Association of Country Entertainers was formed, complete with a screening committee, and pop stylists were not invited to apply.

In California a long-time favorite (tinged with pop associations) strengthened his country credentials early in the 1970s. By the time Rick Nelson performed at the now-legendary Richard Nader Rock and Roll Revival in Madison Square Garden on October 15, 1971, his Stone Canyon Band had recruited steel guitarist Tom Brumley from Buck Owens's Buckaroos, adding an even deeper country slant to its sound. In the Garden that night, with Bo Diddley, Chuck Berry, Bobby Rydell, and the Coasters, Rick sang early hits along with some newer material. He made no effort to look or act like "little Ricky."

The exact events that followed are in contention, but biographer Joel Selvin explains that while Rick was performing "Honky-Tonk Women," the crowd began to boo, but not at Nelson. Fans were actually incensed at security guards who were rousting some rowdies in the audience. The singer and his band didn't know this until after the performance. As a result, during those moments when he thought he was being rejected Rick was able to project his feelings into a song he titled "Garden Party," considered by many to be one of the finest he ever wrote.

Among fans, though, a story circulated that the song had been written because Nelson had been booed off the stage when he refused to perform only his old hits; that version certainly didn't hurt sales of the record. Rick continued touring, and his acceptance within the country-music community kept growing although his general popularity waned. Nonetheless his recordings of "One Night Stand" in 1974 and "Dream Lover" in 1979 made the charts, and he seemed at last to have transcended the former teen-idol image that had for so long haunted him.

Gram Parsons meanwhile left the Flying Burrito Brothers in 1970 and pursued a solo career. After convalescing from injuries suffered in a motorcycle accident, he recorded two albums at Capitol's Hollywood studio that secured his reputation: GP (released in January 1973) and *Grievous Angel* (released in January 1974). His work was livened by Elvis Presley's sidemen, including James Burton, and the sessions featured exceptional country and rockabilly backing. He also hired Hugh Davies, Haggard's mixer and recording engineer, leaving little to chance. Pedal steel player Al Perkins recalled, "Gram had a vivid impression of certain people like Elvis, Merle, and others, and he tried to follow their footsteps, right down to the musicians."

"Still Feeling Blue," the opening cut of GP, was straight country: fiddle, guitars, singing steel, and Parsons's own sensitive vocal; it set the album's tone, as did his harmonizing with the gifted Emmylou Harris. When he was still part of the Flying Burrito Brothers, Gram had met Harris in Washington, D.C. He had recruited her and eventually sent her a plane ticket to Los Angeles. Once there, she sang harmony on his two albums, and the duo is now considered by some to have been one of modern country's finest. Tony Scherman goes so far as to assert that despite Parsons's accomplishments, his "biggest contribution may have been to convert a twenty-one-year-old Joni Mitchell–style folk singer named Emmylou Harris to country music." Harris has remained perhaps Parsons's greatest advocate. "If there's one thing in my life that I really want to do," she explains, "it's get Gram's music out in the open where it should be. A lot of people who would've appreciated him never got to hear him."

➤   ◄ ➤   ◄ ➤

A Fallen Angel

Gram Parsons is one of those figures who has excited far more interest since his death than he did during his professional life. He was born Ingram Cecil Connor III in Florida in 1946 and was reared in Waycross, Georgia. He became "a pawn in a southern family deeply embedded in alcohol, suicides, betrayals, and good money gone bad," writes biographer Ben Fong-Torres. Gram matriculated briefly at Harvard University, but he was a cipher for the mid-1960s: "Acid was the major reason I dropped out— I had taken so much of it. Remember, I was interested in psychedelic trips, so I checked into them on my own and dropped out of Harvard."

He then formed the International Submarine Band. Rhythm guitarist Barry Tashian knew Parsons and the Submarine Band in New York. "They'd be rehearsing, and they were playing Buck Owens's stuff," he told writer Cecilia Tichi. "It was just wonderful." Tashian suggests that Parsons brought "a more rhythmic approach" and "a rock atti- tude" to country. He also brought a Jerry Lee Lewis–like sense of the interrelationship between the sacred and the profane, using prominent religious imagery.

Gram and the Submarine Band moved to Los Angeles in 1965. Three years later he joined the Byrds, and the addition of Parsons gave the group a distinct country tilt. The Byrds had previously revealed that inclination with *The Fabulous Byrd Brothers*, and late in 1968, with Gram contributing two major songs ("Hickory Wind" and "I Am a Pilgrim"), the band then cut *Sweetheart of the Rodeo* in Nashville and performed a cut from the album, the satiric "Drug Store Truck Drivin' Man," to an unappreciative audi- ence on the "Grand Ole Opry."

In 1969 Parsons quit the Byrds after only four months, and Chris Hillman soon did, too. Together with Pete Kleinow, Joe Corneal (both former Byrds), and Chris Ethridge, they formed the group with which Gram's name is most frequently linked: the Flying Burrito Brothers. The release of the Burritos' first and finest album *The Gilded Palace of Sin* that year established this hippie-honky-tonk band as something special, probably as good a fusion of country and rock as would be achieved. Hillman and Parsons con- tributed their own versions of high duets, and Kleinow's steel runs were pure country. While younger, previously disinterested fans began to pay attention to the Burritos' version of this music, conservative country fans little noticed the newfangled songs. Perhaps traditionalists were turned off by the Burritos' Nudie Cohen outfits, complete with sequined marijuana leaves.

Between the studio sessions that led to his final two albums, Gram formed a band called the Fallen Angels—Emmylou Harris, Neil Franz, N. D. Smart II, Kyle Tullis, and Gerry Mule—and toured. One result was *Gram Parsons and the Fallen Angels, Live, 1973*, recorded before an audience in Hempstead, New York. With a Confederate flag unfurled behind the bandstand, this California transplant remained a son of the South.

Some of his songs, such as the poignant "Hickory Wind," which he wrote with Bob Bachanon, were traditional in their sentiments. Many of Gram's contemporaries saw great depth in that lyric. Wrote Marley Brant in 1990: "'Hickory Wind . . .' addresses his own complex emotions regarding his southern roots while evoking the poignancy that touches each one of us who has ever felt a longing to be somewhere else other than where we were." More than a few old-line country music fans, on the other hand, considered the song to be another not-quite-that-complex entry in the established lineage of rural romanticism that included everything from "Detroit City" to "Take Me Back to the Sweet Sunny South." In fact arguments have been made that Parsons's songs, while artistically satisfying, were less original or radical than was the fact that a long-haired, pot-smoking, young southerner was performing them. Identification, that defining characteristic of so many fans, in this case opened the music to a new audience, itself young, long-haired, and often pot-smoking.

His songs reflected the many contradictions in his (and his generation's) soul. As Chet Flippo has written, "I don't think we'll ever again see such a textbook example of a promising pupil teetering on the great divide between perdition and redemption, between Sin City and Heaven itself." To many of his contemporaries Gram remains a central figure; biographer Fong-Torres calls him "perhaps *the* pioneer of country rock." No one can know what Gram Parsons might have accomplished if he hadn't died of a drug overdose at Joshua Tree, California, on September 9, 1973, not quite twenty-seven years old.

◄ ►　　　◄ ►　　　◄ ►

The traditionalism within the nonconformity of many of Gram Parsons's songs—long before Willie Nelson, Waylon Jennings, and the rest developed their own "outlaw" image—created a dilemma for some fans. Country conservatives recognized his music but not his style. He included explicit Christian references in many numbers, and more than a few were distinctly influenced by gospel music—this at time when longhairs were still called "hippies" and considered to be complete hedonists.

California's most visibly hedonistic country-rock band had been formed in the Bay Area during 1973, Nick "Chinga" Chavin's Country Porn. A former Haight-Ashbury poet, the self-nicknamed Chinga, who had migrated from Texas and who then taught English at Richmond High School, decided to take country as far as it would go during those libertine years. The group's unsubtle sexual satire and raunchy lyrics immediately demonstrated who the *real* outlaws were in country music. Performing Chavin-written songs such as "Asshole from El Paso," "Sit, Sit, Sit (Sit on My Face)," and "Head Boogie," the group shocked audiences—walkouts were common—but they also achieved cult status. Their self-released album *Country Porn* became a collectors' item, and when that title was eventually released by Attic Records in Canada, it went gold.

Country Porn, a tight ensemble of good musicians, was a precursor of the 1980s cowpunk movement. Chavin vocalized with an exaggerated nasal twang and played a red toilet-seat guitar. He also "interacted" on stage with pornographic movie star Gina Fornelli, while accompanied by such sidemen as Jelly Roll John Baker and Beaver Bob Hermann, as well as his female backup singers the Muffettes (Sue Gruenwald and Lotta Cash). Miles Hurwitz called this "a killer band" in *BAM*.

The country-rock–country-pop border also produced the Eagles, one of the most commercially successful musical groups of all time. They became in fact one more defining group, eventually creating a new kind of country-influenced pop music that rankled some rock and country aficionados just as it engaged a great many more fans. Founded by Glen Frey, Don Henley, Bernie Leadon, and Randy Meisner, the Eagles had no native-born Californians. All members, however, lived in musically dynamic Southern California. ("The whole vibe of L.A. hit me right off," recalls Frey.) The band spun out of one assembled in 1971 by producer John Boylan for backup on Linda Ronstadt's *Silk Purse* album. Everyone's musical credentials were first-rate, and from the beginning, these musicians planned to avoid the internal ferment that had destroyed so many other promising ensembles. Frey told Cameron Crowe of *Rolling Stone*, "We had it all planned. We'd watched bands like Poco and the Burrito Brothers lose their initial momentum. We were determined not to make the same mistakes. This was gonna be our best shot. Everybody had to look good, sing good, play good, and write good. We wanted it all. Peer respect. AM and FM success. Number one singles and albums, great music and a lot of money." To a great degree they accomplished all those things.

Their debut album *The Eagles* (1972) contained three chart singles, "Take It Easy," "Witchy Woman," and "Peaceful Easy Feeling"; both the album and "Take It Easy" won gold records, an auspicious start indeed. The gang followed with western-themed *Desperado* (1973), which contained two more essential hits: "Tequila Sunrise" and the title track. It was not as great a commercial success as *The Eagles* had been, but critics were impressed, and it certainly helped confirm that the group might become a major factor in the musical world.

Linda Ronstadt joins the Eagles in concert: (from left) Randy Meisner, Glen
Frey, Don Henley, Jackson Browne, Ronstadt, Bernie Leadon. From the Gid
Tanner Artist File #NF1996, The Southern Folklife Collection, Wilson Library,
The University of North Carolina at Chapel Hill.

Already the Eagles's soft-country sound—they actually performed in a
number of styles—was reaching a considerable audience. Still, as had
happened to many of the other country rockers during that period of
proletarian posing, the Eagles were criticized for not including social
commentary in their songs. Most listeners, however, were wearying of social travail, so they didn't seem to mind; enjoyable music drew them to
the group's performances.

For their third album *On the Border* (1974) the Eagles added guitarist
Don Felder. This was their first collection recorded in Los Angeles, and it
achieved gold-record sales. By then the band's concerts had become
enormously popular. They followed *On the Border* with the platinum-
winning *One of These Nights* the next year, and it contained yet another of

their major hits, "Lyin' Eyes." A year later their third consecutive number-one album *Hotel California* was released. It featured a number of different styles and types of songs, and both "New Kid in Town" and the title tune became hits.

"During the mid-'70s," reports *The Rolling Stone Encyclopedia of Rock and Roll*, "the band could do no wrong, achieving status of mega-group with across-board appeal." By then critics were correct to largely identify the Eagles with pop music, but the group was clearly redefining that genre to include significant rock and country elements. The Eagles disbanded in 1981 to pursue solo careers with mixed results; their many followers fell into a funk. "It seems like nothing can stay good in rock," said a caller to a San Francisco radio talk show.

Rarely mentioned—or even recognized at first by many fans—was that soft rock's influence was contributing to the growing homogeneity and decreasing distinctiveness of country music. As younger, often better-educated, and more affluent listeners were drawn to the Eagles and other soft-country favorites, older, often blue-collar fans in the state continued to support the unvarnished southwestern rhythms of the California Sound. Ironically, within many bars and clubs, a social change was afoot because a number of previously all-white jobs had been opened to all comers. Slowly more nonwhites began to spend time and money where their white coworkers did. "We'd always had some Spanish people where we played," recalls Bill Woods, "but after about 1970 or so it got to be a real big bunch at dances." Resident Latinos—almost always called Mexicans or Spanish—had been part of the western music scene from its inception, especially in traditional ranching areas. Old prejudices lingered of course, and in general African-Americans were much less welcome than Hispanics. Nevertheless one gifted singer bucked that tide and became this state's first important "black" country artist.

Stoney Edwards—of African, Irish, and Seminole extraction—was one of many California singers whose style revealed not only deep country roots but also the considerable influence of Lefty Frizzell. A native of Oklahoma, he had moved to the Bay Area in the early 1950s and worked as a machinist for nearly twenty years, relegating his music to avocation. An industrial injury changed that in 1969, but at first things didn't go well. He admitted to *Country Music* magazine writer Glenn Hunter, "I had my bag packed one night and was ready to leave when my little girl came in

Stoney Edwards. Courtesy of Kenneth Edwards.

with this ole windup toy I'd bought her. 'Daddy, if I can't go, how come you get to go?'" That incident led Stoney to write his first song, "Two Dollar Toy," which later became one of his hits.

He pursued his music more aggressively, and in 1971 Capitol released his first album *Stoney Edwards: A Country Singer*. He soon became a favorite in the Golden State, where his intense, bluesy honky-tonk style was much appreciated, and his records began appearing on national charts. His version of "She's My Rock" in particular more than held its own with George Jones's, and he achieved the upper levels of popularity with "Mississippi You're on My Mind," "Cute Little Waitress," "One Beat at a Time," and "Hank and Lefty Raised My Country Soul"—the last a valedictory written by Dallas Frazier and A. L. Owens.

After the success of "Hank and Lefty," Stoney encountered Frizzell, whose career had fallen into eclipse. They were in a bar, and Lefty had just heard the number on the jukebox; the older man actually appeared to have been weeping. Afterward Edwards reported, "This guy [in the bar] told me he'd overheard Lefty say, 'Why that song's a tribute to me . . . and here I didn't think nobody cared a shit about me anymore. And wouldn't you know . . . it had to be a black man.'" Precisely because critics also paid far too much attention to Stoney's color, most of them missed the fact that he was a major talent.

The career of Freddie Hart also blossomed about the same time Stoney's did. Hart was raised in poverty in Alabama, where his uncle made his first guitar out of a wooden cigar box and coil wire from a Ford. He had served a long apprenticeship in this business. After World War II (he had been only fourteen years old when he enlisted in the Marine Corps) Freddie eventually worked for both Hank Williams and Lefty Frizzell, then became a strong favorite on "Town Hall Party" from 1953 until 1956. Hart appeared so often on rival "Home Town Jamboree" that many viewers thought he was a regular there, too. In fact Freddie performed on virtually every country-music show in Southern and Central California and was popular everywhere he appeared. He came to be considered a journeyman singer and songwriter, a regional favorite, but a guy who couldn't get a break or a major hit.

Then in 1971 after twenty-five years in the business his *California Grapevine* album was released by Capitol, and one cut, "Easy Lovin'," shot to number one on the country chart and also achieved number fifteen on the pop list. Capitol soon changed the album's title to *Easy Lovin'*. Virtually every record the Southern California resident made for a good while after that climbed the upper reaches of popularity; after nearly three decades he was an "instant" star.

The Bay Area hosted yet another top exemplar of no-nonsense music, Cal Smith. Born in Gans, Oklahoma, and raised in Oakland, Smith became "one of the most brilliant hard country singers to emerge in the late '60s and early '70s," according to *Country Music* magazine's Michael Bane. Today Smith is often identified with Oklahoma and Missouri, where he has since settled and established businesses, but his big break occurred when he was working as a disc jockey in San Jose, and Ernest Tubb heard him sing "I'm Walking the Floor over You." E. T. was so impressed that he invited the younger man to join his group the Texas Troubadours.

Eventually Cal was named most promising male artist of 1968 by Nashville's *Music City News*. He didn't hit his stride, though, until the 1970s. In 1974 his version of Don Wayne's "Country Bumpkin" won both the annual Country Music Association's and the Academy of Country Music's awards for both single and song of the year. Many fans, including current superstar Garth Brooks, consider that record to be a genuine classic. Among Cal's other chart records was "It's Time to Pay the Fiddler," also a number one. Throughout his career he remained true to hard-country styles.

Back in the late 1940s when Bill Woods's Orange Blossom Playboys were the premier country group in the Bakersfield area, his bass player was Buster Simpson. Buster's younger brother Red, who as a kid hung around nightspots with a shoe-shine box (and once put black polish on Tex Ritter's expensive green boots), developed into a top songwriter and a performer of note, too. Whiteside calls him "perhaps California's greatest songwriter, after Haggard and Tommy Collins." He was for a time also California's best-known performer of truck-driving songs when that subgenre thrived; his "(Hello) I'm a Truck" was number one on radio playlists and reached number four on charts in late 1971 and early the next year. Red recalls that when Visalian Gene Breeden of Portland Records proposed that he cut the song, he had replied, "Hello, I'm a *what?*"

Red's family had moved to Bakersfield from Higley, Arizona, when he was only three, so he grew up in the Kern County town. While he won awards as a singer—and still performs regularly—he has since his youth been primarily a writer of songs. Fiddler Oscar Whittington says Red is "one of the most talented songwriters I know," and Woods remembers, "every time he came home on leave from the navy, he and I would spend all night many times sitting on the floor and writing songs." Later, after Red's discharge from the military, he began performing locally; "he would work in the Bakersfield night clubs for a while," recalls Woods, "but when it interfered with his writing, he'd quit in order to get some songs written." Eventually Simpson penned hits such as "You Don't Have Very Far to Go" (with Haggard), "Love Me Again," "Roll Truck Roll," "Close Up the Honky Tonks," "Sam's Place," and "The Kansas City Song," and his pieces would be recorded by Shelly West, Rosanne Cash, the Flying Burrito Brothers, Roy Clark, Connie Smith, Wynn Stewart, Haggard, and Owens (who has cut thirty-five of them).

Stoney, Freddie, Cal, and Red had all paid their dues in this honky-tonk or on that stage, and tough experience layered their songs. In a real sense, then as now, the small local venues in which those four scratched out their livings were a fertile base of country music. To a greater degree than most other forms of popular music, country music's foundation remains in the countless local singers and bands to which fans dance. Those entertainers and places—whether Cathy Slack and the Cadillacs, the Durhham Brothers, or Harvey Brown and his Sidewinders, whether at Trout's Bar in Oildale, Bonnie Price's Foothill Club in Signal Hill, or the Five High Club in Salinas—have represented the music's endurance and its vitality.

The why of California's fierce retention of hard-country styles in the face of soft country's national domination remains uncertain. Some say it is a breath of harsh reality in the face of the state's own inaccurate soft image. "Let some of them east-coast guys chop cotton in 1 1 2 degrees, or buck pig iron all day on a drilling rig in that oil patch, then tell me about soft life in California," challenges Lee "Brownie" Brown, a retired oil well driller. "We'll find out who's hard and who's soft real quick, pardner." In part, too, hard country has clearly been a reaction against both Nashville's and Hollywood's promiscuous quest for pop dollars. Perhaps its popularity here has been more driven by the good luck of having performers like Owens, Haggard, Rich, Simpson, Edwards, Mooney, Hamlett, Nichols, and the Mosbys in residence.

By the 1970s, however, more and more young artists were feeling they had to relocate to Nashville to really have a chance in this business. Asked why he moved there, Bakersfield songwriter Buddy Mize said simply, "because this is where it's at." In California meanwhile with country music still perceived as somewhat marginal by the arty elite, many musicians and fans alike have yearned for and pursued variations of older, deeper country patterns as a way of reinforcing roots, a nearly sacred return via contrary forms of expression.

Class and cultural allegiance, the tendency of upwardly mobile people not to reject their origins, also continues to play an important part here. The Californian sense of eased limits, thus of expanded creative possibilities, has allowed artists to enrich rather than disdain older styles, as the work of Owens and Haggard, in particular, exemplifies. As a result, a distinctive brand of hard country has ruled: the Bakersfield Sound, the California Sound with its rockabilly and honky-tonk association—the twanging steel, the pounding bass—whether played by the Buckaroos, the Strangers, or the Mosbys.

It was thus not surprising that the most powerful merging of rock and country occurred in the Golden State. While that had little immediate impact on most traditional country audiences, it certainly brought some rock fans toward country music. It also once more distanced the West from musical styles in the South. Said Linda Ronstadt, "There's such an enormous difference between country music in Nashville and country music in California. . . . I don't really play country music—I play very definitely California music." Many in the Volunteer State would have agreed, but Linda's language reveals the power of Nashville: if it ain't from there, it ain't country, or so some had come to believe. In fact, both Tennessee and California produced country, but their styles were (and are) often dissimilar.

In the late 1970s another unexpected surge of interest in an older country style arose on the West Coast, this one driven by a rockabilly renaissance. Suddenly it was again *hot*, especially in Southern California. In 1976 "Jungle Rock," a song recorded eighteen years before by Los Angeles's Hank Mizell, was a hit abroad, and clubs around the state featured unembellished rockabillies. In Santa Monica, for example, the Alligators played "Flying Saucers' Rock and Roll"; down the street Jackie Lee Waukeen Cochran performed and Mac Curtis, too, while Ray Campi, the "King of Rockabilly," could be heard at the Palomino Club. Veterans such as Glen Glenn, Carl Perkins, and the remarkable Rose Maddox were touring. All of them often sounded as though they had arrived directly from Memphis in a 1957 time capsule.

At least some of this interest was energized by "Rockin'" Ronnie Weiser with his fan magazine and record label, both called *Rollin' Rock*. Weiser loved the blending of rhythm and blues and country music that had roared out of Memphis twenty years before. After graduating from UCLA in 1970, Weiser settled in Southern California and began his "fanzine." He then started receiving questions about where various out-of-print rockabilly recordings might be obtained, so he initiated a search for original tapes to reissue.

Virtually everything he eventually later released (cuts by veterans such as Jimmy Patton, Cochran, Curtis, and Campi, for instance) was sold to collectors. Curtis's "Ducktail" and Campi's "Tore Up" soon appeared on international best-seller charts, and Weiser also began to record neo-rockabillies such as Billy Zoom, Colin Winski, Johnny Legend, and Sarah Harris. In 1978, as critics worldwide were dubbing electronic pop "new wave," the sanguine Weiser declared, "Rockabilly is the music of today and tomorrow. This is the real new wave."

A particular California beneficiary of the rockabilly revival was Campi, a transplanted Texan who had first moved to Los Angeles in 1959. He had been a pioneer of rockabilly in his native state, cutting his first record there in 1954. Not until interest in the style reintensified in the 1970s, however, did he score his first big hits. Weiser released an album of Ray's solos, *Rockabilly Rocket*, and Campi organized his Rockabilly Rebels. They played top venues such as San Francisco's Mabuhay Gardens, and both the Whisky A Go-Go and the Palomino in the Los Angeles area. Although Ray still didn't crack the country establishment's veneer or radio playlists, he did gain a considerable international audience; the 1977 *Melody Maker* magazine rockabilly poll named him number one.

All the various mergings (or reunitings) of rock and country throughout the 1960s and '70s forced a recognition that rockabilly had always been part of the country universe—a love child disowned in Nashville but not in Los Angeles or San Jose. In the meantime many other fans had been led toward country by the likes of Bruce Springsteen's reprise of "Wreck on the Highway," Tom Petty's "Louisiana Rain," or Elvis Costello's album *Almost Blue*. Of course the country-rock connection in the state was blurred when groups like the Eagles slipped into the homogeneous pop mainstream. The initial impulse of rock and roll, like much original country, had been distinctly countercultural, driven in rock's case by the emergent youth culture's increasing demand for independence. By the 1970s, however, mutants like pop rock and pop country didn't really address that need.

The connection of country and folk music also endured into the 1970s, but it became a niche market rather than the strong force it had been a decade earlier. Successful singers such as Juice Newton, Emmylou Harris, and Linda Ronstadt, who began their careers as "folkies," moved more solidly into country or pop styles.

Newton (called Judy Kay then) started in the 1970s as a California folk singer before moving to countrypolitan. In the next decade she scored hits with the Grammy-winning "Break It to Me Gently" (1982) and "Angel of the Morning" (1981). Harris had become a country rocker when Gram Parsons brought her to California. After establishing herself as a major singer—winning five Grammys—with her electrically amplified Hot Band, she would switch to all-acoustic backing with the Nash Ramblers in 1990. Harris is now a member of the "Grand Ole Opry." Ronstadt, who began performing with the folkish Stone Poneys in the late 1960s, gravitated to musically diverse Los Angeles, where she became a folk-rock soloist with a strong country flavor. Her 1974 *Heart Like a Wheel* album thrust her into country prominence. With a strong voice and marked presentation skills, she managed to turn country tunes into widely accepted crossovers—"I Can't Help It (If I'm Still in Love with You)," "Crazy," and "When Will I Be Loved," for example. "Linda Ronstadt's music resists categorization," points out *The Illustrated History of Country Music*, because she "had grown up in a musical world in which crossover and cross-pollination were the rule rather than the exception." Amen.

One distinct country-folk talent developed during the decade. Kate Wolf had been much impressed with the Bay Area's rich folk-music scene in the 1950s. Married and the mother of two children, her professional career started in the late 1960s when she was twenty-seven years old. Her marriage broke up, and she moved north to rural Sonoma County late in the decade, dedicating herself to music. She married guitarist Don Coffin in 1974, and they formed a band called the Wildwood Flower. In Northern California, Wolf soon attracted a heterogeneous audience of farmers and ranchers, back-to-earth hippies, suburbanites, and, increasingly, feminists. Kate's own feminism was unabashed but not shrill, and Judy Anderson, a teacher in Sebastopol, recalls, "Her sound and her subjects were so fresh. I'd never heard anyone quite like her."

The singer's appeal expanded first into the urban Bay Area, then well beyond, especially after her albums *Back Roads* (1976) and *Lines in Paper* (1977) were released by her own label Owl Records. Kate later observed with some lingering wonder, "A big shift occurred where people wanted to hear my songs. It was amazing. It just kind of made its own way. They dragged us out of Sonoma County down into the Bay Area, and then we got airplay, and we started traveling further and further." Her music itself had developed into a synthesis of folk and country, called the Sonoma County Sound: clean acoustic string music from guitar, fiddle, mandolin, and bass in the southern tradition, embellished by poetic lyrics. Her words combined considerable life experience with a genuine gift for verse; Anderson called them "grown-up songs for grown-up people."

Through the aegis of Utah Phillips, Kate began touring nationally and internationally in 1977. She appeared at various folk festivals and developed a significant following in Canada, all at a time when no commercial company had yet signed her. Kate remained fiercely independent, with ownership not only of Owl Records but also of Another Sundown Publishing Company. Not until 1979 did she sign with Kaleidoscope Records, which then released *Safe at Anchor*.

Kate's performances continued to be intimate despite surging popularity. Saying, "there's no way I'm going to put out a slick record," she not only refused to "go commercial," but she also refused to "go southern," singing her country-style songs in her unadulterated California dialect—no fake drawl for her—while topflight accompanists provided music far more traditional than commercial country was recording. As the decade closed, Wolf's career seemed to be on a rapid up escalator, energizing varieties of old-time music on the West Coast.

In fact because California remained a destination for entertainers and a musical mix as a result, many major acts from elsewhere had at least some connection with this arena. Earlier, stars such as Bob Wills, Lefty Frizzell, and Johnny Cash had dwelled here at least for a time. That list came to include younger standouts such as Lefty's brother David and Shelly West, whose pairing by veteran producer Snuff Garrett led to hits such as "You're the Reason God Made Oklahoma" and "I Just Came Here to Dance"; Cajun Jo-El Sonnier, who once won a talent contest at the Palomino Club and who bounced from his Louisiana home to Los Angeles then to Nashville and back between 1972 and '80; Lacy J. Dalton, the sultry-voiced singer from Pennsylvania, who lingered on the California scene for several years before hitting it big in Nashville in 1979; Oregonian Susan Raye, a Buck Owens protégé, had four top-10 singles plus a winning duet with Owens, "The Great White Horse." Even better known are Diana and Christina Ciminella, mother and daughter, the former a Kentucky native, the latter growing up in the Golden State. They began singing together in Southern California in the 1970s. Eventually they changed their first names to Wynonna and Naomi, and adopted mom's maiden name: Judd. By the mid-1980s, the Judds' sentimental and often nostalgic songs with acoustic backing produced hits, thanks in part to producer Brent Maher and arranger Don Potter; the mother and daughter were stars. This short list only scrapes the surface, but as has long been true, most of the country performers connected with this state have migrated from elsewhere, and most have in recent years headed for Nashville once they became (or in order to become) hot properties.

The Tennessee capital continued tightening its national hammerlock on country during the 1970s. An "outlaw" movement, centered in Texas and headed by Waylon Jennings, Willie Nelson, and Tompall Glaser, among others, thumbed its nose at Nashville's near monopoly and growing monotony just as Buck Owens had earlier. But as Owens faded on television's "Hee Haw," so did California, despite efforts to promote new talents such as Raye and Buddy Alan.

Nevertheless thanks to Jennings, Nelson, Haggard, Kris Kristofferson, and Johnny Cash, the false, squeaky-clean image of country entertainers was at least loosened, if not totally undone. Country's public relations gurus have worked for years to hide some realities from the public. They've sought to maintain the music's highly marketable image of rural virtue, but reality hasn't always cooperated. The musicians have been mainly young men, and then as now for even minor celebrities, sex was readily available and readily accepted. According to biographer Joel Selvin, for example, candid country-rocker Rick Nelson told a friend, "I love pussy. That's why I tour so much." Another forthright star, Buck Owens, told a *People* magazine reporter, "For an entertainer, there's no end to the girls; you just pick up the phone." Bob Wills's biographer Charles R. Townsend explained that Wills developed "a deep distrust of women, particularly those who frequented dances. Over the years he had seen so many women at dances make eyes at, flirt with, and even proposition him and his musicians that he lost confidence in most of them. Some were wives of their best friends." Female country groupies—called "Buckle Bunnies" or "Snuff Queens," among other things—have never been far from entertainers. Ace guitar player Roy Nichols, discussing life on the road, remembered, "I got a lot of girls."

As for Haggard, by decade's end he seemed to be carrying California country almost single-handedly. His complex persona eventually became an important part of his songs and of his public image, too, so an *auteur* identification arose that created an almost familial sense among his followers. He contrasted sharply with the fake "badass" image long cultivated in the rock and country worlds. Asked by reporter Mark Rose about the rowdy reputation of Gram Parsons, Hag responded with characteristic frankness:

> Gram would've had to get up three times as early as I did to be as wild as I was. He was a pussy. Hell, he was just a long-haired kid. . . .
>
> I thought he was a good writer. He was not wild, though. . . .
>
> That's what's funny to me. All these guys running around in long hair talk about being wild and rolling stones. . . .
>
> I don't know what the Rolling Stones do, but I don't know what avenue they can possibly travel down that I haven't been down. I betcha I can show them a couple of things.

No doubt. A former classmate in Oildale said, "He [Merle] wasn't the toughest guy around—he wasn't big enough for that—but he was damn sure willing." Then he added, "That one bunch can sing about a street fightin' man and all that, but Merle really did it . . . plenty."

Merle Haggard ascended as an artist at a time when children of the Dust Bowl migration were making their artistic marks—fiction writers such as James D. Houston, Raymond Carver, and Ken Kesey, for example, or poets like Wilma Elizabeth McDaniel, DeWayne Rail, and Dorothy Rose. The Oildale native was part of this surge, as were other songwriters—Red Simpson, Dallas Frazier, and Buddy Mize, among them.

Merle's parents had still been kicking the dust of Oklahoma off their boots when, on April 6, 1937, the boy was born in Bakersfield. He is thus old enough to have been touched by legendary hard times and to have developed profound empathy for the downtrodden. He is also old enough to have created some even harder times for himself when he embarked on his adolescent, born-to-raise-hell stretch. "I just wanted to grow up too fast. I wanted to work, not go to school."

Merle was the third child—after Lowell and Lillian—of James and Flossie Haggard, a family that had left Checotah, Oklahoma, in 1934. James found work as a carpenter for the Santa Fe Railroad, obtained a boxcar, then converted it to a house for his family. The boy was raised in Oildale, adjacent to the Kern River oil fields north of Bakersfield. Says writer Bill Barich, "That is one hardscrabble town." It was also a white, blue-collar community with relative homogeneity, so it offered few hints at the generosity of vision and the artistic scope that Haggard would develop.

Even the good schools there had small impact on Merle after his father died in 1946. Mrs. Haggard had to become the family's breadwinner, working as a bookkeeper. Those events cut the bright, athletic Merle loose from virtually any social moorings. He became a stranger even to his own family. "I was basically on my own from age ten," he remembers.

Contrary to rumor, Merle was not raised in abject poverty; his circumstances were about average for his blue-collar neighborhood, although few other kids there were supported by a widowed mother. The loss of parental attention, not destitution, more than likely accounts for young Haggard's antisocial behavior. The boy was also caught between his rural southwestern heritage (Oildale itself was then defined by Texas, Arkansas, Missouri, and Oklahoma memories) and the more cosmopolitan California myths that surrounded him. Bakersfield, which loomed a long mile to the south, was growing from town to city, and Los Angeles's considerable influence was penetrating.

Young Merle seemed to be trying to live a version—perhaps a romantic one—of his lost father's Oklahoma roots. James Haggard had been a musician in the Sooner State, and Merle gravitated toward music early. He remembers riding his bike to Beardsley Ballroom, not far from his house, where he would stand outside and hear major acts like Bob Wills and the Texas Playboys or the Maddox Brothers and Rose. The prophecy for his junior high school yearbook in 1951, written in a retrospective past tense, said, "Donald Warren, Kelly Epps, and Merle Haggard formed a vocal trio."

Merle's pal Bob Teague told reporter John Teves that he met the future superstar this way: "I was just walkin' down the street [in Oildale] one day and I heard somebody pickin' at a guitar." Bob slipped down an alley and peeked over a fence: "There was ol' Merle."

"Hey, you know how you play one of these things?" Haggard called when he noticed Teague, who was four years older. Bob did, and he helped Merle learn how to play. "We were pretty tight after that," says Teague.

Those two, along with other pals, were as likely to be found at Bunkie's Drive-In as at school. Haggard's brother Lowell remembers that Merle and his buddy Teague "headed off to school together" in those years, but he says, "I'm not sure they ever got there." In fact the youthful Haggard became the kind of character country songs are written about.

The southern rovers' mystique of country music gripped Hag early on; he seemed to want to live the songs and to a degree he did. While still in grade school, he hopped trains on the tracks that ran near his house. Later he took advantage of the pass he had been given by the Santa Fe Railroad following his father's death and traveled here and there. But railroads

Mrs. Phair's fifth-grade class at Standard School, Oildale, 1946–47. Merle Haggard
stands fourth from left in second row. Gerald Haslam is second from left in third
row. Photo by Rountree, Oildale. Gerald Haslam Collection.

weren't his only fascination; he admits joyriding in more than one stolen
car, and at fourteen he hitchhiked to Texas with Teague .

This all may have been part of Haggard's somewhat romanticized fascination with the 1930s.

> There were so many things I loved about the thirties, he admits. I could
> find many reasons for wanting to live back there. Such as trains was the
> method of travel; the glamour of trains always appealed to me. And Amer-

ica was at the dawn of an industrial age, coming out of a depression into a war.

Then again, the music was young. So many things were being done in music; it was wide open back then, electronics had not yet been involved, and basically it was *real*. Sure, I'd have liked to have visited those days and at least seen it happen. For musicians of that generation, such as Eldon Shamblin and Joe Venuti, it was an unbelievable period to live in; they saw it all.

Another part of Merle seemed intrigued by the southwestern infatuation with "honorable" outlaws—Pretty Boy Floyd, Bonnie and Clyde, even Jesse James. He found ways to stay in trouble, principally by breaking rules others kids accepted without thought. "Why do I have to go to school?" Merle might demand, "Who says I can't go in a bar?"

During his early teen years the handsome Haggard seemed preternaturally mature to neighborhood kids, a Huck Finn unencumbered by formal education and unintimidated by authority; he escaped seven times from various reform schools (that tally would eventually rise to seventeen). He was in fact envied by many of his male peers and endlessly alluring to young women. Hag had already become singular. Some of his pals even had trouble understanding him, but nonetheless they found him to be an exciting companion. He had also by then begun a series of sprints toward or away from something. In the early 1950s young men could readily find seasonal farmwork, so life on the road was a possibility.

On one such venture when he was still fourteen, Merle and eighteen-year-old Teague did men's work, bucking hay on a ranch near Modesto. More importantly, a joint called the Fun Center on Crows Landing Road became the first place Haggard ever performed professionally. "The Fun Center was the kind of place where they didn't give you a glass when you ordered a beer," he told Peggy Russell, "just slapped the bottle down on the bar. You got the distinct feeling that it would not be in your best interest to ask for a glass, either."

Merle and Bob screwed up their courage and asked if they could perform there. After a few songs the bartender invited them to play the rest of the evening for all the beer they could drink plus $5. "Hell, I felt like we'd hit the jackpot," Merle recalls.

Not everyone recognized Merle's musical potential. His neighbor and contemporary Patricia Puskarich laughs when she recalls that Hag, Leroy

Knick, and her brother Donnie were singing together on the porch one afternoon. The harmony wasn't working, so her brother finally suggested, "Merle, why don't you just play the guitar and not sing." Apparently, vocal standards were high in that neighborhood.

Haggard kept chipping at music then, practicing his guitar, idolizing Roy Nichols, the teenager who picked with the Maddox Brothers and Rose ("He didn't have to go to school. He was makin' a livin' with his music."). Merle loved Jimmie Rodgers's songs, was a great fan of Wills and the Texas Playboys; like most of his peers, he was especially taken with a newcomer from Texas named Lefty Frizzell. He also was familiar with local acts, everyone from Cousin Eb Pilling and his Squirrel Shooters to Bill Woods and the Orange Blossom Playboys.

Teague figured prominently in another early high point of Merle's musical life. As Haggard tells it, he and Bob had gone to see one of their favorites perform at the Rainbow Gardens in Bakersfield. During an intermission, Teague "was ballsy and brassy enough to drag my ass backstage to meet Lefty Frizzell." Bob found the star and said, "Hey Lefty, this guy can sing nearly as good as you can. You need to hear him sing." Lefty said sure, and loaned the sixteen-year-old Haggard his guitar.

After a couple of songs "he was sincerely knocked out with my singin'," Haggard says now, still a little awe-struck at the memory. "I could see that in his face. . . . There was nobody who could tell me different." Lefty was impressed enough to insist that Merle be allowed to sing onstage.

> I walked out there and sang the only thing I could think of to sing that I knew that was not Lefty Frizzell songs, and that was Jimmie Rodgers music.
>
> I remember looking down seein' Frizzell's guitar and I'm highly impressed, man. . . . The man I started singin' for likes the way I sing. And when I got through singin' . . . with his guitar, his band . . . there was 3,000 screamin' kids and they screamed for me in the middle of his show. They screamed for the local kid. Everything was right, and I was hooked.

Hooked, yes, but he had not yet connected the relationship of work and persistence to success. His yearning for independence, plus his maturing masculinity, still dominated: some beer here, a fistfight there, a compliant lass or three, and some guitar strumming. There were more rumors of breaking and entering and of cars borrowed; there was a supposed armed robbery, a burglary or two, some pranks that grew too rough—all the grist of legend now. While most of his peers finished Standard School, then Bakersfield High, Merle was attending penal facilities like Camp Owens and Preston School of Industry, his rap sheet a tangle of commitments, paroles, revoked paroles, and escapes—the word *incorrigible* typed prominently near the page's top.

From ages ten through twenty-three, he now admits, "I didn't seem to be at rest where I was at. . . . It was an interesting childhood to say the least. Probably not like anyone else's." He was in the midst of an increasingly grueling personal odyssey, and a song memorializing those years is titled "I've Done It All." He may or may not have actually done it all, but he certainly did plenty.

Merle was smart, and he could be charming, characteristics that compounded the trouble he got into. By 1958 he ended up in maximum-security San Quentin Prison. By the time he was sent there, he was also four years into a passionate, adversarial marriage to Leona Hobbs, whom he had wed when he was seventeen, and he was the father of two children.

No one knows for certain what was going on in him then, not even Merle in all likelihood. "You know how it is," he told writer Peter Guralnick, "one thing led to another. . . . I finally wised up, and I got out of it." Today the usually candid—even blunt—Hag prefers not to discuss those bad times, principally because of the trouble he caused others, especially his mother. Life has hardened him to his own discomfort, and he does not avoid responsibility.

In retrospect, however, it seems that Haggard's genius—and his work truly merits that label—was built upon the accumulation of all his formative experiences, good and bad. Hitchhiking and riding the rails, bucking hay and picking fruit, sweet talking gals and fighting guys, all of it, merged with the southwestern music his family loved, then generalized into expressions of tribal values and human yearnings. Like other bards Merle has somehow made his experience communal. He has become *our* voice. Says singer Alan Jackson, "He's the real deal. He's the music. He's not showbiz."

Shortly after the young Haggard returned from San Quentin, he was talking with Bill Woods and some other musicians on the street outside

Lewis Talley's recording studio. Woods, who had met Merle's mother while her son was still in prison, recalls:

> You know we'd always shoot the bull after a session's over and all that. But the thing that stands out in my mind—there was another kid that I had met . . . and he saw Merle there, and said, "Don't you remember me?" Merle said, "Yeah, you look familiar." And he said, "Yeah, I used to whip your ass every day at school." And you know what Merle did? He looked at him, just as calm and said, "Well, do you think you can still do it?" And that was the end of the conversation. Merle he was kind of broke in by then.

The path of his career after being released from San Quentin has been charted in many places. He returned to Bakersfield in 1960, at a time when country music was jumping: Cousin Herb Henson's television show seemed poised to go national; Buck Owens released "Under Your Spell Again" and "Above and Beyond," establishing himself as a star; the Hollywood Argyles' version of Dallas Frazier's "Alley Oop" gave that Bakersfield songwriter a number one on the pop chart; Ferlin Husky had another number one of his own with "Wings of a Dove." And a bar called High Pockets on 34th Street hired Merle Haggard to play guitar at $10 per night.

"At first I just intended to work at nightclubs and make a living in Bakersfield," Merle recalls. "Back then I didn't have any idea that I could record. My dream wasn't that large." His talent was, though, and by 1995 Haggard had written forty-two number-one songs, the second-largest total in the history of this music and produced perhaps the finest repertoire written by anyone in country, since many of his best songs did not benefit from radio play and become generally popular. Hag's route to such accomplishments was interesting, for he has been a rebel in a realm that claims to respect rebellion.

Early in his career, it became clear that Haggard was an artist who refused to be limited to musical categories, overtly including elements of blues and jazz in his repertoire. "That's not really my own idea," he told writer Mark Rose and credited Jimmie Rodgers instead. "He did a lot of the same thing. He recorded a lot of songs where he had a jazz band. . . . I'm a music fan. I like most kinds of music." He added, "I don't like all of country music. In fact, I like very little of it."

Asked Rose, "You mean you don't like contemporary country music? You like the more traditional sound?"

"Well, I don't like smooth, perfect studio-manufactured music of any type," Haggard replied. "I like to listen to something that sounds like they weren't trying to make a record. In other words, like somebody was fortunate enough to be there to record it."

Haggard called his music country jazz, and in 1980 he became the first country artist to grace the cover of *Downbeat*, the esteemed jazz magazine. By then Merle was already being acknowledged to be one of country's greatest. Buck Owens said, "My considered opinion of the best singer, songwriter, performer of all time is Merle Haggard." Many peers agreed.

But a well-publicized aspect of Haggard's career has loomed large: the continued economic and personal problems that have plagued him and kept him on the cusp of hard times even during his periods of grand success. Asked to compare Merle and Buck Owens as businessmen, Bill Woods said, "Hell, Merle's probably the best singer ever—him and Marty Robbins—but he ain't *no* kind of businessman. How can you compare 'em?" On top of that Merle seems to be generous to a fault, more than merely repaying the help he once received, but the results of his largesse have not always been pleasant. One sad night at a concert in Santa Rosa, the Internal Revenue Service even seized his buses. Such financial misfortune led Merle back to the club and county fair circuits.

Moreover Hag's recording career drooped in the early 1990s, as he battled Curb Records in court (he had previously recorded for Tally, Capitol, MCA, and Epic). He told Jason DeParle in 1993 that despite having won fifty-six BMI awards to go with having written all those number-one hits—more than Hank Williams and Willie Nelson combined—he was $5 million in debt and struggling to pay creditors.

As a result of such travail, Haggard remained closer to this music's roots than any other superstar by playing those clubs and fairs and by seeing fans' faces up close. Old pal Billy Mize and former wife Bonnie Owens were like family, touring with him then, and he observed, "Being vocal, disgusted, and emotionally drained—those things lend themselves to good music."

Merle Haggard. From the Gid Tanner Artist File #NF1996, The Southern Folklife Collection, Wilson Library, The University of North Carolina at Chapel Hill.

As the lyrics of so many of his songs verify, problems in his personal life have also plagued the talented Haggard. His love life, for example, resulted in many stories about girlfriends as well as in multiple marriages. Yet Merle is a man with a strong commitment to family, and he displays great concern for his five children. But until recently he has not managed to remain involved in a long-term nuclear family. He is also reputed to have occasionally performed when less than sober; indeed, rumors that he has serious drinking or drug problems surface periodically, the stuff of tabloids. His health has not been good of late, either.

Asked about working with him, long-time members of his entourage all assert that they've enjoyed the experience. Dean Holloway says, "He runs with his crew and not above them. He'll sit and talk to you for hours to make sure you're happy with what you're doing." Bonnie Owens summarizes: "One thing about [working with] Merle Haggard, it is never, ever dull." Band members agree, too, that loyalty is the major virtue to Haggard. "I want my people to trust me," he says.

Bonnie, who still occasionally sings harmony with him, summarizes their ongoing relationship this way, "I probably know Merle Haggard as well as anybody. You can't put your finger exactly on who he is or what he is, because just about the time I've got him figured out, he becomes somebody else."

Merle's problems with commercial acumen and perhaps personal relationships have almost certainly allowed him to remain in touch with hard-times past. Bonnie's analysis rings true: "There's a little boy in him, and there'll always be a little boy. He's the type of person that got the feeling that while he was climbing the mountain of success . . . he liked the climb better than sittin' up on top. 'Cause he'd like to do everything he could to fall down again so he could climb back up."

Haggard has managed over and over to transform his experiences into widely attractive lyrics, for he harbors an artist's ability to somehow share the universal. Many songwriters mistake rhymed words and nice melodies for significance. Haggard doesn't. A thoughtful, open-minded man, he defies many expectations. Asked by DeParle about violence and race relations and other contemporary problems, for example, he avoids clichés and replies, "Everything that we probably are concerned about is caused indirectly from over-population."

Earlier in his career he seriously considered alternative messages during the Vietnam War, a rarity in the world of country music. Over the years his lyrics have dealt with race and race relations, with economic inequities, with disabilities, with other subjects conventionally avoided by commercial music. As Paul Hemphill has written, "Merle Haggard's songs come straight up from the gut in the tradition of the purest country songwriters and singers." As of 1996 he had written or cowritten just under 350 songs, with precious few clunkers, "country music's greatest body of work since that of Hank Williams, Sr.," opines writer Tony Scherman.

When he was inducted into the Country Music Hall of Fame in 1995, Haggard stood before the excited crowd and created what writer Jonny Whiteside has called "one of the great iconoclastic moments in country music history." He unfurled a vast thank-you list and said, "First of all, I'd like to thank my plumber Andy Gump—you're doin' a great job of keepin' my toilet workin'." Many in the audience were amused and others were offended, but few were really surprised. ("That's just ol' Hag.") What many didn't realize is that Haggard is a deeply sensitive man but hardened in the old southwestern manner so that he doesn't easily reveal his feelings except in songs.

His performance at the Hall of Fame induction revealed not only that he was aware of the mild absurdity of the semicanonization but more importantly that he was protecting himself from his own feelings. This is the boy whose friends did not see him weep when his father died and who became tough in inverse proportion to his own vulnerability. This is the man who twenty years into his career admitted, "I don't believe I've ever settled down," and wrote songs like "Driftwood" and "I Keep Running from Life." This is also the man who has on occasion simply disappeared; he told Mark Rose, "Sometimes this business gets to closing in on you. . . . when I get all I can pack, I just climb aboard [my bus] and get the hell out."

Merle's past is not entirely behind him but is instead a kind of living summary that remains emotionally unavoidable, so this is also the man who could write and mean "I Can't Hold Myself in Line." Moreover the soul he puts into songs like "Mama Tried," "Hungry Eyes," or "You Don't Have Very Far to Go" is rooted in his suffering, perhaps in his fears, and sometimes in his joys. Haggard's autobiographical songs are consistently his most powerful, and that is as good as it gets in this music.

He may indeed be—or have been—what a classmate once called him, "a tough little Okie," but he isn't an insensitive or an unintelligent one. And that unexpected combination has allowed him to become perhaps the greatest ever in this music.

In 1980 Hollywood produced the hit movie *Urban Cowboy*, which triggered an explosion in neocountry disco music. Various accoutrements of the film—mechanical bulls, feathered cowboy hats, and sexy tank tops—sprouted in bars all over California and the nation, including many swank locales. Mickey Gilley, a journeyman Texas singer best known as Jerry Lee Lewis's cousin, was a sudden star, as was his pal Johnny Lee. The sales of country music at record stores rocketed to $250 million in 1981. Between 1979 and 1984, 900 radio stations nationwide joined the ranks of full-time country or neocountry pop programmers. Like most sudden trends, however, this one had no legs, and by 1984 country music sales had dropped below 1979 figures.

But pop variations of country seemed increasingly to rule the airwaves. While Kenny Rogers and Alabama were producing what one writer called "Country Lite," some significant performers, including Ricky Skaggs, George Strait, Steve Earle, Emmylou Harris, Randy Travis, and John Anderson, were questioning the middle-of-the-road direction of this music. These performers and others created the new traditionalism of the mid-1980s. The reinvigoration of orthodox forms in California grew out of the dogged work of the old traditionalists Haggard and Owens, plus a "roots music" revival that by the end of the decade produced Dwight Yoakam.

One new traditionalist, Rosanne Cash, had connections in both places. The daughter of Johnny Cash was raised by her mother in Ventura, California. With her husband, Rodney Crowell, she became a central figure in that small but powerful movement to liberate country music from pop-style limitations. Along with a circle of musicians, singers, and writers like

Paul Kennerly, Albert Lee, Hank DeVito, Tony Brown, Harris, Crowell, and Cash brought a literary seriousness to highly individualistic work, while still honoring roots music. "Old," as it turned out, didn't have to mean out of date when it came to musical presentations.

Ronald Reagan, something of an older urban cowboy himself, was elected president in 1980. From California's perspective his promise to increase military spending was vital, because by then the state housed the world's largest military-industrial complex. California's economy did indeed benefit, for fully a fifth of all Department of Defense funds were then spent in the state, while NASA sent a third of its money to the state. Southern California in particular thrived. As Richard Rice, William Bullough, and Richard Orsi wrote in *The Elusive Eden*, "A majority of the state's largest companies were centered in the Los Angeles area, where cumulative income surpassed that of all but three other *states* [my emphasis], and the region accounted for one-eighth of the total gross domestic product (GDP) of the United States and a large majority of the state's population growth."

The affluence that followed the election of Reagan, however, didn't tend to be well distributed: the rich got richer, while some in the middle-class felt themselves slipping toward marginal existences. More than a few of those threatened folks were country-music fans, who, in turn, found themselves connecting with Haggard's 1973 anthem, "If We Make It through December."

Still this decade was generally prosperous in the Golden State. To the north, for example, Silicon Valley flourished as the computer revolution erupted. Yet some folks began to sense that changes might be occurring too quickly, even for California. During much of the decade the state's voters also supported a conservative Republican governor and a liberal Democratic legislature. As the 1980s closed, positive international events signaled hard times for the Golden State: the Berlin Wall was pulled down, the Soviet Union collapsed, and California would enter the 1990s sliding into its worst recession since the 1930s.

Merle Haggard dominated country music here and continued as a major force nationally. With his singing, his musicianship, and his songwriting, he had confirmed his status. Kris Kristofferson said simply, "With Haggard, we're not talking about this year's Country Music Association awards. We're talking about *posterity*."

Hag expanded his vocal range—the tenor of his youth could be deepened to a resonant baritone—and he became even more of a white soul singer without having to imitate black vocalists. As writer Robert Hilburn pointed out, Merle "possesses the quintessential voice in modern country music." Haggard's songwriting also deepened, so that the albums he recorded during this decade are arguably the finest series ever released by a country artist in so brief a period, with one startling song or performance after another. A reason for this was that his arrangements of numbers became more musically complex, particularly after Don Markham's emotional sax was added to the Strangers.

In 1980 Merle released *Back to the Barrooms Again*, and it included "Misery and Gin," "Make-Up and Faded Blue Jeans," "I Think I'll Just Stay Here and Drink," "Can't Break the Habit," and "Leonard," the last song a tribute to Leonard Sipes (singer Tommy Collins) who had aided a young Merle years before. *Big City*, released in 1981, stayed on the charts for nearly two years because of cuts such as "My Favorite Memory," "Are the Good Times Really Over?" and a remake of his old hit "You Don't Have Very Far to Go," as well as the album's title song.

Hag's idiosyncratic views on many matters by then baffled observers, since he indeed wore his own kind of hat. The astute Bill C. Malone, for example, wrote that in "Big City" the songwriter "delivered a mixed message that commented on urban anonymity, wage inequities, and inadequate government support ('so-called social security')." Then Malone added a mild slap at the incipient romanticism that occasionally surfaces in Merle's songs: "Haggard's solution—a flight to the wilds of Montana—was a fantasy that working people may have shared but that only someone like a millionaire singer could realize." But Malone seems to have taken the song too literally; like so many country lyrics, it is about working people's dreams and aspirations, not about their reality. The idealized Montana of the song is yet another version of one of this music's major themes: pastoral longing.

A year later Hag would add "Shopping for Dresses," another of his quirky classics, and in 1983 he released the gripping "Some Day When Things Are Good," then followed it with an insider's favorite, "Let's Chase Each Other around the Room." While these were by no means all commercial hits—most received virtually no airplay—they invariably knocked the britches off other songwriters and singers, who appreciated their virtuosity. A list of Hag's potential classics from the 1980s could be much longer—"Kern River," "Old Flames Can't Hold a Candle to You," "Natural High," "I Wonder Where I'll Find You at Tonight," and on and on. It was a golden decade for him and for California's country music as a result. His live performances featured everything from western swing to honky-tonk, plus some undefinable creations of his own.

Merle moved his home base to the Lake Shasta area near Redding in the 1980s. Although Bakersfield, his long-time home, remained relatively prosperous thanks to agriculture and oil, the "Nashville West" scene there was dissipating like the mirage it had always been. Buck Owens suggests why: "Let me put it this way: just about everybody—everybody in the music business, for sure—once they got something going, they moved away from Bakersfield." In 1981, for example, guitarist Eugene Moles, who had been playing at Trout's in Oildale, left for the Palomino in North Hollywood. He explained, "A lot of it [success] comes down to hanging around in the right places. You can't stay in a bar in Wasco or Oildale for five years and expect someone from RCA to come in and sign you."

There was more to it than that of course. Some of the reasons, such as altering population and economic patterns, have little directly to do with music. As country pioneer Jimmy Thomason also pointed out, Bakersfield had developed no major media draw, no "Grand Ole Opry" or "Austin City Limits"; before long, the town's most famous honky-tonk, the Blackboard (or Black Board, the sign out front changed), was closing its doors, as was its heir apparent, Tex's Barrel House. Because facilities were nearby in Los Angeles and possibly because of the intimidating presence of Blue Book Music and Buck Owens' Enterprises, no major record companies settled there. Those reasons are not merely theoretical; the business side of California's country scene, as earlier noted, has tended to be dominated by a few powerful, savvy businessmen like Cliffie Stone, Ken Nelson, and, yes, Buck Owens.

Most galling of all to locals, Bakersfield remained overshadowed by the entertainment complex in Los Angeles, where country music itself was dwarfed. Because of all the national publicity that had been generated about the Kern County town, though, many folks lost sight of the fact that Los Angeles was far from quiet during the period when "Nashville West" supposedly dominated. Reports guitarist-producer Pete Anderson, "When I came here and started playing in bars in the early '70s, Southern Cali-

PETE ANDERSON

Pete Anderson. Photo by John Scarpati.
Courtesy of Little Dog Records.

fornia had a really strong country-western bar scene." And of course through this period "Bakersfield East" in Tennessee had continued solidifying its hold on country music nationwide; radio playlists grew tighter and ever less attainable for West Coast artists. Little wonder so many California performers felt that they had to make the pilgrimage to Nashville to succeed.

Despite the power concentrated there, a new cadre of listeners was growing fed up with soft country, as well as with the direction of rock and roll. Younger fans, the very sort who had once been attracted to rock's rebellion and to its defiant image, were searching for other, less-contrived modes of expression. Many sought out what came to be called "roots rock"—traditional music anchored in ungimmicky, honest presentations and styles, including honky-tonk, rockabilly, western swing, and bluegrass. As a result records by long-forgotten country and blues masters as well as jazz greats also enjoyed renewed popularity.

Rick Nelson was one beneficiary of this trend. In 1981 Capitol released *Playing to Win*, what many considered his return to rock and roll. Four years later, on September 20, 1985, Nelson participated in what has come to be considered the greatest late gathering of rockabillies. Along with other standouts (including the Judds, June Carter Cash, Dave Edmunds, John Fogerty, and Marty Stuart) he joined the remaining big guys from Sun Records: Roy Orbison, Jerry Lee Lewis, Johnny Cash, and Carl Perkins. Those four had spent a week cutting the album *The Class of '55*, and its culmination would be an even larger group singing Fogerty's "Big Train from Memphis." Rick shared a microphone with his long-time idol Perkins, and the resulting cut was a tour de force.

There would be time for few other such high points for Nelson because he was killed in a fiery plane crash on December 31, 1985. Two years earlier he had recorded what were called "the Memphis sessions," a series of rockabilly numbers that once more made explicit his artistic link to the Memphis pioneers. The set was released posthumously, but only after a Nashville producer was paid to "improve" it. "What CBS did on that album was exactly what Rick hated about Nashville," said guitarist John Beland. "They took those tracks after the artist died and over-dubbed them. When we cut Memphis, we wanted a rockabilly album, not a country album."

When Rick was inducted into the Rock and Roll Hall of Fame in 1987, Fogerty told Sun Records's Sam Phillips, "he even gave you a run for your money." He continued, "those records were so valid and such high quality and captured the heart and soul of rockabilly. . . . he could have been putting those records out on Sun." Musician and writer Marshall Crenshaw agreed with Fogerty: "Rick deserves to be remembered by rock 'n' roll and country music fans," he wrote, "for the great records he made, for his stylistic contributions, . . . and for the influence of all the above on many rock and country artists."

One Los Angeles group that reflected Rick's deep rockabilly style was the Blasters, which also created music from elements of hard rock, Tex-Mex, Cajun, blues, and honky-tonk. Their songs, especially those written by Dave Alvin and sung by his brother Phil, reflected the abundance of musical riches that kids coming of age in Southern California in the 1960s and '70s had experienced. Formed in Downey in the late 1970s by the Alvin brothers, drummer Bill Bateman, and bassist John Bazz, the Blasters became prototypes of what was called "the Los Angeles Renaissance."

Pianist Gene Taylor, a later addition to the band, reveals one of its sources: "in the '60s there was a rediscovery of blues masters. You could hear Howlin' Wolf on KMET next to the Grateful Dead, Otis Redding on top 40 stations. We got the benefit of that growing up." But after tight playlist programming gelded so many major outlets in the area, the Alvin brothers "discovered older music when nothing good was on the radio."

They did that by taking advantage of records and of the abundance and variety of live performances in culture-rich Southern California. Dave Alvin recalls, "Within a 10-minute drive from our home in Downey we could see a blues show in Compton or a norteño band in Pico Rivera or a country singer at the Tumbleweed Club in Bell Gardens. The east-south-east side of Los Angeles County was, at one time, a great musical melting pot—all of it going on in small neighborhood bars." A pugnacious underdog's sense like the one that had originally motivated much country music also hardened the core of the Blasters, making it easier for them to ignore not only musical boundaries but also elitist critics.

Roots meant a great deal to the Blasters, but they were not revivalists. Instead Dave explains, "We stressed original material in the older, traditional styles—we wrote our own blues. . . . The country influence in our work came out when I tried to combine my twin loves—country and black blues—into something that reflected where we grew up—orange groves and tract homes (as opposed to southern cotton fields)—and the people we grew up with." An additional impact of the Blasters was that other bands, which had previously settled for performing old-time blues, began composing new songs in the same vein, but few had a writer as talented as Dave Alvin.

This band seemed to "go national" in a hurry, but that was an illusion.

As Dave explains, "We spent a lot of time playing for nothing in bars or being booed off stages—having beer bottles, ashtrays, firecrackers, and even a knife thrown at us—to being 'overnight sensations.' . . . It was almost impossible to get a gig west of the Harbor Freeway—meaning west Los Angeles where the trendy music scene was."

Nevertheless they "went from nowhere to having our first album [*The Blasters*] in the top 10 in *Time* magazine," Dave recalls, "and after that, the goals got kind of different." That would lead Dave to leave the group and strike out on his own.

East Los Angeles is credited with having produced Los Lobos, a more enduring band than the Blasters. Drummer Louie Perez, guitarist Cesar Lozano, bassist Conrad Rosas, and accordionist David Hidalgo had met at Garfield High School in 1973 and for a time played in various different ensembles around the city, performing at everything from weddings to Saturday night dances. In the mid-1970s, however, they—like the Blasters—discovered "old" music listening to their parents' favorites. "The records were around the house," says Perez, "but once we really got into it, we found ourselves going through record stores, filtering out the really good stuff and learning from it." They learned well indeed, and their music made them the first California group to combine Tex-Mex or *norteño* with rockabilly, western swing, along with some jazz and rock and roll riffs.

The end product was a unique, varied music that was literally without peer. Los Lobos has managed to remain distinctly and proudly Mexican-American without limiting its own appeal, no small feat. Hidalgo's accordion, for example, evokes strong flavors of Tex-Mex sensation Flaco Jiminez, yet it moves in other directions, too, with flourishes that Dick Contino would admire. Their vocals sound like Richie Valens on a few cuts, Buck Owens or Chuck Berry on others, but mostly like themselves.

Like many artists emerging from definably "ethnic" backgrounds, these young men faced charges of selling out in direct proportion to their acceptance by non-Chicano audiences. Perez counters such nonsense, "There's no question the name of the group is Los Lobos; that doesn't sound like anything else but Spanish. There's no question that we're four Mexican bodies onstage when we perform and no question that we do traditional music in Spanish as well as American rock and roll. People have to realize that what we're doing is just finding our place in this country as a viable source of artistic contribution." It is difficult to imagine a more proudly and unambiguously Chicano band or one that more effectively merges its two major cultural roots: Mexican and American.

The four might liven their sets with everything from a *norteño* traditional like "Anselma" to their own "What Can I Do." "The stuff we write," explains Perez, "is a blend of a lot. It's not pure." That remark could summarize much of the diverse Los Angeles cultural scene during the decade and of Californian culture in general: "impure" in the best sense.

A new social scene had developed internationally during the late 1970s and early 1980s, another stage of the youth culture. Alienation coalesced musically, especially in London and New York, into a strong punk scene with kiss-my-ass styles of hair, clothing, and behavior. In Los Angeles's nightclubs that surge was profoundly felt; it then combined with traditional country music, especially honky-tonk and rockabilly, as well as with hard rock, leading to what was called "cowpunk." That merging in turn produced one of California's most interesting musical scenes, highlighting young performers who—what else?—ignored labels and merged music.

Punk in Los Angeles was well represented by groups such as the one-letter wonders, X. This band played what Mark Leviton in *BAM* magazine called "an imprecise amalgam of rockabilly and punk." Guitarist Billy Zoom was credited with dominating the band's style, and drummer D. J. Bonebrake provided rhythm. John Doe played bass and sang with a notable vibrato, while vocalist Exene Cervenka wrote startling lyrics and sang in a tough monotone style that many later alternative rock soloists would imitate.

In the mid-1980s Exene, John, and D. J. joined Dave Alvin and Jonny Ray Bartel in a casual group called the Knitters. In 1985 they released the album *Poor Little Critter on the Road* on Slash Records. X began to move toward country after the Knitters started playing Merle Haggard and Johnny Cash material. Some followers hated it but the band loved the new direction, and it opened a door to country music for many young fans. Recalls Alvin, "It was pretty incredible to look out at an audience of punk kids, who had little or no positive experience of country music, being hypnotized by John Doe singing Haggard's 'Silver Wings.'"

After stints with both the Knitters and X, Alvin became a soloist, specializing in the performance of his original numbers. Gerald Locklin, an

Dave Alvin. Photo by Beth Herzhaft.
Courtesy of HighTone Records.

acclaimed author who teaches at California State University, Long Beach, observed, "Dave is one of the finest poets in this area. He's a terrific songwriter, too. In fact, he can just flat-out write." Alvin's performances and crisp songs created the same dilemma of classification as had the Blasters. He said after *Every Night about This Time*, his first album, was released, "in rock 'n' roll I'd be considered a traditionalist, and in country I'm a revolutionary, so where do you play this record?" The answer was that most radio stations didn't, but many fans did.

268

Writer Susan Hayden, a youthful participant in the club scene at that time, remembers that there was then a genuine excitement and a sense of the possible in the region.

> There were brilliant people coming to L.A., and some of them were sleeping in cars, but they knew it *could* happen, and it did for at least some of them. . . . the scene could be really weird, too, but really exciting. Punks with spiked hair dyed half-black, half-green dancing with urban cowboys, pierced and tattooed biker-types with pseudo-starlets. Sometimes the sidewalks outside clubs were more fun than the dance floors inside. A lot of alternative lifestyles were coming out into the open then, too. It was a hoot.

There was more to it than a hoot of course: "A lot of kids didn't really like the world their elders had built," she says, "so they determined to build their own with music. That was a medium they could control." The youth culture, whose first clarion had been the merging of rockabilly and rhythm and blues in the mid-1950s, was alive and vigorous three decades later in the southland.

Hayden also remembers that there was a general disillusionment with the dullness of most radio music and with rock's continuing slide toward pop blandness. Those things led bands to seek cultural autonomy from earlier generations. "Recognizing country music for the earthy, gritty root that it is," points out writer Paul Kingsbury, "young audiences in Southern California flocked to see such cowpunk bands as Rank and File, Lone Justice, and the Beat Farmers."

Loud, fast-tempoed, and defiant, cowpunk found that expanding audience especially among kids in myriad venues in both Southern California and the Bay Area. Some young musicians began employing the straightforward lyrics and twanging licks of country, imitating a group most of them had never heard of, the Maddox Brothers and Rose, those prototypical cowpunks. At their worst, new ensembles emphasized everything from pop anarchism to barnyard humor, but they also unlocked possibilities not visualized by established producers such as Chet Atkins or Lee Gillette.

More importantly some also opened the ears of more new fans to the satisfaction available in deep country, in hard country, in California country music, just as the music itself was being enriched. Guitarist David "Doc" West says,

> For years now country music has been the place where you can play all kinds of music. Country, despite its reputation, is actually very freewheeling. Every music gets its turn at being the melting pot of American music, like jazz was in the '20s and '40s, and rock was, maybe, for a while, country is now. You get a chance to rock like Little Feat and swing like Charlie Christian and twang like Duane Eddy. So for the players it's the most fun. And despite the fact that it's the most open to change of any American music, it has a real definable tradition that you can constantly refer to keep your ground.

Rank and File has been credited with exploring the country sources of rock's roots in California. Tony Kinman of the band asserts, "It took us to kick that door open." Rank and File's first album *Sundown* (1983) featured vocal harmony by Kinman and his brother Chip—both former members of the punk-rock Dils—and it included nihilistic numbers with a country twang. Their second collection *Long Gone Dead* was closer to traditional country, and one cut, "The Sound of Rain," became an underground standard. By 1988, though, the group had drifted back toward punk rock; Tony explained, "what comes out now when we put on our guitars is more overt rock 'n' roll. When you're dealing with a hybrid sound, which is what we were doing, you can only jiggle around with the elements so much."

San Diego contributed perhaps the most outlandish and longest-lived of those groups, the Beat Farmers with Country Dick Montana. Although personnel changed over the years the core of this innovative band was guitarist Jeff Raney, bassist Rolle Love, guitarist Joey Harris, and drummer Country Dick. All contributed vocals, especially Montana, the perhaps funkiest *basso profundo* ever associated with this or any other music.

Serving their apprenticeship in the San Diego club scene and popular in Los Angeles and the Bay Area, too, they played music on the cusp of hard rock and hard country. They wrote many of their own songs but also favored the creations of long-time comrade Paul Kamanski. Some of their original numbers—"The Girl I Almost Married," for instance, or "King of Sleaze"—danced on the edge of good taste to the delight of their youthful fans.

Those same kids helped the whole irreverent cowpunk movement to thrive. In 1982 Lone Justice became an immediate favorite of Los Angeles fans. Considering Los Angeles's great wealth of talent by the 1980s, that was a considerable accomplishment. A year later the band was receiving rave reviews in the region's newspapers, and its personnel had settled: Marvin Etzione on bass, Don Willens on drums, Ryan Hedgecock on lead guitar, and a gifted young vocalist Maria McKee on rhythm guitar. They also had developed a clear vision of their musical goal. While musically unique, Lone Justice was a group beholden to distinctly American roots, and country was a major source.

"The real early country music is so passionate and so raw," said McKee. "If we could mix that with the elements of the raw punk-rock energy and instrumentation, it could just be so phenomenal." Actor Christopher Allport remembers, "they were the ultimate garage band: high energy, talented, but with that rough edge." Hedgecock's driving guitar—a distinct bluegrass-rockabilly sound—dominated the music of Lone Justice, and McKee's singing elevated them. The youthful Maria was also the band's leading songwriter, and her undeniable country tastes kept Lone Justice on that track, performing with a gospel beat one moment, a twangy honky-tonk rhythm the next. In numbers like "Soap, Soup, and Salvation," "Pass It On," and "After the Flood" the country feel was undeniable.

In the Bay Area at that time rockabilly Buck Naked and the Bare Bottom Boys—the leader usually (un)dressed in a cowboy hat, boots, and a G-string with a plumber's plunger placed strategically over the pouch—succeeded Country Porn for outrageousness and became immediate club favorites with youthful audiences. Among their most popular songs was "Bend Over Baby and Let Me Drive." Such groups, like the punk rockers that paralleled them, were attempts to offend "the establishment" and to belittle hypocrisy; in fact, they often appeared to court ire for its own sake. As one young San Francisco fan explained, "Our folks used Elvis and Jerry Lee Lewis to rebel, but that was old stuff by the time we came along. We had to find something that was ours, and we did."

Another popular performer, Rosie Flores, had spent the first twelve years of her life in San Antonio, Texas, before coming of age in San Diego. When she began to perform professionally in the 1970s, Rosie brought a feel for Tex-Mex as well as dashes of Tammy Wynette, Buck Owens, Elvis Presley, and Creedence Clearwater Revival to the Los Angeles scene. By the time she was fronting Rosie and the Screamers late in that decade, she had become a powerful rockabilly. She also performed for four years with an all-female cowpunk band called the Screaming Sirens. Eventually Rosie "started breaking off into my own thing."

Her versatility as a soloist was impressive, although rockabilly always livened her performances. Rockabilly was in fact enjoying yet another revival in Los Angeles; Flores explained, "There had been a real big resurgence of rockabilly coming over from England . . . this was before the Stray Cats. A big part of the punk scene moved over into a rockabilly scene, and from there grew a love of the roots of rockabilly: country. Real early stuff like Rose Maddox and the Louvin Brothers." Working with guitarist Greg Leisz and drummer Donald Lindley, Rosie cut a series of critically acclaimed albums, first for Los Angeles's Warner Brothers/Reprise and later for Oakland's HighTone Records.

About the same time the most commercially successful of California groups during the 1980s, Highway 101, was created by manager Chuck Morris. He assembled drummer Scott Moser, bassist Curtis Stone (Cliffie's son), guitarist Jack Daniels, vocalist Paulette Carlson, and composer Morgan Stoddard. Stoddard departed early, but Carlson proved to also be an outstanding songwriter and the band thrived. In the California tradition this country-rock offshoot retained a hard-country edge, as its early recordings, such as "Whiskey, If You Were a Woman" and "Somewhere Tonight," revealed. The latter climbed to the top of the country chart, and it was followed by two more number ones: "Cry, Cry, Cry" and "(Do You Love Me) Just Say Yes." "I'll tell you what, that 'Whiskey, If You Were a Woman' was a great song!" says California State University, Long Beach, professor, Rafael Zepeda. "They were really good, but they sounded more like Nashville than L.A." The group's live performances were especially popular.

By 1990 Highway 101 had become perhaps the best known nationwide of all California-based ensembles—honored as top vocal group by both the Academy of Country Music and the Country Music Association—but it suffered from personality and artistic differences. Carlson departed and launched a solo career in late 1990. Nikki Nelson, another fine singer, replaced her, and the band moved more toward pop-style numbers, including the 1991 hit "Bing Bang Boom."

The Desert Rose Band was perhaps the most important unit formed in the mid-1980s, this one with major historical country-rock credentials. Former Byrd, former Burrito, former Golden State Boy, and landmark country rocker Chris Hillman founded the group in 1985 with guitarists John Jorgenson and Herb Pedersen, drummer Steve Duncan, bassist Bill Bryson, and pedal steel ace J. D. Maness. From the start they would be recognized as a major touring band, winning three annual Academy of Country Music awards in that category. Moreover they produced a series of top recordings, including "I Still Believe in You," which topped charts in 1989. In the next decade, though, personnel shifts changed the band and for a time also diminished its popularity.

By the mid-1980s the Los Angeles scene had produced not only the Blasters, Los Lobos, Rosie Flores, Highway 101, and the Desert Rose Band but also locally famous groups such as X, Lone Justice, Rank and File, the Long Ryders, the Lonesome Strangers, and the Cruzados, some a little country, others a lot. The area had become one of the most exciting and diverse musical milieus in the world, and California's next major country star was already there.

"Between about '81 and '85, it was a great time in L.A. for music in general," recalls singer Dwight Yoakam. "It was a very eclectic scene, and that's very healthy for artists. And it's healthy for any form of music to have that kind of cross-pollination." As for himself, "it established a grassroots following for me that was diverse—more so than if I had just gone to Nashville and garnered a record deal via exclusively a studio route." In the course of the decade, Yoakam went from paying dues as a club singer in Los Angeles to the brink of stardom, and he stepped well over that brink in the 1990s. As writer Rich Kienzle aptly summarizes, "It took Yoakam and his hard-boiled, hard-hitting West Coast brand of neo-honky-tonk and hillbilly music to telegraph the message to Nashville that the Kenny Rogers leisure suit era of country music was over, and if Music City didn't wake up, it was about to miss out on something big."

Dwight bumped the leisure-suit era in more ways than one, as it turned out, since he celebrated another California country-music tradition: dandified western outfits. In 1985 Manuel Cuevas made a "bolero jacket dripping with rhinestones" for Dwight, and as clothing historian Tyler Beard has written, "That one jacket is what got rhinestones rolling again."

PHOTO CREDIT: Steve Jennings

DWIGHT LIVE

© 1995 Reprise Records/Permission to reproduce limited to editorial uses in newspapers and other regularly published periodicals and television news programming.

Dwight Yoakam in action. Photo by Steve Jennings.
Courtesy of Reprise Records.

Dwight's friend and producer Pete Anderson explains that the singer and his band "wanted . . . really expensive jackets and funky blue jeans, like the Flying Burrito Brothers used to wear. When we started, nobody was wearing those jackets anymore, with piping, the roses and all. Not that we invented it, but we brought it back." In regard to the other major element of Yoakam's style he adds, "Dwight had owned the hat from the beginning."

◄ ►   ◄ ►   ◄ ►

Rhinestoning the Cowboys

Many a country entertainer has performed in an outfit that seemed more fitting for popes and emperors, thanks in no small measure to the renowned Hollywood tailor and clothier Nudie Cohen, who died in 1984. California has been central to that sartorial splendor; without the movies' reach and the work of some tailors in Southern California, there would be no papal vestments on Hank Snow, Porter Wagoner, Judy Lynn, or the rest. In this case the stereotype seems to be true: the glitz started here, and it has become as essential as guitars to this scene.

When Glen Campbell sang "I'm a Rhinestone Cowboy," he might have been celebrating Nudie. "I think we were the first ones," Cohen agreed, and he acknowledged that he really did make it big when he began putting rhinestones on his creations.

After ricocheting around the country as a semiprofessional boxer and sometime movie extra—and all the while an aspiring tailor—he opened Nudie's Rodeo Tailors in 1946. While working mainly for movie studios, Cohen was hired by Tex Williams to create custom suits for his band. That led to work with such stars as Roy Rogers, Dale Evans, Rex Allen, and Gene Autry. Writer Kienzle explains, "His [Nudie's] idea was to come up with a gimmick that corresponded with an artist's name or personality. . . . He designed a suit for Porter Wagoner that was decorated with wagon wheels." Tyler Beard reveals that early in the 1950s when Roy and Dale wanted more striking clothing for outdoor appearances, "Nudie . . . solved the problem with rhinestones and more fringe, which reflected light and waved in the breeze as the performers rode in on [their horses] Trigger and Buttermilk."

By the 1970s he reportedly had captured three-quarters or more of the market for attiring country performers. Cohen explained that he wondered why some entertainers "perform in worse clothes than the people who pay to see them. As long as I can remember, show business has been just that—show business." To prove his point he cited Elvis Presley: "As popular as he was, he always wore rhinestones and flashy clothes. As much in demand as he was, he could have gotten up there in a pair of shorts! But he knew he had a responsibility to act like a showman and look like a showman!" Nudie had created a $10,000 twenty-four-carat gold-lamé suit for Elvis, and as Beard explains, "The only reason a suit would cost that much in the late 1950s would be for publicity. Nudie said his profit was about $9,500."

Nudie's views on showmanship were of course more than a little self-serving, but he probably did convince himself that singers should look like Russian Orthodox icons.

Perhaps his outfits for the Flying Burrito Brothers, with their naked women embroidered on the lapels plus embroidered pills, acid tabs, and marijuana leaves on the rest
of the suits, placed the whole phenomenon in perspective.

Cohen wasn't the first tailor to the country stars of course, although he was the
first to achieve stardom himself. "Nudie crossed all boundaries of fashion. He influenced the western-wear industry for nearly forty years," writes Beard. "Country music
would never have been the same without Nudie, and the golden age of western wear
might never have been."

Nathan Turk preceded Cohen, and no one ever produced more spectacular costumes than he did. Beard describes Turk as "truly the epitome of an Armenian Old
World Tailor—polite, soft-spoken and a real gentleman." In fact the young Nudie had
worked in Nathan's Los Angeles shop and certainly learned much of his craft there.
Turk achieved his greatest fame among California country musicians when he designed
and crafted the remarkable costumes of the Maddox Brothers and Rose. Mel Marion
recounted to Beard the day he wore a Turk shirt to visit Nudie, who was in the hospital. Nudie said, "Lean over here. I *thought* that was a Turk. We never *could* get our
arrows that fine."

Viola Grae was another early major figure in the western clothes market in Los
Angeles. In a career dating to the dawn of horse operas, Grae became most noted as
an embroiderer for stars of rodeo, movie, and stage. Manuel Cuevas describes her as
"a lovely little blond woman, full of energy, piss, and vinegar who ran her shop with an
iron fist."

Manuel has unofficially succeeded Nudie, who was his father-in-law for eleven years.
After briefly working for Turk, Grae, and another noted Hollywood tailor, Sy Devore,
Cuevas was hired by Nudie in 1960. When he left to open his own shop in 1974,
singer Freddie Hart provided him with $10,000 to help. Manuel's first order came from
Mel Tillis: $70,000 worth of clothes for himself and his band. Cuevas—who, like his
mentor, usually employs a trendy, single-name moniker, Manuel—recalls, "While at
Nudie's or my own shop, during my years in California, I made clothing for every star
you can think of," from Bob Dylan to Janis Joplin to Mick Jagger to Hank Williams, Jr., to
Elvis Presley. In 1977 he acquired N. Turk's shop when that stalwart retired, giving Turk
a blank check because, as Beard explains, "he could not bring himself to put a price on
this man's work"; the check was never cashed. Eight years later Manuel made a "bolero
jacket dripping with rhinestones" for Dwight Yoakam, and Beard writes, "That one
jacket is what got rhinestones rolling again."

In 1989, perhaps in recognition of the Golden State's diminishing role in the country-
music scene, Manuel relocated to Nashville. Since then he has clothed stars such as

Wynonna Judd, Travis Tritt, Alan Jackson, David Allan Coe, the Desert Rose Band, and Linda Ronstadt. The Los Angeles area has not been left without a source of boutique cowboy clothes, however. Jaime Castaneda, who also had apprenticed with Nudie, then served as Manuel's head tailor for seventeen years, remained in Southern California. He has since built his own list of Tennessee and California clients, the most prominent of whom is Yoakam, perhaps country's leading contemporary clotheshorse. The beat, or the bead, goes on.

◄► ◄► ◄►

At the opposite end of the sartorial pole was folkish Kate Wolf with simple attire, acoustic instruments, and few flourishes. Although her music remained difficult to classify, she was nominated for and won several awards in the 1980s—most frequently in the folk category—as her popularity continued to expand. One of her prizewinners was the 1983 album *Give Yourself to Love*, titled for what became her signature song. Increasingly Kate was being credited with having pioneered a distinct style of music that bridged traditional country and commercial folk and added a touch of bluegrass. That same year, 1983, she once more illustrated her independent nature when she took a sabbatical from her entertainment career in order to spend more time with her family. "The road is wearing me down," she explained. "I feel my health slipping."

When she returned several months later, she scored a hit when she appeared on "A Prairie Home Companion," recorded a new, award-winning album called *A Poet's Heart*, and toured the East. Her career continued blossoming with a remarkable performance on "Austin City Limits"; the live-performance album that followed (*Kate Wolf: An Evening in Austin*) is considered by many to be her best for it captures not only her voice and her musical accompaniment but also her warm stage presence. Those accomplishments confirmed that this wife and mother with no contacts in the industry had indeed beaten the odds against achieving success.

Just as it seemed she was about to become as triumphant commercially as she already was artistically—a singer's singer, a songwriter's songwriter—Wolf was diagnosed with leukemia. A remarkable public outpouring followed. All over Northern California "Give Blood for Kate" signs were posted at hay-and-grain stores, head shops, natural food emporiums, bars, and colleges, and that campaign actually expanded her

Kate Wolf. Courtesy of Max Wolf.

musical popularity. Benefit concerts were performed nationwide while the artist herself fought for her life. Before she lost that battle, Wolf did manage to assemble a ten-year retrospective album *Gold in California*, selecting all the cuts and even writing notes for the cover. It was her final project; she died on December 10, 1986.

Kate Wolf demonstrated, among other things, that country songs need not be sung with a southern drawl or a pinched style, while she retained what was being called "old-timey" acoustic string accompaniment significantly more traditional than most of what was passing for country music at that time. Perhaps equally important, she was one of that cadre of writers who contributed high-quality poetry with their lyrics.

By the decade's close, despite mavericks such as Wolf and Yoakam, most young Californians, such as the band Highway 101, conceded that Nashville was the place to be to seek a career in country music. The long shots who could make it big while remaining in California were seen as exactly that: long shots. Only then did the accomplishments of Buck Owens and Ken Nelson in the 1960s become apparent; they had overwhelmed the Tennessee juggernaut. And thanks to Yoakam, Owens himself was back on stage by 1989, as lively as ever.

Still, California's impact on country music was dwindling. In fact fewer and fewer people even realized the state had once contributed so mightily to this music, that gap due largely to dominance in Nashville and indifference in Hollywood. An advantage, however, was that, as Patrick Carr explains, the Tennessee capital's "embrace of mass-pop goals created opportunities for smaller operators elsewhere." Regional labels—HighTone, Rhino, Arhoolie, Enigma, and others—were again energizing local performers. Moreover some southern performers who wouldn't conform became expendable to major labels, so those independent record labels were able to recruit a number of the most distinct and best country voices. Oakland's HighTone, for example, recorded such established singers as Gary Stewart, Joe Ely, and Billy Lee Riley.

Another advantage was that just as California acts had been unaided by Nashville connections they had also been uninhibited by Nashville conventions. For instance, two albums, *A Town South of Bakersfield* (Enigma Records, 1985) and *A Town South of Bakersfield 2* (Enigma Records, 1987), both produced by Pete Anderson and Dan Fredman, illustrated how spicy and varied (if unknown beyond the region) the "alternative country" scene in Los Angeles had become. The 1985 record not only offered the first major exposure for Dwight Yoakam but also included such talents as Rosie Flores, Albert Lee, Katy Moffat, George Highfill, and the Lonesome Strangers. The second edition added a number of other crisp talents: Jim Lauderdale, Anne Harvey, and Lucinda Williams (also a sterling songwriter) among them.

In the 1980s California performers did not conform to country mainstream styles. Diverse talents provided a varied and exciting, if shadowy, scene, a kind of anti-Nashville attitude that rewarded innovation and independence. An article in *Country Music* magazine dismissed Yoakam as "cowpunk chic." The tone of such a remark seemed to emanate from a lingering fear that country music might once again be lost to the complex, amorphous, and heterogeneous West. Los Angeles was the enemy, portrayed as Gomorrah in more than one Nashville song. This fear was, suggested educator Dick Kirkpatrick, "a control thing."

In 1995 *The Encyclopedia of Country Music* wrote more perceptively of Yoakam, "He was a monster in Nashville's closet: a legitimate major country star, creatively important and commercially more successful than 95 percent of the field, who didn't officially exist—not at all as far as the Country Music Association and its awards were concerned, and hardly at all on country radio." That observation could have applied to the entire California scene by the late 1980s, which drooped even though Merle, Dwight, and the revived Buck were its apexes.

DWIGHT YOAKAM

Dwight Yoakam entered the highly competitive Los Angeles club scene as a twenty-year-old fresh from a frustrating stint in Nashville. Asked why he relocated there, Dwight said he had been aware of California's country-music tradition—"Rose Maddox and the Maddox Brothers, Tommy Collins, Wynn Stewart, the whole Ken Nelson scene that he started over at Capitol . . . Buck Owens . . . Merle Haggard. . . . That legacy was here." As a result, he "just thought the environment would be more conducive to me performing live if I came to California, and that proved to be the case."

At first it seemed as if Los Angeles wasn't ready for Dwight's particular brand of deep country, but he hooked up with a gifted guitarist named Pete Anderson, one of the most fortuitous musical parings since Don Rich and Buck Owens. "We found musical conspirators in each other," says Dwight. Anderson, who has not only played lead guitar with Yoakam's band but has also produced Dwight's records since the 1980s, recalls their rocky start in clubs:

> We kept getting fired for playing Hank and Merle and Bill Monroe songs and some of Dwight's own songs, when the audience wanted to hear Alabama and other popular bands of the day.
>
> I told him [Dwight] that if he sang the popular songs every once in a while, he'd get the gigs. But he didn't want to. We decided to perform free in clubs where we could play what we wanted to and make our own record.

The scene was varied in those years, and of course it influenced the open-minded singer, who was Ohio-raised but who had roots in the Kentucky hills. He had previously been impressed with everything from Mo-

281

town to Bill Monroe, and in Los Angeles he found a place for both of those and many other styles, too, some of them still unnamed. He told writer Todd Everett, "My music is hard country"; it was so hard that it returned him to one of the roots from which rockabilly and eventually rock and roll had emerged and did so without ever losing authenticity. His style, then still developing, included so much vocal "breaking" that his words at times were difficult to understand. Still says Susan Hayden, "He sounded good . . . and he looked great."

He and his band played gutbucket honky-tonks in the San Fernando Valley one night and rock clubs in North Hollywood the next—the Corral or the Horseshoe, then the Whisky A Go-Go or Club Lingerie—rubbing elbows with the Blasters, X, Ray Campi, Los Lobos—the whole crew. "It was a great time to be part of the scene," he acknowledges; "it probably always will have an influence on what I do musically."

What he and Anderson did in 1984 was record *Guitars, Cadillacs, Etc., Etc.*, a six-track, extended-play record paid for with a borrowed $5,000. Dwight was then economizing by sleeping on the floor in Pete's utility room, and the two mixed the record at a studio during the cheap hours between midnight and morning to shave expenses. At first the record received airplay only from alternative rock stations, principally those anchored on local college campuses, where middle-class kids considered the sound of his honky-tonk deliveries to be as original and unexpected as Buddhist chants.

A welcomed boost occurred when, as Dwight explains,

> Johnette Napolitano [later to front the band Concrete Blonde], who was working the front desk for the man who pressed the extended play, put copies in a box with a bunch of punk-rock albums the man was promoting, and sent it to reviewers across the country.
>
> The *Chicago Tribune*'s Jack Hurst did a review that was syndicated all over the country, and followed that with a phone interview that got even more attention. We got a chance to go on the road with the Blasters, which got us attention in New York City, Houston, and Austin.

Yoakam's national reputation began to build from that point.

In 1985 Anderson coproduced the first of three *A Town South of Bakersfield* albums with bassist Dan Fredman, all highlighting the mostly under-

Dwight Yoakam steps into the spotlight as Showcase Artist Of The Month during June on CMT Europe, coinciding with his European concert tour.

Dwight Yoakam. Courtesy of Country Music Television, Europe.

ground country-music scene in Southern California. Dwight was signed—fittingly enough perhaps—by the Nashville branch of Los Angeles–based Warner Brothers Records. In the tradition of Buck Owens, he and Anderson insisted on using their own band in the studio the next year, on retaining the six original cuts from their self-published, extended-play recording, and on remaining true to their original sound. This album, also titled *Guitars, Cadillacs, Etc., Etc.*, became a West Coast, then a national, sensation, selling a million copies (when 100,000 constituted a major hit). It also gave the singer two top-5 singles: "Honky-Tonk Man" and the title song.

That success prompted Bob Allen, an editor of *Country Music* magazine, to write, "It's hard to recall any artist during the 1980s whose debut album caused as much stir in Nashville as did Dwight Yoakam's *Guitars, Cadillacs, Etc., Etc.* in 1986. This is particularly telling when you consider that Yoakam's first album was made in Hollywood rather than on Music Row."

"Dwight walked in through that little crack in the door," fellow singer Dave Alvin pointed out, "when they didn't know what was going to be the next thing." His emotive style—with its dramatic, yodel-like vocal breaks as the singer swept from high to low ranges, then back again—was distinct, marking him as a truly singular stylist. His appearance—handsome, with painted-on jeans, a stylish short jacket, and a white hat—sure didn't hurt. How had the mainstream's talent scouts missed him and why? The answer is that he was too much deep country, too much original country, and certainly too damned independent.

In the pattern that has characterized the careers of previous California-based stars such as Owens, Haggard, and Rose Maddox, Dwight remained an outsider in the eyes of some, as is illustrated by the fact that his records, then as now, are by no means automatically added to radio playlists. Nashville-based writer Bob Millard points out, "The country music establishment and many critics hated him—out loud—which may just have contributed to a generation of hip, young fans falling in love with his barely intelligible, nasal renditions of classic post-WWII honky-tonk music."

What exactly had Yoakam said or done to so offend the establishment? Well, things like "today we are tragically close to eliminating pure country music entirely. Hillbilly music, white American hillbilly music, is real close to extinction. . . . I think that's not the audience's choosing or doing; it's the marketing structure that's been established in the record business." It's ironic that in country music, where lyrics have so often cut through the fog, that so accurate a statement would bruise thin corporate skins. Buck Owens, also notably forthright, saw the "Yoakam phenomenon" somewhat differently. He said,

I think Dwight's a tremendous credit to country music and the entertainment industry, period.

I've seen Dwight's audiences, the people with the orange spiked hair, and I admire that because Dwight is covering a huge spectrum. He's drawing people to country music and introducing them to country music, where they might never have heard country music otherwise. They get into it simply because they're digging Dwight.

Despite his inarguable honky-tonk approach, Yoakam has more recently been labeled "Hillbilly Deluxe," after the title of his second album and his own propensity to speak of country music using that term: "I think that country lost its coolest side, though, after Buck Owens stopped recording in Los Angeles. Those records of his in the mid-sixties were in-credible—the zenith of American hillbilly music." Clearly Dwight's use of *hillbilly* is not semantically conventional but more like a generalized term for the eclectic music—at least as much southwestern as southeastern—that has dominated West Coast country. Despite Yoakam's unambiguous love of mountain memories, his performances seem to have been more influenced by Memphis rockabilly, Los Angeles rock, and Bakersfield honky-tonk.

He does indeed have a genuine link to the South's hills, but it seems more emotional than musical. Nonetheless it has led to some of his most powerful songs like "Readin', Rightin', Rt. 23"—"Written for and lovingly dedicated to my mother Ruth Ann; and to my aunts Margaret, Mary Helen, Verdie Kay, and Joy; and to my uncle Guy Walton." In numbers like that, Yoakam's roots are revealed by the emotive power of performance; clearly he does not feign the feelings that drive the song.

Dwight himself says, "I know what it was like for all those families who went North to find work after World War II, left their whole world behind them." Like the best in this business, he sings with a bard's collective voice. Living in a transitory society in Southern California—not inherently transitory of course but historically so for many people—helps him retain his emigrant edge.

But by no means are most of his songs so traditional. A thoughtful man, Dwight recognizes that "we are categoric animals. We intellectually make distinctions. So I think it's valid to make musical distinctions." But the slipperiness of definitions of popular music is manifest when Yoakam speaks; he says of Johnny Cash, "Although he would be considered country for the most part, . . . the emotional aesthetic that he brought to what he did was as much rock 'n' roll. There's a *rawness* to what he did."

That kind of emotional *rawness*, which most people identify with soul singers or rockabillies, has for a long, long time actually been a characteristic of country music in California, especially as performed by singers like Owens, Haggard, Maddox, or Yoakam, which may simply mean that shared roots dominated here. As Dwight points out, "I came out of the rock clubs here in L.A., so I think the music lives anywhere . . . and everywhere." Producer Fredman probably sums matters up best when he observes, "Dwight was doing country music, but with a punk attitude. . . . The audience didn't care what you called it: it was just great music, with an attitude."

Yoakam has enjoyed his considerable success against the odds: "At first, living here was an impediment as far as communicating with the political establishment in Nashville," he explains. "I don't think they understood quite what we were up to." In Tennessee he is sometimes scornfully called a "Hollywood singer," as though the place, not the man or his music, is primary. Such accusations are actually funny when one recognizes that Dwight remains close to country's heterogeneous roots, while—except for the new traditionalists—Nashville recordings seem to be drifting far, far away. Says Yoakam, "The game plan is really trying to make the best possible music I can, period." What he makes and how he makes it are very good, and his style remains unique.

Dwight's identification with earlier superstar Owens is by no means coincidental. Yoakam had dedicated his *Hillbilly Deluxe* album to the then-retired Buck, and he had previously spoken publicly of his admiration for Owens and the Bakersfield Sound. When Dwight played at the Kern County Fair in 1987, he visited Buck's office unannounced. As Owens recalls it,

> My secretary came in and says, "There's a guy here who says he's Dwight Yoakam." I'd been hearing a little bit of his records. Two or three records he had out, "Honky-Tonk Man," "Guitars and Cadillacs." And I said, "Well, is it Dwight Yoakam?" And she said, "Well, I think it is." And so I said, "Let me see that dude." And so he came in and we talked and he was appearing at the fair, so. . . .

At the show that night Dwight invited Buck onstage. "I felt very comfortable with Dwight. He and his band knew several of my songs, so Dwight and I did a little medley there. There was something that happened and you could feel it. I could feel it with the audience. They liked what Dwight and I did that night."

Like it the audience certainly did, and so did the performers. As it turned out so did the industry. "In December [1987] CBS called and said they wanted to do *Thirty Years of Country*," Buck explains. "They wanted Hag and I to do something about Bakersfield. . . . [but] Hag couldn't come, wouldn't be able to be there. And so I said, 'Let me bring Dwight Yoakam.' They said, 'Okay, fine. Bring something you guys could sing together.' So I took 'Streets of Bakersfield,' because they wanted something representing California. So that's how Dwight heard it."

The 1988 remake of "Streets of Bakersfield"—Buck had included the song on his 1973 *Ain't It Amazing, Gracie* album—also featured another musical legend, accordionist Flaco Jiminez. This sparkling version not only reached number one—Dwight's first, Buck's twenty-first—on the country-music chart, but it also became one of those rarest of records, an instant classic. The relationship with Yoakam also prompted Owens to revive his own performance career successfully, to the delight of his fans. "I'm actually excited about all this again," he told writer Holly Gleason. "And I can thank Dwight for that." (He adds an unstressed syllable when he says the name, "Da-wight.") "You know, we have a father-son relationship, but we also have a friendship—and I'm enjoying that so much. I can't begin to tell you."

Like Hank Snow's fabled "big eight-wheeler," Dwight Yoakam is still movin' on. His 1993 *This Time* album, with its boundary-busting selections, not only went double platinum, it also produced six hit singles, including the Grammy-winning "Ain't That Lonely Yet." It was honored on many rock-and-roll critics' best-album lists, too. His Los Angeles–inspired versatility has served him well. *BAM* writer Bill Holdship suggests that "in many respects, Dwight Yoakam is sort of that California Cosmic Cowboy that Gram Parsons must've often seen in his fondest dreams."

In a sense Yoakam takes the country-music story in California full circle: The transplanted son of an Ohio service station owner and the grandson of a Kentucky coal miner, he is a profoundly urban singer with a profoundly rustic yearning. He is also fiercely independent, a reminder of country-music roots that have been largely lost. And he is a singular, if increasingly imitated, stylist whose merging of rock and rural is shadowed by his realization that life for hillbilly coal miners long ago turned wretched.

Don McLeese wrote in *Rolling Stone* that Yoakam "has no contemporary peer." That is certainly true of Dwight as a stylist. He remains in many ways a modern link in the long chain of southern disillusionment and desperation that contributed so much to the emergence of this national music in the 1920s.

Early in the 1990s Merle Haggard's career symbolized the diminished commercial condition of country music in California. While his artistry remained intact, Hag's recording career dwindled as he battled in court against Curb Records, which then controlled his releases. Merle explained the consequences of that prolonged legal squabble to Jason DeParle in 1993: "It's real frustrating, and . . . it's really a big financial valley for me because I'm used to having records out, and records cause things to happen—and the same thing in reverse, if you don't have one. It's caused me to go to bankruptcy, Chapter 11. . . . They've got all my assets tied up. You know, I can't liquidate anything. I can't sell a goddamn guitar." Late that year Hag was at last able to peddle the publishing rights to most of his songs to Sony-Tree Music to clear his Chapter 11 and to pay most of his debts.

Buck Owens continued to perform into the 1990s but only selectively—"It's a young man's game," he said—and a new generation awakened to his special brand of music. Buck's considerable business interests —publishing company, radio stations, booking agency, and more— continue to thrive. The poor boy from Sherman, Texas, has ridden hard work a long, long way.

Also in the 1990s a homogeneous and commercially safe version of country—little innovation, scant originality—and performance styles adopted from rock have catapulted the contemporary version of this music to previously unimagined marketing heights. "Some people call it cookie cutter," says Owens. "You can call it what you want." National Songwriters Hall of Fame member Dallas Frazier adds, "There is a lot of polish now, and I don't know if it's good polish."

Writer Robert Price calls contemporary country "an entertainment Godzilla"—America's most popular music in record sales, in radio play, and in virtually any other vendible category. Country concerts, resembling the rock fiestas of thirty years earlier, are packed with young listeners; the new forms of this music have cracked the youth market in part because performance styles have been so influenced by rock and roll's up-front showmanship and pop's lavish production styles. By 1996 contemporary Nashville artist Garth Brooks, complete with Stetson and special effects, became the best-selling recording artist in American history. With the exception of songs by new traditionalists and some Texas and West Coast mavericks, however, there seemed to be a continuing loss of country music's distinctiveness in something like direct proportion to its acquisition of that vast audience.

Many Californians in that throng were, like Haggard, feeling financially squeezed in the early 1990s. The state entered the decade in the grip of an economic recession, and the median wage fell 3.3 percent from 1992 to 1994. In fact society was again bifurcating: the rich growing much richer, while the poor were growing poorer still. This shame was not merely regional: according to *New York Times* columnist Bob Herbert, one of every four children in the richest nation on Earth was born into poverty. Working-class disillusionment intensified, and many of Haggard's earlier songs of poverty—"Some Day When Things Are Good," "If We Make It through December," and others—now touched folks who may have been financially secure before.

Those conditions led Roger Hickey and Robert Borosage, codirectors of the Campaign for America's Future, to use language that might have made its way into country lyrics a generation or so ago: "The measure of the economy is whether it works for working people. It is not sufficient for the wealthy to prosper, speculators to strike it rich, corporations to profit, if working people are not sharing fully in the rewards produced by their labor and productivity." By the mid-1990s, this state's economy was recovering—it had become the seventh-largest economy in the world—but the distribution of bounty remained disproportionate.

With such economic uncertainty came the attendant regression into racism and nativism, especially by whites, that seems always to characterize hard times. By then it was widely recognized that California itself had, or soon would have (given the number of illegal aliens residing here), a nonwhite majority for the first time since Europeans had decimated the native population. Los Angeles, for example, hosted more Hispanics than Costa Rica, Puerto Rico, or Nicaragua and more Mexicans than any municipality other than Mexico City. San Francisco also seemed daily to become more a Pacific Rim metropolis, with a distinctly Asian flavor.

Such developments baffled many whites still harboring middle-American illusions. Martha Jackson, who had arrived in 1937, recalled, "We thought we were just 100 percent American. I had never heard of an Armenian, I had never met an Italian, and I had never seen Chinese or Japanese or Mexican people. . . . We thought their grandparents didn't fight in the Civil War or Revolution." Some southwestern migrants had trouble fathoming that in California nonwhites have been substantial and enduring pioneers, building much of the state and that it has long been clear, particularly in California, that the United States is a world country, not merely an extension of Europe, let alone of Britain. This ain't Kentucky; this ain't Georgia; this sure ain't Tennessee.

Over a half-century after the Okie migration that brought Martha Jackson to California, the progeny of that relocation had disseminated throughout the society, intermarried with various other Californians, and developed fierce pride in their heritage. The Okies had also changed what it meant to be a Californian and so did their favorite music, as will the latest arrivals from Vietnam, from Russia, from Guatemala, from everywhere.

For all the new arrivals, as for other Californians, Nashville pop now dominates, although country's traditional base remains both varied and deep here. Predictably many new groups and individuals imitate what is selling and yearn for the phone call that will beckon them to Tennessee. They are willing, as so many talented southern acts have been, to become new versions of Garth Brooks. Others are not; for example, the continuing success of bluegrass groups in California ignores the limitations of the dominant commercial vision.

Music writer Dave Samuelson points out, "Despite being shunned by the country music industry, radio programmers and many retail record chains, bluegrass has thrived into the '90s." Indeed it has, and festivals

Rose Maddox. Photo by Ken McKnight. Courtesy of Jonny Whiteside.

here are frequently sponsored by the lively California Bluegrass Association or the closely related California State Old-Time Fiddlers Association. "Old-time" music's fan base seems to be both loyal and large, supporting literally scores of bands, ranging from amateur to professional, including favorites such as Good Ol' Persons, Piney Creek Weasels, the Cache Valley Drifters, Past Due and Payable, and until recently even occasional appearances by the legendary Rose Maddox. Bluegrass and old-time fiddle competitions also remain popular all over the state.

One competitor, Steve Emanuels of Lemoore, says, "Many of our fiddlers are Dust Bowl folks. A common thread is that they learned to fiddle as youngsters, gave it up when they came to California and/or entered the army for WW II, and then took it up again when their children grew up and left home. I hear that tale time and time again." Fortunately enough young people are also involved to prompt a "generation-gap" editorial in the *Soundpost* (the fiddlers' newsletter) on proper attire. It said in part, "Those most comfortable in cutoffs, bare feet and other very casual styles are usually our younger members, and we certainly need to encourage and motivate as many young fiddlers as possible."

This controversy is revealing because those young folks see themselves as Californians, not transplanted Oklahomans, Arkansans, or whatever. They never experienced the disdain that some of their elders from the Dust Bowl endured, so they don't share the compulsion to dress up the public image of old-time music. That fact is itself a lesson: that music in their lives has simply been accepted as one more component of California's cultural blend. Variety remains the rule.

But that fact certainly isn't reflected in the recent proliferation of country-radio programming, which has paralleled the pop-rock push from Nashville. By 1996 approximately 2,600 radio stations nationwide featured country formats (there were only 81 in 1961). As the nation's dominant radio format, country has captured 42 percent of all listeners and far outstripped the competition. Eight of the ten states with the most country-music stations are in the South; the other two are California and Oregon. In 1996 some 70 million folks were tuning in to the corporate, pop version of country, perhaps one more hot, short-lived fad.

Although the figures are fluid, it appears at present that Texas and California host the largest number of major all-country stations. But do those outlets play what would have been recognized as country a generation ago? Many don't. No concrete figures are available, but estimates of stations now dominated by national playlists rather than by local tastes range from 60 percent to 85 percent. Dwight Yoakam points out one consequence of contemporary programming: "People like Ricky Skaggs and myself are the last generation to be exposed to real country music on the radio. Kids today can't hear the real stuff, the hard-core honky-tonk music, the Bakersfield Sound, all that great country music."

The "Iconization" of Bakersfield

Long a target of jokes within the Golden State, Bakersfield's less-than-sterling image may have been a reason it was credited with being the state's center of "Okie music"; that wasn't intended as a compliment. Some burghers there have certainly hated and resisted that Okie identification and still do. But something unexpected occurred on the way to the next one-liner: Bakersfield—the image, not the place—came to symbolize in the minds of hard country's fans most of that music's admirable traits: grit, pragmatism, loyalty, honesty, genuineness, in general, as well as resistance to Nashville's countrypolitan sound. It became, in the eyes of some, sacred ground.

As a result those admired characteristics can now be evoked by mere mention of the Kern County community's name. Why? Largely because it remains so associated with Owens, Haggard, and the Dust Bowl migration and because it rose to prominence just as Nashville seemed to be sliding further and further from traditional country. "When you listen to Buck and Merle," says local music legend Bill Woods, "you hear guys that really *did* pick that cotton or do that jail time, not some Nashville or Hollywood 'package.'"

A Bakersfield of the mind, virtually a reversed version of its old stereotype, now dominates, and it prompts a national response. Nowadays when new acts from that area are introduced—whether in Nashville or New York—the crowd's inevitable response is revealing: "Welcome from Bakersfield, California . . ." ROAR! (The announcer must pause.) "Big House." ROAR! Moreover productions such as *A Town South of Bakersfield* (volumes 1–3 [1985, 1987, 1992]), the great success of Owens's and Dwight Yoakam's "Streets of Bakersfield" in 1989, and the 1996 release of a fine hard-country CD, *Bakersfield Bound*, by the Desert Rose Band's Chris Hillman and Herb Pedersen, and even "Dwight Yoakam's Bakersfield Biscuits"—available at your nearby supermarket—illustrate how the city's name has come to connote things that don't necessarily have much to do with its reality.

What began as a snobbish dismissal of country music and its fans in the state—associating them with a supposed rube locale—has actually led to an iconization of Bakersfield or of a version of it anyway. "Who knows," grins Kern County writer William Rintoul, "maybe they'll have to add a Bakersfield theme section to Opryland so there'll some real country music there."

◄ ►   ◄ ►   ◄ ►

Despite national playlists that exclude them, independent labels are still producing outstanding country cuts. They have also developed their own Independent Country Music chart, but their chances of gaining widespread airplay remain next to nil. For example, Rick Shea's CD *The Buffalo Show* on the ironically named Major Label Recordings was called by Los Angeles writer Jonny Whiteside "one of the strongest local country releases in years," yet it was ignored by broadcasters. The country-music establishment seems to resent outsiders, no matter how talented or innovative.

In fact nowadays older cuts are more likely to gain airplay than are new recordings from unconnected labels, because some stations are now making time slots available for "country classics" as a way of assuaging fans of traditional music. In the 1990s Rhino Records—begun by Richard Foos and Harold Bronson in Westwood in 1978—has become a major player on the increasingly important country-classic scene, rereleasing sides by Willie Nelson, Johnny Cash, Haggard, and Owens in 1990. They followed with *The Buck Owens Collection*, a definitive set, in 1992. In 1993 they released *Troubadours of the Folk Era, Vols. 1–3*, then *The Sun Records Collection* in 1994, and the five-volume *Hillbilly Fever!* in 1995. When its pop and soul rereleases are factored in, this California label, the offshoot of a record store, has indeed earned its designation as "the music industry's premier pop culture archival company."

As a result of companies like Rhino, Bear Family, HighTone, Arhoolie, and Little Dog, "the real deal" is a long way from dead in this music. Beyond the rediscovery of classic cuts, younger artists in the South and the West have continued developing more traditional forms, often pursuing trends that flirted with extinction until classic country found new publishers and new fans.

To acknowledge both varied music and arbitrary classifications, one of the radio industry's major trade magazines, *Gavin*, based in San Francisco, invented a new musical category "Americana." in 1994. Explains Chris Marino, program director of Atlanta's WMLB-FM, "We play a lot of singer-songwriters, rockabilly, and older country that's been cast aside. . . . It's a wide range. That's the appeal of it." As a result old-time music, folk music, traditional and alternative country, and other nonmainstream sounds had their own album-based chart. Among the first to enjoy number-one status was 1994's *Tulare Dust: A Songwriter's Tribute to Merle*

Haggard from HighTone Records. Also quickly acknowledged were underground country favorites such as Allison Krauss, Junior Brown, and Laurie Lewis. Americana records began to receive more airplay once that category took hold, and programmers grasped that that music and those musicians boasted a substantial fan base, thus were a lure for advertisers.

Four albums from independent companies, all ignored by mainstream "country" radio but ripe for that Americana listing, have traced the continuing distinctiveness of country music in California in the early 1990s: *Points West: New Horizons in Country Music* (HighTone, 1990), *Lazy Loud and Liquored Up* (Shindig Records, 1990), *A Town South of Bakersfield 3* (Restless Records, 1992), and *Tulare Dust: A Songwriter's Tribute to Merle Haggard.* Their collective message is clear: country in its many guises is alive and well in the Golden State, airplay or no airplay. Despite Dwight Yoakam's success, "utter distinctiveness, it seems, is a career inhibitor in country's new age of sonic regimentation," writer Patrick Carr asserts, and these albums reveal much distinctiveness.

The remarkable *Points West* was bolstered by three world-class talents: Gary Stewart, Joe Ely, and Jimmie Dale Gilmore, but its less-celebrated contributors were in their own ways no less compelling: Heather Myles, Buddy Miller, and the Lonesome Strangers, in particular. *Lazy Loud and Liquored Up*, subtitled (without capital letters) *the san francisco alternative country compilation*, highlights such club favorites as Buck Naked and the Bare Bottom Boys, the Zacharies, and the Legendary Stardust Cowboy, among others. *A Town South of Bakersfield 3*, with its reflection of the Los Angeles cow-punk-blues-rockabilly nightclub scene, features such talents as Dale Watson and the Lone Stars, Ronnie Mack, Mary Lyn Dias, and Patty Booker (singing a real winner entitled simply "99"). *Tulare Dust: A Songwriter's Tribute to Merle Haggard* was released to commemorate Hag's October 1994 induction into the Country Music Hall of Fame. It offers a virtual who's who of country and roots rock performers associated in some fashion with the Golden State.

Writer Peter Guralnick has observed of Haggard, "The body of work he has created is absolutely staggering." So is *Tulare Dust's* repertoire. Performances on it are heterogeneous, vital, and savvy, singers giving Merle the gift of their own creative visions and unique artistry rather than imitating his arrangements. Another good album, *Mama's Hungry Eyes: A Tribute to Merle Haggard*, appeared concurrently from Arista/Nashville. It featured a better-known cadre of stars performing a selection of hits, most of which were arranged much as Haggard had originally performed them, and the contrast between the two collections is informative. With few exceptions Arista/Nashville's performances are smoother and far more obvious in their production values, with fine voices backed by the gifted sidemen who distinguish much contemporary country. In fact it exemplifies the electronic perfection that has smoothed what used to be a creatively imperfect music. As writer Tony Scherman points out, now "it's as spontaneous as a Super Bowl half-time show."

Those *Tulare Dust* cuts from California, on the other hand, are downright rough in places, and the vocals, arrangements, and background music are far more varied: hard and perhaps deep country. Katy Moffat's lovely "I Can't Be Myself" is, for example, accompanied only by the singer on acoustic guitar and Dave Alvin on electric lead guitar. Dwight Yoakam's moving version of "Holding Things Together" is backed only by his own acoustic guitar. Steve Young's strong performance of "Shopping for Dresses" features just the vocalist's acoustic guitar and was recorded, according to liner notes, "at Steve's house."

In its variety, its earthiness, and its authenticity, *Tulare Dust* bespeaks the health and rich sweep of this music in the Golden State. Genuine creativity and taking chances are clearly still welcome. The album also illustrates the endurance of deep traditional country here. The home base of Haggard, Owens, and Yoakam certainly isn't part of country's contemporary mainstream. On the other hand, performers *do* enjoy freedom from the musical uniformity of countrypolitan dominance. They retain their individuality, which seems to be the trade-off. They are allowed, even on their recordings, to sound like flawed but genuine human beings expressing the human condition.

In spite of, or because of, California's outsider status in the national country-music world and of country's outsider status within the state, this music that spread, in part at least, as an anthem for outsiders during the urban migration following World War I retains its traditional hard edge here. California's country still attracts iconoclastic performers from elsewhere. Oakland's HighTone Records, for example, has shown a commitment to offering opportunities to country stars displaced by Nashville's pop thrust; the label recently signed Johnny Rodriguez, Marty Brown, and Bobby Durham. It also works at developing fresh talent such as Chris Gaffney, Dale Watson, Rev. Billy C. Wirtz, and Big Sandy and his Fly-Rite Boys. Cofounder Bruce Bromberg noted, "There's plenty of talent out here, and it's sad that all commercial country music has to be made in Nashville because everything [there] pretty much sounds alike. In the '50s, when I was a kid, you had stuff coming from everywhere. Now, no matter where you come from, you gotta go there. I think the irony of ironies is that most of these young Nashville guys are trying to sound like Merle Haggard, who was from out here."

The release of Rosie Flores's *After the Farm* (1993), *Once More with Feeling* (1994), and *Rockabilly Filly* (1995) exemplifies HighTone's commitment to California's country music. This last collection in particular was a historic release, since it included Rosie's duets with Janice Martin and Wanda Jackson, two original and preeminent female rockabillies.

HighTone's list by no means summarizes the state's country standouts. The great Rose Maddox performed here until her death in 1998, and cowboy songs continue to be honored in the performances of such groups as the Sons of the San Joaquin, while Big Sandy and his Fly-Rite Boys present their version of western swing. Jody Stecher and Kate Brislin represent the "old-timey" acoustic tradition of mountain-style music. The Bakersfield area has two new winners in the Smokin' Armadillos and Big House. Along with Boy Howdy they have scored in Nashville, as have a bright pair of Southern California natives known professionally as the Sweethearts of the Rodeo.

The Smokin' Armadillos, all local boys, quickly established themselves in their hometown with a country-rock style and original songs. Within months of their professional debut the photogenic young men ranging in age from sixteen to twenty-four—Jason Theist, Scott Meeks, Josh Graham, Aaron Cassida, Rick Russell, and Darrin Kirkindoll—found themselves reaching large audiences when they were invited to open for major stars. They then followed Yoakam's lead by producing their own initial album *Out of the Burrow* (1994), which included two hits: "My Girlfriend Might" and "Red Rock." The latter leaped to number one on the Independent Country Music chart. Their successful second CD *Let Your Heart Lead Your Mind* in 1996 was released by MCG\Curb Records. In the tradition of many earlier stars they toured radio stations nationwide from October 1995 through February 1996, making the contacts necessary to open doors.

And it worked; stations used their limited discretionary-play slots to play cuts by the Armadillos.

If that group features youth, the other Bakersfield band that has risen to the top, Big House, features experience. Its members—Monty Byrom, Chuck Seaton, David Nuehauser, Sonny California, Ron Mitchell, and Tanner Byrom—are journeymen musicians edging toward middle age. They've seen several sides of this business and paid their dues, so theirs is a triumph of good music over mere country image. Big House seems in fact to have slipped into a reactionary niche in Nashville (they record for MCA there) since they do not project the current trendy country-politan superficiality. Mavericks' bassist Robert Reynolds says, "If you're worried about sameness in this industry you only have to look to them [Big House] to find a band that can make a difference." Big House's "soul country" is an overt rockabilly–rhythm-and-blues style that links the group closely to this state's country-music past, just as it does to the Delta South's heritage: a country root recovered.

Boy Howdy is based in Southern California. Bassist Jeffrey Steele recalls that they first played together "at a chili cook-off about 1989. We . . . just kind of looked at each other and went, 'Man, this is going to be good.'" They were right, but they, too, paid their dues, for they were long a fixture at Southern California clubs such as Santa Ana's Crazy Horse Steak House, Anaheim's Bandstand, San Juan Capistrano's Swallow Inn, plus the redoubtable Foothill Club in Signal Hill.

Like Steele, guitarists Larry and Cary Park and drummer Hugh Wright were all established musicians when they formed the band. In 1992 the young men broke that barrier against independent labels when "A Cowboy Born with a Broken Heart" on Burbank's Curb Records crashed into the country chart's top 10. Late in 1993 they proved that their first hit was no fluke when influential music writer Robert K. Oermann chose the title tune of their Curb album *She'd Give Everything* as his "single of the day." By January the collection was among the top five nationwide, and suddenly the Southern Californians were performing in Tulsa, Austin, and, of course, in Nashville. Of Boy Howdy's eclectic repertoire Steele says they play for people who "cut their teeth on *both* rock and country."

Kristine Arnold and Janis Gill—the Sweethearts of the Rodeo—were born in Torrance and raised in Manhattan Beach, and for many years

these sisters performed in the area. Although they became locally popular, participating in the country-rock scene of the 1970s and the blue-
grass-newgrass revival of the early 1980s, the limitations of being
country-music entertainers in California finally wore them down. The
women came reluctantly to accept that even good country music is still
treated as low class by many entertainment bigwigs in the state.

Explains Arnold, "Janis and I had been beating down doors trying to
get somebody interested in our music in L.A. for years. . . . We were
burned out, and we thought, 'I don't want to do this anymore. I want to
have my family.'" For a time Kristine (married to guitarist and songwriter
Leonard Arnold) and Janis (married to singer Vince Gill) left music to
have children, but when Gill's husband's career took them to Nashville
and Kristine followed, the Sweethearts quickly observed the difference in
opportunities for country artists in the Tennessee town and in Los Angeles

After winning the 1985 Wrangler Country Showdown, they were
signed to a contract by Columbia Records. Their solid 1986 debut album
Sweethearts of the Rodeo contained four top-10 hits, which may illustrate as
much about the role of promotional clout as it does about quality, since
theirs was always high. It was in any case called one of the year's best by
Billboard. The women followed that success with *One Time, One Night* (1988),
Buffalo Zone (1990), *Sisters* (1992), and *Rodeo Waltz* (1994 [Sugar Hill
Records]), their popularity starkly illustrating the degree to which a Tennessee connection is now necessary to energize the careers of even such
talented performers.

California no longer boasts great country clout, but with a population
approaching 33 million, it can support entertainers who don't manage to
develop huge national reputations, as it did the Beat Farmers, for instance. That band boasted a generous following among other musicians.
The members' playing and singing became uniformly admired, and their
albums, such as *Poor and Famous* (1989) and *Loud and Plowed and . . . Live!!*
(1990), both on Curb Records, quickly became collectors' items. However, Country Dick Montana's unexpected death while performing in
1995 finally gutted this popular group.

The country-folk scene also endures in California. Utah Phillips, now
of Nevada City, still links the spirit and songs of Goebel Reeves to the contemporary world. A card-carrying, idealistic Wobbly, Phillips keeps the
proletarian faith. He sings labor songs, union songs, cowboy songs, songs

Utah Phillips (left) with Kate Wolf. Courtesy of Max Wolf.

of workers, thus tapping a root of country that has long since been abandoned by the southern mainstream. He is as a result almost universally
classified as a folk singer, with all the resulting political connotations. But
when asked about the relationship between folk and country, he answers,
"The same roots! That's what brought me to California, or part of what
brought me. We may not choose to sing with southern drawls, but we're
closer to real country music than Nashville if the songs're what really
counts."

Phillips has never forgotten that lyrics can be powerful weapons in the
struggle for equality in the United States. Probably no single element of
his work more separates him from contemporary country than his continued presentation of labor songs. Utah has spoken with clarity about the

contrast between the popular "cultured" version of folk music and the earlier proletarian root of country music actually written for and sung by workers:

> This [proletarian] music is not great poetry . . . it had to be simple because people didn't speak a lot of English, or hadn't been to school. But it's not like your modern protest music which tends to be introverted, a lot of it very poetic, hard to understand though, a middle-class music written for middle-class consumption. . . . What I'm saying is that there's a lot of difference between "How many miles must a white dove sail / before it can rest in the sand" and "Dump the bosses off your back!"

Iris DeMent, whose compositions are as traditional as Phillips's but whose style is distinctly southern, is a performer who easily slides from country to folk and back. "She has the best voice I've heard in a long, long time" says Professor Roxanne Dunbar Ortiz of California State University, Hayward. "She's one of those special talents." Many others, including Merle Haggard, agree. The clear, emotive voice of DeMent is rendered more intense by a slightly constricted delivery that carries strong southern memories. In fact the Arkansas native was raised in Long Beach and Buena Park in Southern California from the age of three until she was seventeen, and that style represents both a family tradition and a conscious artistic decision.

Her 1992 debut album *Infamous Angel* (Philo) brought her immediate attention; its unabashed spiritual tone troubled some but pleased many others. "Because of the way I was raised," the singer-songwriter explains, "I learned to look at the world and talk about it in a certain way. I grew up very religiously and feel that I am basically a religious person." Introducing a duet with her mother on that first album, Iris credits that lady for teaching her that music was "a path to higher ground." Although mainstream AM-radio stations avoided her records, she became a favorite on alternative (often public) radio stations, where her poetic lyrics attracted listeners not normally attuned to country. When *My Life*, her second album, was released in 1994, many feminists praised her portrait of a woman's dull lot in "Easy's Gettin' Harder Every Day."

Explaining her songs, DeMent told Bruce Robinson, "Sometimes I tell my own story, and sometimes I just tell somebody else's story. . . . A lot

Iris DeMent. Photo by Mark Tucker. Courtesy of HighTone Records.

of times something just pops into my head and I just go with it." Like Haggard, who seems to have influenced her writing, Iris DeMent's work remains firmly rooted: "My feet are still, a lot of the time, in the dirt, so I guess that makes me down to earth."

Down to earth in a somewhat different and perhaps even more amazing way are the Sons of the San Joaquin, their name a tribute to the Sons of the Pioneers. This singing group was formed "just for fun" by brothers Jack and Joe Hannah, and Joe's son, Lon, in the late 1980s. The older Hannahs, both coaches and educators, had established themselves as avocational singers in the Fresno and Visalia areas over the years; says Jack, "we've sung in so many venues—bar mitzvahs, weddings, Rotary club meetings, and all that—I can't remember 'em."

Lon actually urged his dad and uncle into professional performing. Their break came when they were invited to sing at the 1989 Cowboy Poetry Gathering in Elko, Nevada. Timing is said to be everything, and just as cowboy poetry was becoming increasingly popular, here was a singing group capable of not only reprising the great numbers of the Sons of the Pioneers and the original Riders of the Purple Sage but also of producing their own songs, such as Jack's "From Whence Came the Cowboy." The western part of country and western had been all but forgotten by many fans, but after the Sons of the San Joaquin's appearances on television shows such as "Grand Ole Opry," "Austin City Limits," and "Nashville Now," this trio—their background music enriched by accordionist Dennis Mack and fiddler Richard Chon—have once more infused country music with its legitimate western heritage.

Thanks to varied performers such as Flores, DeMent, the Smokin' Armadillos, Boy Howdy, Highway 101, Big House, and the Sons of the San Joaquin, California's country music scene has enjoyed an expansion of its audience. This has happened in two distinct ways: first, a large group of people with no knowledge of or concern with the music's history has been lured by the pop versions of country, by line dancing, by neowestern, and even by lingering urban cowboy styles. Second, and more interesting over the years, has been the social and ethnic broadening of the culture as working people of both sexes and all colors accept versions of country as roots music.

Related to the second phenomenon has been that widening economic gap between haves and have-nots in the not-always-golden state. Peter Schrag, political editor for the California-based McClatchy newspapers, explains that while "upper-level incomes are rising somewhat faster than they are in the rest of the nation . . . California's poor, to put it simply, have been getting poorer faster than those in the nation as a whole." The haves, of course, enjoy many choices, and more than a few yuppies and DINKS (double-income, no kids, couples) find themselves drawn to variations of this once-rebellious music. The sight of an Asian-American ur-

SONS OF THE SAN JOAQUIN

Sons of the San Joaquin. Photo by David M. Graham.
Courtesy of Scott O'Malley and Associates.

ban cowboy two-stepping with an African-American cowgirl at an upscale
Silicon Valley nightspot may war with the old Okie-music concept, but
that sight is a new aspect of contemporary California. Social, economic,
and educational class frequently supersede race and ethnicity among the
successful, and among some of them country music still retains a delicious, largely illusory edge of cultural slumming. How can you slum
with the nation's most popular music sung by millionaires in designer
jeans?

There are, of course, still plenty of neighborhood bars that can justly be called Okie joints where fancy cowboy duds would seem as out of place as white wine and ferns. Those taverns, like their upscale variants, are essentially the product of socioeducational class—people of similar affluence and education comfortable together. Hard country's contrarian tack still seems to appeal to a variety of folks. "I love my country, but I fear my government!" reads a bumper sticker outside the Tejon Club in Oildale. Says traditionalist singer Dale Watson, "The big corporations, that's the worst thing that ever happened to country music. That and line dancing."

For many Californians, country carries much historical baggage, remaining associated with Okie music, with redneck bars, with social outsiders: the Others. A well-heeled lady said after attending an Anne Murray concert in Santa Rosa: "She was *wonderful*, but the audience was noisy and rude, hooting between songs and carrying on. It was embarrassing, and I just *know* Anne didn't like it either." Maybe not, but she probably cashed her check. In Tennessee, on the other hand, country is the social establishment's ally.

Echoes of nineteenth-century class and regional prejudice remain in California, and the reasons some "sophisticates" disdain country music still have more to do with the music's listeners than with its actual presentation. Reports of country being the music of choice at rallies of right-wing militias and racist posses nationwide haven't much helped its image either: simple white music for simple white people it ain't, but that nevertheless remains an acceptable stereotype, although many of country's recent stars have worked at correcting that image.

Perhaps as a result California Latinos appear to be joining the previous white working-class fans in large numbers and contributing many performers, too. Suddenly for them as for others country's populist distrust of big shots seems to be as contemporary as computers. The continuing expansion of audience in the state has led, of course, to an expansion of opportunities for performers. Attitudes about who can sing what are slowly changing, so Iris DeMent performing Haggard's "Big City" on the *Tulare Dust* album, for example, is more a revelation than a shock to fans. California country's notoriously male-dominated universe has come to be identified with a sterling group of female performers, including Katy Moffat, Lucinda Williams, Mary Lyn Dias, Heather Myles, Carlene Carter, and Jann Browne, plus those already mentioned.

◄ ►   ◄ ►   ◄ ►

Excerpt from an interview with Rosie Flores—April 4, 1994:

Alexandra Haslam: What does Nashville think of California-based country artists?

Rosie Flores: They're looked at as a different breed. But also, "We will welcome you as long as you're willing to play our game." People like Dwight Yoakam and Buck Owens and Merle Haggard have proved that you don't have to [record in Nashville], but not doing it just makes things tougher for you. . . . I don't blame them for sticking to what they know; it's too risky otherwise.

Haslam: Is it frustrating?

Flores: It was in '87. Right now it's not because I understand the Nashville way and it doesn't frighten me. In some ways I love it. I've been dismissed by certain labels and people in Nashville who don't want to talk to me or hear about me. . . . I don't really have to worry about that in the same way, because I've got a label here that digs what I do anyway. And I've got people in Nashville who dig what I do anyway, so I've got the best of both worlds.

Haslam: How about radio play for a California artist?

Flores: It's gotten better since my first record came out in 1987, but it's still kind of tough. . . . I'm on an independent label, and if the radio station's only going to pick five songs a week [to supplement the playlist], they'll be pulling from the majors. But if I pick a really good song, and release the right one, maybe nothing can stop it. . . .

But if nothing like that does happen, I'm having a lot of fun. . . . I'm getting to record the exact music I want to, so I'm in really good hands and I feel really lucky. A lot of my dreams have come true. I got to play onstage at the "Grand Ole Opry." Got to meet Buck Owens. I got to meet Roy Orbison—that was a real thrill. . . .

I love singing and I love recording.

◄ ►   ◄ ►   ◄ ►

Southern California remains the world's entertainment center, and commercial country music abides as only one small piece of the large mosaic. That lack of attention can be negative, but it does allow considerable cross-fertilization. A noted punk rocker like John Doe, for example, can contribute a splendid version of "I Can't Be Myself" to *Tulare Dust* because roots are roots. The stylistic line between rock, rockabilly, and honky-tonk remains slim and permeable.

To the north, country's position in the Bay Area remains ambivalent. Some towns like Oakland, Richmond, Concord, Vallejo, Santa Rosa, and San Jose have long supported it. San Jose now boasts more country nightspots than does Bakersfield, including the Saddlerack, California's largest, where the enduring Don Cox holds court. A Sacramento roadhouse named Sidekicks, which was known as the Bell Avenue Corral in the 1940s, then the Detour Inn from the 1950s through the 1970s when Okie Paul Westmoreland ran it, remains a local institution. Nearby San Francisco, however, seems still to view country as a curiosity or perhaps as a way to get funky; in that entertainment-rich city, country is often treated as underground stuff. Explaining the indifference to the music there, SF Weekly writer Cary Tennis has written,

> Why do any of us come to San Francisco? Maybe for the same reason that country music isn't all that popular here. Most of the people who make up the hip nightlife crowd have come here from elsewhere, to reject tradition and reinvent themselves in complicated ways. Sure country can be complicated, and subtle. It has range. It's great music. But, really, if you were going to reject tradition and reinvent yourself in a complicated way, would you want country music playing in the background?

As it turns out a generation of well-educated urban cowboys and cowgirls have done just that and are still doing it at the Saddlerack and other upscale honky-tonks around the state, but Tennis's point is well taken. Country music still is not much associated with sophistication in the state, and in San Francisco sophistication is often the pose of choice. Pedal steel player Joe Goldmark asserts that "outside of New York, San Francisco is probably the worst area for country music in the nation." Still some country performers persevere in that locale: Paula Frazier, Gary Wayne Claxton, Jim Campilongo, Gregory Scott Reeves and the Gladhands, Red Meat, and Stephen Yerkey.

Despite the fact that literally scores of Buck and Merle imitators and now Dwight imitators are appearing, the torch here seems to be passing from the old California and Bakersfield Sounds to the increasingly dynamic roots-country–roots-rock scene that developed first in Los Angeles, as well as to cookie-cutter hat acts yearning for Nashville.

Creative leadership appears to rest with Yoakam and Pete Anderson, Dave Alvin and Rosie Flores, Tom Russell and Scott Joss, Lucinda Williams and Jim Lauderdale, and all the rest who are creating new songs, new styles, and, yes, new visions to evoke enduring realities. Like Buck, Merle, and Dwight before them, those others are trying to reinvent the form. Where matters will stand tomorrow is anybody's guess, but California remains one of the few domains that has both the economic and cultural independence to support its own country-music scene, albeit without great national reach.

Russell, for example, has become something of a songwriter's songwriter. Dave Alvin says, "Tom Russell's songs changed my life. . . . There was no bullshit in the songs, no lies, nobody telling you things they thought you wanted to hear just to make a buck." In albums like *The Rose of the San Joaquin* (HighTone, 1995) Russell—who has cowritten with such luminaries at Ian Tyson, Moffatt, and Alvin—demonstrates that he is a notable performer, too. He and Alvin coproduced the remarkable *Tulare Dust* album.

Among the present generation Yoakam has most successfully bucked the system. Dwight has pointed out that country music is an unusually concentrated entertainment genre: the Tennessee establishment dominates and naturally enough wants to continue doing so. Other music— pop, jazz, rock—thrive in many places at once: Los Angeles, New York, London. But Nashville controls one musical game, and that location is the game's core. As a result California-identified (and other independent) performers are resisted or ignored until they relocate (or at least conform). Some have refused to do that. Says Yoakam of the southern bosses, "I don't think they understood quite what we were up to. . . . [that] I don't feel constrained by any musical boundaries."

The soul of traditional country here as elsewhere remains romantically rural, romantically southern, romantically white, and probably just as romantically the anthem of underdogs. It is a medium that is indeed often the message: "*I listen to country to hear something about me!*"

Booking Agent
Little Bear Productions
(403)426-4343

TOM RUSSELL

HIGHTONE RECORDS
220 4th St. #101
Oakland, CA 94607
(510)763-8500

PHOTO CREDIT: BETH HERZHAFT

Tom Russell. Photo by Beth Herzhaft. Courtesy of HighTone Records.

Perhaps that's why California has managed to remain number two in this music now dominated by the South; it is a state where people have come to reinvent themselves: Leonard Slye became Dick Weston who became Roy Rogers; Ferlin Husky became Simon Crum and Terry Preston, then Ferlin Husky again. California is also where country music has several times reinvented itself, thanks to the impact of "cowboy" songs, to the popularity of western swing, to the independence of the Bakersfield Sound, to the defiance of cowpunk, and so on. In this music as in all art there must be a setting that rewards originality at least as much as it rewards conformity. Welcome to the Golden State.

The process continues, and some important country music in California, as in Texas, continues veering in a different direction from the dominant Tennessee version; so does *some* in Nashville. All are legitimate branches of the family, of course, but the commercial Nashville Sound is increasingly believed to be the whole show nationwide, because, as journalist Tony Scherman observes, "popular tastes, including the taste for country music, are less and less freely arrived at, shaped more and more by a few corporations." Gatekeepers who decide what folks *should* hear and limit what they *can* hear—especially over the radio—inhibit country music's ability to continue growing and changing.

A generation (or two) unconnected to Depression roots or World War II is now buying a new country music in what is essentially a new country or a significantly altered one: 36 percent of this music's fans today have postgraduate degrees—the highest among pop music, according to a recently published study. Moreover a third of individuals who earn more than $100,000 a year are now reported to be listening to country. Soon we may have songs about unreliable mutual funds and perfidious personal trainers.

Scholar Archie Green commented, "I'm not sure that California country music, in all its varied forms, counters Nashville in meaningful ways." Probably not, because young singers and musicians here are human; they crave acceptance and success, and for most of them that is spelled N-A-S-H-V-I-L-L-E. The only hope for a truly distinct music here is if local performers think of their work as Californian, descended from Haywire Mac, from the Sons of the Pioneers, from the Maddox Brothers and Rose, from Spade, from Buck, from Bonnie, from Merle, from everything that used to be called West Coast country.

Carloads of country performers no longer pour into California as they did in the 1930s, '40s, and '50s; those days are likely gone forever. Even without those erstwhile musical migrants to the West, though, alternative versions of this music endure as individuals celebrate region, culture, and class with songs. They do so against the contemporary current, because that homogeneity of top-40 country music has led to the leveling of national culture—symbolized by the reach of "tight playlists" on radio and ubiquitous (and firmly controlled) music videos on television.

311

Dwight Yoakam asserts,

What they [the Nashville establishment] did cost a generation the experience of an American ethnic music form that we've almost lost. . . . I'm
tired of them peddling it and soft selling the categories: "Well, country can
be anything." The hell it can. No it can't. . . . You know why? Because it's
back to Dwight Yoakam doin' this for Dwight and a man named Luther
Tibbs [his grandfather] that mined coal in Pikeville, Kentucky, and had to
get up off a chair and had to roll around on the floor to catch his breath
because he had coal dust on his lungs. And I'll be damned if you're gonna
tell me what country music is.

Most outsiders don't recognize the irony that in the Golden State some
of the same psychological conditions that shaped early country music in
the South still exist: disappointment with modern life and yearning for a
bucolic past inspired many of the first commercial songs. Disenchantment
with contemporary life lingers here not because conditions are bad but
because expectations are high, and so many folks bring unrealistic dreams
to California. An inability to realize the state's glitzy image has led many
to yearn for a rose-colored version of the rural past and to listen for lyrics
reflecting similar disillusionment. If conditions were in fact no better in
other places and at other times, at least the fans were younger, so they remember their lives as more hopeful. Traditional country music has connected with such longings.

Of course many folks *have* made it economically in California, or their
kids have, more than a few of them college educated. Their loyalty to traditional music is a statement of unwillingness to succumb to the pervasive forces of homogeneity sweeping the nation; to paraphrase Hag's
anthem, "We Take a Lot of Pride in What We Are."

It's also important to remember that in the not-so-distant past, country music nationwide was considered to be an expression of the Others—
of outsiders, of rebels, perhaps of losers—most often of white folks it was
okay to disdain. The Maddox Brothers and Rose could represent the Others; Buck Owens and the Buckaroos could represent the Others; Dwight
Yoakam still can. Ironically, while poor whites today seem to be about the
only group it's politically correct to ridicule—Okies, hicks, trailer trash,

and so on—today's top-40 country no longer represents, or even vaguely evokes, the Others. Neither does Owens's wonderful new Bakersfield nightclub, the Crystal Palace. The name remains country music, but the lives of many in the audience—the lucky ones in particular—and the music itself have radically altered. The present escape from poverty and bigotry certainly isn't bad, but it is different.

Yet in California the shadow of the Others does linger; a hint of class snobbery endures. "They still don't respect us here," complains a middle-aged Bakersfield woman at the Crystal Palace. "They still think we're Okies. We're still fighting that old prejudice." She did not identify "they." And there are even lingering Gold Rush illusions; a homeless man at a San Francisco shelter says, "I thought California was about somethin', but it ain't about nothin'."

Country music in California had surged in the 1930s, then peaked in the 1940s when the state was national leader and musicians migrated west. It remained at a high level through much of the 1950s but was already beginning a slow decline—younger talent moving south, not west—when Buck Owens had his remarkable run, and Nashville-West was hyped. While the Golden State's greatest native-born performer Merle Haggard dominated in the 1970s and '80s, country was retreating to the margins of entertainment on the West Coast, with fiercely loyal fans but fading visibility. Only the rise of country-flavored rock, an enduring club scene, and the high profile of the Academy of Country Music offered much hope. In the 1990s that fan base seems to be again expanding. But national leadership is long gone, so California has become a locale favored by mavericks, by outlaws, perhaps by romantics. Ironically, local music remains not only original but arguably richer than most of what's heard on top-40 radio.

That is exemplified by Yoakam—his southern memories expressed in southwestern styles much enriched by the state's creative freedom— who has so effectively defied the southern establishment's grip on country music. This locale will likely continue to produce some nonconformist stars, for the Golden State still offers artists a sense of loosened limits and creative encouragement that expands possibilities; it may also provide a sense of frustration or even repression that goads them into expressing their deepest feelings. Like Texas, that other "outlaw" domain, it also defines country music generously and respects its history as much as it respects the bottom line. While two of this music's three most important states have been, in the recent past, thoroughly dominated by the third, Tennessee, each retains or has retained at least a cadre of innovative traditionalists who know what they like and who "ain't give up and ain't give in," whether they are Don Walser in the Lone Star State, Johnny and Joni Mosby in the Golden State, or their many colleagues there and here.

As seems so often the case Haggard has something to say about all this: "Country music is feelin' and *heart*, not a bunch of stuff some asshole says the public wants just because he's made 'an extensive study of the market.' It's enough to make you puke."

BAKERSFIELD, 1995

The headline says it all:

> *Together*
> *Again*
> *Buck & Merle*
> *making country*
> *music history*
> *in the streets of*
> *Bakersfield*

Well, my wife, some pals, and I are together again, too, home for the show. Old friends have saved seats for us in the half-circle of bleachers around a turf "standing room," but we decide to join the crowd closer to the stage. That youthful gang socializes—much flirting and posturing—as it enthusiastically awaits the big stars.

This is a different mix than we'd seen at performances here thirty years before, when spectators were almost exclusively white, dominated by Okies or the progeny of Okies. Tonight at the pavilion on the Kern County Fairgrounds there are many darker faces under Stetsons, evidence of California's increasingly blended culture. Latinos, especially, are mingling, in no way segregated.

A tall black man, his arm around a petite white woman, slices through the throng near us, and an older white man next to me mumbles, "That couple wouldn't've been too popular in the old days." His tone is neutral.

"These ain't the old days," I respond, my timbre flat as his.

"You got that straight," he grunts.

There are few spectators our age or older on the turf, but many in the stands. I recognize some faces, knowing that all of us are caricatures of our youthful selves. I also notice a few folks glancing furtively at my lined mug, trying to remember who I used to be.

Near the beer booth I recognize an old schoolmate. "Hey, Charley," I call, and he stops,

315

squints, then grins.

"Hey, Gerald. I ain't seen you since before we got drafted. What the hell're you up to nowadays?" He's balancing three cups of beer, so we don't shake hands.

"No good."

"I damn sure believe that."

"What're you doin' now?"

"Still in the oil fields," he bobs his head and makes a clucking sound in his cheek. " 'Bout to retire, though," he adds. "You reckon ol' Merle'll be sober?" We three were in the same class at Standard School.

"Will you be?" I counter.

He grins. "Not if I can help it."

"I heard Dwight Yoakam's here, too."

Charley says, "Yeah, ol' Dwight's here. The wife she seen him and his bus out back this afternoon. She said him and Buck and Merle were rehearsin'."

"That's great."

We say so-long and I—trying to remember Charley's last name—wander back toward my wife and pals, who have moved to an area behind low bleachers on one side of the stage; it offers a better view of the musicians. Nearby, a man pushes a wheelchair past us containing a striking young woman. She twitches and rolls in her seat, apparently suffering from cerebral palsy, and he pats her shoulder. The young beauty wears a bright red jacket embossed with a large KUZZ, the call letters of one of Buck's radio stations. I watch them climb a ramp up the low platform before us. It is reserved for folks with physical problems, and ushers help situate them. Next to that couple I notice a man with his arm around a teenage boy who appears to have Down's syndrome; they are conversing and laughing. And close to them in another wheelchair sits an older man, half his face sliding downward like melted wax, the other half grinning.

The crowd is pleasantly noisy; loud guffaws and occasional good-natured shouts echo from it. Subtlety and understatement are not cultural characteristics of this group; that much hasn't changed since my youth. As a warm-up band, the Wichitas, is performing, a large man in pastel golf togs points toward the stage and asks, "Is that guy Dwight Yoakam?"

Some spectators are here tonight because this is Bakersfield's summit, not because they follow country music. Local citizens have every reason to take pride in the community's musical history, and in the public-mindedness of people like Buck Owens. Pioneer local performer Cousin Herb Henson used to sing, "Y'all Come!" back in the 1950s. Tonight many have, but even Herb might be surprised at this diverse audience, although he helped create it.

Examining the bleachers, I see plenty of apparently affluent older folks. I recognize that some are, like me, card-carrying liberals. Hereabouts, we haven't allowed conservatives or reactionaries—or liberals, for that matter—to usurp country music. It belongs to all of us, transcending politics and ethnicity, touching deeper, shared realities, for it is one of many important cultural currents in the remarkably diverse stream that is present-day California.

The standing-room crowd surges toward the stage and tightens when Buck Owens and the Buckaroos appear. The star wears his characteristic wide, black hat and dark jacket. From where we stand he looks little different than he had way back when—droopier in the face, maybe—and his voice remains crisp as he reels off hit after hit, all familiar as breath to most of us.

Dennis pokes me and says, "Buck owns about half of this town, but he's still got that touch, doesn't he?"

"He sure does." In forty-plus years I've never seen Buck give a poor performance. Tonight is no exception. The singer dedicates one song to his high-rolling golf buddies. Hard hands applaud, and so do plenty of soft ones; like Buck himself, many in this crowd have pulled themselves well up the economic ladder.

Near us a young girl—high school age perhaps—moans to another youngster, "I didn't know this was gonna be so Okie," and my pals and I can't suppress laughter. Embarrassed at being overheard, the kids scurry away.

Her remark may indicate a gap growing between the fans of current country-pop entertainers—Trisha Yearwood, Garth Brooks, Mary Chapin Carpenter, and that gang—and the adherents of hard country such as Buck performs. It is likely as much a social and spiritual phenomenon as a musical one. The former group seems, in the main, to be composed of new converts to this music or of youngsters, while a high percentage of hard country's fans here tend to be oldsters like us. Despite this dichotomy, Buck's honky-tonk and rockabilly numbers have everyone bouncing.

Merle's segment of the show begins with a couple of lively Cajun numbers by his band the Strangers. They slide into a ballad, the steel guitar cries, and I shudder: the wail of a steel can break a heart, start a fight, or do both. As usual Bonnie Owens begins the set with a series of numbers, and we older fans especially are enraptured by her. She links the two stars in the minds of many devotees, and she has also been a star in this town since the early 1950s.

When her set seems to extend beyond its expected limit, those same older fans begin to nudge one another and mumble ("Where's Merle at? Is he gonna show or what?"). Many remember other Haggard concerts where the warm-up acts provided most of the entertainment. Nervous laughter and rueful remarks ("You don't reckon the IRS went and took his bus again, do you?") are rippling through the throng when a feisty Hag strides on stage to an enormous ovation. People here love Buck; he is a local institution and often a *public presence. But Merle is the prodigal son who rarely returns, so his greeting is proportionate to his long absence.*

During the applause I notice that the young man who had pushed the wheelchair up onto the platform now sits in it, and the pretty lady with neurological twitches snuggles on his lap. Those two look mighty comfortable to me.

Meanwhile Hag has broken into song—"Mama Tried"—and the crowd has quickly quieted. Merle's mother and father—all of our mothers and fathers, for that matter—had in the 1930s and '40s been part of California's large population of hard-working folks seeking to survive in a changing world, a theme of much country music. And now we're what's left; most of our parents have passed on, but their dreams still live in us.

Merle croons "Hungry Eyes," and Dina is swaying. Her own eyes are half-closed as she sighs, "Sometimes I think he's just in another league."

That nostalgic moment is broken as the outer fringe of the crowd begins surging and shouting: a fistfight has broken out. Police stop it quickly, but I know that it will be only the first bout of the night.

"Welcome home," says Bud, as unsurprised as I am. "Want to make your comeback?"

"That's close," I chuckle. The rest of the evening, police are busy keeping a lid on that outer edge.

When Dwight Yoakam is introduced, it becomes clear that for many younger fans he is the other league, and the pitch of cheers is higher, punctuated by several squeals. The handsome young man joins Buck and Merle, and he fits comfortably with them. Soon they are offering a dynamite version of what has become a local mantra: "The Streets of Bakersfield," with a new verse for Hag—two new ones in fact, one written by him, one written by Buck. The standing-room crowd is involved and energized as it listens to this hymn to hard times.

This song is deep country, and the singers have certainly found the right place to practice it this night because deep country remains more aligned with the state's hard-work reality than with its soft-life image. Bakersfield, with its kick-ass Okie reputation, remains that music's symbolic heart. "Sing that sucker!" cries a craggy man standing near us, the stub of a cigar in his mouth, a John Deere cap askew on his head.

The song ends; Bonnie, who has joined the band behind them, suddenly becomes the target of a series of jibes from her former husbands. Buck starts it when he removes his wide-brimmed hat and says, "See how bad me and Hag look? Bonnie did that to us!"

The crowd roars, and a voice calls, "You guys was ugly to start with!" and another roar follows.

The former wife feigns consternation and the jibes continue. Then Yoakam joins in, saying,

"I don't know how she got stuck with you two losers," and the crowd guffaws, for they know this is inside stuff, special Bakersfield banter.

Hag growls, "Only a young man could talk to me that way," and the guy with the crooked John Deere hat, listing like the leaning tower of Bakersfield, mumbles, "He ain't shittin'."

After Dwight dedicates a solo to Bonnie, there is shuffling onstage, then Merle announces that a music video of the trio singing a new song will now be taped, and "You folks'll be part of it." We cheer.

Hag reveals that the song is named after a spot most oldsters remember well, "Beer Can Hill," and he mentions a second locale called the "Seven Sisters." Kids in the crowd don't seem to know anything about those fabled party zones amid oil fields on the treeless hills north of Oildale, but we sure do. Underage beer guzzling aplenty took place there until the oil companies fenced the area off in the 1960s. More importantly to us, though, it was a prime necking spot in our heated youthful nights. Most of us parked there, and Bud slips between my wife and me, puts his arms around our shoulders, and whispers, "Hell, you two're married because of that hill."

He may be right, so we laugh with him.

Cameras rolling, Hag formally introduces the video's title, speaking into the microphone: "We're gonna do a new song for you called 'Beer Can Hill,'" and on cue we in the audience cheer wildly.

The singing begins, while Bonnie is jitterbugging with Merle's old pal, Bob Teague, on one side of the stage. Midnight approaches and the audience is tired; nevertheless it remains lively, bellowing on cue, laughing and joshing, really into it. When the song ends and applause subsides, there is a pause, then a long-haired, bearded young man wearing a headset walks on stage and whispers to Merle, who nods.

Hag glances at Buck and Dwight, then announces to the crowd, "We gotta do it again." He pauses briefly, then once more announces, "We're gonna do a new song for you folks called 'Beer Can Hill,'" and we laugh and cheer. When this take is over, the young man again walks on stage. Merle grins and shakes his head, then announces, "We're gonna do a new song for you folks...." The crowd laughs.

After the fifth take, however, the natives have grown restless and less responsive, too. The bearded young man once more trots onstage, whispers to Merle, then departs. Hag looks at the audience, pauses, and finally snorts, "They want us to do it again, but I ain't gonna sing that son of a bitch no more." Buck and Dwight, Bonnie and Bob, all break up with laughter, and so does the crowd.

I say to Bud, "You know, ol' Merle hasn't changed all that much, has he."

319

"Oh yeah!" grunts Bud. "Forty years ago, he might've knocked that dipshit into next week," and we all laugh.

Onstage, three guys who have served the hard apprenticeship this music demands—ol' Merle, ol' Buck, and not-so-ol' Dwight—launch into another song. Because they, too, once stood spellbound and threadbare before stages listening to this kind of music, they understand that the deep heart of country is found not on the bandstand but among what might be called—in a quasi-religious sense—the witnesses. In this tradition, the success of singers, players, and listeners is collective, and these three bards have not forgotten that.

(opposite) Record sleeve for
A Town South of Bakersfield.
Photo by Scarpati. 1985
Enigma Entertainment Corp.

Detailed listings for books and articles referred to in this essay may be found in the Selected Bibliography. The following abbreviations are employed:

AQ	*American Quarterly*
BC	*The Bakersfield Californian*
CM	*Country Music*
CSR	*Country Song Roundup*
JAF	*Journal of American Folklore*
JCM	*Journal of Country Music*
JOTC	*Journal of the American Academy for the Preservation of Old-Time Country Music*
JEMF	*John Edwards Memorial Foundation Quarterly*
JPC	*Journal of Popular Culture*
LAT	*Los Angeles Times*
MCN	*Music City News*
PMS	*Popular Music and Society*
RQ	*Request*
SFC	*San Francisco Chronicle*
SRPD	*Santa Rosa Press Democrat*
SQ	*Southern Quarterly*
SO!	*Sing Out!*
WF	*Western Folklore*

One of California's most important contributions to country music was bibliographic and scholarly. The John Edwards Memorial Foundation, possibly the finest collection of country music materials in the world at the time, was established at UCLA's Folklore and Mythology Center in 1962. Moreover, the invaluable *John Edwards Memorial Foundation Quarterly* was published there.

Edwards was an Australian scholar who had collected country records, memorabilia, letters, and so on, but whose Australian colleagues showed only slight interest in his work. When he died in 1960, he willed his collection to scholars in the United States, with Eugene W. Earle as trustee. That in turn led a distinguished group—Archie Green, Fred Hoeptner, Ed Kahn, and D. K. Wilgus—to join Earle in founding the Edwards Foundation and in beginning publication of its quarterly journal. As Bill C. Malone points out, "This was the greatest 'academic respectability' the study of country music has achieved."

The foundation's quarterly provided many of the most valuable references for this book. Its studies of California-based performers are unparalleled. In a change that symbolically augured Californian unwillingness to defend its position in this music—as well as the continuing "southernization" of country music's history—the Edwards's collection was eventually transferred to the excellent Southern Folklife Collection at the University of North Carolina in Chapel Hill, where "prune pickers" and "rebs" are housed indistinguishably.

General Sources

The bibliographic foundation of research for this book is the revised edition of Bill C. Malone's landmark *Country Music U.S.A.* The 1995 edition of *The Illustrated History of Country Music*, edited by Patrick Carr for *Country Music Magazine*, has also been of great value, as have various numbers of JOTC. The best presentation of the West Coast scene can be found in Jonny Whiteside, *Ramblin' Rose: The Life and Times of Rose Maddox.* In addition, contrary to what some people may suppose, abundant material on country music has been published, and the names of several writers occur over and over in the literature: Gerald F. Vaughn, Ken Griffis, Douglas B. Green, Robert K. Oermann, Robert Price, Charles Wolfe, George H. Lewis, and especially Jonny Whiteside and Rich Kienzle. For their work we are most grateful.

Among the other general studies we found to be particularly valuable were Lewis (ed.), *All That Glitters: Country Music in America;* Robert Shelton, *The Country Music Story;* Russell D. Barnard et al., *The Comprehensive Country Music Encyclopedia;* Bob Millard, *Country Music: 70 Years of America's Favorite Music;* Irwin Stambler and Landon Grunlun, *The Encyclopedia of Folk, Country and Western;* Paul Kingsbury and Alan Axelrod (eds.), *Country: The Music and the Musicians;* Nick Tosches, *Country: The Biggest Music in America;* Melvin Shestack, *The Country Music Encyclopedia;* Douglas B. Green, *Country Roots: The Origins of Country Music;* and Fred Dellar, Roy Thompson, and Douglas B. Green, *The Illustrated History of Country Music.* Jonny Whiteside's article "When Country Went Coastal" in *Variety* offers first-rate insights into California's special country-music scene.

Also of consistent value were articles in JEMF, JCM, and JOTC. Three popular articles that appeared while this book was being written were also stimulating: Tony Scherman, "Country," *American Heritage*; Charles Hirshberg and Robert Sullivan, "The 100 Most Important People in the History of Country," *Life*; and Bruce Feiler, "Gone Country," *New Republic*.

Each of the chapters that surveys a decade includes a brief review of high points in California's general history. In writing those sections, we have drawn upon the work of W. H. Hutchinson; Kenneth G. Goode; Carey McWilliams; Walton Bean and James J. Rawls; and Richard Rice, William Bullough, and Richard Orsi. Southernness bears on many chapters; we have consulted C. Vann Woodward, *Origins of the New South*, and his *The Burden of Southern History*; W. J. Cash, *The Mind of the South*; and (more fun) John Shelton Reed and Dale Volberg Reed, *1001 Things Everyone Should Know about the South*.

General sources were also supplemented with interviews, most by Richard Chon. We are particularly grateful to everyone who allowed one or more of us to speak with them, some (such as Owens and Woods) many times:

Bobby Adamson	Dave Alvin
Pete Anderson	Kate Brislin
Sandy Coker	Carolina Cotton
Rosie Flores	Buddy Mize
Ken Nelson	Bonnie Owens
Buck Owens	Jimmy Phillips
Sal Sage	Jelly Sanders
Jody Stecher	Jimmy Thomason
Louise Thomason	Bill Woods
Dwight Yoakam	

We also benefited from letters and conversations with many folks. These were not necessarily conducted or solicited with this book in mind but occurred with friends and fellow fans over a period of approximately forty-five years. We've reproduced them as we remember them, always true to their content if not to their word choices. Thanks are due to

Terry Alexander	Tom Alexander
Judy Anderson	Jess Avalos
Bill Barich	Ken Byrum
Fred Castro	Frank Chase
Francis Clark	Tom Clark
Donnell Cooley, Jr.	Tee Dixon

Fred "Duke" Dominguez	Steve Emmanuels
Charlotte Epp	Peter Epp, Jr.
Pat Fix	Terrence Fix
Steve Fjeldsted	Monty Garth
Merle Haggard	Lorraine Haslam
Spec Haslam	Lew Hedgecock
Tanya Hilderbrand	J. K. Johnson
Ken Johnson	Dick Kirkpatrick
Gerald Locklin	Larry Jay Martin
Clyde Mayfield	Doy Mayfield
Justin Meyer	Buddy Mize
Sharon Mize	Joseph Molinaro
Larry Nelson	Utah Phillips
Don Plank	Mary Pruett
Don Puskarich	Patricia Puskarich
John Renfree	Gary Sposito
Bob Stephens	Clark Sturges
Jim Thomas	Suzanne Tumblin
James L. Wattenbarger	Richard Winn
Robert Earl Wood	Rafael Zepeda

Chapter 1

All the general sources above were consulted for this important chapter (and for most others). Because arguments continue over what exactly distinguishes country music, Chapter 1 seeks to establish our working definition and to briefly outline the music's history as we understand it. We consulted many valuable volumes bearing on these issues, including Malone, *Southern Music: American Music*; Peggy A. Bulger (ed.), *Musical Roots of the South*; Frye Gaillard, *Watermelon Wine: The Spirit of Country Music*; Jimmie N. Rogers, *The Country Music Message: All About Lovin' and Livin'*; John Egerton, *The Americanization of Dixie: The Southernization of America*; Michael Bane, *White Boy Singin' the Blues: The Black Roots of White Rock*; and Paul Hemphill, *The Nashville Sound*. Patrick Carr, *The Illustrated History of Country Music*, was most valuable of all.

Among articles and essays of notable value were Archie Green, "Hillbilly Music: Source and Symbol," *JAF*; George H. Lewis, "Country Music Lyrics," *JCM*; Lewis, "Mapping Fault Lines: The Core Values Trap in Country Music," *PMS*; Melissa Ladenheim, "'I Was Country When Country Wasn't Cool': An Ethnography of a Country Music Fan," *Culture and Tradition*; Marc Landy, "Country Music: The Melody of Dislocation," *New South*; Norman Cohen, "America's Music: Written and Recorded," JEMF; Anne Cohen and Norm Cohen, "Folk and Hillbilly Music: Further Thoughts on Their Relation," JEMF; Charles Seeger, "Music and Class Structure in the United States," AQ; Alex S. Freedman, "The Sociology of Country Music," Southern Humanities Review; Thomas F. Johnson, "That Ain't Country: The Distinctiveness of Commercial Western Music," JEMF; James C. Cobb, "From Muskogee to Luckenbach: Country Music and the 'Southernization' of America," JPC; Chet Flippo, "Country and Western: Some New-Fangled Ideas," American Libraries; John Buckley, "Country Music and American Values," PMS; Sherry B. Ortner, "On Key Symbols," American Anthropologist; D. K. Wilgus, "An Introduction to the Study of Hillbilly Music," JAF; Roderick J. Roberts, "An Introduction to the Study of Northern Country Music," JCM; Richard A. Peterson and Russell Davis, "The Fertile Crescent of Country Music," JCM; and on and on.

Chapters 2 and 3

In addition to all the general volumes and history books cited above we consulted other material. Among the particularly important articles were Norm Cohen, "Transcripts: Interview with Johnny Crockett," and his "Materials toward a Study of Early Country Music on Radio III: Fresno, California," both in JEMF.

Chapter 3 also employed material from "Musical Roots of the South" by Charles Wolfe and "Old-Time and Country Music Traditions" by W. K. McNeil, two chapters in Peggy A. Bulger (ed.), Musical Roots of the South. Perspective on cowboys in film and reality comes mostly from Henry Nash Smith, Virgin Land: The American West as Symbol and Myth; Jon Tuska, The Filming of the West; Don Miller, Hollywood Corral; William Everson, A Pictorial History of the Western Film; as well as Lawrence Zwisohn, "The Western through the Years on Film and Television," Songs of the West, a boxed CD set from Rhino Records. Also of value was William Henry Koon, "The Songs of Ken Maynard," JEMF.

Chapters 4 and 5

Apart from the sources listed above, we most benefited from Gene Autry and Mickey Herskowitz, Back in the Saddle Again, plus an Arts and Entertainment Channel Biography episode on Autry.

Chapter 5 contains the roots of much that endures in this music. All the general sources, plus Ken Griffis, "The Beverly Hill Billies," JEMF, informed the section on that band. Material on the Okie migration came from personal sources, plus James Gregory, American Exodus: The Dust Bowl Migration and Okie Culture in California; and Walter Stein, California and the Dust Bowl Migration. Horse operas (aka, singing westerns) are well surveyed in Douglas B. Green, "The Singing Cowboy: An

American Dream," JCM; Kalton C. Lahue, *Riders of the Range: The Sagebrush Heroes of the Sound Screen*; and Charlie Seemann, "Cowboy Music: A Historical Perspective," included in *Songs of the West*. Cowgirls are discussed in Camille Paglia, "Annie Oakley, Frontier Feminist" in the SRPD. The genesis of commercial folk music and its characteristics may be found in Charles Seeger, "Music and Class Structure in the United States," *AQ*; and his *Studies in Musicology 1935–1975*.

Biography also examined the life of Roy Rogers, and Frank Raskey contributed *Roy Rogers: King of the Cowboys*. The most valuable additional source on the Sons of the Pioneers was Griffis, *Hear My Song: The Story of the Celebrated Sons of the Pioneers*. Our primary source on Woody Guthrie was Joe Klein's excellent biography, *Woody Guthrie: A Life*, plus Guthrie's own, less satisfactory *Bound for Glory*. Many general references also discuss his life and music. The primary source on Jack Guthrie was Guy Logsdon, "Jack Guthrie: A Star That Almost Was," JCM.

The genesis of western swing was explored in Cary Ginell, "The Development of Western Swing," *Devil's Box*. Also of value was "Merle Travis on 'Western Swing,'" JEMF. In addition to the previously listed books and articles, we found the early history of bluegrass in Robert Cantwell's admirable *Bluegrass Breakdown: The Making of the Old Southern Sound*; Steven D. Price, *Old as the Hills: The Story of Bluegrass Music*; and L. Mayne Smith, "An Introduction to Bluegrass," JAF.

Apart from the general sources cited above, which of course consider early honky-tonk, and many other books and articles that don't explicitly mention it in their titles (Roger M. Williams's *Sing a Sad Song: The Life of Hank Williams*, for instance), we relied on studies such as "Honky-Tonk: The Music of the Southern Working Class" in *Folk Music and Modern Sound*, edited by William Ferris, plus a section of Lewis, *All That Glitters*, containing stimulating essays by Joli Jensen, Aaron A. Fox, and Karl Neuenfeldt. The evolution of the guitar as dominant instrument was traced in Kienzle, "The Electric Guitar in Country Music: Its Evolution and Development," *Guitar Player*, and most of the material on Les Paul was derived from Mary Alice Shaughnessy, *Les Paul: An American Original*.

In assessing the early impact of radio and television, which was not covered in such sources as Cohen's "Materials toward a Study of Early Country Music on Radio," George O. Carney, "Country Music and the Radio: A Historical Geographic Assessment," *Rocky Mountain Social Science Journal*, was particularly important, as were Hugh Cherry, "Country DJs Carry Music to People," MCN; Bill Steigerwald, "For Your Ears Only: On the Road with Radio," LAT; Gene Fowler and Bill Crawford, *Border Radio*; Robert Hilburn, "Listeners Are Tuning in to Revitalized Country Sound, . . . " LAT; and Ivan M. Tribe, "The Economics of Hillbilly Radio: A Preliminary Investigation of the 'P.I.' System in the Depression Decade and Afterward," JEMF.

Chapters 6, 7, and 8

This group of chapters examines California's temporary dominance of country music in the 1940s due to western swing and population shifts. The principal source for Chapter 6, other than yarns spun by fellow musicians and fans, was Charles R. Townsend's good biography *San Antonio Rose: The Life and Music of Bob Wills.*

Chapter 7 builds on the western swing sources noted for Chapter 5, plus Gerald F. Vaughn, "Foreman Phillips: Western Swing's Kingmaker," his "That Ozark Playboy: Red Murrell," both in *JEMF,* and his *Ray Whitley: Country-Western Musicmaster and Film Star.* Ken Griffis, "I Remember Johnny Bond," "The Eddie Dean Story," and "The Tex Williams Story," all in *JEMF,* were valuable; as was Jonny Whiteside, "Wesley Tuttle," *JCM;* and Kienzle, "The Checkered Career of Hank Penny," *JCM.* Marilynn Johnson, *The Second Gold Rush: Oakland and the East Bay in World War II,* offered a rich perspective on that part of the state. Further discussion of singing cowboys came largely from Kalton C. Lahue, *Riders of the Range: The Sagebrush Heroes of the Sound Screen;* Charlie Seemann, "Jimmy Wakely," *JOTC;* and Wade Austin, "Hollywood Barn Dance: A Brief Survey of Country Music in Films," *SQ.* Useful material on screen cowgirls was found in Robert K. Oermann, "Mother, Sister, Sweetheart, Pal: Women in Old-Time Country Music," *SQ,* as well as his "Patsy Montana and the Development of the Cowgirl Image" (with Mary A. Bufwak) in *JCM.*

Chapter 8 benefited most from Kienzle, "When a Country Star Turns Murderer: The Strange, Tragic Case of Spade Cooley," *CM;* and Bruce Henstell, "How the King of Western Swing Reached the End of His Rope," *Los Angeles,* as well as suggestions from Donnell Cooley, Jr.

Chapters 9 and 10

Most histories of country music have discussed the genesis and ascendance of Capitol Records, as well as the work of Lee Gillette and Ken Nelson. Kienzle's recent articles "Ken Nelson" and "Lee Gillette" in *JOTC* were excellent.

The emergence of rockabilly—and the development of rock and roll—dominates this chapter. Because people have likely written more about rock than any other popular music, it boasts its own general sources. We consulted the following for this and succeeding chapters: Mike Clifford (ed.), *The Harmony Illustrated Encyclopedia of Rock;* Jim Curtis, *Rock Eras: Interpretations of Music and Society: 1954–1984;* Philip H. Ennis, *The Seventh Stream: The Emergence of Rocknroll in American Popular Music;* Brock Helander, *The Rock Who's Who;* Lorrie Mack (ed.), *Encyclopedia of Rock;* Greil Marcus, *Mystery Train: Images of America in Rock 'n' Roll Music;* Dave Marsh, *The Heart of Rock and Soul;* Jon Pareles (ed.), *The Rolling Stone Encyclopedia of Rock and Roll;* Ed Ward,

Geoffrey Stokes, and Ken Tucker, *Rock of Ages: The Rolling Stone History of Rock and Roll*; and Frye Gaillard, *Race, Rock, and Religion*. Michael Bane, *White Boy Singin' the Blues: The Black Roots of White Rock*, was especially interesting. Rick Nelson is discussed in most of those books, and we consulted also Regan McMahon, "Rick Nelson: Back to School Days," *BAM*; and Joel Selvin's biography *Ricky Nelson: Idol for a Generation*. Memories and conversations played a large role here, too.

Both radio and television are examined in a number of places, including George O. Carney's previously mentioned article, plus Hugh Cherry, "Country DJs Carry Music to People," *MCN*; Kienzle, "The Hometown Jamboree," *JOTC*; J. R. Young, "West Coast Country: Cowboys and More," *JOTC*; Bryce Martin, "Cousin Herb Pioneered Country Music on TV," *BC*; plus interviews with Jelly Sanders, Bill Woods, Buck Owens, Bobby Adamson, and various undated, sometimes unpaginated, materials—press releases, flyers, photocopied articles, and the like. As this book was going to press, *BC* published an excellent series of articles, "The Bakersfield Sound," written by Robert Price.

Along with the general sources, interviews, and conversations, we consulted Don Rhodes, "Jean Shepard—Starting Life Anew"; Richard Luongo, "Ferlin Husky on the 'Comeback' Trail," both in *CM*; and "Tommy Collins," *CSR*, when writing about those three stars. Tennessee Ernie Ford is prominently mentioned in most histories of this music, but the best source of information is Kienzle, "Tennessee Ernie Ford," *JOTC*. Ernie's friend and manager Cliffie Stone is also considered in virtually every history book listed; see also his own *Everything You Always Wanted to Know about Songwriting but Didn't Know Who to Ask* (with Joan Carol Stone); it is filled with anecdotes.

The folk revival of the 1950s has also been much written about. Our principal sources were Anne and Norm Cohen, "Folk and Hillbilly Music: Further Thoughts on Their Relation," *JEMF*; Norm Cohen, "Tin Pan Alley's Contribution to Folk Music," *WF*; David A. De Turk and A. Poulin, Jr., anthology, *The American Folk Scene: Dimensions of the Folksong Revival*; Richard Dyer-Bennett, "Some Thoughts on the Folk Song Revival," *SO!*; Stephen Fiott, "In Defense of Commercial Folksingers," *SO!*; John Greenway, *American Folksongs of Protest*; Fred Hoeptner, "Folk and Hillbilly Music: The Background of Their Relation," *Caravan*; Paul Hood's anthology *Artists of American Folk Music*; Alan Lomax, *Folk Song Styles and Culture*; Bruno Nettl, *Folk Music in the United States*; Pete Seeger, "There's Gold in Them Thar Hills—and Streets," *SO!*; Bill Wolff, "For Cisco Houston—the End of the Road"; and Lee Hayes, "Cisco's Legacy," also in *SO!*

Chapter 10 especially benefited from Whiteside, *Ramblin' Rose*, plus two of his articles: "Maddox Brothers and Rose: The First Hillbilly Punks?" *Goldmine*, and

"The Manifest Destiny of the Maddox Brothers and Rose," JCM, plus Gary Girard, "'Maddox Brothers and Rose' Stir Memories," BC. The interviews with Rose and Fred Maddox on KCET's "Bakersfield Country" were also valuable.

Chapters 11 and 12

These chapters continue the stories of Cooley, Nelson, and rock from the sources listed above. The material on country pop's California emergence derives from general sources: Kienzle, "Lee Gilette," JOTC; the Carr volume; plus the books by Hemphill and Grissim offering interesting glimpses. We also used William Ivey, "Commercialization and Tradition in the Nashville Sound," in *Folk Music and Modern Sound* (edited by William Ferris and Mary L. Hunt); Hughson Mooney, "Commercial 'Country' Music in the 1970s: Some Social and Historical Perspectives," PMS; Ken Tucker, "The Old Sound of New Country," and David Gates, "Are You Sure Hank Done It This Way?" both in Lewis's *All That Glitters*. The material on the California Sound and the Bakersfield Sound— in addition to the sources already cited—came from interviews and conversations (sometimes heated), plus Patrick Carr, "Buck Owens and Others: The Bakersfield Scene," JOTC; Dale Sheehan, "Backwardsfield (An Interview with Bill Woods)," *Country Star News*; Jack Smith, "The Country Music Capital of the West," *Travel and Leisure*; Arnold Shaw, "Bakersfield—City with a Flair for Country Music," LAT. Please see Chapter 16's sources for our references on Haggard. The development of California country rock, as well as its "newgrass" connection, is thoroughly traced in the general rock and country sources listed above.

The core of Chapter 12 came from various sources other than Chon's interviews with Buck and his associates: The best published was Kienzle's terrific booklet accompanying Rhino Records's three-CD *The Buck Owens Collection*, as well as his recent "Buck Owens," JOTC; Jeff Tamarkin, "Buck Owens: All He's Gotta Do Is Act Naturally," *Goldmine*; and Dwight Whitney, "Still Just Pickin' Away," *TV Guide*. Buck's interesting comments on *Bakersfield Country* were also of value.

Chapters 13 and 14

For sources on Haggard, please see essay on Chapter 16. The general books as well as the articles cited above discuss radio playlists. Sammi Smith's career is summarized in the various country music encyclopedias. The continuing stories of country rock groups, and of Rick Nelson in particular, employ the same references cited above, plus Anthony Fawcett, *California Rock California Sound*.

Our primary source on Gram Parsons was the excellent *Hickory Wind: The Life and*

Times of Gram Parsons by Ben Fong-Torres. We also consulted, along with the general books, articles such as Howie Klein, "Emmylou Harris: Progressive Country Is Alive and Well in Sin City," *BAM*, plus some sections of Cecelia Tichi's *High Lonesome*.

Nationally celebrated performers such as Freddie Hart, Juice Newton, Linda Ronstadt, Emmylou Harris, the Eagles, and Cal Smith are discussed in many general books on country music or country rock. More particular to the California scene are many articles culled from *BAM*, which has both Northern and Southern Californian editions: Blair Jackson, "Ray Campi and His Rockabilly Rebels: 'Real Rock' for Now People"; Chinga Chavin, "Chinga Chavin Exposes Self!" (as told to Miles Hurwitz); Steve Stolder, "The Byrds' Reflyte"; Art Fein, "Confessions of a Fanatic"; Davin Seay, "Rollin' the Rock: The Saga of Ronny Weiser"; and so on, all from *BAM* and all useful in this chapter. Stoney Edwards is the subject of two interesting pieces: "Stoney Edwards: A Very Special Person" (no author listed), *CSR*; and Peter Guralnick, "Stoney Edwards: Black Man Singing in a White Man's World," *CM*. The information on Cal Smith is from Michael Bane's essay in Russell Barnard et al., *The Comprehensive Country Music Encyclopedia*.

Kate Wolf's career is considered in Blair Jackson, "Kate Wolf: Home Grown and Easy Goin'," *BAM*; in various liner notes; and in *The Kate Wolf Songbook*, edited by Max Wolf, which includes both "Biography" by Jamie Keller and Max Wolf and "Recollections" by Utah Phillips.

The material on Glen Campbell and Barbara Mandrell in Chapter 14 draws first on general sources. The Grissim and Hemphill books especially examine Campbell's career, as does John Fergus Ryan, "They Knew Glen Campbell before He Was a Superstar,"*CM*. Ryan also wrote "A Visit with Barbara Mandrell" for *CM*, and Genevieve Waddell contributed "Barbara Mandrell: Little Miss Versatility" for *CSR*.

Chapters 15 and 16

All the material on Bakersfield and the Bakersfield Sound has been anchored in a series of interviews and conversations—especially with Bill Woods, Jelly Sanders, Louise Thomason, Jimmy Phillips, Bonnie Owens, and Jimmy Thomason, among others—but other references also contributed. The vertical file at the Beale Memorial Library in Bakersfield contains a wealth of reprinted articles, some of which are not fully identified. A documentary television program, "Bakersfield Country," on KCET–Los Angeles, contains some interesting interview excerpts. Also, incisive articles (by reporters such as Bryce Martin, Rick Bently, Pete Tittl, Richard Chon, and Rick Mitchell) on local music have appeared in *BC*.

BAM, which became the state's primary music magazine after 1976, was, as a result, the primary source for material on Dwight Yoakam and the Los Angeles Renaissance, as were interviews with Dave Alvin, Pete Anderson, and Yoakam, as well as generous correspondence from Dave and conversations with other figures in that scene. The Blasters and Dave Alvin are also well considered in Chris Morris's excellent liner notes for *The Blasters Collection*; Derk Richardson, "Riding High Down Blue Blvd," in the *San Francisco Bay Guardian*; and Alexandra Haslam, "Dave Alvin: Cruising the Boulevard of Broken Dreams," *BAM*. For information on other major groups we consulted—always along with liner notes for various albums and anecdotal material from conversations—Darryl Morden, "Los Lobos Prowl Beyond East LA" (photocopy, source unknown); Mark Leviton, "X Heart of the City: A Journey into the Dark Underbelly of L.A.," *BAM*; plus survey articles in various local publications. Alexandra Haslam's interview with Rosie Flores is the basis for the section on that singer. Highway 101 and the Desert Rose Band are discussed in most of the general sources. Information about attire came largely from Tyler Beard, *100 Years of Western Wear*; and Nudie Cohen was also profiled in Jan Otteson, "Nudie Is the Original 'Rhinestone Cowboy,'" *MCN*; and Jonny Whiteside, "Like a Rhinestone Cowboy," *LA Weekly*. For sources on Dwight Yoakam, please see the essay on Chapter 16.

Although Haggard declined to be interviewed, many of his associates and our mutual Oildale friends did speak about him. Moreover, a series of printed sources were a great help: his *Sing Me Back Home* (with Peggy Russell); articles such as Peter Guralnick, "Merle Haggard: In the Good Old Days (When Times Were Bad)"; and Jason DeParle, "Workin' Man Blues: An Interview with Merle Haggard," both in *JCM*; Mark Rose, "Merle Haggard: Big Wheels Keep Rollin'," *Rolling Stone*; Larry Kelp, "Merle Haggard," *SRPD*; Robert Hilburn, "Merle Haggard: Made in America," *SFC Datebook*; Tony Scherman, "The Last Roundup," *Atlantic Monthly*; and David Bowman, "The Life and Times of Merle Haggard, American Songwriter and Champion of the Working Stiff," *Pulse*. Also of value were the thoughtful interviews with Merle contained in *Merle Haggard: An American Story* on the Nashville Network.

Chapter 17

Information on old-time fiddlers and bluegrass gatherings came from Steve Emmanuels and Steve Fjeldsted. Conversations, newspaper articles, liner notes, and even press releases contributed to the segments on the Sons of the San Joaquin, Boy Howdy, the Smokin' Armadillos, and the Sweethearts of the Rodeo. Alexandra Haslam, "Jody Stecher and Kate Brislin: The Mountain Comes to San Francisco," in *BAM* examined those performers. A conversation with Utah Phillips was the basis of his section, augmented by the liner notes for, and commentary on, several of his albums, especially *We Have Fed You All a Thousand Years*. The brief section on Iris DeMent was derived from conversations and liner notes, as well as Bruce Robinson, "Sweet Salvation: A Rising Star Who's Down to Earth," *Sonoma County Independent*; and Chris Samson, "Blooming Iris: Iris DeMent Brings Heartfelt Melodies to Mystic," *Petaluma Argus-Courier*. Much of the information on country music in San Francisco was found in Cary Tennis, "Lonesome Nights 'n' Haunted Days: San Francisco's Hidden Country Music Scene," *SF Weekly*, and confirmed in conversations.

An interview with Dwight Yoakam by Bill Holdship and Alexandra Haslam is the foundation of our section on that star's California career, and Richard Chon's interview with Pete Anderson is also important. We consulted all the various books dealing with contemporary country music, too, plus articles like Todd Everett, "Dwight Yoakam: Not Just Another Hat"; and Paul Kingsbury, "Dwight Yoakam: Honky-Tonk as Cutting Edge," both in JCM, and Steve Morse's "Yoakam Outdoes Himself, Again," *Boston Globe*.

Abrahams, Roger D., and George Foss. *Anglo-American Folksong Style*. Englewood Cliffs, N.J.: Prentice-Hall, 1968.

Akenson, James E. "Lewis Crook: Learning and Living Country Music." JEMF (fall–winter 1984): 84–93.

———. "Higher-Order Thinking Skills and Country Music: The Curriculum Linkage K–12." *Mid-America Folklore* 16, no. 2 (fall 1988): 109–20.

Allen, Bob. "The View from the LA-Z-Boy: I've Seen It All Before." JCM 16, no. 2 (1994): 15–17.

Alvin, Dave. *Any Rough Times Are Now behind Us*. San Diego: Incommunicado Press, 1995.

American Social History Project (Joshua Freeman et al.). *Who Built America? Working People and the Nation's Economy, Politics, Culture, and Society*. New York: Pantheon, 1992.

Anderson, Robert Mapes. *Visions of the Disinherited: The Making of American Pentecostalism*. New York: Oxford University Press, 1979.

Austin, Wade. "Hollywood Barn Dance: A Brief Survey of Country Music in Films." SQ 22, no. 3 (spring 1981): 11–23.

Autry, Gene. "Three Pals." CSR (January 1950): 15.

Autry, Gene, and Mickey Herskowitz. *Back in the Saddle Again*. Garden City, N.Y.: Doubleday, 1978.

Axthelm, Pete. "Lookin' at Country with Loretta Lynn." *Newsweek* 81, no. 25 (June 18, 1973): 65–68, 71–72.

Bailey, Richard. *Heritage of Kern*. Bakersfield, Calif.: Kern County Historical Society, 1957.

Bane, Michael. *White Boy Singin' the Blues: The Black Roots of White Rock*. New York: Penguin, 1982.

Barnard, Russell D., ed. *The Comprehensive Country Music Encyclopedia*. New York: Random House, 1994.

Bean, Walton, and James J. Rawls. *California: An Interpretive History.* 6th ed. New York: McGraw-Hill, 1993.

Beard, Tyler. *100 Years of Western Wear.* Salt Lake City: Gibbs Smith, 1993.

Bego, Mark. *Linda Ronstadt: It's So Easy.* Austin, Tex.: Eakin Press, 1990.

Benham, Herb. "Kern Country Music Pioneer Plays It Straight with Inmate Addicts." BC (October 6, 1993): B1.

Bentley, Rick. "Dwight Makes Right." BC (May 17, 1991): F1–F2.

———. "Bonnie Owens Stayed Friends with Exes." BC (June 17, 1995): A9.

———. "Together Again." BC (June 17, 1995): A1, A9.

———. "The Bloom Is on the Rose." BC (February 28, 1996): D2–D2.

———. "Big Country." BC (March 8, 1996): E11.

Black, Kris. "Don Rich: The Man We Knew." *The Star from Nashville West* (July 22, 1974): 3.

Blackstone, Cammy. "Iowa Chic—Red Meat: It's Not Just for Heart Disease Anymore." *SF Weekly* (July 14, 1993): 12.

Boehm, Mike. "Boy Howdy Band Is Riding Fast on Comeback Trail." LAT (January 31, 1994): F1, F7.

Bond, Johnny. *Reflections: The Autobiography of Johnny Bond.* JEMF Special Series, no. 8. Los Angeles: John Edwards Memorial Foundation, 1976.

Bowman, David. "The Life and Times of Merle Haggard, American Songwriter and Champion of the Working Stiff." *Pulse* (August 1996): 38–42, 84.

"Boy Howdy." *California Country Music News* (September 1992): 6.

"Boy Howdy." *Pollstar* (December 13, 1993): 3.

Brant, Marley. Untitled jacket notes for *GP/Grievous Angel.* Pasadena: Sierra Records, Books, and Home Video, 1990.

Brewer, Shirley. "The Bakersfield Sound." Unidentified reprint, vertical file. Bakersfield, Calif.: Beale Memorial Library.

Bronner, Simon. "Country Music Culture in Central New York." JEMF 13, no. 47 (winter 1977): 171–82.

Broven, John. *South to Louisiana: The Music of the Cajun Bayous.* Gretna, La.: Pelican, 1987.

Brunvand, Jan Harold. *The Study of American Folklore: An Introduction.* New York: W. W. Norton, 1968.

"Buck-O Turns to Publishing." *Graphic Arts Monthly* (June 1988): 90, 94.

"Buck Owens Roamed While His Fiddler Burned, But Now He's Back on Bended Knee." *People* (July 18, 1977): 31–32.

Buckley, John. "Country Music and American Values." PMS 6, no. 4 (1979): 293–301.

Bufwack, Mary. "The Feminist Sensibility in Post-War Country Music." SQ 22, no. 3 (spring 1981): 135–44.

Bulger, Peggy A., ed. Musical Roots of the South. Atlanta: Southern Arts Federation, 1991.

Burmeister, Eugene. The Golden Empire: Kern County, California. Beverly Hills: Autograph Press, 1977.

Butterfield, Fox. All God's Children: The Bosket Family and the American Tradition of Violence. New York: Knopf, 1995.

Butts, Robert W. "More Than a Collection of Songs: The Concept Album in Country Music." Mid-American Folklore, 26, no. 2 (fall 1988): 90–99.

Campbell, John C. The Southern Highlander and His Homeland. 1921; reprint, Louisville: University of Kentucky Press, 1969.

Cantwell, Robert. Bluegrass Breakdown: The Making of the Old Southern Sound. Urbana: University of Illinois Press, 1984.

Caputo, Salvatore. "For Country Fans, the Garth Moves." SRPD (November 14, 1993): Q31.

Carlin, Richard. The Big Book of Country Music. New York: Penguin, 1995.

Carnal, Jim. "Country Plays Tribute to Mize." BC (March 18, 1994): D2, D19.

———. "Smokin' Armadillos Save Best for Last." BC (September 25, 1994): E7.

Carney, George O. "Country Music and the Radio: A Historical Geographic Assessment." Rocky Mountain Social Science Journal 2 (April 1974): 19–32.

Carr, Patrick. "A Journey with Dwight Yoakam." CM, no. 192 (July–August 1998): 30–34.

———. "Buck Owens and Others: The Bakersfield Scene." JOTC 30 (December 1995): 21–23.

———. "The HighTone Story. CM 27, no. 183 (January–February 1997): 39–42.

Carr, Partick, ed. The Illustrated History of Country Music. New York: Doubleday, 1980.

———, ed. The Illustrated History of Country Music. 2d ed. New York: Random House/Times Books, 1995.

Cash, Johnny. The Man in Black. Grand Rapids, Mich.: Zondervan Books, 1975.

Cash, W. J. The Mind of the South. New York: Knopf, 1941.

Chavin, Chinga (as told to Miles Hurwitz). "Chinga Chavin Exposes Self!" BAM (June 1977): 29–30.

Cherry, Hugh. "Country DJs Carry Music to People." MCN 18, no. 4 (October 1980): 18–19.

Chon, Richard. "Buck by the Numbers: A Conversation with One of Bakersfield's Most Prominent—and Elusive—Public Figures." BC (April 14, 1991): E1–E2.

———. "Farmer Boys Are the Real Roots." BC (March 27, 1992): E1, E6.

Clark, Donald, ed. The Penguin Encyclopedia of Popular Music. New York: Viking, 1989.

Clark, Roy (with Marc Eliot). My Life in Spite of Myself. New York: Simon & Schuster, 1994.

Clifford, Mike, ed. The Harmony Illustrated Encyclopedia of Rock. 5th ed. New York: Harmony Books, 1986.

Cobb, Buell E. The Sacred Harp: A Tradition and Its Music. Athens: University of Georgia Press, 1978.

Cobb, James C. "From Muskogee to Luckenbach: Country Music and the 'Southernization' of America." JPC 16 (winter 1982): 81–91.

Cohen, Anne, and Norm Cohen. "Folk and Hillbilly Music: Further Thoughts on their Relation." JEMF 13 (1977): 50–55.

Cohen, John, ed. The Essential Lenny Bruce. New York: Ballantine, 1967.

Cohen, Norm. "The Skillet Lickers: A Study of a Hillbilly String Band and Its Repertoire." JAF 78, no. 309 (July–September 1965): 229–44.

———. "Transcripts: Interview with Johnny Crockett." JEMF 1 (1965): 18–26.

———. "Materials toward a Study of Early Country Music on Radio III. Fresno, California." JEMF 5 (1969): 7–9.

———. "Tin Pan Alley's Contribution to Folk Music." WF 29 (1970): 9–20.

Cohen, Norman. "America's Music: Written and Recorded." JEMF 16 (1980): 121–30.

Coles Robert. Children of Crisis. Vol. III. The South Goes North. Boston: Little, Brown, 1971.

Cook, Gareth. "Breaking Camp." Sonoma County Independent (January 4, 1996): 10–12.

Corbin, C. Paul, exec. producer. "Merle Haggard: An American Story." The Nashville Network, 1994.

Coriet, Isador H. "Some Aspects of a Psychoanalytic Interpretation of Music." Psychoanalytical Review 32 (1945): 408–18.

"Country-Western Music Accompanied Okies." Unidentified newspaper clipping, vertical file. Bakersfield, Calif.: Beale Memorial Library.

"Cousin Herb's Trading Post Show." Undated press release, vertical file. Bakersfield, Calif.: Beale Memorial Library.

Crawford, Bill, and Gene Fowler. "'Stations between the Nations' Tuning Out." *SFC Datebook* (November 29, 1987): 18–19.

Curtis, Jim. *Rock Eras: Interpretations of Music and Society: 1954–1984.* Bowling Green, Ohio: Bowling Green State University Popular Press, 1987.

Danker, Frederick E. "Country Music." *Yale Review* 63 (spring 1974): 392–404.

Darling, Cary. "The Cruzados: Better Luck This Time." *BAM* (October 18, 1985): 22, 26–28.

———. "Curzados: Hanging Out." *BAM* (September 25, 1987): 8, 12, 14.

Dary, David. *Cowboy Culture: A Saga of Five Centuries.* Lawrence: University of Kansas Press, 1981.

Davenport, F. Garvin, Jr. *The Myth of Southern History.* Nashville: Vanderbilt University Press, 1967.

Davis, Ronald L. *A History of Music in American Life.* Volume III. Malabar, Fla.: Robert Kreiger, 1981.

Dawidoff, Nicholas. *In the Country of Country: People and Places in American Music.* New York: Pantheon, 1997.

Delgatto, John M. Untitled jacket notes for *GP/Grievous Angel.* Pasadena: Sierra Records, Books, and Home Video, 1990.

Dellar, Fred, Roy Thompson, and Douglas B. Green. *The Illustrated History of Country Music.* New York: Harmony, 1977.

DeMuir, Harold. "Night Shift: Dave Alvin Leaves X, Blasters for Allnighters." *BAM* (August 1987): 24.

Denisoff, R. Serge. *Sing a Song of Social Significance.* Bowling Green, Ohio: Bowling Green State University Popular Press, 1972.

Denisoff, R. Serge, and Richard A. Peterson, eds. *The Sounds of Social Change: Studies in Popular Culture.* Chicago: Rand McNally, 1972.

DeParle, Jason. "Workin' Man Blues: An Interview with Merle Haggard." *JCM* 16, no. 1 (1993): 11–15.

De Turk, David A., and A. Poulin, Jr., eds. *The American Folk Scene: Dimension of the Folksong Revival.* New York: Dell, 1967.

Dyer-Bennett, Richard. "Some Thoughts on the Folk Song Revival." *SO!* 12, no. 2 (April–May 1962): 17–18, 20–22.

"Editorial," *Richmond Times* (May 29, 1890), n.p.

Edmonds, Anthony O. "Myths and Migrants: Images of Rural and Urban Life in Country Music." A paper delivered at a conference of the Committee for the Advancement of Early Studies, Ball State University, Muncie, Ind., October 25, 1975.

Egerton, John. *The Americanization of Dixie: The Southernization of America.* New York: Harper's Magazine Press, 1974.

Emrich, Duncan. *Folklore on the American Land.* Boston: Little, Brown, 1972.

Ennis, Philip H. *The Seventh Stream: The Emergence of Rocknroll in American Popular Music.* Macon, Ga.: Wesleyan College Press, 1992.

Epstein, Dena. *Sinful Tunes and Spirituals: Black Folk Music to the Civil War.* Urbana: University of Illinois Press, 1977.

Erlewine, Michael, Chris Woodstra, and Vladimir Bogdanov, eds. *All Music Guide.* 2d ed. San Francisco: Miller Freeman, 1994.

Everett, Todd. "Dwight Yoakam: Not Just Another Hat." JCM 15, no. 3 (1993): 11–17.

Everson, William. *A Pictorial History of the Western Film.* Secaucus, N.J.: The Citadel Press, 1969.

Fawcett, Anthony. *California Rock California Sound.* Danbury, N.H.: Reed, 1979.

Feiler, Bruce. "Gone Country." *New Republic* (February 5, 1996): 19–20, 22–25.

Fein, Art. "Confessions of a Fanatic." *BAM* (August 18, 1978): 28.

Fenin, George N., and William K. Everson. *The Westerns: From Silents to the Seventies.* Rev. ed. New York: Grossman, 1973.

Fenster, Mark. "Under His Spell: How Buck Owens Took Care of Business." JCM 12, no. 3 (1989): 18–27.

Festavan, Bob. "Hopped-Up Country." *American Heritage* 49, no. 2 (April 1998): 38.

Ferris, William. *Folk Music and Modern Sound.* Jackson: University of Mississippi Press, 1982.

Fife, Austin, and Alta Fife. *Cowboy and Western Songs.* New York: Clarkson N. Potter, 1969.

Fiott, Stephen. "In Defense of Commercial Folksingers." *SO!* 12, no. 5 (December–January 1962): 43–45.

Flint, Country Joe, and Judy Nelson. *The Insider's Country Music Handbook.* Salt Lake City: Gibbs Smith, 1993.

Flippo, Chet. "Country and Western: Some New-Fangled Ideas." *American Libraries* 5 (April 1974): 185–90.

———. "Glen Campbell Sounds Off on Country Music, Bryan White, Down Under." *Billboard* (August 10, 1996): n.p.

Fong-Torres, Ben. *Hickory Wind: The Life and Times of Gram Parsons.* New York: Pocket Books, 1991.

Fowke, Edith, and Joe Glazer. *Songs of Work and Protest*. New York: Dover Publications, 1973.

Fowler, Gene, and Bill Crawford. *Border Radio*. Austin: Texas Monthly Press, 1987.

Frady, Marshall. *Billy Graham: A Parable of American Righteousness*. Boston: Little, Brown, 1979.

Freedman, Alex S. "The Sociology of Country Music." *Southern Humanities Review* 3 (fall 1969): 358–62.

Gaillard, Frye. *Watermelon Wine: The Spirit of Country Music*. New York: St. Martin's Press, 1978.

———. *Race, Rock, and Religion*. Charlotte, N.C.: East Woods Press, 1982.

Gardner, Jim. "The Politics of Country." *The Paper* (September 3, 1992): 20–21.

Gavin, Camille, and Kathy Leverett. *Kern's Movers and Shakers*. Bakersfield, Calif.: Kern View Foundation, 1987.

"Gene Autry." *Biography* (television series). Arts and Entertainment Channel. Produced by Del Jack and Cass Darwin. Script by Cass Darwin, Alex Gordon, and Ruth Gordon.

Gentry, Linnel, ed. *A History and Encyclopedia of Country, Western, and Gospel Music*. Nashville: Clairmont, 1969.

Ginell, Cary. "The Development of Western Swing." *Devil's Box* 18, no. 1 (spring 1981): 31–35.

———. "The Development of Western Swing." *JEMF* 20, no. 74 (fall/winter 1984): 58–67.

Girard, Gary. "'Maddox Brothers and Rose' Stir Memories." *BC* (May 27, 1972): n.p.

Gleason, Holly. "Merle Haggard." *Tune-In* 6, no. 2 (February 1988): 4–6, 11.

———. "Sweet Hearts of the Rodeo." *Tune-In* 6, no. 2 (February 1988): 12–13.

Goode, Kenneth G. *California's Black Pioneers: A Brief Historical Survey*. Santa Barbara: McNally & Loftin, 1974.

Green, Archie. "Hillbilly Music: Source and Symbol." *JAF* 78, no. 309 (July–September 1965): 204–28.

Green, Douglas B. *Country Roots: The Origins of Country Music*. New York: Hawthorn, 1976.

———. "The Singing Cowboy: An American Dream." *JCM* 7, no. 1 (1978): 4–61.

Greenway, John. *American Folksongs of Protest*. Philadelphia: University of Pennsylvania Press, 1953.

———. "Country-Western: The Music of America." *The American West* (November 1968): 32–41.

———. "No Talk That God Is Dead." *National Review* (August 11, 1970): 842.

Gregory, James N. *American Exodus: The Dust Bowl Migration and Okie Culture in California.* New York: Oxford University Press, 1989.

Griffis, Ken. "The Ray Whitley Story." JEMF 6, no. 18 (summer 1970): 65–68.

———. "The Eddie Dean Story." JEMF 8, no. 26 (1972): 63–69.

———. *Hear My Song: The Story of the Celebrated Sons of the Pioneers.* JEMF Special Series, no. 5. Los Angeles: John Edwards Memorial Foundation, 1974.

———. "I've Got So Many Million Years: The Story of Stuart Hamblen." JEMF 14, no. 49 (spring 1978): 4–22.

———. "I Remember Johnny Bond." JEMF 14 (August 1978): 110–12.

———. "The Tex Williams Story." JEMF 15, no. 53 (spring 1979): 5–19.

———. "The Beverly Hill Billies." JEMF 16 (1980): 3–17.

———. "Merle Travis on Western Swing." JEMF 16, no. 60 (winter 1980): 215–17.

———. "Hank Penny: The Original 'Outlaw'?" JEMF 18, nos. 65, 66 (spring–summer 1982): 5–13.

Grissim, John. *Country Music: White Man's Blues.* New York: Paperback Library, 1970.

———. "I'm Still Not Sure It Wasn't Planned." *Rolling Stone* 59 (May 28, 1970): 14.

Gritzner, Charles F. "Country Music: A Reflection of Popular Culture." JPC 11 (1978): 861–69.

Grossi, Mark. "A Country-Sized Audience Tunes in for That Sound." BC (August 9, 1981): E1.

———. "A Sound Born in Bakersfield." BC (August 10, 1981): B4.

———. "'Mischievous' Merle Is How Band Member Recalls Him." BC (August 13, 1981): C1.

———. "Texas to Bakersfield: Owens Leaves His Tracks." BC (August 13, 1981): C1

Guralnick, Peter. *Lost Highway: Journeys and Arrivals of American Musicians.* Boston: D. R. Godine, 1979.

———. "Merle Haggard: In the Good Old Days (When Times Were Bad)." JCM 8, no. 1 (May 1979): 39–46, 63–64.

———. "Stoney Edwards: Black Man Singing in a White Man's World." CM 7, no. 7 (May 1979): 42–44, 68.

———. *Sweet Soul Music: Rhythm and Blues and the Southern Dream of Freedom.* New York: Harper & Row, 1986.

Guterman, Jimmy. "What Happened to the New Country Rock?" JCM 11, no. 3 (1988): 6–11.

Guthrie, Woody. *Bound for Glory*. New York: New American Library, 1995.

Hackney, Sheldon. "The South as a Counterculture." *American Scholar* 42, no. 2 (spring 1972): 283–93.

Haggard, Merle (with Peggy Russell). *Sing Me Back Home*. New York: Times Books, 1981.

Hall, Steve. "Seeing Red: Joe Simpson Took a Shine to Country Music." BC, n.p., vertical file. Bakersfield, Calif.: Beale Memorial Library.

Hamilton, Janie B. "West of the Mississippi." *Tophand* 3 (March 1945): 24.

Hammond, Richard, and Nick Zachreson. *The San Joaquin Valley*. Visalia, Calif.: Corralitos, 1979.

"Happy Trails, Roy." *Daily Press* (Victorville, Calif.). Special ed. (July 7, 1998): 1–2, 3–4.

Haslam, Alexandra. "It's a Rough Trade Indeed: The Rugged Road for Independent Distribution." BAM (August 9, 1991): 28.

———. "Dave Alvin: Cruising the Boulevard of Broken Dreams." BAM (December 13, 1991): 36.

———. "City Slickers: Will Country Go Boom or Bust in the Bay?" BAM (October 2, 1992): 26, 28.

———. "Western Underground." BAM (October 2, 1992): 28.

———. "Jody Stecher and Kate Brislin: The Mountain Comes to San Francisco." BAM (April 9, 1993): 46.

———. "Dixie Darlin': Carlene Carter Does It 'Cause She Wants to." RQ (July 1993): 37–38, 59.

Haslam, Alexandra, and Bill Holdship. "He's a Little Bit Country—He's a Little Bit Rock 'n' Roll." BAM (July 14, 1994): 22–23, 32.

Haslam, Gerald. *Voices of a Place: Social and Literary Essays from the Other California*. Walnut Creek, Calif.: Devil Mountain Books, 1987.

———. "The Bakersfield Sound." SFC This World (August 2, 1992): 16.

———. *The Other California: The Great Central Valley in Life and Letters*. 2d ed. Reno: University of Nevada Press, 1994.

Hasseltine, William B., and David L. Smiley. *The South in American History*. Englewood Cliffs, N.J.: Prentice-Hall, 1960.

Hayes, Lee. "Cisco's Legacy." SO! 11, no. 3 (summer 1961): 4–5.

Helander, Brock. *The Rock Who's Who*. New York: Schirmer Books, 1982.

Hemphill, Paul. *The Nashville Sound*. New York: Ballantine, 1970

Henstell, Bruce. "How the King of Western Swing Reached the End of His Rope." *Los Angeles* (June 1979): 126, 128–36.

Hilburn, Robert. "Perryman Heads for Pioneer Roundup." *LAT* Calendar (April 18, 1972): 1.

———. "Listeners Are Tuning in to Revitalized Country Sound." *LAT* Calendar (November 29, 1981): 1, 74–75.

———. "Merle Haggard: Made in America." *SFC* Datebook (March 10, 1991): 39–40.

Hirshberg, Charles, and Robert Sullivan. "The 100 Most Important People in the History of Country." *Life* 17, no. 7 (September 1, 1994): 18–27, 30–39.

Hoeptner, Fred. "Folk and Hillbilly Music: The Background of Their Relation." *Caravan* 16 (April–May 1959): 8, 16–17, 42, and *Caravan* 2 (June–July 1959): 20–23, 26–28.

Hood, Paul, ed. *Artists of American Folk Music*. New York: William Morrow, 1986.

Horstman, Dorothy. "Memories of a Guitar Genius: Merle Travis." *CM* 4, no. 1 (October 1975): 31–34.

———. *Sing Your Heart Out, Country Boy*. New York: Dutton, 1975.

Houston, James D. *Californians: Searching for the Golden State*. New York: Knopf, 1982.

———. "Looking for the Great Central Valley." *Golden State* 1:2 (Autumn, 1984): 38–41.

Hume, Martha. *You're So Cold I'm Turnin' Blue*. New York: Viking, 1982.

Hutchinson, W. H. *California: Two Centuries of Man, Land, and Growth in the Golden State*. Palo Alto, Calif.: American West Publishing, 1967.

I'll Take My Stand: The South and the Agrarian Tradition. New York: Harper, 1930.

Ivey, William. "Commercialization and Tradition in the Nashville Sound." In *Folk Music and Modern Sound*. Ed. William Ferris and Mary L. Hunt. Jackson: University of Mississippi Press, 1982.

Jacks, Jaime. "B.A.D. Bars." *BC* (July 21, 1989): n.p.

Jackson, Blair. "New Riders of the Purple Sage: Back in the Saddle Again." *BAM* (May 1977): 20–21.

———. "Kate Wolf: Home Grown and Easy Goin'." *BAM* (February 1978): 49, 51.

———. "Ray Campi and His Rockabilly Rebels: 'Real Rock' for Now People." *BAM* (August 18, 1978): 24–28.

Jackson, George Pullen. *White Spirituals from the Southern Uplands*. Chapel Hill: University of North Carolina Press, 1933.

Jaret, Charles. "Hits or Just Heartaches: Characteristics of Successful and Unsuccessful Country Music Songs." PMS 8, no. 2 (1982): 113–24.

Jaret, Charles, and Lyn Thaxton. "Bubbles in My Beer Revisited: The Image of Liquor in Country Music." PMS 7, no. 1 (1980): 214–22.

Johnson, Charles. "That Ain't Country: The Distinctiveness of Country Music." JEMF 17 (1981): 75–84.

Johnson, Dirk. "Fleeing Mid-America." SRPD (September 5, 1994): A3.

Johnson, Marilynn. *The Second Gold Rush: Oakland and the East Bay in World War II*. Berkeley: University of California Press, 1993.

Johnson, Stephen, Gerald Haslam, and Robert Dawson. *The Great Central Valley: California's Heartland*. Berkeley: University of California Press, 1993.

Johnson, Thomas F. "That Ain't Country: The Distinctiveness of Commercial Western Music." JEMF 17 (1981): 75–84.

Kahn, Ed. "Hillbilly Music: Source and Resource." JAF 78, no. 309 (July–September 1965): 257–66.

Kearns, Owen, Jr. "Country Music Revisited." BC (August 1, 1981): E1.

Keegan, John. "One Englishman's America." *American Heritage* (February–March 1996): 38, 40, 42, 44, 46, 48, 50, 52, 54, 58–60, 62, 64–67.

Kellog, Stuart. "The Pick-Up." *Victorville Daily Press* (April 24, 1998): D1, D4.

Kelp, Larry. "Disc Reaches into Songwriter's Heart." SRPD (April 9, 1995): Q15–Q16.

———. "Merle Haggard." SRPD (April 9, 1995): Q14–Q15.

Kent, Nick. "A Change of Tune." SRPD (September 5, 1994): B1.

Kienzle, Rich. "When a Country Star Turns Murderer: The Strange, Tragic Case of Spade Cooley." CM 5, no. 10 (July 1977): 34–38, 64.

———. "The Electric Guitar in Country Music: Its Evolution and Development." *Guitar Player* 13, no. 11 (November 1979): 30–41.

———. "The Checkered Career of Hank Penny." JCM 8, no. 2 (1980): 43–48, 61–77.

———. *The Buck Owens Collection* (CD notes). Santa Monica: Rhino Records, 1993.

———. "The Hometown Jamboree." JOTC 26 (April 1995): 8–11.

———. "Jimmie Rivers Day." JOTC 28 (August 1995): 6.

———. "Tennessee Ernie Ford." JOTC 32 (April 1996): 9–11, 34.

———. "Ken Nelson." JOTC 33 (June 1996): 13–15.

———. "Billy Jack Wills: Western Swing with a Modern Twist." JOTC 36 (December 1996): 17, 34.

———. "Red Simpson." JOTC 36 (December 1996): 27.

———. "Buck Owens." JOTC 37 (February 1997): 9–11, 34.

———. "Lee Gilette." JOTC 37 (February 1997): 17, 34.

Killian, Lewis M. "The Adjustment of Southern White Migrants to Northern Urban Norms." *Social Forces* (October 1953): 66–69.

Kingman, Daniel. *American Music: A Panorama*. New York: Schirmer Books, 1979.

Kingsbury, Paul. "Dwight Yoakum: Honky-Tonk as Cutting Edge." JCM 11, no. 1 (spring 1988): 12–14.

———. "The Hard Realities of Hard Country: Conversations with Nashville Label Heads." JCM 11, no. 1 (1988): 15–21.

———, ed. *The Country Reader: 25 Years of the "Journal of Country Music."* Nashville: Vanderbilt University Press, 1996.

Kingsbury, Paul, and Alan Axelrod, eds. *Country: The Music and the Musicians*. New York: Abbeville Press, 1988.

Kirby, Jack Temple. *Media-Made Dixie*. Baton Rouge: Louisiana State University Press, 1978.

Klein, Howard. "West Coast Weirdness Oozes East." CM 5, no. 6 (March 1977): 13.

Klein, Howie. "Emmylou Harris: Progressive Country Is Alive and Well in Sin City." BAM (February 1978): 40, 42.

Klein, Joe. *Woody Guthrie: A Life*. New York: Knopf, 1980.

Kleiner, Richard. "Bakersfield Makes Its Own Kind of Music." Unidentified reprint, vertical file. Bakersfield, Calif.: Beale Memorial Library.

Koon, William Henry. "The Songs of Ken Maynard." JEMF 9 (1973): 70–77.

La Chapelle, Peter. "Country Honors." BC (October 2, 1994): E1.

———. "Dean Holloway: 'I Still Like Him, So I Guess That Says Something.'" BC (October 2, 1994): E2.

———. "Henry Sharpe: 'Man Alive, This Cat Can Sing.'" BC (October 2, 1994): E1–E2.

Ladenheim, Melissa. "'I Was Country When Country Wasn't Cool': An Ethnography of a Country Music Fan." *Culture and Tradition* 11 (1987): 69–85.

Lahue, Kalton C. *Riders of the Range: The Sagebrush Heroes of the Sound Screen*. New York: Barnes, 1973.

Landy, Marc. "Country Music: The Melody of Dislocation." *New South* 26 (winter 1971): 67–69.

Laws, G. Malcolm, Jr. *Native American Balladry*. Philadelphia: The American Folklore Society, 1964.

LeBaron, Gaye. "Country Music Is Nothing New in These Parts." *SRPD* (February 21, 1993): A2.

Lees, Gene. *Singers and the Song*. Oxford: Oxford University Press, 1987.

Leviton, Mark. "X Heart of the City: A Journey into the Dark Underbelly of L.A." *BAM* (September 12, 1980).

Lewis, George H. "Country Music Lyrics." *Journal of Communications* (autumn 1976): 37–40.

———. "Mapping Fault Lines: The Core Values Trap in Country Music." *PMS* 9, no. 14 (1984): 7–16.

———, ed. *Side-Saddle on the Golden Calf: Social Structure and Popular Culture in America*. Pacific Palisades, Calif.: Goodyear, 1972.

———, ed. *All That Glitters: Country Music in America*. Bowling Green, Ohio: Bowling Green State University Popular Press, 1993.

Liberatore, Paul. "Country Porn." *Penthouse* (September 1976): 120, 122, 172–73.

Logsdon, Guy. "Jack Guthrie: A Star That Almost Was." *JCM* 15, no. 2 (1993): 32–38.

Lomax, Alan. *Folk Song Styles and Culture*. Publication number 88. Washington, D.C.: American Association for the Advancement of Science, 1968.

———. *Cantometrics: A Method in Musical Anthropology*. Berkeley: University of California Extension Media Center, 1976.

"Lord, They've Done It All." *Time* (May 6, 1974): 51–55.

Lovejoy, Sandy. "Bonnie Owens Talks about Merle Haggard." *Tune-In* 6, no. 2 (February 1988): 7, 11.

Luongo, Richard. "Ferlin Husky on the 'Comeback' Trail." *CM* 2, no. 7 (March 1974): 20.

McCarthy, John D., Richard A. Peterson, and William L. Yancey. "Singing along with the Silent Majority." In *The Sounds of Social Change*. Ed. R. Serge Denisoff and Richard A. Peterson. Salt Lake City: Goodyear, 1972, 56–63.

McCulley, Jerry. "Saved: Maria McKee's Career Is Born Again." *RQ* (July 1993): 33–35.

McCulloch, Judith. "Hillbilly Records and Tune Transcriptions." *WF* 26 (October 1967): 225–44.

MacIntosh, Laurie. "Sidekicks—a Big Ol' Roadhouse, Pure and Simple." *Sacramento Bee* (November 7, 1997): from the worldwide web page: http://www.sacbee.com.

Mack, Lorrie, ed. *Encyclopedia of Rock*. New York: Schirmer Books, 1987.

McMahon, Regan. "Carlene Carter: A Long Way from Nashville." *BAM* (December 14, 1979): 28.

———. "Rick Nelson: Back to School Days." *BAM* (January 16, 1981): 14–17.

McQueen, Wes. "The Elegant Stranger." *The Star from Nashville West* (n.d.): 3.

———. "Real Nice People in Dim Light, Thick Smoke and Loud, Loud Music." *The Star from Nashville West* (n.d.): 14.

McWilliams, Carey. *California: The Great Exception.* Santa Barbara: Peregrine Smith, 1979.

Malone, Bill C. *Southern Music: American Music.* Lexington: University of Kentucky Press, 1979.

———. "Honky-Tonk: The Music of the Southern Working Class." In *Folk Music and Modern Sound.* Ed. William Ferris and Mary L. Hart. Jackson: University of Mississippi Press, 1982.

———. *Country Music, U.S.A.* Rev. ed. Austin: University of Texas Press, 1985.

———. "From Bluegrass to Newgrass." *JCM* 10, no. 2 (1985): 2–19.

———. *Classic Country Music.* Washington, D.C.: Smithsonian Institution Press, 1990.

———. *Singing Cowboys and Musical Mountaineers: Southern Culture and the Roots of Country Music.* Athens: University of Georgia Press, 1993.

Malone, Bill C., and Judith McCulloh, eds. *Stars of Country Music: Uncle Dave Macon to Johnny Rodriguez.* Urbana: University of Illinois Press, 1975.

Marcus, Greil. *Mystery Train: Images of America in Rock 'n' Roll Music.* New York: Dutton, 1990.

———. *Dead Elvis.* New York: Doubleday, 1991.

Marsh, Dave. *The Heart of Rock and Soul.* New York: New American Library, 1989.

Martin, Bryce. "Truck Driving Songs Lead to Red Simpson's Success." *BC* (April 1, 1973): n.p., vertical file. Bakersfield, Calif.: Beale Memorial Library.

———. "Bakersfield's Quiet King of Country." *BC* (August 19, 1983): D1–D8.

———. "Bill Woods: If You Want to Sing Country, Go See Woods." *BC* (August 19, 1983): D1–D2.

———. "Who's Who in Bakersfield Country?" *BC* (September 9, 1983): n.p.

———. "Cousin Herb Pioneered Country Music on TV." *BC* (December 2, 1983): D1–D2.

Millard, Bob. *Country Music: 70 Years of America's Favorite Music.* New York: HarperPerennial, 1993.

Miller, Don. *Hollywood Corral.* New York: Popular Library, 1976.

Mitchell, Rick. "The Bakersfield Sound Is Back." *BC* (January 29, 1988): n.p.

———. "California Country." *RQ* (May 1993): 32–37.

———. "Hillbilly Deluxe." *RQ* (May 1993): 28–31.

Mooney, Hughson. "Commercial 'Country' Music in the 1970s: Some Social and Historical Perspectives." *PMS* 7, no. 1 (1980): 208–13.

Morgan, James. "Conversations with the Cowboy King." *TWA Ambassador* (October 1976): 38.

Morris, Chris. Liner notes for *The Blasters Collection*. Los Angeles: Slash Records, 1990.

Morse, Steve. "Yoakam Outdoes Himself, Again." *Boston Globe* (November 2, 1995): 69, 74.

Morthland, John. "Changing Methods, Changing Sounds: An Overview." *JCM* 12, no. 2 (summer 1989): 4–8.

Moseley, Andy. "Mr. and Mrs. Country Music Joe and Rose Lee Maphis." Undated press release from Moseley Publications, vertical file. Bakersfield, Calif.: Beale Memorial Library.

Murphy, Reg. "Not Since Jefferson and Madison." *Saturday Review* (September 4, 1976): 8–11.

Nash, Allana. *Behind Closed Doors: Talking with the Legends of Country Music*. New York: Knopf, 1988.

Nass, Martin L. "Some Considerations of a Psychoanalytic Interpretation of Music." *Psychoanalytic Quarterly* 40 (1971): 303–13.

National Arts. Produced by Mike Baker and Peter D. Marshall. WNTV (Northern Virginia Public Television), 1994.

Neal, Roger. "They Come to Work." *Forbes* (March 11, 1985): 76–77, 80, 82.

Nettl, Bruno. *Folk Music in the United States*. 3d ed. Detroit: Wayne State University Press, 1976.

Oermann, Robert K. "Rockabilly Women." *JCM* 8, no. 1 (May 1979): 65–94.

———. "Mother, Sister, Sweetheart, Pal: Women in Old-Time Country Music." *SQ* 22, no. 3 (spring 1981): 125–31.

———. *The Conway Twitty Collection*. Universal City, Calif.: MCA Records, 1994.

———. *America's Music: The Roots of Country*. Atlanta: Turner Publishing, 1996.

Oermann, Robert K., and Mary A. Bufwak. "Patsy Montana and the Development of the Cowgirl Image." *JCM* 8, no. 3 (1981): 18–32.

Ortner, Sherry B. "On Key Symbols." *American Anthropologist* 75 (1973): 1338–45.

Oster, Harry. *Living Country Blues*. Detroit: Folklore Associates, 1969.

Otteson, Jan. "Nudie Is the Original 'Rhinestone Cowboy.'" MCN 15, no. 8 (February 1978): 13.

Paglia, Camille. "Annie Oakley, Frontier Feminist." SRPD (March 19, 1995): G1, G6.

Palmer, Robert. *Deep Blues*. New York: Viking, 1995.

Pareles, Jon, ed. *The Rolling Stone Encyclopedia of Rock and Roll*. New York: Schirmer Books, 1987.

Parsons, Clark. "Chasin' That Neon Rainbow." JCM 16, no. 2 (1994): 11–15.

Parsons, James J. "A Geographer Looks at the San Joaquin Valley." *Geographical Review* 76, no. 4 (October 1986): 371–89.

Peterson, Richard A. *Creating Country Music: Fabricating Authenticity*. Chicago: University of Chicago Press, 1997.

Peterson, Richard A., and Russell Davis, Jr. "The Fertile Crescent of Country Music." JCM 6, no. 1 (spring 1975): 19–25.

Peterson, Richard A., and Paul DiMaggio. "From Region to Class, the Changing Locus of Country Music; a Test of the Massification Hypothesis." *Social Forces* 53 (1975): 497–506.

Phillips, Ulrich Bonnell. "The Central Theme of Southern History." *American Historical Review* 34 (October 1928): 30–43.

Poe, Randy. "Song Roundup." CD notes in *Songs of the West*. Los Angeles: Rhino Records, 1993.

Pond, Steve. "Beverly Hillbilly." US (May 1993): 70, 72.

Price, Robert. "Back When Ferlin Was Terry and Terry Was It." BC (June 22, 1997): A8.

———. "The Bakersfield Sound." BC (June 22, 1997): A1, A6.

———. "It All Comes Back to Bill." BC (June 22, 1997): A8.

———. "The Man Who Could've Been." BC (June 22, 1997): A7.

———. "The Blackboard: The Honky-Tonk, Bar None." BC (June 29, 1997): E1, E9

———. "From Boy Wonder to Burnout: Don't Count Out Frazier." BC (June 29, 1997): E1, E9.

———. "The Man Who Let Buck, Merle 'Act Naturally.'" BC (June 29, 1997): E1, E10.

———. "The Other Cousins on Country Television." BC (June 29, 1997): E11.

———. "Y'all Come—and, for Herb, Y'all Did." BC (June 29, 1997): E11.

———. "Fender-Bender: Roy Made Telecaster Ring." BC (July 6, 1997): E6.

———. "The Truck-Drivin' Man Who Wasn't, or the Ballad of the Green Boots." BC (July 6, 1997): E1, E7.

———. "When Mosrite Was Lead Guitar." BC (July 6, 1997): E1, E7.

———. "Bakersfield Born, Memphis Bred." BC (July 13, 1997): F1, F11.

———. "It's in the Genes." BC (July 13, 1997): F9.

———. "Just Saying No to Cowboy-Pop." BC (July 13, 1997): F10.

———. "King of His Own Country." BC (July 13, 1997): F1, F11.

Price, Steven D. *Old as the Hills: The Story of Bluegrass Music.* New York: Viking, 1975.

Pugh, Ronnie. "Ernest Tubb's Performing Career: Broadcast, Stage, and Screen." JCM 7, no. 3 (December 1978): 67–83.

Quaglieri, Al. *Spadella! The Essential Spade Cooley.* CD notes. New York: Columbia Legacy, 1994.

Randall, Stephen A. "Barbi: The Superbunny Bides Her Time." CM 3 (1975): 37, 61.

Raskey, Frank. *Roy Rogers: King of the Cowboys.* New York: Julian Messner, 1955.

Reed, John Shelton, and Dale Volberg Reed. *1001 Things Everyone Should Know about the South.* New York: Doubleday, 1996.

Rhodes, Don. "Jean Shepard—Starting Life Anew." CM 2, no. 7 (March 1974): 18–20.

Rice, Richard, William Bullough, and Richard Orsi. *The Elusive Eden: A New History of California.* New York: Knopf, 1988.

Richardson, Derk. "Riding High down Blue Blvd." *San Francisco Bay Guardian* (March 4, 1992): 29–30.

Roberts, Roderick J. "An Introduction to the Study of Northern Country Music." JCM 7, no. 1 (January 1978): 23–28.

Robinson, Bruce. "Sweet Salvation: A Rising Star Who's Down to Earth." *Sonoma County Independent* (September 29, 1994): 17.

Rogers, Jimmie N. *The Country Music Message: All About Lovin' and Livin'.* Englewood Cliffs: Prentice-Hall, 1983.

Rooney, James. *Bossmen: Bill Monroe and Muddy Waters.* New York: Hayden, 1971.

Rose, Mark. "Merle Haggard: Big Wheels Keep Rollin'." *Rolling Stone* 90 (October 24, 1980): 22–25.

Rumble, John W. "Country Music and the Rural South: Reminiscing with Whitey and Hogan." JCM 10, no. 2 (summer 1985): 11–53.

Russell, Tony. *Blacks, Whites, and Blues.* New York: Stein and Day, 1970.

Ryan, John Fergus. "A Visit with Barbara Mandrell." CM 2, no. 5 (January 1974): 32–34, 68–73.

———. "They Knew Glen Campbell before He Was a Super Star." CM 2, no. 7 (March 1974): 68–73.

Sakol, Jeannie. *The Wonderful World of Country Music.* New York: Grosset & Dunlap, 1975.

Samson, Chris. "Blooming Iris: Iris DeMent Brings Heartfelt Melodies to Mystic." *Petaluma Argus-Courier* (September 23, 1994): 6B.

Samuelson, Dave. "Woody Guthrie." JOTC 36 (December 1996): 13–15, 34.

Savage, William W., Jr. *Singing Cowboys and All That Jazz: A Short History of Popular Music in Oklahoma.* Norman: University of Oklahoma Press, 1983.

Scherman, Tony. "Country." *American Heritage* 45, no. 7 (November 1994): 38–57.

Schrag, Peter. "California's Comeback." SRPD (May 11, 1997): G1–G6.

Seay, Davin. "Rollin' the Rock: The Saga of Ronny Weiser." BAM (August 18, 1978): 26.

Seeger, Charles. "Music and Class Structure in the United States. AQ 11, no. 3 (fall 1957): 281–94.

———. *Studies in Musicology: 1935–1975.* Berkeley: University of California Press, 1977.

Seeger, Pete. "There's Gold in Them Thar Hills—and Streets." SO! 11, no. 5 (December–January 1961): 65.

Seemann, Charlie. "Cowboy Music: A Historical Perspective." CD notes in *Songs of the West.* Los Angeles: Rhino Records, 1993.

———. "Jimmy Wakely." JOTC 27 (June 1995): 17.

Selvin, Joel. *Ricky Nelson: Idol for a Generation.* Chicago: Contemporary Books, 1990.

———. "Ricky Nelson: I'm Walkin'." JCM 13, no. 2 (1990): 9–15.

———. *Summer of Love.* New York: Penguin (Plum Books), 1994.

Sharp, Cecil. *English Folk Songs from the Southern Appalachians.* Ed. Maude Karpeles. 1932, reprint, London: Oxford University Press, 1960.

Shaughnessy, Mary Alice. *Les Paul: An American Original.* New York: Morrow, 1993.

Shaw, Arnold. "Bakersfield—City with a Flair for Country Music." LAT Calendar (August 24, 1969): n.p.

Sheehan, Dale. "Backwardsfield (An Interview with Bill Woods)." *Country Star News* (September 1977): n.p

Shelton, Robert. *The Country Music Story.* Secausus, N.J.: Castle Books, 1966.

Shestack, Melvin. *The Country Music Encyclopedia.* New York: Thomas Y. Crowell, 1974.

Simon, George T. *The Big Bands.* Rev. ed. New York: Macmillan, 1971.

Skinner, Chris. "Teenage Idol, Travelin' Man." *JCM* 15, no. 1 (1992): 62–63.

Smith, Henry Nash. *Virgin Land: The American West as Symbol and Myth.* Cambridge: Harvard University Press, 1970.

Smith, Jack. "The Country Music Capital of the West." *Travel and Leisure* (April–May 1973): W2–W3.

Smith, L. Mayne. "An Introduction to Bluegrass." *JAF* 78, no. 309 (July–September 1965): 245–56.

Smythe, Willie. "A Preliminary Index of Country Music Artists and Songs in Commercial Motion Pictures (1928–1953), Part 4." *JEMF* 20, no. 73 (spring–summer 1981): 8–18.

Soberanes, Bill. "Smile away the Years with Singer Dorothy Rae." *Petaluma Argus-Courier* (August 29, 1995): 4b.

Stambler, Irwin, and Grunlun Landon. *The Encyclopedia of Folk, Country, and Western.* New York: St. Martin's Press, 1984.

Steigerwald, Bill. "For Your Ears Only: On the Road with Radio." *LAT* Calendar (November 29, 1981): 3.

Stein, Walter. *California and the Dust Bowl Migration.* Westport, Conn.: Greenwood Press, 1973.

Steinbeck, John. *The Harvest Gypsies.* Berkeley: Heyday Books, 1991.

Stolder, Steve. "The Byrds' Reflyte." *BAM* (December 14, 1990): 27–28, 30.

Stone, Cliffie (with Joan Carol Stone). *Everything You Always Wanted to Know about Songwriting But Didn't Know Who to Ask.* North Hollywood: Showdown Enterprises, 1991.

Stone, James H. "Mid-Nineteenth-Century American Beliefs in the Social Value of Music." *AQ* 43 (January 1957): 38–49.

"Stoney Edwards: A Very Special Person." *CSR* 27, no. 189 (April 1975): 10–11, 44.

"Strictly by Ear." *Time* (February 11, 1946): 48–49.

Sutton, Horace "The South as New America." *Saturday Review* (September 4, 1975): 8.

Synan, Vinson. *The Holiness-Pentecostal Movement in the United States.* Grand Rapids, Mich.: William B. Eerdmans, 1971.

"Taking Stock of the Nineties Boom." *JCM* 16, no. 2 (1994): 10.

Tamarkin, Jeff. "Buck Owens: All He's Gotta Do Is Act Naturally." *Goldmine* (February 9, 1990): 7–8, 10, 12, 14, 16, 18, 93.

Tennis, Cary. "Lonesome Nights 'n' Haunted Days: San Francisco's Hidden Country Music Scene." *SF Weekly* (July 14, 1993): 11–13.

Teves, John. "Snapshots from a Country Extravaganza." BC (June 17, 1995): A8.

Tharpe, Jac L., ed. Elvis: Images and Fancies. Jackson: University of Mississippi Press, 1979.

Thaxton, Lyn, and Charles Jaret. "Country Music and Its City Cousin: A Comparative Analysis of Urban and Rural Country Music." PMS 6 (1979): 307–15.

Tichi, Cecelia. High Lonesome: The American Culture of Country Music. Chapel Hill: University of North Carolina Press, 1994.

Tittl, Pete. "It's a Long, Hard Road If You're Going to Be a Star." BC (January 17, 1981): D10.

———. "When Every Corner Had a Guitar Player." BC (September 11, 1982): D14–D15.

"Tommy Collins." CSR 7 (n.d.), vertical file. Bakersfield, Calif.: Beale Memorial Library.

Tosches, Nick. Country: The Biggest Music in America. New York: Stein and Day, 1977.

———. Country: Living Legends and Dying Metaphors in America's Biggest Music. New York: Scribner's, 1977.

———. Unsung Heroes of Rock 'n' Roll: The Birth of Rock in the Wild Years before Elvis. Rev. ed. New York: Harmony Books, 1991.

Townsend, Charles R. San Antonio Rose: The Life and Music of Bob Wills. Urbana: University of Illinois Press, 1976.

Tribe, Ivan M. "The Hillbilly Versus the City: Urban Images in Country Music." JEMF 10 (1974): 41–51.

———. "The Economics of Hillbilly Radio: A Preliminary Investigation of the 'P.I.' System in the Depression Decade and Afterward." JEMF 20, no. 71 (fall–winter 1981): 76–83.

Totten, Melissa, producer. Bakersfield Country. Los Angeles: KCET-TV, 1991.

Tucker, Stephen R. "Progressive Country Music: 1972–1976." SQ 22, no. 3 (spring 1981): 93–110.

———. "Pentecostalism and Popular Culture in the South." JPC 16 (winter 1982): 68–80.

Turner, Al. "Swinging West: 1940s Western Swing from Southern California." CD notes. London: Krazy Kat, 1997

Tuska, Jon. The Filming of the West. Garden City, N.Y.: Doubleday, 1976.

"The Unseen Hand: How Producers Shape the Country Sound." JCM 12, no. 2 (1989): 2–3.

Vaughn, Gerald F. "Foreman Phillips: Western Swing's Kingmaker." JEMF 15, no. 53 (spring 1979): 27–29.

———. "Ray Whitley: County Musicmaster and Film Star." Newark, Del.: Self-published.

———. "Ray Whitley: Cowboy Singing Star." *Western Film Collector* 2, no. 3 (July 1974): 36–52.

Vaughn, Gerald F., and Douglas B. Green. "A Singing Cowboy on the Road: A Look at the Performance Career of Ray Whitely." *JCM* 5, no. 1 (spring 1974): 2–16.

Vaughn, Jerry. "That Ozark Playboy: Red Murrell." *JEMF* 17, no. 61 (fall 1981): 119–22.

Ventura, Michael. *Shadow Dancing in the U.S.A.* Los Angeles: Jeremy P. Tarcher, 1985.

Wacholtz, Larry E. *Inside Country Music.* New York: Billboard Publications, 1986.

Waddell, Genevieve. "Barbara Mandrell: Little Miss Versatility." *CSR* 26, no. 181 (August 1974): 8–9.

Wakely, Linda. *See Ya Up There: The Jimmy Wakely Story.* Jenks, Okla.: Frontier Music, n.d.

Ward, Ed, Geoffrey Stokes, and Ken Tucker. *Rock of Ages: The Rolling Stone History of Rock and Roll.* New York: Summit, 1986.

Westmoreland, Paul. Interview by Tom Norris. May 23, 1983. Sacramento: Sacramento History Center.

White, John I. *Git Along Little Dogies: Songs and Songmakers of the American West.* Urbana: University of Illinois Press, 1975.

Whiteside, Jonny. "Honky-Tonk Man." *BAM* (December 4, 1987): 20.

———. "The Manifest Destiny of the Maddox Brothers and Rose." *JCM* 11, no. 2 (summer 1988): 6–15.

———. "Maddox Brothers and Rose: The First Hillbilly Punks?" *Goldmine* (February 9, 1990): 46–47.

———. "Wesley Tuttle." *JCM* 13, no. 2 (1990): 4–5.

———. "Hank Penny, 1919–1992." *LA Weekly* (May 1, 1992): 79.

———. "Like a Rhinestone Cowboy." *LA Weekly* (September 9, 1994): 150.

———. "Academic History." *Variety* (May 5, 1995): 19, 22, 26.

———. "When Country Went Coastal." *Variety* (May 5, 1995): 20, 26.

———. *Ramblin' Rose: The Life and Career of Rose Maddox.* Nashville: Vanderbilt University Press, 1997.

Whitney, Dwight. "Still Just Pickin' Away." *TV Guide* (November 7, 1970): 14–18.

Wilgus, D. K. "Current Hillbilly Recordings: A Review Article." *JAF* 78, no. 309 (July–September 1965): 267–86.

———. "An Introduction to the Study of Hillbilly Music." *JAF* 78, no. 309 (July–September 1965): 195–203.

Will, George. "Richer, Healthier and Upset." *SRPD* (January 19, 1996): B4.

Williams, Roger M. *Sing a Sad Song: The Life of Hank Williams*. Garden City, N.Y.: Doubleday, 1970.

Winters, Donald E., Jr. *The Soul of the Wobblies: The I.W.W., Religion, and American Culture in the Progressive Era, 1905–1917*. Westport, Conn.: Greenwood Press, 1985.

Wolfe, Charles. "Vernon Dalhart." *JOTC* 27 (June 1995): 8–11.

———. "Skeets McDonald." *JOTC* 27 (December 1995): 19, 34.

Wolf, Max, ed. *The Kate Wolf Songbook*. San Francisco: Another Sundown Publishing, 1987.

Wolff, Bill. "For Cisco Houston—the End of the Road." *SO!* 11, no. 3 (summer 1961): 8–13.

Woods, Bill. "Our Favorite Red-Head: Red Simpson." *Country Star News* (April 1976): n.p.

Woodward, C. Vann. *Origins of the New South*. Baton Rouge: Louisiana State University Press, 1951.

———. *The Burden of Southern History*. Baton Rouge: Louisiana State University Press, 1960.

Wren, Christopher S. "The Great White Soul Sound: Country Music." *Look* 35, no. 14 (July 13, 1971): 11–13.

Young, J. R. "West Coast Country: Cowboys and More." *JOTC* 18 (June 1993): 21–24.

Zimmer, Dave. "Lonesome Strangers: Riding the High Country." *BAM* (April 21, 1980): 42.

Zwisohn, Lawrence. "The Western through the Years on Film and Television." CD notes in *Songs of the West*. Los Angeles: Rhino Records, 1993.

Page numbers in boldface refer to pages containing photographs.

Designer:	Steve Renick
Compositor:	Integrated Composition Systems
Printer:	Data Reproductions
Binder:	Data Reproductions
Text:	Johanna; Gill Sans Light
Display:	Stymie Bold; Decotura